The Other Half
of My Soul

Includes Essays by:

Matthew Fox
Thomas Keating
Wayne Teasdale
Rupert Sheldrake
Thomas Berry

Foreword by
The Dalai Lama

The Other Half
of My Soul

Bede Griffiths and the
Hindu-Christian Dialogue

Compiled by Beatrice Bruteau

QUEST BOOKS
The Theosophical Publishing House

Wheaton, IL U.S.A./Adyar, Madras, India

The Theosophical Publishing House
P.O. Box 270
Wheaton, IL 60189-0270

A publication of the Theosophical Publishing House,
a department of the Theosophical Society in America

*This publication made possible with
the assistance of the Kern Foundation*

Library of Congress Cataloging-in-Publication Data

The other half of my soul : Bede Griffiths and the Hindu-Christian dialogue /
compiled by Beatrice Bruteau.
    p.   cm.
"Quest Books."
A festschrift.
Includes bibliographical references.
ISBN 0-8356-0717-8
    1. Christianity and other religions—Hinduism.   2. Griffiths, Bede, 1906–   .
3. Hinduism—Relations—Christianity.   4. Religions—Relations.   5. Contemplation—Comparative studies.   6. Monastic and religious life—Comparative studies.   I. Bruteau, Beatrice, 1930–   .   II. Griffiths, Bede, 1906–   .
BR128.H5065   1996
261.2'45—dc20   95-49267
                                                                              CIP

    9 8 7 6 5 4 3 2 1 * 96 97 98 99 00 01 02

Printed in the United States of America

Nivedanam

Contents

THE DALAI LAMA

Foreword

I am pleased to know that the book entitled *The Other Half of My Soul: Bede Griffiths and the Hindu-Christian Dialogue*, will soon be published.

I have always believed that all the major religions of the world propagate love and altruism and attempt to transform their followers into better human beings. Essentially they all have the same message. I therefore have much admiration for the life-long work of Father Griffiths for interreligious understanding, and for helping people open their hearts and minds to gain a sense of peace and utility to further the cause of goodwill among all peoples.

If we religious practitioners emphasize the importance of such qualities as love, tolerance, forgiveness and humility, we can then make the betterment of humanity our main goal. When we are able to do that we can easily work and contribute constructively for world peace, which everyone is talking about.

August 6, 1993

Preface

Beatrice Bruteau

Dom Bede Griffiths' aspiration was toward a Unity that would preserve and enhance harmonious diversity and complementarity. He wanted to see such an ideal manifested in the relations among religions, between masculine and feminine values and images for the divine, and between religion and science.

These interests have suggested the architecture of this book. It begins with personal memories, and general appreciations of Bede and his predecessors in the quest for bonding between Christianity and the Vedanta. Pieces that give the general flavor of his spirituality and show how it is being developed by his disciples according to their special talents follow next. The middle portion of the book is devoted to Bede's main concern during most of his life—the interreligious dialogue and the question of how to reconcile the personalism of Christianity with the nondualism of Hinduism. Toward the end of his life, the whole world of the Feminine came strongly into Dom Bede's consciousness, and he was also deeply interested in the relation of religion to science and in ecological issues. These facets are represented by the concluding essays and poetry. I have also appended a bibliography and Father Bede's favorite scripture passages, which I feel will be most meaningful to the reader in the light of the foregoing studies.

Father Bede brought together a number of the outstanding issues of contemporary spirituality, as this volume shows, and he worked on them not only theoretically but concretely. His monastery is a living example of fruitful exchange between Christianity and Hinduism, including the important roles of feminine values and imagery in both traditions. It has been a nurturing place for research and composition, where guest scientists and artists have developed their creative works. It is a magnet for visitors from all over the world, who evidently feel that it represents a new way for religion, science, art, and social relations whose time has come. Dom Bede himself believed that a new form of religious (or monastic) life is now needed that will dissolve the distinction between "professional" religious and "lay" persons. He felt that monasticism needs to take into account recent cultural developments, especially in the sciences, and that it will find itself in the world in terms of the new planetary consciousness that is clearly in our future. Several of his friends are engaged in generating such monastic communities in his lineage.

The contributors to this volume are each involved in work along these lines, some of them very extensively. Wayne Teasdale and I would like to thank all of them for joining us in this salute to our mutual friend. We also thank Father Douglas Conlan and Judson Trapnell for making the fine photographs available.

A special word of gratitude is extended to the Dalai Lama, with whom Dom Bede had several private conversations, especially when they were together in Australia in 1992. We are most grateful to His Holiness for sending his Foreword.

Beatrice Bruteau
January, 1996

Acknowledgments

The article by Thomas Keating, "Meditative Technologies: Theological Ecumenism," appears by permission of *The Way*, Heythrop College, University of London.

Excerpts from the poem *Jonah*, by Albert LaChance, appear by permission of the author, who retains the copyright.

Parts of the essay, "Christ and the Buddha Embracing," by Michael von Brück, were presented as the P. Wattson Endowment Lecture at the University of San Francisco on January 25, 1993.

Earlier versions of parts of "God as Feminine: Experiencing Wholeness," by Felicity Edwards, were published in the *Journal of Theology for Southern Africa* 37 (1981), 23–37, and in *Sexism and Feminism in Theological Perspective*, ed. W. S. Vorster (University of South Africa Press, 1984), 36–57, and material from these publications is used with permission of the editor and the University of South Africa, respectively.

The essay by Judson B. Trapnell, "Multireligious Experience and the Study of Mysticism," has been published in largely similar form in *Philosophy & Theology* 7, no. 4 (Summer 1993), pp. 355–379, as "Bede Griffiths, Mystical Knowing, and the Unity of Religions."

The essay by Thomas Berry, "The Ecozoic Era," was originally presented as an E. F. Schumacher Society Lecture (October 19, 1991) and is taken from a chapter in a book to be published as *Essays of Thomas Berry*. It appears here by permission of the author, who retains the copyright to it.

Introduction: Bede Griffiths as Visionary Guide

Wayne Teasdale

We owe to Wayne Teasdale the idea of creating this book in celebration of Dom Bede Griffiths' life and work. Having gathered most of the contributors, he then asked me to be the editor. I have relied on his knowledge and advice throughout and have consulted him on many points. Because of his personal background and because he was a close friend of Bede's, he was the logical one to invite to write the Introduction. In it, he provides the background and sets the stage for the pieces that follow, by explaining the significance of what Dom Bede has done for monasticism, interreligious dialogue, and the renewal and expansion of Christian spirituality in both mystical and cosmological dimensions.

Teasdale received a doctor's degree in Theology from Fordham University and wrote his doctoral dissertation on Bede. He is also an oblate of Saccidananda Ashram and was initiated into sannyasa by Father Bede. His early publication, Essays in Mysticism, *was followed by* Toward a Christian Vedanta *(1987).[1]*

very age has its prophets, those unique figures who arise to meet a need for vision that gives clarity in a time of confusion and transition. They often point the way to a new direction or they give strong moral leadership as to what should or should not be done by nations, religions, organizations and individuals. Such prophetic voices have existed and do exist in each culture and religious tradition. Indeed, there is never a lack of them, the Spirit responding to the demands of every time and special set of circumstances. Guides on an ocean of life, they set the course for countless generations to come after them. Certainly this is true of the great founders of the world religions, but it is equally true of all those who represent these traditions in later ages, and especially in our own. It is no less true of a Vivekananda, a Mother Teresa, a Thich Nhat Hanh, a Martin Luther King, or a Ramana Maharshi, than of an Augustine, a Benedict, a Shankara, a Nagarjuna, or a Francis of Assisi.

As the last decade of this tumultuous twentieth century advances toward the third millennium and the agony of conflict still haunts dozens of nations in virtually every area of the world, the figure of a gentle Englishman and Benedictine monk, Bede Griffiths, looms large on the horizon. He represents a sign not simply for peace but for the transformation of the entire global order as we know it. In book after book, in his lectures and homilies, but especially with his life, Father Bede has eloquently and clearly presented a new vision of humanity, detailing its various elements. More than a prophet, Bede the sage and spiritual master has skillfully and untiringly set forth his understanding of the demands of the future—what is required to bring the planet to sanity, wholeness and harmony.

FATHER BEDE'S HISTORY

Born as Alan Griffiths on December 17, 1906 to a middle-class British family of Anglican background, Bede enjoyed a happy home life. Gifted intellectually, he easily established himself in school as exceptional. During his school days, before going to Oxford, he was vaguely agnostic, but a mystical awakening to nature while he was still at school inclined him decisively toward nature-mysticism, or the religion of nature. This became his opening to faith and his eventual entrance both into the Catholic Church and into monastic life. These two latter events followed his years at Oxford, where his friendship with C. S. Lewis, his tutor, assumed a significant role in his conversion and the process of his own spiritual maturation. As it turned out, he played the same role in Lewis' life.

In early 1933, about a month after his acceptance into and whole-hearted embracing of Catholicism, he entered Prinknash Abbey, a Benedictine monastery founded by former Anglicans at Glouster in central England. In a CBS News interview in 1979, Father Bede remarked that Prinknash was the only place in all of England where he ever really felt at home. For the next twenty-four years he was to remain a monk in Britain, taking his solemn vows in 1936 and ordination to the priesthood in March, 1940.

Bede began a serious study of Eastern scriptures—the Vedas, the Upanishads, the Bhagavad Gita, the Tao Te Ching, Chuang Tsu's writings, the Dhammapada, and others. This reading was deeply formative for him, reinforcing a fascination with the Orient. But it was actually the influence of a friend, Toni Sussmann, one of Jung's first disciples, that proved to be decisive for him in the development of his passionate interest in Asia. Her husband was a German Jew, and they had left Germany at the time of Hitler and settled in London. It was there in the early 1940s that Bede met them, and the three became great friends. Toni had opened a yoga and meditation center in London, and this was the context of their initial meeting. Toni's own interest in Eastern spirituality and the activities of the center had a profound impact on Bede.

SHANTIVANAM

Then, in 1955, at the invitation of Father Benedict Alapatt, an Indian Benedictine, he set out for India to establish a Benedictine monastery in the Bangalore region of South India, an experiment that ultimately failed. Bede then tried again with Father Francis Mahieu, a Belgian Cistercian; together they established Kurishumala Ashram at Kottayam in Kerala state, again in the south. Although it was Cistercian, Kurishumala followed the Syriac Rite in liturgy. Bede stayed at Kurishumala for the next ten years, functioning as novice master and professor. But in 1968 a dramatic change took place in his life. He was asked to take charge of Saccidananda Ashram, dedicated to the Holy Trinity at Shantivanam, Forest of Peace, a monastery not far from Trichy in neighboring Tamil Nadu state, where Swami Abhishiktananda had been since 1950. Abhishiktananda, the surviving founder, had permanently retired to his hermitage in the north of India at Uttarkashi.

Shantivanam had known little real growth since its establishment in 1950, and the other founder, the saintly Jules Monchanin, died in 1957. Many prospective candidates came to join the community, but none actually persevered. Part of the reason for this was no doubt Abhishiktananda himself, whose heart was divided between Shantivanam and his hermitage for which he longed; he had always felt a deep sense of ambiguity and anxiety about Shantivanam. The source of these emotions was his own confusion about his vocation—his ultimate call to be totally immersed in the mystical life of India, the life of the sannyasin, the wandering ascetic "clothed only in the wind," and his role in the Shantivanam community.

Shantivanam was a Christian Benedictine monastery, an ashram somewhat open to dialogue with Hinduism. But it was still terribly limited and constrained by theology and ecclesial obligations from taking the plunge into the spiritual stream of Indian contemplative wisdom. Abhishiktananda remained a Christian until the end of his life in December 1973, but he always felt an irresistible attraction to the advaitic experience—the pull to pure unity or nonduality with the source. Abhishiktananda pursued his own quest for the Absolute with an intense passion and he did so within an equally passionate commitment to sannyasa, the life of total renunciation. He went all the way into Hinduism, and Shantivanam became an obstacle in his path. Those who came to explore a vocation there must have discovered the great unease of his soul, his dividedness, and so left.

The arrival of Bede Griffiths at Shantivanam in 1968 brought a fundamental change in the character and spirit of the ashram. As Bede settled in to the rhythm of Indian style monasticism, the life of the ashram began to improve and ambiguity was banished. The faith was completely Christian, but the lifestyle completely Indian. Numerous Indian vocations developed over the course of his tenure, and many of these stayed on. In 1993 the community had about fifteen members, all Indian—of course with the exception of Bede.

In 1980 Dom Bede officially joined the Camaldolese Order, which itself had joined the Benedictine Order in 1962, and in 1982 Shantivanam became part of Camaldoli. The first ordinations occurred in January, 1982, when Amaldas and Christudas, two of Bede's disciples who had left Kurishumala to follow him, received Holy Orders at Shantivanam from the bishop of Trichy. Amaldas, who was to have been Father Bede's successor, died quite suddenly of a heart attack in May 1990, forcing Bede to remain as superior longer than anticipated.

Dom Bede died peacefully while napping on May 13, 1993 at 4:30 p.m., following two crippling strokes some months earlier that had left him incapacitated but miraculously still able to speak. Father Christudas today serves as administrator of the ashram, but not as prior. Father Bede groomed Brother Martin John Kuvarupu as his successor in the role of superior or prior of Saccidananda Ashram (Shantivanam). Brother Martin, a South Indian from the state of Andra Pradesh, is well versed in both Christian and Hindu spirituality, and is endowed with a spirit similar to his English spiritual master's.

Since 1968 Shantivanam has become an important center for dialogue and retreat; it has gained an international reputation for its openness to all who come in large numbers from every corner of India and every part of the globe. Father Bede had been thrust into the role of guru and focus of attraction for those making the journey to Shantivanam. It was precisely because of him that the ashram has become so prominent. People came from everywhere to be inspired by his wisdom and his example, and to be touched by his love and his presence—called *darshan* in India.

Under his leadership, Shantivanam has become completely "inculturated." Inculturation, a fruit of Vatican II, means the attempt to express the Christian life and mystery in the form of the particular culture in which a community finds itself. Shantivanam assumed Hindu forms in style of life, such as vegetarianism, sitting on the floor or ground, eating with one's fingers, living in simple huts with little furniture, and following utter simplicity in all things, free of the telephone, the radio, and the television. The monks wear *kavi*, the saffron color of sannyasins, or Hindu monks. Some Sanskrit prayers from the Vedas and the Upanishads have been incorporated into the public worship, though not into the Eucharistic liturgy itself. The chapel is built in the classical style of a Hindu temple.

Shantivanam, in these ways, has become both Christian and Hindu, but in a very profound sense that defies either description or analysis.

FATHER BEDE'S SPIRITUAL LEGACY

Bede's vision has been presented in person to audiences all around the world. He made many trips to Europe, where he is well known. Australia received him enthusiastically in 1985, and he visited America on six occasions (1963, 1979, 1983, 1990, 1991, and 1992), where his impact is well recognized. Bede also participated in many Asian conferences, including the monastic gatherings at Bangkok in 1968—the one at which Merton died—and at Bangalore in 1973. These and many other meetings provided opportunities for him to offer his insights and intuitions to the global spiritual atmosphere. This wisdom has formed a body of discourse that is elaborated in his various books.

Father Bede wrote ten books during his lifetime and more than three hundred articles, gave several dozen major interviews, and was the subject of at least ten documentaries. His books, most of which have been translated into several languages, include:[2]

> *The Golden String: An Autobiography* (1954)
> *Christ in India: Essays Towards a Hindu-Christian Dialogue* (1968)
> *Vedanta and Christian Faith* (1973)
> *Return to the Center* (1976)
> *The Marriage of East and West: A Sequel to the Golden String* (1982)
> *The Cosmic Revelation: The Hindu Way to God* (1983)
> *River of Compassion: A Christian Commentary on the Bhagavad Gita* (1987)
> *A New Vision of Reality: Western Science, Eastern Mysticism, and Christian Faith* (1989)
> *The New Creation in Christ: Christian Meditation and Community* (1992)
> *Universal Wisdom: A Journey through the Sacred Wisdom of the World* (1994)

When Bede was preparing to leave for India in 1955, he wrote to a friend that he was going out to India "to seek the other half of my soul." This is, I think, the key to his life's work—integration of the rationality of the West, symbolized by science, with the intuitive capacity of the

East, represented by Hindu and Buddhist mysticism, and more generally by India itself. The rational tendency is a more masculine approach, while the intuitive tendency is more feminine. The intuitive aspect—"the other half of the soul"—is the contemplative dimension, the depth side of our nature, and has its roots in the unconscious. India lives more from the unconscious—this intuitive capacity of human nature. It was this that Bede wanted to bring into harmony with his rational life—his intellectual ability, which was already highly developed.

For the last two centuries European thought has been dominated by the masculine tendency, disregarding the feminine intuition—the great strength of India and other Eastern cultures. In a very real sense, Father Bede sought a balance of these two capacities; in himself first and then in the world at large, to which he tried to be an example. This balance or integration is a major theme in his thought and a constant one, one of the deepest meanings of his life—a life that can only be described as essentially inspired by and devoted to Wholeness.

The process of searching for the other half of his soul in the Indian context gave Bede a rare perspective on his former Western culture. This revealed to him the shadow side of its obvious powers: its complexity, its alienation from and dominance over the natural world, its over-emphasis on analytic reason, its technological frenzy, its overactivism and lack of contemplative awareness, its noise, confusion, disintegrated unfocused consciousness, its profound injustice (at times) and its totally secular mentality, a mentality with no tangible sense of the sacred. He clearly perceived its overindulgence and consumerism, its addiction to having more and more things, its neglect of spiritual values—except in a very superficial sense, often sentimental—its overemphasis on industrial development with its devastating effects on the ecology of the planet, not to mention the social side effects of urban poverty, homelessness and the erosion of village, town, and family communities.

At the same time, he appreciated the positive and beneficial aspects of Western civilization: advances in medicine, education, a higher standard of living, better working conditions, more leisure time, stable government based on democratic ideals and a commitment to peace, while collaborating with like-minded societies. Western achievements in art, music, science, literature, philosophy, and theology were unassailable. The West's commitment to social action and a rudimentary kind of justice were equally impressive.

In contrast to this experience of the West, he discovered the very special values of India and the East as a whole. He found that in India everything was reduced to simplicity—life there was not as cluttered as elsewhere, notably in Europe, America, and Japan, where excess was prominent. Needs in India are basic: just food, shelter, and clothing. Very few Indians have cars or air conditioners; the average Indian is likely to use a bicycle for transportation, since only the very rich, government and industry officials have cars at their disposal; houses are simple, both in design and contents, with no need for eating utensils. The pace of life is much slower. Community seems to exist everywhere, especially in the village, and the lives of people are more integrated than in the West. There is a profoundly real sense of the sacred surrounding everything: the land or places; actions such as bathing, eating, sleeping and working; relationships; and the prevalence of religious rites such as offering the temple puja (sacrifice), ritual purification, almsgiving, and pilgrimage. Everything, in fact, is considered sacred, and God is acknowledged in everyone. Even the standard way of greeting one another is more profound: "Namaste" ("The God in me salutes the God in you") has sacred meaning, compared to our secular "Hi! How are you?" Bede lived and breathed the spiritual culture of India, a culture that is infinitely deep when compared with most any other, especially American—while he observed the shallowness of Western culture and its values that exist today.

THE BEDEAN SYNTHESIS

Bede was able to assimilate the insights of the Asian traditions into his spiritual conception by distinguishing between cosmic and historical revelation. In Christian theology the stress has always been on historical revelation as the only valid form. There is virtually no sense of a cosmic or more general type of revelation, though one could make a case for it from scripture, something that Bede does in passing. All revelation culminates in Christ, but the cosmic revelation is itself an ongoing process of the Divine Reality revealing Itself in the universe, nature, and in all beings. Cosmic revelation is theophanically dynamic, that is, it is by its very nature based on an outpouring theophanic function of the created or mediated universe. The cosmos itself is the outward thrust of the cosmic revelation. There is also an inward or subjective thrust in this revelatory process in which the divine is discovered in the depths of the heart, the most inward center of consciousness.

The cosmic revelation is the basis of the Asian faiths in their inner experience, unity being one of the determining notes of this kind of revelatory experience. The cosmic revelation is also present in the so-called "primal" societies. The inward thrust of the primordial revelation, its explosion in the depths of consciousness in mystical revelation, is the core reality of Hindu and Buddhist spirituality. Parenthetically, the cosmic unity, glimpsed in the primordial revelation, is an advaitic and even nirvanic experience. Both bear some inner relation to the cosmic unity, and in some sense are a further and deeper awareness of it. This inward life of the cosmic revelation is the focus of meditation in these traditions, and meditation itself is a way into it. Cosmic revelation is thus ongoing, perennial, and always accessible to us.

Another important theme in Bede's synthesis, one that is closely associated with the notion of cosmic revelation in his thought, is that of myth—its place, nature, and value. For Bede, myth was a sort of symbolic theology, which expresses the experiences and intuitions a people have of the cosmic revelation, and represents their original cosmology or worldview. The symbol makes the reality present, and the recitation of the cosmic myth recreates the origin or makes it present again; it propels consciousness into the timeless origin, the eternal present. Myth comes from a very deep experience, something that Mircea Eliade and others were able to grasp and that Bede himself understood since his first years in India.

Along with Eliade, Bede came to realize the substantial reliability of mythic thought as a repository of the most significant experiential insights into the nature of life and the basic tentativeness of Western thought on these same questions, especially contemporary philosophy. The West's earlier, uninformed view of myth as equivalent to falsehood, imagination, wishful thinking, or just plain unsophisticated thought, proved to be grossly inaccurate and self-serving. Ironically, these negative qualities might be more appropriately applied to much of contemporary Euro-American philosophy, rather than to "primitive" cultures that philosophy has tried to denigrate.

Bede's own synthesis began to crystallize as he read extensively the works of such seminal thinkers as Fritjof Capra, Ken Wilber, David Bohm, Rupert Sheldrake, Sri Aurobindo, Abhishiktananda, Raimundo Panikkar, and the mystics of both Christianity and the Asian traditions. He was able to achieve a clear understanding as to the general shape of the new synthesis, one that also included myth and the cosmic revelation. This synthesis had been unfolding in his thought since the late sixties, and reached a final expression of clarity and depth in one of his later works, *A New Vision of Reality*.

The subtitle of this important book—which, I believe, is the best statement of his overall position—provides the key to the general direction of his synthesis: *Western Science, Eastern Mysticism and Christian Faith*. It should be observed, parenthetically, that it is Bede's capacity for synthesis that is one of the distinguishing characteristics of his contribution. He always had a genius for seeing implications, the basis of a sound synthetic construction. In this later work he stretched that ability very far, and offered a striking picture of a new approach to knowledge, one that seems to overcome the skepticism and fragmentation of contemporary Western philosophical thought, with its devastating effects on culture, morality, faith, and life.

When Bede spoke of "Western science," he meant that constellation of new ideas brought about by the revolution in physics, biology, and psychology. As Newton's physics and reductionistic mechanism have been enriched by speculations about implicate orders and morphogenetic fields, an entirely novel vision of reality has become possible. The organic model of the cosmos emphasizes the interrelationship of all reality, the fact that the universe is a unitary system. The organic insight opens the door to a reconciliation of religion and science. This is because the implications indicate a mystical significance to the phenomenal universe and to reality as experienced in human consciousness that is consistent with the deepest experiences and insights of the mystics from various traditions, notably the Hindu, Buddhist, Christian, and Sufi.

Bede felt that the ultimate significance of the cosmos is a mystical one, in the sense that the universe itself is a vehicle leading the mind to the Divine. His view is much like the medieval Franciscan view of creation as a great book from which we can learn the essentials of being and life. Because of this, science, as well as both Eastern and Western mysticism, is part of the larger synthesis that Bede conceived.

At the same time, he regarded Christian faith as providing the third element in his vision, the new synthesis. The Incarnation gives direction to the vision, or rather, demonstrates the direction of reality and history. This has to be understood in the Teilhardian sense, for the Incarnation is the crown of creation, the ultimate goal toward which the universe, all beings, and human history move. Bede was quick to point out that this Christian faith includes a mystical, or spiritual, dimension, as all genuine religious awareness does. It has, in fact, a very profound contemplative tradition, on which rests much of the Bedean synthesis. To neglect it would be to fall into the old problem of science, the Enlightenment, and Rationalistic philosophy: gross inadequacy in worldview and metaphysics, and cosmological incompleteness.

Science, mysticism, and the Gospel of Christ offer the elements that, working together in their proper place, give us a more accurate account of the nature of the universe and the meaning of our lives. Bede's position is Christocentric, but it is a Christology from below, and it is consistent with Teilhard's intuition of the Omega Point—that Jesus as the Image of the Invisible God is the model of what we can all become, what is in fact our ultimate destiny. The consciousness of Jesus, as totally awake to his relationship with the Ultimate Source, which he called his "Father"— a relationship of communion and love—is the goal of all human life. To become rooted in and transformed by Divine Love, to be this Love, as Christ is, is the heart of Bede's Christology. In this sense, his thought and life were Christocentric.

Bede's Christocentrism makes room for genuine pluralism. He rejected both the old exclusivism (our religion is true; the others are false) and the more modified inclusivist view (there is truth in the others, but they are preparations for the Gospel), instead embracing a Christianity dynamically open and related to the deepest truth in the various other religions, an attitude that the conciliar document *Nostra Aetate* encourages. Bede accepted the reality and validity—with some nuances—of non-Christian forms of mysticism, particularly Hindu, Buddhist, Jewish, and Sufi forms, as well as nature-mysticism. It is from this mystical level that his thought—his great synthesis—emerges.

The Advaitic Problem

Anyone who enters into the Hindu tradition in any depth, who studies it in an open, unbiased way, soon realizes the authenticity of Hindu mysticism. One cannot escape the fact that here we are encountering genuine experiences of real insight. Christians may, and often do, argue with the representatives of contemplative Hinduism, but they cannot ignore them, just as they cannot ignore those representatives of Buddhism who have become, in their own way, living icons of its spiritual validity, wisdom, and effectiveness.

Most educated Hindus today are advaitins. They follow the pure advaitic (nondualist) doctrine summed up so powerfully by Shankara in the ninth century. Advaita is the experience and the notion of identity with the Divine Reality, the experience of nondifference. It is the view that the difference, or ontological distinction, between God or Brahman and our own deepest self, Atman, is not real or absolute; they are not actually different. Although there are many interpretations of advaita, some of which are compatible with the Christian faith and religious experience, it can be regarded as a problem for Christianity. Certainly Abhishiktananda thought so.

Abhishiktananda spent many years of his life in India—almost until he died—trying to reconcile advaita and Christian faith. He had been caught in the vortex of advaitic experience that carried him along in the power of its inner awareness. Bede incorporated much from Abhishiktananda on this issue, though he resolved it in his own way. Abhishiktananda, in a very telling chapter of his important work, *Saccidananda*, entitled "The Advaitic Dilemma," characterized advaitic consciousness and pinpointed the challenge to Christianity posed by the existential truth and intensity of the experience.[3]

> When the Self [Atman/Brahman, God] shines forth, the I that has dared to approach can no longer recognize its own self or preserve its own identity in the midst of that blinding light. It has so to speak vanished from its own sight. Who is left to *be*, in the presence of Being itself? The claim of Being is absolute.[4]

"The claim of Being is absolute"! There can be no identity separate from it. Here our dualistic language fails; the subject/object dichotomy disintegrates in the overpowering presence of the ultimate subject, the Supreme Identity. We have no language to name this union. The state of oneness with the Absolute comes at the price of our sense of a separate individual identity, but this does not mean that we have no real identity. All along we have "leaned" on the Godhead to be; we are totally dependent beings. Little did we know that our dependence is internal: a dependence of being, of consciousness, of identity. In the presence of the Divine, human identity is barely a shadow ontologically, or so it would seem from the experience of unity itself. The experiencing consciousness is so saturated by unity that it can no longer experience or know itself as different or separate from God, the Brahman, the Godhead. It is completely absorbed into the unity, an absorption that takes it beyond the limitations of individual selfhood, freeing it into the Totality. All distinction is gone; all separate selfhood is overcome.

In one of the last talks before his death—one that he never actually gave but did prepare for the Bangalore monastic gathering in 1973—Abhishiktananda put it in the most emphatic of terms. Referring to his own advaitic experience, and generalizing from it, he boldly declared:

In this annihilating experience [of advaita] one is no longer able to project in front of oneself anything whatsoever, to recognize any other "pole" to which to refer oneself and to give the name of God. Once one has reached that innermost center, one is so forcibly seized by the mystery that one can no longer utter either a "Thou" or an "I." Engulfed in the abyss, we disappear to our own eyes, to our own consciousness. The proximity of that mystery which the prophetic traditions name "God" burns us so completely that there is no longer any question of discovering it in the depths of oneself or oneself in the depths of it. In the very engulfing, the gulf itself has vanished. If a cry were still possible—at the moment perhaps of disappearing into the abyss—it would be paradoxically: "But there is no abyss, no gulf, no distance!" There is no face-to-face, for there is only That-Which-Is, and no other to name it.[5]

Advaita is first of all the total transcendence of the ego, the collapse of selfhood in the empirical sense—that is, in the sense of a self defined and established in being by its finite relations to other finite selves who *know* and *experience* one another as *objects* relative to themselves as *subjects*. The whole subject/object dichotomy, a distinction of ordinary consciousness, is superceded. This is the "return to the Source," to the original Ground, the primordial condition of pure being, beyond multiplicity and every distinction.

Second, like the nirvanic consciousness of the Buddhist tradition, a-dvaita is often said by its adherents to be impersonal, or what we might currently call transpersonal. The "personal" in this context, and as a category of being, implies finitizing relationships. But it is surely true that *person*, in a more ultimate sense—something that came to Hinduism as late as the Bhagavad Gita—is a significant part of the Godhead and therefore escapes finitude, while still maintaining the note of relationship. The Godhead is both *impersonal*—as not partial or particular—and *personal*—as full of nonobjectifying knowledge and love. Does not the *Brahman/Atman/Purusha* triad point to this truth? The notion of person is not inconsistent with advaitic experience, since advaita also includes further levels of interiority, where communion is discovered at the heart of unity. To deny this is to admit a limit in one's experience of advaita itself, to fixate at an earlier stage where pure unity predominates.

This suggests how reconciliation might be approached. But for Abhishiktananda advaitic experience was a serious challenge to the Christian faith, and yet he maintained the necessity to integrate it into Christian understanding. That is at once the problem and the task, both of which require an interior appropriation of the advaitic consciousness in its experiential intensity.[6]

Bede clearly grasped the problem and the task, and made significant progress in his own life and thought toward resolving the "advaitic dilemma" for Christians and others. This is a continuous theme in his literary efforts, his lectures, homilies, his interviews, and even in his letters. Often he said—echoing Jules Monchanin—that the aim is to relate advaita and the Trinity, and it is an equation he never tired of making. Over some years in India, as he pondered this question, he discovered the point of contact between advaita and the Trinity, and so developed a Christian form of advaita.

Bede saw in the Trinitarian intuition the same mystery of nonduality, the same emphasis on unity as ground of Being. There is relationship in the Godhead as Trinity; there is distinction of Persons, but there is no difference, no multiplicity. In Bede's view the unity of nature—of divine nature between the "Father" and the "Son"—is evident from the Gospel of John. The seventeenth chapter of John in particular offers a decisively advaitic text. There we read:

> . . . may they all be one: as you, Father, are in me, and I in you, so also may they be in us, that the world may believe that you have sent me. The glory which you gave me I have given to them, that they may be one, as we are one; I in them and you in me, that they may be perfectly one. [John 17:21–22]

Bede correctly pointed out that Jesus never claims that he is the Father, only that he and the Father are one. Jesus thus goes beyond mere identity or unity and reveals that within the unity there is a relationship of knowledge and love.

The unity is dynamic and personal.[7] The person, in Christian terms, is a capacity for relationship and *is* relationship. It is a dynamic capacity for communion, a communion of presence or being, of consciousness or knowledge, and of love or bliss. As beings-in-relationship, persons are also *processes* and *acts/activities* toward loving presence to and in other persons, especially in the Persons of God, culminating in total mutual indwelling communion.

Communion is the heart of the Godhead and is the essence of Being. Advaita, in this interpretation, is compatible with the ontological reality of the Trinity, and the Trinity represents a further secret of the Divine Mystery, a more ultimate depth in the pure advaita of the spirit. Love is the content of the dynamism of relationship in the unity of the Godhead. Love is the fullness of unity expressed in communion. Bede said, "The Father knows himself in the Son and communicates himself in the Spirit. . . . It is this Spirit that is communicated to our human spirit, so that we participate in that love, which is the very being of the Godhead."[8]

According to Bede, we share in this primal condition of nonduality with the Trinity, and that is one of the main points of chapter seventeen of John: our unity with the Divine Persons and with one another. In a very real sense—and certainly this is one of the implications of this insight— we are related to the Godhead, advaitically, in much the same way as the Divine Persons are related to one another. Christian advaita follows the intrinsic dynamic principle of Bonaventure: *bonum diffusivum sui*. Thus the

Divine Persons "diffuse themselves" to one another and to us, and we also, being persons, "diffuse" ourselves to one another and to them.

Father Bede verified this dynamic, communitarian nature of the Godhead in his own experience. Surely this same dynamic quality is present in the fuller development of the advaitic doctrine expressed in the notion of *Saccidananda*, the great metaphor for the Trinity at the summit of the Hindu tradition: *sat*—being, or pure existence; *cit*—pure consciousness of existence; and *ananda*—the bliss of being totally conscious of the act of existence. Bede spoke of it as "Being, or Reality, experienced in pure consciousness, communicating perfect bliss."[9] Perhaps it should be noted here that by "pure" consciousness is meant consciousness without form, object, content, or concept. It really implies transcendent consciousness, nonfinite and nonrelative, though still relational because of the absolute "self-diffusion," or love character of the Persons.

Christian advaita thus goes deeper into the mystery of unity, of non-duality, and awakens to its ultimate identity as *dynamic relatedness of being*. In this it completes both the Hindu advaitic experience/doctrine and the Buddhist notion of nirvana. Bede had a very deep insight, proceeding from an equally profound experience, of how this completion is true. In early 1990 he suffered a stroke that left him in a strange state of consciousness transcendent to this realm of ordinary consciousness. It went on for months, and the inner changes in him seemed to be permanent. In one broad move, his inner experience had traversed and unified two spiritual universes: the Buddhist and Christian, the East and West, but equally the advaitic and the Trinitarian, unity and communion, the self-comprehension and self-communication of Unity itself.

BEDE AND THE FUTURE OF CHRISTIANITY

Another very significant theme in Father Bede's thought is the idea of a truly universal Christianity that is genuinely open to the other traditions and that learns to "speak" their inner languages. This is a recurring theme that appears in all his writings and public discourses, not to mention his letters. The need for such a development—a massive project, without question—shows in a stubborn fact: the real failure of the Christian missionary effort in Asia. After several centuries of missionary activity, only two percent of the Orient is Christian. The meaning of this statistic became clear for Bede, and for many others in the course of dialogue and living in India. Christianity in its Western cultural expression is really unintelligible and unappealing to the vast majority of Indians, as well as the Chinese, Japanese, Thais, and so on. If Christianity is to be made available to the Asian people, then indigenous forms of Christian theology, liturgy, and ecclesial structure also have to be introduced, as they have been to a limited extent on the subcontinent.

Christianity has been and still is eurocentric, and its eurocentrism grew out of still more narrow cultural heritages: the Semitic worldview, reinforced and polished by the Greco-Roman configuration. Greek philosophy then became the foundational support of Christian theology, giving it a vehicle, while Roman law and organizational skills became the paradigm for Canon Law and Church government. Father Bede believed that this system has reached the end of its usefulness; it is no longer either meaningful or beneficial, save for those who have a vested interest in preserving it along with their own power. The present system has imprisoned the real Church, which is totally of the Spirit.

The Church, then, must open herself up to the presence of God in other religious traditions and seek to integrate their insights, their wisdom, into her own self-understanding and view of reality, thus becoming universal in a more than geographical sense. She must make the truths of these other systems of faith her own. Bede summed it up in this way: "Christianity cannot grow as a religion today unless it is willing to abandon its Western culture and its rational masculine bias and learn again the feminine intuitive understanding that is characteristic of the East."[10]

The exclusivist position regarding Christianity's role developed out of a mentality that had precious little exposure to or sympathetic understanding of other traditions. The great temporal power of the papacy and the Church managed to solidify eurocentrism in theology and ecclesial culture, while at the same time negative experiences with a militant Islam served only to erect a bastion-type mentality of a Christianity under siege. As a consequence, Catholicism became increasingly xenophobic, more rigidly Latin, a living fossil of the Greco-Roman world. There were no studies done of other traditions, though Nicholas of Cusa did give some attention to Islam and the need for reconciliation in his progressive treatise, *De Pace Fidei*. Apart from the example of Cusanus, the Christian world has been dominated by a negative attitude to non-Christian faiths, and this attitude has been the basis of the Church's continuing eurocentric focus, a focus that is deeply ingrained and will be mitigated—let alone dissolved—only by great effort.[11]

The road to universality in the Christian tradition by entering into new relationships with the other traditions, notably with the Asian faiths— especially Hinduism, Buddhism, Taoism, and Confucianism—has been an unsteady and irregular affair. The path has not been sufficiently trod. The very promising experiments of Matteo Ricci (1551–1610) in China and of Roberto de Nobili (1577–1656) in India ultimately fell victim to the eurocentric predicament, though these experiments were immensely valuable in their accomplishments and valid in their direction.

Both men had followed the route of inculturation and both became respected scholars of the sacred texts of their host cultures: Ricci of the Confucian and Taoist classics, de Nobili of the Hindu canon. Ricci, by this means, was able to convince the Confucian scholars of the imperial court that the Gospel actually completes Confucian ethics; he virtually had the emperor and his family converted. Roberto de Nobili, meanwhile, was having great success with his program on the subcontinent. He was the first non-Hindu ever to read the sacred scriptures and the first European to learn Sanskrit. The Brahmins had enormous respect for him, especially since he lived in utter simplicity after assuming sannyasa, the life of total renunciation of the Indian ascetic. De Nobili had something visible developing, but he was bitterly opposed at every turn by local authorities of the Church, particularly the Portuguese segment of the Indian Church, which was militantly conservative. His work, like that of Ricci, was suppressed by those who feared that Christianity in a non-European dress would not be the true Christianity.

Another crucial figure in the movement for an Indian Christian theology, spirituality, and monasticism was the fiery nationalist and Bengali, Brahmabandhab Upadhyay (1861–1907). He was a brilliant metaphysician, a journalist and political activist, and one of the fathers of Indian independence. Upadhyay was a Brahmin who embraced Catholicism and then went on to become a Christian sannyasin. He has inspired many Indian Christian theologians since his time, introducing some of the technical language of Indian theology and indicating a path for future development. For instance, it was Upadhyay who first suggested the word *Saccidananda* as a term for the Trinity. It was also Upadhyay who wanted to substitute the Vedanta for Scholasticism (that is, for Thomism) as the metaphysical foundation of an Indian Christian theology. Upadhyay also established an Indian Christian *matha* (monastery), exclusively for Christian sannyasins. His approach was suppressed by Archbishop Ladislas Zaleski, the Apostolic Delegate to India at the turn of the century, a persistent opponent of Upadhyay's innovations.

Today in India there are hundreds of native Christian theologians who grapple with some of the issues and challenges Upadhyay raised, but they still do so in a climate clouded by conservatism. The Indian Church is an enigma, though, for while so many bishops, priests, and laity are stuck in the past, there are yet some extraordinary advances. One is the rise of the ashram movement and the emergence of Christian sannyasa, both of which are monastic ventures and have witnessed the fruitful participation of Father Bede. It has to be said that the dream of an inculturated Christianity in the Indian context, with its more universal character, has been realized primarily on the monastic level, and there only imperfectly.

Bede and his immediate predecessors, Jules Monchanin and Henri Le Saux/Abhishiktananda, took up the monastic experiment where Upadhyay left off. Shantivanam is thoroughly Indian and Christian at the same time. It is Hindu/Indian in culture and style of life but Christian in faith, though exposed and sensitive not only to Hinduism but to Buddhism and other great traditions. Bede's ashram has evolved into something capable of reconciling East and West.

In the classical understanding of ashramic life, Shantivanam is a center devoted to the search for God and one's true self. There is a dynamic openness to people from every corner of the world. Shantivanam provides a space for something to happen within the depths of the heart, on the contemplative level of being. It also offers a model for how the various world religions can meet on this level, this mystical meeting point common to them all—a meeting point at the center of subjectivity where we are already one. Here, in the "cave of the heart," facilitated by the simplicity and peace of the ashram which strip away all our distractions and pretentions, we can explode into awareness and spiritual wisdom. Shantivanam never fails in this regard, at least in my own experience. It is this mystical awakening that has to spread in the Church, and India can do much to encourage that type of inner growth. Thus the Church can be renewed in the deepest dimension of her being as she flows forth from the Spirit.

Christianity has the same contemplative depth as Hinduism and the other Eastern traditions; it possesses vast mystical, psychological, and moral wisdom. What India can contribute is a spark to ignite contemplative renewal on a vast scale, a reorientation of the Church toward a rediscovery, and indeed a recovery, of her mystical life, her precious spiritual treasures; for as we become receptive to the riches of the East we *do* recover our contemplative being, even though the journey to the East is not the only way to accomplish this. Within our own house we have such gems as Meister Eckhart, Ruysbroeck, Dionysius, Cassian, *The Cloud of Unknowing*, the great Carmelites and many others, all tremendous resources for self-discovery and for dialogue.

In a video interview conducted by Laurence Freeman, Director of the World Community for Christian Meditation, Bede summed up the whole aim of interreligious exchange in his experience, what Matthew Fox calls "deep ecumenism," and what is actually an instance of existential convergence. Bede observed that what Christianity has to do is understand itself anew in the light of the East, while the Eastern religions—Hinduism, Buddhism, and the others—are invited to rediscover *themselves* in the light of the Christian mystery, that is, in the light of Christ.[12]

It should be kept in mind that this is a two-way street, as Bede unambiguously stated and as his experience verified. As a spiritual master, Bede had and continues to have many Hindu followers who see in him a genuine saint and guru. Bede and his approach to spirituality are having an impact in India among certain educated circles of Hindus, but not on the masses. His "experiment" was so fruitful that conservative Hindus—just like, ironically, conservative Catholics—took notice, and not always in the most flattering way![13] Nevertheless, what Bede and others have started represents a seed within Christianity and within Hinduism, a seed that will bear fruit in time.

Finally, Father Bede has been part of the development of an Indian Christian spirituality that draws upon the insights of yoga, meditation, and the Tantra, the latter highlighting the role of the body in spiritual formation. He felt that the body must be incorporated into prayer, something that has not been emphasized in Christian spirituality up until now. Yoga can prepare the body for meditation and for great breakthroughs that can occur in the meditative state of contemplation, but Tantric yoga can unite the body with the mind in the effort of prayer.

Here the Christian tradition has serious limitations, since the body has often been rejected, at least in recent centuries. This can be aptly illustrated by a medieval Cistercian saying, "When you enter the monastery, you must leave your body at the gate." India and the Tantric school of yoga, a school that actually antedates both Hinduism and Buddhism, go in the opposite direction altogether, epitomized in the Tantric aphorism, "That by which we fall is that by which we rise." Bede emphasized this teaching again and again. The whole aim of life on earth is to integrate the body with the mind and then to surrender these to the Spirit.

FATHER BEDE'S LAST DAYS

Father Bede's two strokes—one in December 1992 and the other in February 1993—left him emotionally vulnerable and quite spontaneous. His sense of ego-identity had dissolved, and this condition gave him the freedom to express feelings that British reserve had previously kept in check. His response to anyone close to him was with genuine affection—hugging and kissing them. These spontaneous manifestations of love really communicate his ultimate teaching so well, and reinforce his role as a Christian thinker, spiritual teacher, and saint. This eloquent teaching concerns the reality of love that Bede came to incarnate in his life and example. Russill and Asha Paul D'Silva, who were very dear to Father Bede, wrote in a wonderful circular letter to their friends dated Holy Thursday (April 8, 1993), of their impressions of Bede in terms of this depth of love. One morning, in early April, shortly after their hurried arrival from America, Bede said to them tenderly, "I feel that God has created a love and understanding in us that I have never experienced before and that has completed my life. It is a plan of total love, of total self-giving in love."

Bede had gone through a complete inner transformation that established him more deeply and totally in the spontaneous flow of divine Love. This process of transformation had begun a few years earlier after the first stroke.

For some months, an inner process of profound change took place, and in a letter to me in the Spring of 1990, he revealed: "I find myself in the Void, but the Void is completely saturated with Love." It has often struck me how this inner awareness of his—this mystical consciousness—actually unites the deepest experience of Christian mysticism with the deepest experience of the Buddhist tradition. However we may wish to name or describe Bede's mysticism, it thoroughly remains within this great school of affective spirituality.

Russill and Asha, in their moving letter, characterize the nature of Bede's transformation in a final observation:

His [Bede's] words and teachings are very simple and straight from the heart—devoid of all theology and intellectual prisms. His speech is full of love and his eyes shine with an inner light whenever he says anything. His face, although wizened and pale, nevertheless reflects that glory which comes from communion with God. He only speaks of love. Love seems to be the central experience of his consciousness and it is all that comes through whether he sleeps or wakes. He has the aura of a baby, and many a time we have experienced a strong sense of a sacred energy when we are with him. Without any doubt we can say that he has reached a very high level of being.

Bedeji had achieved what his Indian name, Dayananda, means—the Bliss of Compassion, really the Bliss of Love.

Bede Griffiths' approach and method of working was essentially grounded in his intuition of the complementary nature of the world religions, that is, that they enrich and complete one another. They have to be seen together and not in either opposition to, or isolation from, other traditions. Bede had a firm commitment to a pluralistic vision that is confident of the ultimate metaphysical and mystical harmony of the various spiritual paths in the one Spirit uniting us all. It is in the Spirit that we are one, and it is in the same Spirit that each path finds its eventual fulfillment. We all meet, as Swami Abhishiktananda says so eloquently, "in the cave of the heart."[14] It is because Bede advanced intercultural dialogue in this cave of the heart, and so contributes to the realization of our unity in the Spirit, that we offer this volume to him.

NOTES

1. Wayne Teasdale, *Essays in Mysticism* (Lake Worth, FL: Sunday Publications, 1985); idem, *Towards a Christian Vedanta* (Bangalore: Asian Trading, 1987).

2. The only existing biography of Bede Griffiths is Kathryn Spink's, *A Sense of the Sacred* (1968).

3. Abhishiktananda, *Saccidananda: A Christian Approach to Advaitic Experience* (Delhi: ISPCK, 1974, rev. 1984).

4. Ibid., p.45. For a really fine treatment of the problem, see Sara Grant, "Christian Theologizing and the Challenge of Advaita," in *Theologizing in India*, ed. M. Amaldas, T. K. John and G. Gispert-Sauch (Bangalore: Theological Publications in India, 1981).

5. Abhishiktananda, "Experience of God in Eastern Religions," *Cistercian Studies*, vol. 9, nos. 2 & 3 (1974), pp. 151–152.

6. Abhishiktananda, *Saccidananda*, p. 47.

7. Griffiths, *The Marriage of East and West*, p. 99.

8. Ibid.

9. Ibid., p. 89.

10. Griffiths, *The Marriage of East and West*, pp. 198–99.

11. I remember a conversation a few years ago with Father Felix Wilfred, an Indian theologian of considerable note, who remarked to Father Bede and me that there would be an intense struggle in Rome and in the Church at large over the issue of interreligious dialogue, that the battle over *Humanae Vitae* would pale into insignificance in comparison with this upcoming struggle. One could remark that the first salvo was perhaps fired with the promulgation of the Vatican Letter on Meditation in November 1989, which takes a rather negative view of those Eastern techniques that are not in themselves Christ-centered.

12. Video interview of Bede Griffiths by Laurence Freeman, *Christ in the Lotus* (Benedictine Priory of Montreal, with Concordia University, 1990). Contact: Department of Religion, Concordia University.

13. In March of 1987 I gave a talk in Madras to a group of Hindu intellectuals on Bede's spirituality and interreligious views. It was reported in the *Indian Express* with a rather unfortunate summary. This touched off a storm of protest by radically conservative swamis. Of course, more reasonable ones came to Bede's defense.

14. See Abhishiktananda, *Hindu-Christian Meeting Point: Within the Cave of the Heart* (Delhi: ISPCK, 1969).

Part One:

Personal Memories

The Four Rivers of Bede

Sunder Wells

Sunder Wells' poem commemorates the significant stages of Bede's life as a crossing of symbolic rivers, to reach each time a "further shore." The poet is the founder of the New Monk Project, an experimental form of contemplative vocation welcoming members from all religious traditions or those with no formal affiliation. Dom Bede was one of the Elders.

J
Conversion

Daring!   This day I invoke you, daring
to cross the bridge of bones
where brother slaughtered brother
and in anger slaughters still
since Henry tossed his gauntlet
at the foot of Peter.

My son, be warned
   this river is of blood still flowing
   and its fierce defenders
   yet may rise to strike you down.
Beware!

But the word came down: Dig deeper!
   And you crossed the River of Blood.

JJ
Emigration

Daring!   Once more I invoke you, daring
to cross the straits of time
where drifts of years in millions
turned our faces in the four directions
fanning us to infinite variety.

Far oceans you must cross on floes of ice
   while ghostly voices call through racial
   strictures collared white and order you:
Turn back!

Once more the word came down: Dig deeper!
   And you crossed the River of Ice.

ℑℑℑ
ℑmmersion

Haven!   This day I invoke you, haven
          warmed with blood of sun
          orange and ochre flowing edgeless
          vespered in the velvet dusk,
          heartbeat bared
          to water, earth, and air,
          dark eyes and gentle hands
          around me now.

      But north winds curl the edges
          of your dream and launch cold shafts
          against the garment of your peace.
          My son! they wail,
          the beauties of this land
          have lulled you with their
          opiate of bliss. Rise up
          and flee its perfumes while
          you still have feet to fly!

The word came down in silence, and you sat as one
with warmth of earth, digging ever deeper as flames
rose high to circle you

And motionless
      You crossed the River of Fire.

IV
Emergence

Rising!   This day I invoke you, rising
taut as bow string from the couch of this
bright cave. For I hear voices more than hairs
upon my whited head. They call me from across
the western sea. Various they cry while hands
of many hues tug pleading at my robe.

*Not one voice of warning, not one
    voice but calls you on
    through stream of narrow winding
    through rich fields destined for harvest
    in a land you never knew.*

*This land is parched, its people thirst,
    the stream flows deep and crystal; it
    bursts its banks to wake the dormant seed.
    The crystal swirls around you now,
    your staff upholds you strongly*

And the River that you cross is named Compassion.

A Tribute

Raimon Panikkar

Raimon Panikkar was a personal friend of the "three gurus" of Saccidananda Ashram, Abbé Jules Monchanin, Swami Abhishiktananda, and Dom Bede, all of whom were dedicated to the interreligious quest. Panikkar is himself an incarnation of the union of spiritual traditions that is our center of interest. Born of an Indian Hindu father and a Spanish Catholic mother, he has devoted his life to finding fruitful conversations among the world's religions. Gifford Lecturer (1989) at Edinburgh, he is the author of twenty-nine books in several languages, including The Silence of God: The Answer of the Buddha *(1989).[1] His contribution, "A Tribute," was occasioned by Dom Bede's death and replaces (at his request) his piece in the first edition of this book, "A Good Theologian Should Be a Lover of Myths."[2]*

J would like to join my voice in tribute to Swami Dayananda, which is the Indian name of Dom Bede Griffiths. Father Bede reached the final stage of his individual pilgrimage a week before the Ascension on May 13th, 1993, the anniversary of the first appearance of Our Lady of Fatima. With him the Saccidananda Ashram, or "Cenobium" of the Holy Trinity, had completed its trinitarian leadership: Jules Monchanin, the founder, Abhishiktananda, the transformer, and Griffiths, the reformer. The three were so different that the friends of the first were rather critical of the second, and the followers of the second were not "tuned in" by the third. And yet these men were great and holy—as a friend of all three I can attest to this!

Still fresh in my memory is the entire day I spent with Monchanin discussing the Trinity; in one of my meetings with Le Saux (Abhishiktananda), he sang Breton songs and cried; I also spent the first six months of Bede's stay in India with him, and in our last meeting, just a few months before his full resurrection, we cried, embraced, and blessed each other. In addition to the three men mentioned above, I also include two others with a similar mission: Father Lambert of the Mother of God (1912–1968), who in a quiet way was received into the sannyasa order of the Saraswati Dasanamis without ceasing to be a most orthodox Carmelite, and the still living Francis Acharya, the founder of Kurishumala in Kerala, an ashram that revives the ancient spirituality from the first Christian centuries. The life and witness of these spiritual giants is a plain refutation of the cliché about the foreign missionary obsessed with conversions and implanting a spirituality alien to India. In fact, three of the five named above acquired Indian citizenship.

"Le roy est mort, vive le roy!" was a past slogan of traditional monarchies. The King was perceived as the symbol of a divinely established institution, more than the particular human individual who filled that role at any given time. In contrast, in the traditional Indic sense, the ashram *is* the guru. It is not an institution that perdures. When the guru is no longer there, the ashram either disappears or transforms itself. This is the reason why many modern Indian ashrams try to keep the "presence" of the guru alive—it is often essential to its continuing existence.

Shantivanam has had *three* gurus. They had something very fundamental and humble (*humus*) in common, which is overlooked sometimes, influenced as we are by Cartesian ways of thinking. They had in common the place. The *genius loci* is powerful.

Now, for the first time, a "native son" of Shantivanam will maintain and sustain the ashram. Love of guru and the spirit of humility may be enough encouragement simply to try to follow the example of the master and keep his memory and his teaching alive. However, history shows us the power of both place and time. For instance, Peter and Paul, to recall an important Christian example, changed after the death of Christ, and changed again after they moved to Rome, as also did their immediate followers. As Shantideva said, "One dies and another is born." Shantivanam is in the Orient—it is in India, Tamilnadu, the banks of the Kavery. These are essential geographical, historical, and human categories that influence its nature. With Bede's passing, the umbilical cord with the West has been cut. This is the occasion to establish other kinds of links. Shantivanam, like a true martyr or witness of the three saints, is now called to be a cradle of new spirituality for a country and for the world.

None of Shantivanam's three masters was a fanatic. None of them was an exclusivist Christian or blind follower of imported spiritualities. The expressed freedom of the three was astonishing, up to the point of scandalizing many who cannot imagine that Roman Catholics could be so bold, so free, so fearless. The fresh spirit that they brought to Christianity is their witness for many others.

"Unless a grain of wheat falls into the earth and dies, it remains alone; but if it dies, it bears much fruit" (John 12:24): Now is the time to collect the "harvest" of these three, or rather to be prepared for this collection after the immediate "monsoon" is over. I am not saying that we should busy ourselves with creating a synthesis of their three approaches to spirituality, but rather suggesting that we should wait in .expectation—with patience and a great receptivity, but also with unbounded confidence in the fruits of the earth. "Whether Paul or Apollos or Cephas . . . ," it is God who gives the increase.

Bede's extraordinary gift (and I know how much it cost him) was one of tolerance. This was his special spirit that pervaded Shantivanam during the years of his tenure. He did not judge anybody or anything. Everyone felt immediately loved. He seemed unaware of the concrete existential evil that torments so many people, without being blinded to the objective evils in the world. He looked for the good. On the level of ideas, as well, he tried to take positive steps. He foresaw the "marriage of East and West" and the fruitful dialogue of science and spirituality. He knew that a new world is coming, that profound adjustments will have to be made, and he made his contribution toward opening the way for that new world. His spirit, therefore, is a spirit of self-transcendence, a spirit that would go beyond itself, that would do new things. In this spirit, may we go forward and take our own further steps into the future.

NOTES

1. Raimundo Panikkar, *The Silence of God: The Answer of the Buddha*, trans. by Robert R. Barr, in Faith Meets Faith Series (Maryknoll, NY: Orbis Books, 1989).

2. See Beatrice Bruteau, ed., *As We Are One: Essays and Poems in Honor of Bede Griffiths*, 1991.

"At Shantivanam" and "Evening Meditation"

John F. Baker

Michigan writer and poet John Baker composed these two poems after a meaningful visit to Father Bede's ashram.

At Shantivanam

My love is like a lotus flower
in the night,
deep beneath the surface
of the pool,
its petals closed,
the drunken bee within
drowned.

Evening Meditation
(Shantivanam)

Smell of dung and sandalwood,
the river's silence.

A stick of incense gazes
from the darkened corner.

The race of mental images
subsides at last.

My heart a breathed-on ember
opens, opens . . .

Bede Griffiths at Apple Farm: A Personal Memory

Helen Luke

Helen Luke gives us a personal glimpse of Father Bede—an account of his 1992 visit to the Apple Farm Community, which she helped found near Three Rivers, Michigan, in 1963. British born, Luke read modern languages and literature at Oxford, then trained as a Jungian therapist in England before coming to the United States to open practice in Los Angeles. Author of four books, including her study of Dante's Divine Comedy *entitled* Dark Wood to White Rose *(1989), she has been a frequent contributor to* Parabola *magazine, whose editors have published* Kaleidoscope *(1992), a collection of Luke's best essays and book chapters. At Apple Farm she continued until her death in 1995 to offer opportunities to discover "the transforming power of symbols" in a Jungian context, and it is from this perspective that she shares her own "memories, dreams, and reflections" as they relate to Father Bede.*

It was only a few days before Father Bede Griffiths' death that I received a letter from Dr. Bruteau asking me if I would write something in his honor for this book. It is a particular joy for me to do this, since here at our small community of Apple Farm we were greatly blessed by a visit from him during the time which, as we now know, was to be his last in the United States.

Father Bede gave a talk in our small meeting house, to which about fifty of our friends came, and his particular message shines in our memory, while the impact of having been in his presence touches the eternal spark in each of us. Others have spoken of his prophetic words about religious groups among lay people as being essential guardians of the Spirit in our time, and of their work of restoring the sense of the sacred on every level of our daily lives—a sense that has been almost completely lost here in the West. In the dark ages that followed the complete breakdown of the law and order established by the Roman Empire, he said, the great monasteries were the keepers of the flame through the centuries. But Father Bede laid great stress in his talk with us on an essential aspect of such groups in this our time of a new and terrible dark age of violence and loss of meaning: these groups must remain *small*. This had a particularly deep meaning for us here at Apple Farm, and we felt a profound gratitude that somehow we had intended from our beginning in 1963 that we not do what many of the small groups and communes starting at that time did, which was to set out with as much publicity as possible and appeals for money from foundations, etc., with the obvious hope of support from collective institutions and the attraction of new members. Most of these groups that we knew of came to an end and faded away after a very few years. Many of our respected advisers had put pressure on us to do something of this kind, but we insisted that we were simply a group of friends, whose particular experience of life, and of what C. G. Jung has called the way of individuation, could perhaps be shared with other individuals who either could not afford or were not in need of clinical analysis, but yearned for meaning in their inner lives through listening to the voice of their dreams. Our way is indeed based on the same attitude as that which Father Bede called "the sense of the sacred" in all the smallest happenings of daily life—in its often seemingly meaningless conflicts and hurt feelings, its experiences of darkness and of light, of happiness and pain. We have remained small, simply a focal point, a meeting place, for mutual support and discussion. We have never sought to have more than four guests at a time, but through the years people sharing our basic attitude have come to settle nearby, living their own lives and joining in meetings at the Farm, seeking the sacred in their chosen way. We have, of course, a non-profit charter.

The hunger for a renewed sense of meaning in life, for the restoration of that which transcends space and time and the small ego in each of us, is now "erupting," one could say, everywhere. That which is sought is called by many names, though ultimately unnameable by the consciously rational mind. In our tradition it is God, or more deeply, the "I am." The hunger is real and often desperate, but the state of consciousness that has taken over since the enormous increase in rational, extraverted knowledge in the West has brought with it a terrible loss of feeling values, and the result is the worship of quantity at the expense of quality on every level of being. All success, so-called, is identified with large numbers: larger businesses, larger congregations in churches, larger groups, larger bank accounts. The more has become the better, even in the evaluation of good works. And this is most dangerous of all in the hunger for "spiritual experience"—that lonely thing, destroyed by any sort of mass thinking. When a man or woman *identifies* with a strongly numinous experience, followers may be sought and often come in large numbers, and a cult begins. The extreme horror of this may result in a Jonestown disaster or something similar.

I think it is important to be careful of the word "religious," especially as applied to communities. The "religious life" has meant for so long the life lived by a community, usually large, within the structure of a particular church, and therefore to apply it to such groups as ours would give a wrong impression. It is true, of course, that such small focal points, if real, are religious in the true and basic meaning of the word. The word *religious*, in Father Bede's teaching, refers to that deepest essence that is finally the unity beyond all the many approaches to religion inside and outside the churches of the world. C. G. Jung, as is well known, said that no psychological neurosis was ever truly healed (made whole) in a person unless he or she found a religious meaning in life—in Father Bede's words "the sense of the sacred." One passage I greatly love is in T. S. Eliot's "Little Gidding" in his *Four Quartets*: "All shall be well and all manner of thing shall be well by the purification of the motive in the ground of our beseeching."

That is the life-long inner work in every human being. It is very hard indeed to discover and purge the ego-centered motive at the root of all the superficial choices that proliferate within us, until we may come, at least in glimpses, to that "condition of complete simplicity costing no less than everything" ("Little Gidding") which shines out of Father Bede's sacred humanity.

I would like now to say a little of the two hours or so of private conversation that I had with Father Bede during his visit to Apple Farm, which left me with such a sense of joy and unity, and of the true marriage of East and West incarnate in him. I knew already from having met him some years earlier, when he came to speak at St Gregory's Abbey (Anglican Benedictine, only a mile or so distant from Apple Farm), of his introduction to yoga and the East by Toni Sussman in London, of which he often spoke. She and her husband were Jewish refugees from Hitler's Germany. While in Berlin she had had much experience in Hindu thought and practice, and had become a Roman Catholic. She also was one of C. G. Jung's early pupils and was a Jungian analyst. I, too, had met her in those years of the Second World War, and to me, too, she opened the door to the depths of Eastern religion, as well as taking me on as a student of Jung's way. An enormous enrichment came to me at that time through reading the Upanishads, the Bhagavad Gita, the Tao Te Ching, and the I Ching, and this has increased and deepened through all the fifty years since and in all my work in Jung's psychology, which turned out to be my vocation. Father Bede told me that at that time, when traveling, he often carried Jung's *Memories, Dreams, Reflections* in his luggage. Then, last year during our conversation we again remembered Toni, and he said that she had tried at one point to steer him into Jungian work! But his vocation, of course, was abundantly clear. We also had quite a number of English things in common from our youth. Our years at Oxford, for instance, overlapped in the twenties, and although I never met C. S. Lewis, he was a very prominent and influential person in the University during those years. So I could share memories and laughter and that strangely deep meeting that comes through roots in the soil of the country of birth, as well as feeling the radiance of his spirit beyond words.

The affirmation of the kinship of all life beyond duality will grow in those individuals all over the world who, without evasion, consent to suffer the darkness of the extreme tension between opposites, supported by the spirit and the all-embracing love of such great ones as Father Bede. So the light shines still in the darkest places, each of us carrying our tiny unique candle, and thus there may come to our world by grace the global healing of earth and spirit, of the dark and the light, in the oneness beyond and including all opposites.

I end with a vivid dream that came to me on the night after I heard of Father Bede's death. In this dream I saw him lying on his bed and surrounded by a growing number of young people and children. Each one of them was holding out a hand to him in grief and sadness at his going. And then I heard his voice, low but very clear, saying to them, "You have, I know, each one of you, come here in Love; and please remember that in Love there is always joy."

A Way of Initiation

Odette Baumer-Despeigne

The contribution of Odette Baumer-Despeigne, who lives in Frauenfeld, Switzerland, is a double one. She tells her own story of meeting the three men who made Saccidananda what it is today—Abbé Jules Monchanin, Swami Abhishiktananda, and Dom Bede—and of her close association with them, especially Abhishiktananda. She has prepared many of Abhishiktananda's posthumous works for publication and continues to make his life and spiritual ideals known through her lectures and writing. In this piece, joining in the gift to Dom Bede, she has Abhishiktananda himself speak by selecting passages from Swamiji's works (many of these from his as yet unpublished writings) that illumine the familiar lines of the Lord's Prayer. She has noticed that the "Our Father," if read in reverse order, provides a succinct guide to our inner experiences in the spiritual life. She interweaves a golden thread throughout this tapestry by adding Abhishiktananda's discourse on advaita (nondualism), presented as if revealed by Jesus himself from his own experience.

Before bringing my gift to lay at the "lotus feet" of Dom Bede Griffiths, the one we honor in this volume, let me explain how I came to know and be deeply committed to the Shantivanam monks and the new/old spirituality that they lived. Just as scientists say that all things in the universe are interrelated, so we can affirm that the same is true in the spiritual world. An Eastern saying is that all beads or gems of a necklace are strung on a single thread. Three precious gems on the thread of my life have been Abbé Jules Monchanin (1895–1957), Dom Henri Le Saux/Swami Abhishiktananda (1910–1973), and Father Bede Griffiths (1906–1993). Abhishiktananda is the one whom I have known best, being introduced to him by Abbé Jules Monchanin, with whom he founded the Shantivanam Ashram in 1950. And then, through Shantivanam, I came to know our revered Father Bede.

Let me begin this journey with my own biography. In 1927 I was in a boarding school in Brussels. The chaplain of the convent gave a course on the Holy Trinity, at the end of which he declared, "Mesdemoiselles, at present you know all that is possible concerning God." I was horrified and began to weep, thinking that if at the age of seventeen I already knew all that is knowable about God, what am I going to do during the rest of my life?

Fortunately, this "teaching" was enlarged months later by Professor Pierre Charles, S.J., then holding the first chair of Missiology at the University of Louvain. His topic was "How to present Christianity to non-Christian religions." When he began to talk on the Hindu way of approach to the Divine, it was as though I had been struck by lightning. From then on I knew what would be my interest in life—I had discovered my vocation!

In 1936 I came across the name of Jules Monchanin in an article, "The Church and Indian Thought," in the *Bulletin des Missions*, No. 4. Three years later I had the joy of meeting him during his last stay in Louvain, just before his departure for India. I was fascinated by his personality—so much nobility allied with simplicity and abundant serenity, with a great love for India, and above all a bright intelligence and extensive culture allied with humility. In fact, he said: "I have no plan; I just want to be a humble priest among Indian priests. . . . My wish is to see contemplative monastic life surging from the very soil of India and to be one of those monks trying to rethink Indian culture as a Christian and Christianity as an Indian."

In a recently edited book, *Abbé Monchanin, Letters to His Mother*,[1] there are sayings that clearly reveal the continuity of spirit between Father Bede and one of the founders of Shantivanam. For instance, Abbé Monchanin expressed his wish that "from the soil and the soul of India also there should arise a monastic life vowed to contemplation."[2] He also said, "I think that the mission of India in the Church is to sink a well—to the very depths of the abyss—into the contemplation of the Holy Trinity! and that I myself may contribute to this in my feeble way, and in this my life will have all its meaning."[3] "It will be necessary that India herself create her own unique form for men and women of contemplative life . . . by way of exterior and interior modes that are purely Indian."[4]

It was with great enthusiasm that I read, shortly after its publication in 1956, *Ermites du Saccidananda, Un essai d'intégration chrétienne de la tradition monastique de l'Inde*, by Jules Monchanin and Henri Le Saux.[5] This is how I discovered the existence of Father Le Saux, the second "gem" with whom I would become deeply familiar, from 1966 through 1973, during the last seven years of his life. We first met by correspondence (seventy-eight letters), and finally I met him in person in India. I wrote to him first after attending a series of lectures on Hindu spirituality, given by a Hindu sannyasin from Rishikesh, which put me in an unclear situation vis-à-vis my Christian faith. When at last we met face to face, it was in Indore at the Nursing Home of the Franciscan Sisters, where he had come after his severe heart attack and where he passed away "to the Further Shore." Of course, Abhishiktananda was not in his natural Hindu environment, but the privilege of meeting him after his deep spiritual experience that occurred while he was undergoing his heart attack was a grace granted to very few. His whole being was, as it were, transparent to the inner mystery of the Divine Presence. The radiance of his eyes, wide open in wonder, cannot be described in words.

After his death, Abhishiktananda's archives, especially his spiritual diary, were entrusted to me. It took me years of work to publish the posthumous writings, to decipher the diary and to prepare a first selection from it. The latter was published in French, with an introduction by Raimundo Panikkar, under the title, *La montée au fond du coeur, journal intime d'un moine chrétien-sannyasi hindou*,[6] in 1986, but has not yet been translated into English. The second most important work also remains untranslated into English: *Intériorité et Révélation*, published in 1982;[7] it contains various theological essays. Besides these two volumes, there are thousands of pages of correspondence awaiting publication.

In the meantime, I have dedicated much of my life to the spread of interreligious dialogue, presenting the ideas of Swami Abhishiktananda and present-day Shantivanam in many monasteries and lay spiritual centers in the United States as well as in Europe. I know Shantivanam quite well, having stayed there three times.

Those are the deep connections I have had and continue to have with those pioneers, not trying to make "commentaries" on their work but simply trying to transmit their messages plainly and faithfully, leaving the further work to the Holy Spirit in the heart of every hearer or reader.

I now would like to make my contribution to the celebration of Father Bede Griffiths. The following contains a text that is mine in conception and organization, but which extensively uses quotations from Swami Abhishiktananda taken from all of his works, published and unpublished (especially the two mentioned above and not available in English), and from many private letters. In my eyes, this text represents the most intimate core of the spirituality of the "three gems" I spoke of at the beginning.

This is a "Meditation on the Lord's Prayer," seen as a "Way of Initiation." It is a kind of consideration of the Our Father, read in reverse order, the last verse becoming the first and vice versa. I discovered that when read in this manner, the Lord's Prayer exactly follows the steps of the "inner pilgrimage to the Source" that we learn through the upanishadic approach to the divine Mystery. There are three steps on this pilgrimage: 1) the Dialogue with the Master, or Guru; 2) the Monologue of the Awakened One; and 3) Ultimate Silence, the Void exploding into Fullness. It is my hope that presenting the message in this way may enable it to touch both Western and Eastern hearts.

MEDITATION ON THE LORD'S PRAYER
FIRST STAGE: DIALOGUE WITH THE GURU

[In the following, much of the text is the words of Swami Abhishik-tananda. My own contributions are set in italics.]

Once Jesus was in a certain place praying, and when he ceased, one of his disciples said to him, "Lord, teach us to pray as John taught his disciples!" [Luke 11:1]

The teaching of the master, the guru, does not consist of words to be meditated on, or to be fixed in the mind but should lead to an experience to be "felt." The whole teaching of the guru conceals a dart which causes the fountain in the depth of the disciple's heart to gush forth. The meeting with the guru is the essential encounter that is the decisive turning point in the life of a man. The [true] guru is one who knows by personal experience, one who is capable of establishing contact with the inmost soul of his disciple, and of communicating to him mysteriously, by his "grace," that same experience. That is the experience of the "Further Shore, beyond darkness" (Chandogya Upanishad 7).

The disciple must be pure and transparent, so open and teachable that the words uttered by the guru can penetrate to his inmost heart and then spring up like a fountain of living water. Problems present themselves only at the level of our reason, which desires to grasp conceptually that which cannot be expressed in conceptual terms. Hence, the only true solution is to learn the language of silence.

It is precisely this language that the Lord's Prayer, meditated on in reverse, will teach us.

AMEN: SO BE IT

Jesus appeared in the world not to teach ideas but to impart to men an experience, his own personal experience of being Son of God. Following on from this experience of his and by its efficacy, he undertook to bring others to realize and integrate in their own awareness that condition which is theirs also, of being children of God.

Man's essential task is to rediscover his Ground, to rediscover his own origin at the center of his being, to rediscover in the source of the self the Self of the Source.

In the Vedic Tradition this ultimate mystery of being is called *Brahman*. . . . the ineffable reality which lies hidden behind all things and at the same time penetrates all things, that which is at the source of everything that exists, the Absolute—at once beyond and within what is limited. It is the sacred, the numinous, that which is revealed in the ultimate secret of all (cf. Kena Upanishad).

DELIVER US FROM EVIL

This is also the petition that every disciple in India addresses to her or his guru when prostrated at the teacher's feet.

Eradicate my fault, this evil that I have committed. [Maha Narayana Upanishad 93]

From darkness lead me to light. From death lead me to immortality. [Brihadaranyaka Upanishad I.3.28]

The whole of life is a mystery of passing over. The fundamental step in salvation, or conversion, is taken at the level of the human heart, that is to say, at the deepest center of our being. This conversion, the *metanoia* of the Gospel, is the abandoning of all self-centeredness, of all egoism; it is a total turning back of the whole being to God. In other words, it is to place oneself in the presence of the guru, the Savior.

Jesus is Savior principally by his presence in the midst of humanity. He is Savior also by the teaching and example which he gave to mankind concerning the means of salvation here and now. For salvation is not primarily something belonging to the future, a kind of celestial survival, for which one has to prepare to the best of one's ability while on earth. It is above all, a reality to be found here and now, at this very moment of time. For the very fact that "In Him, I am" has for me the value of eternity. As St. Paul says, "In him we live and move and have our being" (Acts 17:28).

Salvation does not consist of an idea, but requires a change of level in the soul. It is a remorseless process of dying to oneself, dying to the inherent dualism of the human mind and to the bondage of the ego which is the fundamental obstacle to the "taking in charge" of the human being by the Spirit, as announced in the scriptures.

The essential work is the abandonment, the handing over (the *surrender*) of the peripheral self to the interior Mystery, the abandonment of the phenomenal self which man takes as the center of his being, whereas this center is independent of all localization, psychological as well as physical.

This is why the true experience, whether it is reached by starting from the Upanishads, from Zen, from Christianity, or from Islam, demands first of all a drastic purification of the whole mentality and of the self, and this purification is the most urgent need of our age, in all the Traditions.

"Go, sell all your goods," Jesus has said, "then come, follow me." [Matthew 19:21]

"Leave all things behind you, come to me, the only refuge," Krishna has said in the Bhagavad Gita. [18:66]

"Uproot us from evil," Chouraqui has translated this petition. In the Katha Upanishad we read: "No one who has not desisted from evil ways . . . can reach the supreme Spirit [Atman]" (I.2.24).

Evil, the state of sin, is the pretense of being distant from God. As long as unconsciousness of the Presence of God is not an insupportable weight on the heart, an anguish impossible to contain, man knows nothing. The state of sin is to wish to remain unconscious of the non-distance of God. Life is the experience of the Presence of God.

Remember what the Dominican, Tauler, said in the fourteenth century: "It is a great sin and a shame that we benighted people, who are Christians and who have received so much help in the form of God's grace, the faith, and the Holy Sacrament, are still turning round and round like blind hens, not knowing ourselves and what is in our inner being."

The Prashna Upanishad, more than seven centuries before Christ, has already said: "If one meditates on the Supreme Person. . . . just as a snake sheds its skin and is freed, so one is released from one's sins" (5.5).

So, I abide in this Within, in this place sacred to the Divine Encounter, there where alone in the *presence of God*, I am.

Such is the first step on the path of spiritual Awakening.

—ᴧᴧᴧ—

Do Not Subject Us To Temptation

Lord, after we have felt our face brushed by the burning breath of the Spirit, may we preserve its indelible mark, and may nothing ever again obstruct that inward thrust which is the Spirit in us.

It would take very little to turn the last verse of the Isha Upanishad into a magnificent Christian prayer to the Spirit: "O Agni [Divine Fire], lead us by the right path . . . O Thou who knowest every path, drive far from me the sin which leads me astray" (15.18).

It is at this moment in his journey toward God that the Call of the Absolute in man becomes tormenting, the call of that Mystery which transcends him and which he does not know how to name. It is a call to recollection, a call to detachment, as much from the spiritual as from the temporal. It is a call to faith. Faith is just this: to accept that there is something beyond the rational, for the experience of Christ as that of advaita—the nonduality of the Upanishads—is supramental, and our conceptual apparatus can never perceive more than its impact; we are prisoners of our Greek categories of thought.

Do not let us succumb to temptation: give us the courage to go forward, to face the test.

A journey into the unknown is certainly involved for any man who enters wholeheartedly upon this pilgrimage to the source of being. "Go not outside, return into yourself; the Truth dwells in the inner man," wrote St. Augustine in the *De vera religione* (1.39).

Jesus himself taught that a man has to abandon everything, to put everything at risk, if he is to enter the Kingdom. The Gospel is essentially a renunciation of and an uprooting of the self, of the ego, leaving it behind and following in the footsteps of the Master.

Man is afraid of his essential mystery, afraid of penetrating to the bottom of his heart face to face with himself, afraid of penetrating to the depths of the heart of Christ, there to encounter face to face the Father, the living God, fountain of life; there to encounter beyond all symbols, in his reality, the One who IS. Man is afraid, for God is a devouring Fire, and how can the human ego endure before this devouring fire? "No man can see God and live" (Deut. 4:24; 5:26).

If the ego does not survive, it is because it never was! Yet the self clings to everything, and the "I" refuses to let itself fall away, for it wants to live what it, itself, calls "living."

These painful convulsions of the ego which refuses to die, this agony and distortion of the self, are the "nights" of St. John of the Cross. But this struggle is also a progressive liberation; it means the gradual evaporation of whatever put it in a relation of otherness with essential Reality.

In order that there may no longer be anything to inhibit that interior burst of energy that is the Spirit in us—the One who is the very Presence of God to all things and especially to oneself:

Let us say from the bottom of our heart,

Pardon Us Our Offenses As We Also Pardon Those Who Have Offended Us

From the point of view of Jesus, neither my neighbor nor God nor Jesus is an "other." I live in a communion that is both human and cosmic. The Last Judgment will not depend upon our acts of notional faith but upon our recognition of the theandric mystery which Jesus is in each human person. "I was hungry, and you gave me to eat. . . . Lord, when did we see you hungry and feed you? Inasmuch as you did it for one of the least of my brothers, you did it for me" (Matt. 25:37ff). The Presence shines through my neighbor as truly as it shines in Jesus.

Jesus, like the Buddha, taught no philosophy but a practical way of life: All for God and all for your brother. God in your brother, and I in your brother.

[*Let us make peace with all our brethren, with all men, for*] peace is the essential condition set by Jesus for participating in the divine filiation: "Blessed are the peacemakers, for they will be called children of God" (Matt. 5:9).

In the Yajur Veda, which precedes the Gospel by at least a thousand years, we find already this prayer: "May all beings look on me with the eye of a friend; may I also look on all beings with the eye of a friend; may we look on one another with the eye of a friend" (26.2).

The man who lives at peace is he who lives in the present and has integrated the past without frustration. His gains and his losses are admitted and accepted, mistakes are forgiven and, as he has forgiven those wrongs which his neighbor has committed against him, so he has forgiven himself for having sinned. . . . The man who is at peace has neither fear nor desire, nor does he project himself into any future whatsoever. He is totally himself in the totality of the present moment, and so the future offers him no problems.

In fact, there are no problems; there are only makers of problems! The problem is resolved when the maker of problems has evaporated, for every problem lies essentially in its connection with the ego, the "I-maker." When the ego flies away, the problem goes too!

In my passage of faith into Christ, I participate (as if in a mirror) in his experience of being Son of God, and in this experience of Jesus my nonduality (advaita) with my brothers expands into communion, into *koinonia*. The Christian experience is truly the experience of advaita lived in the human community; it is the Holy Spirit who makes men brothers and unites them around this unique archetypal, cosmic Purusha (Supreme Person) of which Jesus is the privileged expression.

Love is the only way in which man can enter into a true relation with God and with his neighbors. The act of love, or disinterested service toward others, is what awakens a man to himself, to God. There is no Awakening to Being at the foundation of oneself which is not an Awakening to Being in all beings, in the whole history of the cosmos.

It is absolutely necessary that humanity put itself at peace with creation in its entirety, and that humanity confess its sins, not only sins against the natural elements of the cosmos (pollution of the air, of the water), but also the grave sins that humanity has committed in shamefully exploiting the plants and the animals. This is the second step on the path of Awakening.

GIVE US THIS DAY OUR DAILY BREAD

Now that the "knots of the heart have been loosened" (Mundaka Upanishad 2.2), humanity can express its supreme desire: to receive the grace of the guru, the Bread of Life.

The mystery of grace is the Spirit who, when I look outward, envelops me, and when I look inward, permeates me. The Bread Jesus gives is his Spirit. This Bread does not bring forth a change of ideas about God or man, but a change of level of consciousness. Grace is the perception of the totality of the mystery in everything that reflects it here on earth.

—☆—

The mystery of grace is the Spirit who overturns everything: a fire, a mighty wind, power from on high—what the Hindu tradition calls *Mahashakti*, the *dynamis* of the New Testament. It is the Spirit who, according to the promise, is to "teach us all things," beginning with the essential matter: to put God there where he is, and first of all not to "put" him at all, for he is there. HE IS.

God is not in the concept; the concept has been fabricated. God is the Given. He is the very search for him. In fact, there is no such thing as a search for God. He is himself the One who gives the light, always essentially present. One might as well search for the sun at high noon!

God is in the common reality which I touch; he is in the texture of space and time which I touch in my days and in my nights; he is in this very moment in which I perform this act of writing.

God is not in the *object* of thought but in the very *act of thinking*, of speaking, of writing, of walking, of living.

[*Eating this daily bread*] is the Awakening to the Real, beyond and in the silence of the ego. No word can encompass it. God is an "I" before whom every "I" must keep silence: the "I am the one who is" of Horeb.

The saint, the sage, is one who—[*if I dare to say so, has "digested" the bread*]— has integrated the divine Presence into his consciousness, whereas the ordinary man has failed to do so even though he lives in the Presence. The awakened man no longer projects God before him as an Other, but integrates him into that depth of himself which is God, and by so doing gives to his awareness its ultimate dimension.

No sooner has the disciple consumed the Bread which the Master has given him, than the Master mysteriously disappears: "It is to your advantage that I go away, for if I do not go away the Spirit will not come to you" (John 16:7). He will teach you everything you need to know (1 John 2:27) and will make known to you all that you have been incapable of understanding until now (John 16:12). He will guide you into the whole truth, even to the most inward meaning of my words.

"All that I have heard from my Father, I have made known to you" (John 15:15). All that the Father has given me I have handed on to you. When God gives, he can only give himself, and not just a part of himself, for he is indivisible.

Too often Christians are afraid of statements in the Bible that seem to them overbold: they dare not believe that God could have truly meant to say this, or do that, to confer on them such a high dignity. For example, take 1 Corinthians 6:17: "He who unites himself with the Lord becomes one spirit with him." Or again, "All who are moved by the spirit of God are children of God" (Romans 8:14).

Jesus, the Incarnate Word, received from the Father the Spirit in full measure, precisely in order that he might be in a position to communicate the Spirit to those who were his own, to communicate to them God in His wholeness. The aim of the mission of Jesus, then, was the sending of the Spirit, "the Spirit who joins with our spirit to testify that we are God's children" (Romans 8:16).

For the Hindu tradition, the Spirit, the Breath of life, is the Atman, the Self, the ultimate principle of being that resides in, who is, the very ground of the soul.

> *It moves and it does not move,*
> *It is far and it is very near.*
> *It is within all that is, all this.*
> *It is truly outside all this.*
>
> *[Isha Upanishad vs. 5]*

The Spirit is this cosmic, universal, impalpable Presence. It assumes a face in every human face.

Therefore, I can only say that I abide in the deepest center of my heart, there where FROM God, I am.

On the road to Awakening, this is the third step. With the eating of "the Bread of Life" the First Stage of the spiritual journey—the dialogue with the Guru—is completed. The Second Stage begins.

SECOND STAGE: MONOLOGUE OF THE AWAKENED ONE

Once the dialogue with the Guru has ended, the disciple asks nothing more for herself or himself. Having abandoned everything into the hands of the vanished Guru, the disciple can only begin to sing the song of the "Further Shore."

—⟆⟆—

May Thy will be done, as in heaven so on earth.
May Thy Kingdom come.
May Thy Name be sanctified.

For the Christian mystic, as for his Hindu brother, the moment comes when the center of gravity shifts, when everything, including himself and the world, is seen from the viewpoint of God and no longer only according to his *idea* of the viewpoint of God. He can only murmur, "For me everything, all prayer, all adoration, every act, now consists in entering the Depth, the Depth of my heart, there where ALONE GOD IS."

This is the whole mystery of the One and of the Facing each other. Everything is burned away: even the humility of the repentant sinner has no more place in myself by which I might recognize myself as a sinner.

After this bewildering experience of the Truth, God can only be spoken of in paradoxes. The Gospel is paradoxical, and so are the Upanishads, and even the term "the Awakened One" is only an image.

THY WILL BE DONE ON EARTH AS IT IS IN HEAVEN

This acceptance of the Presence of God manifests itself in the alignment of the human will with this Presence which is the Spirit.

The Greeks wanted to reduce the Gospel to a set of notions. But the Gospel is, above all, and for every man, a confrontation with Jesus, the archetype of the God-man relation. Jesus realized all his virtualities as a man, and especially the supreme one: his nonduality with God. He is that above all: "The Father and I are one."

As for myself, in the depths of my heart I discover an Other with whom I am totally united [advaita] and with whom I am no less fundamentally face-to-face. The only true duality is that of the Father and the Son. It springs forth and is achieved in nonduality; it is the eternal Awakening of the Son to the Father in the unity—advaita—of the Spirit.

May your will be done, O Lord! Man should take stock of himself in the eschatological context of death. What humanity has need of are witnesses to the eschaton—to the Further Shore, people who bear the marks of having been burned in an encounter with the Absolute, like the encounter of Naciketas with Death—Mrityu—in the Upanishad and the encounter of Jesus with the Cross and Death. This is advaita; this detaches you from everything.

The great lesson that our Lord teaches us is that man's salvation passes through the Cross. Whether salvation takes place in a Christian milieu or a non-Christian one, there is no direct passage from man to God. One attains God only in death, in real death, for which bodily death is only a sign.

THY KINGDOM COME

The Father is encountered only when man's "I" has passed into the "I" of Christ.

Little by little the disciple is thus brought into that state of pure disponibility and expectation, of conceptual, volitional and affective emptiness, of simple transparency which permits him to repeat with St. Paul "It is no longer I who live, but Christ who lives in me" (Gal. 2:20). Or, one might say with the rishi [seer]:

> I know this mighty Person of the color of the sun, beyond darkness. Only by knowing him does one pass beyond death. [Svetasvatara Upanishad 3.8]

The Purusha is the archetypal Man, the cosmic Man; he is the nondual interiority of man and God.

In biblical language this experience is the Kingdom to which faith has given entry beyond all eschatological and apocalyptic images. The entry into the very mystery of God is the summit of the spiritual life, the coming of the Holy Spirit for which we ask every day in the Lord's Prayer when we say, "Thy Kingdom come."

The Kingdom of God does not come from anywhere; it just happens, just is [asti]. Yes, it does occur, but simply from the point of view of the flux of time. By coming in time it establishes time in eternity; or, rather, it delivers the eternal into the flux of time.

> How can it be discerned other than by saying, "it is"? [Katha Upanishad 6.12 (II.3.12)]

> Yahweh said to Moses, "I am the One Who Is." [Exodus 3:14]

In order to attempt to explain more clearly the depth of the human psyche at which this fundamental intuition is to be found, through which man comes to himself at the level of the essential mystery, I must specify that it is not a question of a transforming union that takes place in every awakening. It is the passing over from a state of dreaming to that of wakefulness.

Awake, O sleeper, and rise from the dead and Christ will give you light. [Eph. 5:14]

It is by an awakening that he is attained, it is a lightning flash . . . the eye blinks—Ah! [Kena Upanishad 4.4]

This transforming awakening, this rebirth in the Spirit, is precisely the same as the *metanoia*, that total conversion required by the Gospel of every man who wants to enter the kingdom:

Truly, truly, I say to you, unless one is born anew, he cannot see the kingdom of God. . . . unless one is born of water and the spirit, he cannot enter the kingdom of God. [John 3:3, 5]

This awakening consists in piercing through the egoistic center of oneself and passing beyond to the deepest center; it is the nuclear explosion of the individual and the passing over to the absolutely Other who is *not* an other.

I continue to believe that baptism in water was never "thought of" by Jesus as essential for entry into his Church. What was expected was a baptism *in spiritu et igni*, in spirit and fire. This was the baptism experienced by the disciples at Pentecost and by other early Christians, described in Acts by the words "the Spirit fell upon them" (e.g., Acts 10:44.)

When the "Kingdom" has thus come upon a person, so that she or he has become liberated-while-yet-in-the-body, as it is said in India—a jivanmukta—the person can only stammer with the prophetess Hannah, the mother of Samuel: "Nothing IS but God" (1 Sam. 2:2).

May Thy Name Be Sanctified

"From the rising of the sun to its setting my NAME is great among the gentiles, and in every place incense is offered in my NAME." [Mal. 1:11]

In the Hindu tradition the prayer of the Name is called *namajapa*. It consists of repeating continuously the name of God in one of its many traditional forms, such as Shiva, Krishna, Devi (Goddess, Divine Mother). By repeating the Name, the mind becomes more and more one-pointed; distractions diminish and then vanish almost entirely. Some images no doubt will float across the firmament of the soul, but they are like those light clouds which pass across the sky without being noticed by one who is gazing at the sun. Once the mind is thus firmly fixed and established, it can only point toward its center.

The nearest equivalent among Christians to the Hindu namajapa is what the spiritual tradition of Hesychasm calls the "Jesus Prayer," whether this be a simple repetition of the Name of Jesus or some more elaborate formula which includes the Holy Name. For the believer, the uttered Name contains, as it were, a distillation of the mystery in its fullness. The Name is the supreme mental icon of the mystery. It is in the person of Jesus that salvation can be attained. It is his secret Name that saves and not any of the names given to him by men. His real Name is: I AM. "In truth I tell you. . . . I AM" (John 8:58).

The Christian prayer of the Name of God comes from an ancient tradition. Its origin can be traced to the Egyptian monks. "Let the remembrance of Jesus be present in every breath you draw, and you will come to know the value of solitude," wrote St. John Climachus in the eighth century.

The prayer of the Name has different levels. The highest stage is reached when the prayer, or rather the Name, is placed in the heart. At this stage there is no longer any movement of the lips or the vocal cords, nor even, at the highest degree, any movement of thought. The prayer is lodged there at the very center of the being. From there it sheds its light and glory in every direction. This is truly the experience of the Holy Spirit, as the Russian saints often say. This glory, the very light of the Transfiguration, sometimes overflows upon the whole body, as in the famous visions and ecstasies of St. Seraphim of Sarov.[8] When the Name has taken up its dwelling in the heart, then it has reached its true place; the sign has returned to the Reality from which it issued.

Finally, only by silence can He be praised, that silence which is no longer even a look but rather the supreme *shunyata*, the emptiness, the essential Void. What is its identity? ask the logicians. Pantheism, declare the theologians. Advaita, simply nonduality, respectfully suggest the Rishis, those who have penetrated to the secret of the root. All otherness, all duality, will have at last disappeared, all that can be expressed in human language.

Man must come to the point where all reflections cease, where every attempt to imagine, every attempt to think, is ineffectual. It is the place and the moment of the *sva-prakasa atman*, the self that shines with its own light.

> The sun shines not there, nor the moon and stars, nor lightning— much less this fire. Every thing shines only after that shining Light . . . *Brahman* without stain, without parts. . . . His shining illumines all this world. . . . That is what the knowers of the Self know. [Manduka Upanishad 11.2.10–11][9]

Compare Revelation 21:23: "[The heavenly Jerusalem] does not need the sun or the moon for light since it is lit by the radiant Glory of God." In that Final Day, says the glorified Christ to those who "have kept my word and have not denied my name . . . Behold . . . I will write on [them] the Name of my God . . . and my own new Name" (Rev. 3:8, 12)—the I AM of Horeb. Is not this "the name confided in secret" to the one "who knows the place where all things have their common origin"?[10]

OUR FATHER WHO ART IN HEAVEN

Jesus does not allow anything to stop at himself but bears all things to the Father. He is essentially a road to the Father; he is God within our range in order to lead us to God in his mystery—"the mystery wrapped in silence from eternity but now made manifest" (Romans 16:25).

The last word of all is the bosom of the Father, prefigured in the sign of the Vedic *pada* (place), the *guha* (cave) of the Upanishads, the most inward recess of man's heart. The Taittiriya Upanishad tells us Brahman is known "in the secret place of the heart and in the highest heaven" (11.1.1). This is the mystery which is inaccessible in its very proximity, close at hand and yet transcendent, both interior and exterior, yet not reducible to any notion of "within" and "without"—"beyond all" (Isha Upanishad 5).

> He is our tie of kinship, he is our Father, for he knows the inner workings of whatever exists. [Maya Narayana Upanishad, 59]

It was in the mystery of the Father that Jesus experienced in the depths of his own being his own inward mystery, and this experience, like all experience at the level of the Ground, the Source, at once precedes and transcends all expression of it. The Name of the Father is itself a symbol (in the sense in which it is used in depth psychology). In Himself the Father is ineffable; He has no name. He is beyond all naming. In finding the Father, Jesus has not discovered an Other. "The Father and I are one." In one Spirit he has discovered his nonduality with Yahweh.

It was in his baptism in the Jordan that Jesus experienced the disappearance of the separation, the dividing chasm, when the omnipresent Spirit annihilated the separation. In the Spirit, he understood the Voice which called him "Son" out of the original *padam*. When he replied, "Abba," he realized his oneness with the Father.

This was the *Tat tvam asi,* That thou art, of the Chandogya Upanishad (VI.8.7).

The baptism was perhaps the most important event in the life of Jesus. Easter was only the unfolding of the mystery. At Easter he passed over to the Father in his manifested form, but at the Jordan he realized that he was the I AM of Yahweh.

This is the fundamental experience of Jesus, expressed in terms of the biblical tradition. In a Psalm (89:26) we read, "He shall cry to me, Thou art my Father," but in his Jordan experience Jesus passed through and beyond those terms like a laser beam. For Jesus there is himself, the Father, the Spirit. The Trinity, for him, is not a mystery; it is his "I," the firmament of his "I," the summit of his "I," which is manifested in "Three."

It is in the light of this mystery of the Father and Son that, immersed in the Spirit, man integrates in his own awareness the mystery of his own abyss, and realizing it, is in turn immersed in the abyss of God, of Being, of the Self.

It is interesting to observe that the name "Father" was chosen by Ramana Maharshi to designate God at the beginning of his great spiritual experience. In a note left before secretly departing from his family, he wrote: "In search of my father, and to obey his call, I leave this place."

OUR FATHER

Here we have reached the end of our spiritual Journey. We have arrived at the "Further Shore." At this point we can read again the words already cited on page 46:

Jesus appeared in the world not to teach ideas but to impart to men an experience, his own personal experience of being Son of God; following on from this experience of his and by its efficacy, he undertook to bring others to realize and integrate in their own awareness that condition which is theirs also, of being children of God.

Finally, we come to the realization of St. Paul's vision of all creation waiting "with eager longing for the revealing of the sons of God. . . . for creation itself will be set free from its bondage to decay and obtain the glorious liberty of the children of God" (Romans 8:19, 21) here and now.

THIRD STAGE: ULTIMATE SILENCE—EMPTINESS EXPLODES INTO FULLNESS

The Further Shore: man reaches it only through the fission of the self, the violent breaking open of the deepest center of himself. And that cannot be measured in terms of any rite, any formula, any prayer, any law whatsoever. The light of God is too strong for anything to hold before Him. It simply disappears, swallowed up in the Source which is Light—*jyoti*.

In this experience of the Source, everything, the entire body and the entire soul, is carried off. Then how can we pray? Adore? One can only BE.

Faith has come to fulness in the experience of wisdom, which is knowledge by connaturality.[11] Thus man knows by experience what the Savior taught in the Gospel and revealed both in his life and his words. The unity of the Father and the Son does not prevent their distinction: face-to-face at the heart of the advaita. At the heart of BEING—of SAT—nonduality and distinction are not contradictories.

The Spirit is the mystery of the inseparability of the Father and the Son. The Spirit is infinite Love which opens up Being in a face-to-face so that Love may express itself, and which closes it in *advaita* so that Love may be consummated.

To conclude this meditation, here is a yet unpublished account given by Swami Abhishiktananda to some of his friends, of his own experience of his return to the Source.

There are touches of the Spirit on the soul—often fleeting and gentle, but at times searing and bewildering—which prepare it for the ultimate revelation.

The first mention of his spiritual breakthrough goes back as far as 1952, when he was living in a cave on the mountain of Arunachala. Abhishiktananda wrote in his spiritual diary:

Illumination, satori (in Zen language), is to have realized this total all-pervading Presence of God in my actions as in my being and as in all things. . . . Deep joy, deep peace.

This Awakening was to reach its climax in 1973, when a very serious heart attack caused Abhishiktananda to fall to the ground in the bazaar of Rishikesh in the Himalayas. He wrote:

Really a door opened in heaven when I lay stretched out on the pavement. But a heaven which was not the opposite of earth, something which was neither life nor death, but simply "being." An Awakening beyond all myths and symbols. . . . This Awakening is a total explosion. It was an extraordinary spiritual adventure which left me hanging for marvellous minutes beyond every circumstance of death and life, rejoicing in the simple joy of being. . . . An Awakening—the existential discovery that life and death are only particular circumstances. Awakening is the return to the Father.

The awakening has nothing to do with any situation. It has nothing to do with what one sees at the moment of Awakening. The place of the Awakening is there where I am.

I have discovered the Grail! And the Grail is neither far nor near. It is outside all location. Man needs only to open his eyes for the "take off," and the quest is over! This is Galahad's discovery of the Grail in its ultimate truth, his direct sight of the interior of the vessel, no longer one only being fed by the Grail. Then it became very clear that there had been for me a fundamental break in my life. After several weeks, routine naturally reasserted itself, but the thought of the grace of those days is always a light that glows.

Here Swami Abhishiktananda, Dom Henri Le Saux, has literally realized what he had written many years before concerning the experience of the sage.

The wise one, the jnani, is someone who has made the great leap forward which brings a man to the Further Shore of himself. . . . and he has recognized in the secret of his self the mystery of God in His Epiphany. In the words of the Taittiriya Upanishad (III.10.4), "He who is here in the person and who is yonder in the sun, he is one."

God is all in all. [1 Cor. 15:28]

On the Eve of the Feast of the Immaculate Conception, in 1973, Swamiji entered the Final Silence in which Emptiness explodes into fullness, in the Fullness of the Source.

NOTES

1. Abbé Monchanin, *Lettres à sa mère* (Paris: Le Cerf, 1989).

2. Ibid., November 1938, p. 228.

3. Ibid., January 1939, p. 249.

4. Ibid., March 1939, p. 264.

5. J. Monchanin et H. Le Saux, *Ermites du Saccidananda, Un essai d'intégration chrétienne de la tradition monastique de l'Inde* (Tournai: Castermann, 1956).

6. Henri Le Saux/Swami Abhishiktananda, *La montée au fond du coeur, journal intime d'un moine chrétien-sannyasi hindou*, 1910–1973, Introduction et notes de R. Panikkar (Paris: O.E.I.L., 1986).

7. Henri Le Saux, *Intériorité et Révélation* (Sisteron: Présence, 1982).

8. St. Seraphim of Sarov (1759–1833), Russian Orthodox priest and monk, lived twenty-five years as a forest hermit, after which he returned to an active pastoral ministry. He was reputed to work wonders and to read hearts. He was the first to extend to lay persons the monastic method of contemplation leading to ecstatic mystical experience, which he claimed was within the capacity of any earnest Christian. On numerous occasions he was observed surrounded by light, as if the glow emanated from within himself. See, e.g., Constantine Cavarof and Mary-Barbara Zeldin, *Modern Orthodox Saints V* (Belmont, MA: Institute for Byzantine and Modern Greek Studies), pp. 24–25, 37–38.

9. Cf. Katha Upanishad, I.3.15; Svetasvatara Upanishad VI.14; Bhagavad Gita, XV.6.

10. Maha Narayana Upanishad, 55, 57.

11. St. Thomas Aquinas, Summa Theologiae II-II. 45.2.

In the Beginning Was Music

Russill Paul D'Silva

Russill Paul D'Silva was a close disciple of Dom Bede's and can be considered a spiritual heir. He is also a cross-cultural explorer, specializing in music and its relation to spirituality. Knowledgeable in both classical and popular Indian and European/American music, he also plays a number of instruments and is a singer and composer. He and his wife Asha, a musician, traveled with Father Bede and led the chanting that preceded meditations during retreats and other presentations. They offer their music and knowledge of the spiritual life to those who feel called to this area of development, through Matthew Fox's Institute of Culture and Creation Spirituality. In the following piece, D'Silva tells of his training under Father Bede in Saccidananda Ashram and of the particular powers of music to influence the human soul.

T

his article serves as an acknowledgement of the graces in my life that have come through my relationship with Father Bede Griffiths. His patient guidance has brought me to where I am today, both musically and spiritually.

We first met in October 1984. Having decided to leave behind a career and studies in Western music as well as a professional course in engineering, I entrusted myself to his direction. During the five year period I spent at his Christian ashram in Southern India, he guided my studies, not only in the spiritual and monastic life but also in the arts. He encouraged me to study Sanskrit and South Indian classical music, along with yoga and other meditation practices. This had profound consequences in my life.

During my years at the Ashram I experimented with groups and individuals using a mixture of Eastern and Western music, sacred poetry and spiritual practices (particularly yoga) in various formats. This provided a marvelous opportunity for an exploration of music therapy with a strong spiritual base. Through this process I was prepared for the work that I now do with the spirituality of music and the mysticism of sound in the West, termed *shabda yoga*.

Shabda is sound in the very deepest sense of the word. It is that primal cosmic vibration that is the source of all creation and that *is* all creation. It is the Divine word, the *vac*, the logos through which all creation issues forth. It is *shruti* [that which is heard] the source of all revelation and thus the essence of all scripture. It is Nada Brahma, the sound of God, the form of the formless. Yoga of course is unity, integrity, and total fulfillment of being on every level. It is a practical way of experiencing and becoming one with the great cosmic mystery.

Nearly all religious traditions of the world use sacred language and chanting as well as music and singing in their spiritual practices. Music, though, is more than just a practice—it is a self-expression of the highest order and reflects the Divine principle in all things. It feeds contemplation and leads to a deep and powerful inner experience that later overflows into music once again. One keeps feeding the other, leading into an ever deepening experience of oneself, the universe, and that inexpressible mystery we call God. Authentic music uses both sound and silence in a way that constantly alters and transforms our consciousness, from the gross to the subtle.

Western Music

Western music is essentially *horizontal* in character. It has an intrinsic expansive quality that by its very nature causes it to go outwards. This is typical of the Western culture, which is basically extroverted. Religion in the West, particularly Christianity, primarily advocates a going out of oneself, towards one's fellow human beings and towards nature. Western music facilitates this process. Are we not meant to feel a burning desire to do good deeds for others after a worship service?

The power and beauty of Western music lie in the principle of harmony, which is the relationship of simultaneous musical sounds. This musical principle expresses the inner laws of the universe as well as those of human nature and its relationship with the earth and the rest of the cosmos. The sounds of birds, the river, the wind, and the night can all be expressed better musically through the use of harmony. The very word *harmony* reflects the principle by which diverse entities can coexist in mutual support of each other, for harmony enhances life, growth, beauty, and love. Harmony is such an important expression of the soul because it objectifies one's connection with all of life and creation. It enables the coming together of human beings and nature in a very special way. In addition, harmonic music strengthens family solidarity, helps build community spirit, facilitates the channeling of romance and sentimentality into a subtler form of love and provides us with the energy to be more compassionate. It can awaken a great joy in us that can be shared with others in celebration, especially celebrating the gift of life.

This is not to say that melodic music sung in unison does not accomplish something similar. However, harmonic music does it more completely; this is the great musical gift that the West has to share with the rest of the world. Harmony is a late discovery in the history of Western music. Previous to this, music was essentially melodic and was sung in a group without harmony.

One of the great drawbacks of Western harmonic music is that it can be fragmenting. At times there can be so many elements to listen for that the listener's attention becomes divided. Different themes, and variations on these themes performed with embellishments and accompaniments, make the whole process of listening quite complicated. However, there is no doubt that this is exactly what the music is intended to be and do—that is, to create an expansive quality in the mind and in the heart.

The real problem occurs when a composition or performance of music becomes more of an exposition of the ego than an expression of the spirit. This danger exists in non-Western traditions of music as well, whenever the emphasis is on being too clever. The result of this kind of performance is that the listener is left spellbound and very impressed by the music. Also, the musician tends to look upon the composition or performance as an achievement. It is to a certain extent an achievement, but the danger is that the performance can easily be a powerful prop for the ego of the musician and the listener: it takes both of them away from a more holistic experience of the music and limits the experience to the intellect. Instead of encouraging a journey beyond oneself, the music confines one to the ego. Musical education today unfortunately encourages this attitude towards music.

One of the most profound passages in Herman Hesse's novel *Siddhartha* is when the Buddha cautions Siddhartha to *beware of too much cleverness*. This is the great lesson of our times. We appropriate too much to ourselves and give ourselves more credit than we deserve. We often forget that at each moment, our life and all its faculties is a gift from God.

Today in the West (and most Eastern countries imitate the West) popular music, when presented live, has many elements that distract attention from the music itself: dramatic stage props, dancers, fancy costumes, lighting, and showmanship that is often wild and obscene. Music is only one-sixth of the presentation in this format! This is not necessarily wrong, but it does reveal how much the original function and purpose of music has been obscured in our times. There is also an exaggerated use of electronics in modern music. This has advantages, but a lot of spirit and consciousness is filtered out because of their use. We need to rediscover the meaning and purpose of music, and reintegrate the musical values we have discovered in our time with all the knowledge of music we have accumulated throughout history. Fortunately, this seems to be happening.

Another limitation of Western music is its emphasis on precision and perfection. This is not wrong or bad as it is certainly necessary to communicate the spirit of music effectively. But the danger is that the music can lack that *magical* quality of spirit that is also essential to authentic music. Music is often considered to be one of the great powers of magic remaining from that time in evolution when human beings discovered their capacity for self-transformation. The original power and purpose of magic is self-transformation, and this is what music is all about. It is about the transformation of matter, energy, and consciousness into the evolving condition of the universe, a natural process that we are all capable of. Music is at the very heart of our being. Without the transformational power of music we can create stumbling blocks for ourselves and for the universe.

Music communicates consciousness, and it is important that we be aware of the kind of consciousness a particular music is communicating to us. Stevie Wonder opens his song "Sir Duke" with: "Music is a language by itself, it is a language we all understand!" We need different kinds of music for various purposes. It has been observed in recent times that a lot of Western classical music was not composed to heal the listener. There is also a fair amount of classical music that simply communicates the consciousness of a superficial level of society and strives desperately to impress the listener. There are other kinds of music that communicate sexual perversion or emotional frustration, and some that stimulate physical violence. Real music, however, always points to something beyond itself. It is one of the clearest signs we have of the absolute mystery of our being. Great Western composers, such as Bach, Handel, and Mozart, and Indian composers, such as Thyagarajar, Dikshitar, and Narayana Thirtar, reveal this through their music. What they communicate is profoundly spiritual and touches the heart and soul on a very deep level. We cannot fail to notice a sense of awe and wonder when listening to their music.

MUSIC OF THE MONASTERIES

The depth, beauty, and power of Western music can be experienced in the ancient Plainchant and Gregorian music of the monasteries. It is a music that is simple, yet profound, which strives not to impress the listener, or to prove the skills of the singer, but to elevate them both to the level of the spirit. Like most ancient music it developed as an important element of religious rites and functioned to heal the soul. The Gregorian modes awaken different moods and can be compared to the subtle *ragas* of Hindu music.

The Latin texts that are used in such music are *mantric* in nature. (Mantras are powerful spiritual sounds that communicate spiritual experiences beyond the rational mind.)

In my experience, I find that the mantric effects of Latin act only on the upper chakras, that is, from the heart upwards. This is somewhat indicative of the disregard and negation in Christianity of the value and spiritual power of the lower chakras (which involve sexuality and the primal energies), as they are considered to be "of the flesh." But wasn't it this very "flesh" that was transformed in the resurrection? Sadly, the association is that it must be "killed" in order that it may be transformed, and this is perhaps true in some cases, but it is certainly not healthy for the human psychology of our times. Fortunately we realize today, through the efficacy of Eastern mystical practices, that there are nonviolent and systematic methods of transforming and sublimating these energies. The complex consonants of mantric Sanskrit, for instance, affect these "lower" energy centers quite dramatically. It was wonderful that Father Bede included these sounds in the prayers and liturgies at the Ashram, for they helped stimulate the entire chakra system during prayer.

Ancient languages had musical and spiritual power in their sounds. The sounds of the universe were contained in the sounds of the language, and the music of the universe could be heard when they were spoken. We can still experience something of this nature when listening to the chanting of languages such as Sanskrit, Latin, African, or Aboriginal. The greatness of these languages also lies in their tremendous suggestive power. They do not simply communicate an intellectual idea by itself, isolated from the whole. Instead they awaken rich symbolism in thought, image, and feeling; they communicate the experience along with the idea. In contrast, modern languages tend to be rather abstract. Such forms of language are useful but we should not lose touch with the depth, power, and beauty of ancient languages.

Gregorian music has the capacity to stretch the soul. It creates a certain elasticity in the singer and the listener. The stretching of the soul paves the way for the primal sounds of the universe contained in the Latin language to take root in the depths of one's being. Over time the music of the universe unfolds in the individual and overflows into the community.

The Christian monks (like all monks) who sing the beautiful Gregorian modes in praise of the Divine, live in a world of the sacred, and this world swells in their hearts with the tones and modes that they use in their music. These are sacred scales that have the power to harmonize us with ourselves, with nature, with the cosmos, and thus naturally with God. This subtle music causes the ego to be transformed and has a strong link with the ancient sacred music of the Hindus and perhaps other sacred cultures. Having substituted the vernacular, to the almost complete expulsion of Latin, the Western Church today lacks the transformative power and aura of mystery that is so essential for it to be a genuinely spiritual force at work in the world.

As already observed, genuine music transforms. Through such music the smallness of the ego is expanded so that it becomes aware of the rest of creation and is made sensitive to the realities of the cosmos. We open up to the depths of the womb of creation and are filled with the awe and mystery of our being. The greatness, the vastness, the glory of the cosmos is contained in the subtle melodies of Plainchant and other sacred music. Why? Because the composers of such music literally *heard* these melodies in the depths of their being. Their whole lives were centered on listening. Sacred music was never composed with the aim of making money or with the intention of taking it to the big stages and impressing large audiences. This music is born from the experience of God in the human heart and the ability to sense this presence in all of nature and the cosmos. Composers of such music will always acknowledge that the music came *through* them and not *from* them.

INDIAN MUSIC

Indian music is essentially *vertical* in nature, meaning that it is internal, reflective of a drawing inwards. Like the Eastern culture and religion, it is introverted. Eastern religions advocate the need to look within oneself and discover the inner reality and mystery of one's being. Eastern music facilitates this process.

The power and beauty of this vertical music lie in *melody*, which is the *relationship* of successive notes. Melody is essentially a means of connecting the human with the Divine. It works through the psychic levels of an intermediate world that is hard to define, because it exceeds the boundaries of normal existence and consciousness. It is a world of the unconscious, of dreams and deep moods, images and sounds, of the inner senses—those mystical dimensions of the human psyche that are either overdeveloped or underdeveloped in most of us.

Indian music, and all contemplative music, strives to balance these dimensions as it unites the human with the Divine through the psychic levels. There is a grounding in the matter and energy of the universe as well as an ascension into the heights and airiness of the *Akasha* (the etheric planes), which symbolizes the Absolute. Music has a way of simplifying and tuning the levels of our being to the underlying unity that holds it all together.

One of the images that often comes to my mind when performing Indian music is that of everything being spun together into a fine thread—something very fine with very subtle results. This music facilitates the unification of our consciousness and the integration of our being. It enlarges and intensifies our awareness.

India's music was born out of her profound spiritual heritage. It is said to have originated in the ancient seers who meditated on the mystery of the universe and heard the sounds that became the seven basic intervals of the octave. The seven *swaras* [*swara* = note; *swara* literally means "that which makes its own sweetness"] represent the seven energy centers that govern the human being. Thus, using the swaras in various combinations, one can awaken the chakras and stimulate them to their maximum potential. [Chakras are vortices of energy located in various parts of the body. The most important chakras known to us are located along the line of the spinal cord.]

The various musical intervals are located within the octave, at specific mathematical distances. Indian musicians over the ages discovered how these intervals are connected with moods. They learned to combine the swaras that occur at these intervals in various ascending and descending patterns that they called *ragas*. Ravi Shankar, the musician who made Indian music popular in the West, termed the *raga* a "coloring of the Spirit." It is the tonal or modal expression of a basic mood or feeling in the human being that corresponds to a similar mood or feeling in nature. Certain ragas are more powerful at certain times of the day or night and serve to awaken particular moods in us.

Each raga is a world of its own. An experienced musician knows all the permutations and combinations of a raga, and knows when to use them effectively in order to bring about a union. This union is called yoga, and the process of using a raga to obtain it can be called *raga yoga*. It is a way of harmonizing the levels of our being into peace and unity, and this brings joy, or *ananda*.

In the experience of a raga, parts of the brain that have been dormant can become activated. This induces a sense of knowledge and well-being that is full of power and vitality. The cells, tissues, and muscles of our body become vibrant and the heart swells with love and compassion for all creation. Our mental processes are slowed down, sometimes to the point of being apparently stationary. Remaining in this state of emptiness (discursive emptiness) one can be receptive to the subtle sounds and movements that occur at deeper levels of our being. We are completely in the moment. Time is full of meaning and purpose, for there is that sense of being beyond all time. All time seems to be contained in the moment. It is a sense of the sheer *isness* of things. Just as harmonic music is spatial and expansive, melodic music unifies time into an eternal moment. This is the ultimate experience of the raga.

Ragas, in this way, can be extremely powerful, and when used correctly, their effects can be quite amazing. Ragas are said to be capable of creating effects in nature such as fire, lightning, storms, and thunder. By using the intervals in certain combinations, musicians are able to awaken their chakras and those of their audience. In employing ragas for this purpose, the music is not planned but created in the musician, and in his or her interaction with the environment in which the performance is taking place.

In order to express fully the power and feeling of the raga, the musician must first meditate and develop a sense of how everyone is feeling. Next, a raga that adequately expresses this feeling is selected and performed through various stages of development. As time passes, the feeling is channeled from the unconscious into the conscious. The *nadis* (nerve channels) in the body, located along the spinal cord, channel these energies from the depths of one's being to the top of the head. Along the way they meet and dance in the chakras, awakening them to their full power. The bliss of this unity and integrity is offered to the Divine consciousness at the level of the highest chakra, located at the crown of the head. Finally, the effects of this process are allowed to penetrate every level of one's being, from the top of the head to the base of the spine. Father Bede was very particular about this. He advised that after every spiritual experience, the effects of it should be allowed to penetrate one's being to the very roots. The experience needs to be grounded in the body and in the earth, making every level sacred and permeated with the consciousness of the Spirit.

Music as Yoga: The Way of Harmony, Healing, and Integrity

Many are familiar with the music of Hildegard of Bingen. Apart from being an amazing composer of music, this remarkable woman of the middle ages was also an artist, theologian, mystic, and healer. It was undoubtedly the wholeness and profundity of her life that made her music so powerful. Some say that her music was composed five hundred years ahead of her time. One thing that is so interesting about her music is the fact that Hildegard utilized her knowledge of healing in her compositions. When I first began working with her music, I had a sensation of feeling feverish whenever singing her songs. Later it dawned on me that her compositions were stirring up all the toxins in my psyche and that I was being healed by her music. Hildegard utilized her knowledge of scales (which are really ragas) to the fullest. Her music is definitely a way of yoga, for so much of the breath and spine are involved. It is also quite sensual, stimulating the lower chakras in a subtle way.

Music has played an important part in the healing rituals of many cultures throughout history. Much of the healing that needs to take place in our lives today comes through balancing and integrating the male and female sides of our nature. This means bringing together within us the rational and the intuitive, the audible and the visible, action and meditation. It seems clear that we have been overemphasizing the male, the rational, the visual and the active, particularly here in the West. The East is looking to the West with its knowledge of science, technology, and structure for its balance, while the West seems to be turning to the East for its knowledge of interiority, receptivity, and feminine wisdom. This marriage of the East and West was Father Bede's message to the world and also the secret of his personal integrity. The marriage is taking place on a global level as much as it is struggling to take place within each one of us. It is our call today to facilitate this process within us, through our relationship with the earth and with each other. Music and spirituality can be our most valuable tools in accomplishing this task successfully. For me, personally, this expresses itself in my efforts to specialize in diverse styles of music and also to blend them with each other, not just technically, but emotionally as well. It is a form of interspiritual dialogue with a sensitivity to avoiding syncretism.

The marriage of opposites takes us beyond the world of duality that has dominated us for so long. The great mystics had a mode of perception called *advaita* (nonduality), and they taught a variety of spiritual practices to enable us to develop this vision. We are becoming increasingly aware of the fact that the opposites are not contradictory but complementary. The sense of the opposites as being antagonistic to each other has caused enough harm to cultures and civilizations in the past and we cannot allow this understanding to continue, for it will be to our own destruction. Nicholas of Cusa, a great Christian mystic and scientist, said that the opposites conflict only on the surface, giving us our dualistic perception. This concept of reality, based on our visual perception, is important for our understanding of reality. However, when we go deeper or beyond, we see the opposites contained in a cosmic whole. This brings peace and the ability to love all things.

In order to balance these opposites and go beyond them, the way of sound is perhaps the best method we have today, since we have overemphasized the visual for so many generations. The way of sound as mysticism is a feminine form of spirituality because it is based on receptivity, on listening. The Taoist teachers of ancient China had a profound understanding of this balance of the male and the female, which they termed as the yang and yin respectively. In Hindu cosmology, *Shakti*, that primal, undifferentiated energy that is present in the void, is seen to be constantly manifesting as the evolved cosmos and then withdrawing itself in dissolution, *pralaya*. In Christian terms, the Father, the Source, manifests love and creation in the Son, the Word, and this returns to the Source in the Spirit. These understandings communicate that the seed of one opposite is always potentially present within the other and it begins to unfold when the latter has reached its climax. The way of harmony is to keep either of the opposites from going to its extreme. We realize this today more than ever as we sense the need for balance on so many levels. Evolution seems to flow through periods of extremity followed by periods of stabilization. This cycle seems to characterize both the cosmos and our personal lives.

This is a natural cycle and we should cooperate with it in order to be one with the Tao, the Rita, the cosmic order of the universe. The universe is demanding that we grow and that we develop the neglected aspects of our psyches. Growth demands change, and we are being challenged to change our forms of worship, our understanding of music, our concepts of God, the universe and our very own selves.

We are living in powerful times—perhaps on the edge of a major paradigm shift. The marriage of opposites is taking place on a global level. Never before has the need for yoga, the way of harmony, been more urgent. The establishment of so many thousands of yoga centers all over the world witnesses to this. The way of yoga appeals to so many because it is cyclic as well as linear; it can be compared to a spiral—interconnected ascending and descending circles. Nothing is lost in the process, but everything grows together with the whole.

We all have a need to learn from each other, to appreciate each other and to mutually nourish one another with our religions, our cultures, our wisdom, and our music. A lot of cross-cultural work is occurring in the fields of music and spirituality. Music and spirituality are two sides of the same coin and are the main forces of bonding disparities in our societies today, just as they have been for so many thousands of years. The marriage of opposites is reflected in a lot of music today, and music often sets the tone for our development into the future. Musicians and all artists are called to be prophets, priests, healers, and mystics (yogis). Art has been separated from spirituality long enough and a reconciliation needs to take place if we are to emerge from our fragmented life-styles to one of wholeness and integrity.

MUSIC: OUR HOPE FOR THE FUTURE

Music will play a powerful role in uniting the peoples of the world in this process. "We Are the World," "Ebony and Ivory," and many other similar songs that have touched such deep chords within us, the powerful appeal of New Age music, and the new world music that fuses ethnic styles are all indicative of the role of music in the formation of a new world order.

Music can help bring religions and cultures together in a peaceful way, since it transforms through the emotions and is not limited to left-brain understanding alone. In our era of science and technology, we often forget that as human beings we have strong feelings that are directly linked to our spiritual being, which is our deepest identity. Music constantly serves to remind us of this. Music is also a creative way of expressing our pain and negativity, for it is capable of resolving our differences without letting our minds get in the way. It connects our minds and hearts, and enables us to celebrate the gift of life as one family. Most of all it can communicate our experiences as experiences, and is without question one of our best languages for spirituality.

As a people we need to learn to listen again. The feminine side of all of us (including women) needs to be developed, and music can help us do this. We need to listen to each other more intently and feel each other's music more deeply. In interreligious and intercultural dialogue, music can be a wonderful way of bringing about a deep communion between the peoples of the world.

Just as music can take us a step beyond words, silence can take us a step beyond music. It is in silence that we most profoundly realize our communion with each other, with the universe and with God. It is important to recognize that silence is not a negation of sound or music. In fact it is full of sound and music. Mystics have called this "the roar of silence." Silence is simply another order of sound, just as stillness is another form of movement. Silence is implicit sound and contains all sound, all music. We know today that every note contains all the other notes. Each vibration contains and affects every other vibration in the universe. The whole is present in every part.

In the beginning was the Word. The Word, of course, is a sound, and sound as we have just seen is nothing but implicit music. Therefore we can say with equal conviction that "In the beginning was Music!" Creation is the unfolding of this music. All of us belong to this majestic musical expression; it is the Great Music! Our musical knowledge and sense is derived from it— the Divine expressing itself in melody, harmony, and rhythm (movement).

We see and hear this expression in the sounds of the wind and ocean waves, in the cycle of day and night, the songs of the birds and the cries of beasts. How true is the saying: "A life without music is a life without God." For God is Music and Music is Love.

Part Two:

A Bridge Between
East and West

The Monk as a Bridge Between East and West

James Conner

Father James Conner, O.S.C.O., is abbot of Assumption Abbey in Ava, Missouri, and is a long-time student of the spirituality of Thomas Merton. He is a board member of the Monastic Interreligious Dialogue (MID), this continent's branch of the worldwide Aide Inter-Monastères, which facilitates shared experiences between monastics of the different world religions. He is presently the editor of the board's Bulletin. Here Father James develops the theme that we are all called to return to our original oneness beyond gender, language, and culture by suggesting that it is especially the vocation of the monastic to lead the way. He uses extensive quotations from three examples of such personal culture-bridges—Thomas Merton, Swami Abhishiktananda, and Father Bede Griffiths—to show that they each share this view of the function of the monastic in today's world religious milieu.

The book of Genesis expresses the concept of the creation of Adam and Eve as being "in the image of God—male and female He made them." The early Church Fathers, following an earlier, pre-Judaic myth, saw this as telling us that Adam was originally created containing both sexes in the one person, and that the split or "creation" into two came as a result of sin. The final fulfillment of this is seen in Paul when he tells us that "in Christ there is neither male nor female, Jew nor Greek, free nor slave" (Gal. 3:28). Genesis also tells us how human language was originally one and that the division into many came as a result of the curse of God on the Tower of Babel. Yet this original unity of sex, language, and culture is still present within our human roots. It might be seen as the Buddhist expression of the "Original Face." The purpose of life for all peoples and for each individual is to return to that original unity from which we have strayed, in order to restore that "image" in which we were created.

If this is the purpose of life for every person, it is even more directly the purpose of the life of the monk. Consequently, when the Secretariat for Non-Christian Religions asked the Benedictine family to serve as a "bridge" between East and West—which share common traditions of monastic life— it was perhaps expressing more than merely an historical phenomenon. It was perhaps coming closer to the very heart of the monastic vocation. This purpose can be seen in the lives of three monks who became acutely aware of the underlying unity and the call for us to enter into that reality in a lived experience.

THOMAS MERTON (1915–1968)

Thomas Merton both spoke and wrote of this return to oneness. In a talk in Calcutta shortly before his death, he said: "My dear brothers, we are already one. But we imagine that we are not. And what we have to recover is our original unity. What we have to be is what we are."[1] He had earlier defined a monk as one who "withdraws deliberately to the margin of society with a view to deepening fundamental human experience."[2] This fundamental human experience is that of our unity with all. According to Merton it is "not that we discover a new unity. We discover an older unity."[3]

It is a unity that highlights the irrelevancy of all that seems to distinguish one from another. As Merton emphasized, "The marginal person accepts the basic irrelevance of the human condition, an irrelevance which is manifested above all by the fact of death."[4] In fact, all that seems to be taken from us in death is basically irrelevant to who we really are. All that we tend to posit as our identity—gender, race, language, belief, state of life, even religion as an expression of human history—is ultimately irrelevant. These will all pass away in death. And if that is the case, then they cannot be the criteria for defining who we are and who we see ourselves or others as being. Merton thus maintained that "the office of the monk or the marginal person is to go beyond death even in this life, to go beyond the dichotomy of life and death and to be, therefore, a witness to life."[5]

Life in this sense is that which makes each one of us to be who we truly are in relation to God and in relation to one another. We are, as Merton said, to "find relevance in Him. And the relevance in Him is not something we can grasp or possess. It is something that can only be received as a gift. Consequently, the kind of life that I represent is a life that is openness to gift, gift from God and gift from others."[6]

In addition, with regard to the spiritual life, Merton felt that "the basic condition for this is that each be faithful to his own search."[7] Merton thus reiterated what Christ himself said—that life is a search for the pearl of great price, for the lost drachma, for the lost sheep, for the kingdom of God. And yet while there is a fundamental sense of something lost, there is also a faith in that which is present even though not seen, not found; it is known to be more real, more valuable than anything that can be seen or experienced more immediately. It is this true reality, seemingly lost, that ultimately binds all together most effectively—and there are always people who dare to seek for this reality. As Merton said: "Among these people, if they are faithful to their own calling, to their own vocation, and to their own message from God, communication on the deepest level is possible. And the deepest level of communication is not communication, but communion. It is wordless. It is beyond words, and it is beyond speech, and it is beyond concept."[8]

Merton had written of something similar to this in an article on the concept of "final integration." Elaborating on the work of Iranian psychologist Dr. Reza Arasteh,[9] he developed this idea in relation to the monastic and

Christian life of today. "Final integration" is an expression used to denote the process by which a person realizes the limitations of our common experience of life and personhood and breaks through to a "new birth" on a level that is closer to the original unity of Adam. According to Merton:

> The idea of "rebirth" and of life as a "new creature in Christ in the Spirit," of a "risen life" in the Mystery of Christ or in the Kingdom of God, is fundamental to Christian theology and practice—it is, after all, the whole meaning of baptism. All the more so is this idea central to that peculiar refinement of the theology of baptism which is the monastic *conversatio*— the vocation to a life especially dedicated to self-renewal, liberation from all sin, and the transformation of one's entire mentality "in Christ."[10]

The monk is called to be a bridge because he or she is called to become universal. It is not even that one is called to be that which one is not; rather, the calling is to recognize what we are, to set aside the illusion of what we are not.

Fulfilling our spiritual potential as manifested in the concept of rebirth, which Christians interpret as a rebirth in Christ, is found in many world spiritual beliefs. Merton commented on this when he stated:

> The notion of "rebirth" is not peculiar to Christianity. In Sufism, Zen Buddhism and in many other religious or spiritual traditions, emphasis is placed on the call to fulfill certain obscure yet urgent potentialities in the ground of one's being, to "become someone" that one already (potentially) is, the person one is truly meant to be.[11]

All too often when we say that something is "potentially" something else, we mean that it is within the realm of possibility for transformation to take place. In this instance, however, something much more is implied. We are "potentially" the new creature because that is what we were created as, what has divine "power" to unfold in us. We are to become what we are. That which is new is also that which is old, since the "new creature" is identical with the original unity. Merton elaborated this by saying:

> Final integration is a state of transcultural maturity far beyond mere social adjustment, which always implies partiality and compromise. The person apprehends life fully and wholly from an inner ground that is at once more

universal than the empirical ego and yet entirely one's own. One is in a certain sense a "cosmic" and "universal person," having attained a deeper, fuller identity than that of the limited ego-self which is only a fragment of one's being. One is in a certain sense identified with everybody: or in the familiar language of the New Testament, has become "all things to all people," able to experience their joys and sufferings as one's own, without however being dominated by them. The "fully born" has attained to a deep inner freedom—the Freedom of the Spirit we read of in the New Testament.[12]

Several points that Merton makes here deserve to be highlighted. He said that mere social adjustment "implies partiality and compromise." This is true not only of the obvious ways in which one is compromised by human convention and social respect, but more profoundly true of the ways in which we humans almost inevitably limit and compromise ourselves—ways that flow from the very nature of our limited consciousness. We identify ourselves with what we are conscious of while failing to recognize the further dimensions of our own being and the demands that those dimensions place upon us. The one who enters into final integration experiences life "fully and wholly from an inner ground that is at once more universal than the empirical ego and yet entirely one's own." This "inner ground" of our being is by its nature universal, and yet it is what makes us to be who we each are. We share in this gift, and to that very extent we share in every other person and thing.

But to walk and live on this level implies a freedom not only from the limitations of the more superficial levels, but also from the secure moorings of that more familiar territory. One who chooses this path has to walk in an inner poverty and solitude that is greater than merely having little or being alone. Merton described it thus:

The state of insight which is final integration implies an openness, an "emptiness," a "poverty" similar to those described in such detail not only by the Rhenish mystics, by St. John of the Cross, by the early Franciscans, but also by the Sufis, the early Taoist masters and the Zen Buddhists. Final integration implies the void, poverty and nonaction which leave one entirely docile to the "Spirit" and hence a potential instrument for unusual creativity.[13]

This is the kind of inner solitude to which the monk in particular is called. It is not simply a "discipline" that can be imposed from without, but a whole new area into which one is led by the transforming action of the Spirit. And yet this new area is actually our "home." It is the area we were created to live in. In a sense it is the Garden of Eden from which we were expelled by the Fall—and yet a part of us still resides there and recognizes it when we are led into it. Not only that, but we also find all others there, whether they are aware of it or not. To this extent the one who has entered into final integration is more truly at one with all others than someone in the same room with them. We know the others not simply on the level of the partial selves that they present, but on a level where they may not even know themselves, since this level is hidden to them as well.

According to Merton, this recognition of full unity with others allows us to become one with all life:

> The one who has attained final integration is no longer limited by the culture in which one has grown up, but " . . . has embraced *all of life* . . . experienced qualities of every type of life." One passes beyond all these limiting forms, while retaining all that is best and most universal in them, "finally giving birth to a fully comprehensive self." We accept not only our own community, our own society, our own friends, our own culture, but all humankind. We do not remain bound to one limited set of values in such a way that we oppose them aggressively or defensively to others. We are fully "Catholic" in the best sense of the word. We have a unified vision and experience of the one truth shining out in all its various manifestations, some clearer than others, some more definite and certain than others. We do not set these partial views up in opposition to each other, but unify them in a dialectic or an insight of complementarity. With this view of life we are able to bring perspective, liberty and spontaneity into the lives of others. The finally integrated person is a peacemaker, and that is why there is such a desperate need for our leaders to become such persons of insight.[14]

This passage clearly delineates why the monk can serve not only as a bridge for dialogue by words and concepts, but particularly as a bridge for understanding, sharing, experiencing oneness of life. This is what Merton meant when he spoke of the connection between "communication" and "communion." This is also ultimately what is behind the Buddhist notion of "compassion" in its fullest sense. Just as communication implies much more than mere sharing of ideas, so compassion implies much more than mere sharing of feelings. Both come together in this one state of final integration. Only such integrated people can truly enter into dialogue in a way that will build unity—or rather that will recognize the unity that already exists.

To become one of these people, we must undergo the process of losing all that is familiar in order to become at one with all. To this end, again returning to Dr. Arasteh's work on the final integration process in Sufism, Merton redefined the life-purpose of the monastic. He wrote:

> Dr. Arasteh describes the breakthrough into final integration in the language of Sufism. The consecrated term in Sufism is *Fana*, annihilation or disintegration, a loss of self, a real spiritual death. But mere annihilation and death are not enough: they must be followed by reintegration and new life on a totally different level. This reintegration is what the Sufis call *Baqa*. The process of disintegration and reintegration is one that involves a terrible interior solitude and an "existential moratorium," a crisis and an anguish which cannot be analyzed or intellectualized. It also requires a solitary fortitude far from the ordinary, "an act of courage related to the root of all existence."
>
> Seen from the viewpoint of monastic tradition, the pattern of disintegration, existential moratorium and reintegration on a higher, universal level, is precisely what the monastic life is meant to provide. . . . [Dr. Arasteh] will help us recover some sense of the real aim of that monastic *conversatio* which we have not only mentally approved but actually vowed. We have dedicated ourselves to rebirth, to growth, to final maturity and integration. Monastic renewal means a reshaping of structures so that they will not only permit such growth but favor and encourage it in everyone.[15]

Thus Merton proposed that monastic life is intended to lead one into this universal being who is fully at the disposal of God and of all peoples. The monk withdraws from the world only in order to be able to enter more deeply into the heart of all. In this way the monk becomes the bridge to all.

SWAMI ABHISHIKTANANDA (HENRI LE SAUX, O.S.B.) (1910–1973)

The second monk who leads us on this path is Swami Abhishiktananda. This French monk lived in India for more than thirty years and learned how to integrate the Hindu spirit not only exteriorly but also, and particularly, interiorly. He, too, in his writings spoke of the need for becoming a universal person, not simply for the sake of outward dialogue with others, but for a living dialogue that must begin within. Like Merton, he saw this as connected with the very notion of what it means to be the person we are— that it entails a process of death and resurrection to new life. According to Abhishiktananda:

> In the Vedantic tradition *brahma-vidya*, or knowledge of God, is no less costly to obtain. One has to give all that one has. One has to pass beyond all that one is, or rather, all one thinks one is. Otherwise one will remain forever a *brahmavadin*, one who talks or argues about brahman, in other words a theologian—at least in the modern western understanding of that term; one will never become a contemplative, a seer, a *brahmavid*, or knower of brahman.
>
> Whoever still utters an I and a Thou which sets one apart from the brother or sister has not yet left this world nor oneself, nor has one passed to the level of the Real. Whoever still utters an I and a Thou which set one apart from God shows thereby that one does not yet know God.
>
> For whoever knows the supreme brahman truly has become brahman. [Mundaka Upanishad III.2.9]
>
> Henceforth there is no one left to say "I know," or "I have become brahman";
>
> for into the Glory itself that one has vanished who wanted to know the Glory, like the moth which, fallen into the flame, itself became flame and vanished. . . .

This is what it costs for the human to reach one's true end and attain to one's true self.[16]

Abhishiktananda came to the firm conviction that the way for the Church to be open to the riches of India was through a lived experience, not merely a study:

India's secret will be transmitted in the Church only very secondarily by means of the word, writing or university teaching. Rather, what is at issue here is more like an ontological transmission, from depth to depth, soul to soul, in the great silence. Words and writings do not reach to the *depths* unless they already spring from the depths of the individual from whom they issue. They will awaken veritable echoes in souls only if they themselves are bearers of experience.[17]

He saw this as the task not simply of "experts" but of contemplatives:

Any soul that penetrates within, just by doing so, deepens the Church and the Church's consciousness of herself. It thus calls the Church, as though from depth to depth, in the realization of her own mystery. Each Christian, each group of the faithful, in effect, expresses and manifests in itself the *Una Catholica* as a whole, and in her, the only Lord. That is precisely the irreplaceable role, the very *service* of contemplatives in the Church.[18]

In this way, India draws the Christian ever more deeply into that revelation that has come to us from Christ, but that is often missed precisely because of the commonness of the formulas that we have been taught. In fact, Abhishiktananda felt that

India's mystical tradition contributes nothing in itself to the Christian which the latter does not already know. Nevertheless, it is an infinitely precious grace of God bequeathed to His Church so that she might deepen the revealed mystery, that of the Spirit above all, of the correlative intimacy of the Father and the Son, the mystery of the Oneness of the Plenitude, of the Pleroma. To be sure the formulations of the Upanishads will strike anyone who has been raised in other spiritual climes as abrupt and paradoxical: but it is precisely in that way that they jolt the mind and do not allow it indolently to rest in the world of signs and of concepts in which it delights. Above all it is not the words that are of prime importance here, but rather the message which these words, tirelessly but always inadequately, try to convey. . . . They are not words that must be gathered and investigated. They are rather a call that plumbs the depths, that *aspires* to descend to the depths.[19]

Abhishiktananda was also clearly convinced that there is much more to Indian spirituality than monism and pantheism, as is sometimes asserted:

What in effect the Christian should try to take over from Hinduism is not this or that rite, this or that myth, or this or that theological formulation, but before all else the spiritual experience that is the foundation and the reason for being of all these developments. . . . One must never forget the essentially provisional value of any philosophy or theology in India. Here philosophy is not a speculative science, conformed to the contemplation of intelligible forms. It is fundamentally "practical" and tends to experience which alone has a beatifying and salvific value. . . . Words and concepts will never make up for experience, they will always involve antinomies which only direct experience will resolve.[20]

Here Swami Abhishiktananda is making use of the distinction formulated by Raimundo Panikkar between *faith* and *beliefs*. *Faith* is the human being's inner relation to what is beyond us, which is its own light and can never fade and is connected with our very creation in this Beyond. *Beliefs* are those noetic symbols through which faith becomes manifest at the mental level. In Abhishiktananda's expression:

Faith has to do with what cannot be seen. But even though faith is located in the intellect, it far surpasses it; and the intellect, even when enlightened by grace, is unable to comprehend its whole mystery. At the new level to which the believer is brought by the Spirit, one can do nothing except simply surrender to this movement which is beyond all thought and all merely intellectual realization. It is precisely in transcending even the highest reach of the human mind, in passing beyond all symbols and expressions of itself, that faith reveals itself in its essential purity. This is the essential "void" in which alone the human is open to and able to hear the eternal Word.[21]

Abhishiktananda felt that Christianity as a faith, and Christian believers in particular, must be able to assimilate this aspect of India precisely in order to reveal the Pleroma of Christ:

The transition from the Old Testament to the New was also a "passover," a "passage" [Ex. 12:11], a process of death and resurrection. And in fact the Jewish contemporaries of Jesus were by no means ready to accept the refashioning from within of the Mosaic religion which Jesus announced to them. Such a transformation seemed to them to empty it of its supreme truth. However it was only in this way that the Law could be fulfilled. And the same thing has to happen to all the civilizations, cultures and religions which meet with Christ in the course of ages.[22]

Such a transformation will not take place in Christianity in the abstract. It has to begin in the hearts of those who strive to carry out this mission of Christ. Those who enter into dialogue must allow this process of death and resurrection to take place within their own hearts in order to become more universal and so to share more fully in the Fullness of Christ.

Swami Abhishiktananda saw this as comparable to the passing over of primitive Christian experience to its expression in terms of Greek knowledge and Roman law. What saved the Church then was the deep spiritual experience of the Fathers. He saw Christianity itself as being an attempt to formulate the experience of the apostles in their encounter with the experience of Jesus himself, which was objectified in the Gospels. The early Fathers of the Church also rejoiced in their own share in this primal experience. They were much more than mere theologians in a rational sense. They were true contemplatives and even mystics in the fullest sense of the word. Christianity today must return to that original experience and claim it as its own. And, like the early Church Fathers, those who enter into dialogue today must base it on a lived experience rather than merely a rational formulation. Abhishiktananda declared:

> I think that no real theology of the Trinity-Incarnation is possible as long as we do not turn back to the fundamental *anubhava* (experience) which they express. But as long as this experience will remain a *notion* for most theologians there cannot be any hope that a real theo-logia will develop. It is a question not only of a humble and prayerful approach, but of a mental approach completely conditioned by the underlying *anubhava*![23]

He reaffirmed this opinion another time when he said:

> It is the reduction of the mystery of Jesus to a Jewish or Greek concept that makes the dialogue of salvation with non-Christians so difficult. One culture has monopolized Jesus. He has been turned into an idea. People

argue about Jesus—it is easier than to let yourself be scorched by contact with him.[24]

To the very end of his life, and especially after the heart attack that shortly preceded his death, Abhishiktananda felt that any formulation of theology must be based on the fundamental experience of the discovery of the Self. This discovery brings one into a realization of the Self in God and God in the Self in a nondualistic way. His impending transition elicited the following:

Even more after my "beyond life/death" experience of December 14, I can only aim at awakening people to what "they are." Anything about God or the Word in any religion, which is not based on the deep *I*-experience, is bound to be simply "notion," not existential. From that awakening to self comes the awakening to God—and we discover marvelously that Christ is simply this awakening on a degree of purity rarely if ever reached by humans.[25]

In Johannine terms, Jesus discovered that the I AM of Yahweh belonged to himself; or rather, putting it the other way around, it was in the brilliant light of his own I AM that he discovered the true meaning, total and unimaginable, of the name of Yahweh. To call God "Abba" is an equivalent in Semitic terms of *advaita*, the fundamental experience.[26]

This nondual experience is a reflection of the very nature of God, and it is made manifest in humans:

Humanity is so constituted that the whole race is summed up and comes to fulfilment in the individual, while at the same time the individual can only reach fulfilment in the whole. Yet it could not be otherwise since God himself is both one and plural in his mystery—or rather, to put it more accurately, he is not-one, *an-eka*, and also not-two, *a-dvaita*. By its very nature the fullness towards which humanity is moving is also the fullness, *pleroma*, of Christ, since he is the beginning and end of all.[27]

Abhishiktananda saw the monk as being called to live out this reality in a particular way. The monk is to enter into the depths of the Mystery, and in that way to bring all of humanity into that oneness in which it was created. The monk is also to be a living "bridge" within humanity, not in ways that can be seen or explained or demonstrated, but simply in Being. Abhishiktananda epitomized the life purpose of the monk when he said, "It is the monk who has the ecclesial mission of penetrating the depths of Being, much less as a theologian (which is only the first step) than as a *seer*, if seeing can still express itself in words."[28]

BEDE GRIFFITHS, O.S.B. CAM. (1906–1993)

The third monk who elaborated on the path and purpose of monasticism is the one to whom this book is dedicated. Father Bede spent thirty-five years in India working with the variety of religions he encountered there. He said of his experiences:

> It is no longer possible today for one religion to live in isolation from other religions. For many this presents a real problem. Each religion has been taught to regard itself as the one true religion and to reject all other religions as false, so that to enter into dialogue with other religions is not easy. . . . We begin to realize that truth is one, but that it has many faces, and each religion is, as it were, a face of the one Truth, which manifests itself under different signs and symbols in the different historical traditions.[29]

Father Bede saw the difference between East and West in the differing emphasis on the immanence and transcendence of God. The West high-lights the transcendence of God as "infinitely Holy," separate from and above nature, while the East sees primarily the immanence of the Absolute, whether this is called God or Brahman or whatever it may be named. The world does not exist apart from but *in* God; God dwells in the heart of every creature. Father Bede commented on these two differing approaches to spirituality:

> Hinduism, starting from the immanence of God in creation, ascends to the awareness of his infinite transcendence, and in the same way the Hebrew/Christian tradition, starting from the infinite transcendence of God or Yahweh, sees this God descending to earth, manifesting

himself through his angels, speaking his Word to his prophets, and finally becoming "incarnate"—the Word made flesh—and communicating his Spirit to humans.[30]

The Eastern religions are not primarily concerned with theory or doctrine; they begin with experience. Father Bede observed the spiritual benefit of the contemplative approach:

> When the mind in meditation goes beyond images and concepts, beyond reason and will to the ultimate Ground of its consciousness, it experiences itself in this timeless and spaceless unity of Being. The Ultimate is experienced in the depth of the soul, in the substance or Center of its consciousness, as its own Ground or Source, as its very being or Self (Atman). This is an experience of self-transcendence, which gives an intuitive insight into Reality.[31]

Many religions try to express this inexpressible self-transcendence through the language of myth—an image that is real, whether it is historical or not. Myth gives expression to the undivided unity of being and consciousness. It relates the human person to the Ultimate as well as to all the parts of creation, whether experienced as within or without oneself. Father Bede saw the story of Jesus as fulfilling a similar purpose:

> Jesus was a man in the sense that he possessed a human body and human soul like every other human, and he experienced himself through this human body and soul as other people do. But in the depth of his spirit, in that Ground or Center of the soul, which exists in every person, he knew himself as one with that ultimate Reality, which he called God, and he experienced himself in this Ground of his being in the relationship of a Son to a Father. This experience of relationship, which he expressed in terms of knowing and loving the Father and being known and loved by Him, seems to be the unique character of Jesus' experience of God.[32]

When one tries to translate this symbolic language of the Bible into more universal terms, it can be said that the one Reality, God, Truth, Spirit—by whatever name it is called—has been manifesting itself from the beginning in all creation and in every human consciousness. In this way, every human person both hides and manifests this Reality. The same can be said for every religion. Jesus knew himself, in the depths of his own consciousness, as the one who fulfills to a preeminent degree that which all humanity and ultimately all creation is to be. In him sin, which brought a divided consciousness into the world, is overcome, and nature and humanity are restored to their original unity with God. All this was realized through a communion of love rather than a pure identity. The Son is not the Father and the Father is not the Son. Yet both are united in that divine love that is the Holy Spirit. Father Bede eloquently developed this theme:

> This, of course, is "mythological" language, but it expresses a profound metaphysical truth, the truth that Being itself is not only consciousness but also love, that there is a relationship at the heart of Reality. In thus revealing his own relationship to God as his Father in the love of the Spirit, Jesus also reveals what is the destiny of the human person. Every person is destined to discover this relationship of Filiation in the depth of one's Spirit. As we pass beyond our limited rational consciousness and become aware of the depth of the Spirit within, we discover this unfathomable depth of knowledge and love opening up within us and uniting us to one another and to the whole creation in the light of God. And this is not an identity of being without distinction but a communion of love, by which each is "in" the other, as Jesus expressed in his high priestly prayer: "I in them and thou in me, that they may be perfectly one."[33]

In Father Bede's view, the Church then is simply an extension of this fundamental experience:

> The Church in this sense is clearly the communion of those who are united by the love of the Spirit in the knowledge of the Word of God, the Eternal Truth, and through him return to the Father, the Source, the Origin and the Ground of all creation.[34]

When the Spirit came upon the disciples at Pentecost they were given a share in Jesus' experience of the divine Filiation. They were set free from the limitations of our present mode of existence and consciousness and were brought into new life "in Christ." The effect was that they were truly "all of one mind and one heart," and they carried this over into the economic and social aspects of their lives by sharing all in common.

Even though Jesus did establish a rudimentary organization of the institution of the Church, he was not concerned so much with the external aspects of the Church as with the transcendent Reality. Father Bede felt that "the organization of the Church as a human community is necessary for its evolution in history, but it belongs to the world of signs and appearances, not the world of ultimate Reality."[35] This is why he urged an expanded vision of the Church that would include not only all Christians but also all those who sincerely seek God. There is no limit to the grace of God revealed in Christ. The important thing is not the symbol but the Reality. The Church, Christianity, and every religion remain symbols of that ultimate Reality. That Reality is not simply God as God, but God as pouring out in creation and in every person. All symbols remain fingers pointing the way. Father Bede explained the role of the Church as a sign revealing this way:

> Whenever a person encounters God, or Truth, or Reality, or Love, or whatever name we give to the transcendent mystery of existence, even if that person is formally an atheist or an agnostic, that one encounters the grace of God in Christ. For Christ is the Word of God, the expression of God's saving purpose for all peoples. Everyone either in life or in death is brought into contact with that Word, that Truth, in some form or other, and everyone who responds to that Word is a member of that body of redeemed humanity which is the Church. Those who belong to the visible Church by faith and baptism are not an exclusive group of the "saved," but a sign or sacrament of salvation, that is to say, they manifest God's saving purpose for all humanity.[36]

Father Bede spoke of being a sign in relation to his own vocation as a sannyasin, or renunciate. Yet what he said is perfectly in accord with the monk as a bridge between East and West. He described the sannyasin as one who renounces the world in order seek God (the same definition Benedict gave for the monk). Yet this renunciation extends beyond what is ordinarily understood as "world." The monk renounces the whole world of signs or appearances. This includes the Church as a sign, doctrine and sacraments as signs, Christ himself as the "sacrament of God," and even God, insofar as God can be named. In fact, Father Bede stated:

Thus the [monk] is called to go beyond all religion, beyond every human institution, beyond every scripture and creed, till the person comes to that which every religion and scripture and ritual signifies but can never name. In every religion, whether Christian or Hindu or Buddhist or Muslim, it has been recognized that the ultimate Reality cannot be named and the [monk] is one who is called to go beyond all religion and seek that ultimate goal. . . . To go beyond the sign is not to reject the sign, but to reach the thing signified.[37]

Father Bede said that the world needs signs and symbols; he even said that it cannot survive unless it rediscovers the signs of faith, the myth, the symbol in which the knowledge of reality is enshrined. But it is fatal to mistake the sign for the ultimate Reality. This is ultimately idolatry and serves only to divide people from one another. Stopping short at the sign divides, but living in the Reality unites.

If the monk is to be a person who refuses to stop short of the Ultimate, then the monk is already in that original unity, that oneness with all peoples that manifests the very nature of Reality. This is why Merton can say that "we *are* one; we only imagine that we are not."[38] In this way the monk truly becomes a sign of what he or she is, a sign of what every person is—the Kingdom of God in our midst!

NOTES

1. Thomas Merton, *The Asian Journal of Thomas Merton*, edited by Naomi B. Stone (New York: New Directions, 1973), p. 308.

2. Ibid., p. 305.

3. Ibid., p. 308.

4. Ibid., p. 304.

5. Ibid.

6. Ibid., p. 307.

7. Ibid.

8. Ibid., p. 308.

9. A. Reza Arasteh, *Final Integration in the Adult Personality* (Leiden: Brill, 1965), develops the notion of the "transcultural state" and studies extensively the "rebirth" experience in Rumi and in Goethe.

10. Thomas Merton, *Contemplation in a World of Action* (Garden City: Doubleday, 1971), p. 206.

11. Ibid., p. 207.

12. Ibid., p. 211.

13. Ibid., p. 212.

14. Ibid., quoting Arasteh and modified for inclusive language.

15. Ibid., pp. 215–16. For "existential moratorium," see Arasteh, *Final Integration*, p. 152.

16. Abhishiktananda, *Saccidananda: A Christian Approach to Advaitic Experience* (Delhi: IS-PCK, 1984), pp. 7–8.

17. Abhishiktananda, *The Eyes of Light* (Denville, NJ: Dimension, 1983), pp. 72–73.

18. Ibid., p. 73.

19. Ibid., pp. 92–93.

20. Ibid., p. 184, n. 18.

21. Abhishiktananda, *Saccidananda*, p. 199.

22. Ibid., p. 50.

23. James Stuart, *Swami Abhishiktananda: His Life Told through His Letters* (Delhi: ISPCK, 1989), p. 276.

24. Ibid., p. 317.

25. Ibid., p. 349.

26. Ibid., p. 317.

27. Abhishiktananda, *Saccidananda*, p. 135.

28. Abhishiktananda, *The Eyes of Light*, p. 173.

29. Bede Griffiths, *The Marriage of East and West* (1982), p. 25.

30. Ibid., p. 19.

31. Ibid., p. 27.

32. Ibid., p. 33.

33. Ibid., p. 35.

34. Ibid.

35. Ibid.

36. Ibid., p. 38.

37. Ibid., pp. 42–43.

38. Merton, *Asian Journal*, p. 308.

Existential
Breakthrough

Pascaline Coff

Pascaline Coff, O.S.B., was a long-time close friend, disciple, and colleague of Bede's, who on several occasions spent extended periods of time at Saccidananda. She is a member of the Benedictine Sisters of Perpetual Adoration, a board member of MID, and Prioress of Osage Monastery, which she founded to implement the kind of interreligious learning that Dom Bede was urging. The very architecture and furnishing of the chapel at Osage—located in its own "Forest of Peace" (Shantivanam)—speaks of this ideal: the choir is a sunken circle, like a kiva (Pueblo Indian ceremonial house), over which hangs an equally large Buddhist Wheel of the Law. One side altar shelters the Sacrament of Christ, the other shows Nataraj in his Cosmic Dance. And the whole is surrounded by large windows at ground level, so that the forest itself almost seems inside.

Her essay calls for reactivating our intuitive faculty, our sensitivity to revelation through the mythic dimension of the world and its history, so that we become capable of recognizing the Divine in all reality and exclaiming, "Oh, it's You!" Drawing on Hindu and Buddhist sources as well as Western spiritual guides, she examines the role of meditation—to still, clarify, and harmonize body and mind, along with the role of memory—to recreate, heal, and integrate the past, to reveal the Divine Presence that dwells in us from the beginning. She gives examples of how several spiritual traditions have found ways of nurturing the capacity for existential breakthrough, ways of arousing the latent sense of the Divine in ourselves and one another and in all our experiences, so that we open to the realization that we are not separate from God.

Among all the Hindu myths, some of the most popular and much loved are of the ten Avatars or incarnations of Vishnu. When God saw that humankind was in great need, unable to help itself in the midst of the threat of some great evil, Hari, the loving Lord, would assume some form in order to rid the world of the harm and restore peace and harmony. The earliest of these "des Avatars" appears in the Flood Story, usually called the Matsya, or Fish Avatar. In the first half of the story:

Brahma, the Creator, inclined to slumber, one day fell asleep with his mouth open, and Hayagrive, a strong demon, came near and stole the Vedas, the sacred scriptures, from his mouth. Hari, Preserver of the universe, discovered this and therefore assumed the shape of a tiny fish.

Soon after, while Sraddhadevi, a saintly king, was making his libations in a sacred river near his home, he perceived a small fish in the water he had gathered in his hands. The fish made known to the king, who always showed affection to the oppressed, that it did not want to be left in the river. So the king gently placed the fish in his vase full of water and put it under his protection.

But the fish grew so large in one night that it could no longer be contained in the vase. The king removed it from one container to another until it was obvious that it had to be put in a lake. When the fish grew to equal bulk with the lake, the king decided he had no alternative but to cast it into the ocean.

Repeatedly deluded by the fish who had addressed him with gentle words, the king said: "Who are you that beguile me in that assumed shape? Surely it is you, Bhagavan, who appear before me, the great Hari . . . salutations and praise to you, O Lord of creation, preserver from destruction." And the king prostrated himself in adoration of the blazing, golden fish that seemed to fill the very ocean from shore to shore.[1]

This awakening to the Transcendent is what we are made for. In the Christian tradition, it was St. John, the beloved Disciple, who called out from the boat, "It is the Lord! . . . It is you!" Mary Magdalene, too, said, "It is you!" in her utterance of "Rabboni!" Nicholas of Cusa, one of the Christian mystics, cried out: "Wherever I turn there you are!" In other words, "It's you!"

During the sharing of the meal at Emmaus, the two disciples recognized Jesus in the breaking of the bread. The Ultimate Reality is totally present everywhere, in everything, in you and in me. But we cannot ordinarily recognize this Presence, and therefore, we need signs and symbols. God is self-revealing to all—to other peoples, to all peoples. Other religions are filled with gifts and truth that lead to the Divine. Every religion aims at bringing one beyond the "ego," the selfish center, to the Transcendent, the Absolute—to the Lord.

Philip Kapleau, an expert in Buddhist meditation, describes Zen as the actualization of your undefiled True-nature. And in practice you sit in complete faith that the day will come when, exclaiming "Oh, this is it!" you will unmistakably realize this True-nature.[2]

Each religion is embedded in a certain culture and language, with its own myths, stories, rites, and teachings. These can be like searchlights on our own scriptures and teachings. Even some contemplative meditation practices from these other religions can be extremely valuable for us. We of the West have for too long sustained a rational, cerebral, analytical training and badly need to discover and utilize our whole intuitive, contemplative faculties. The seers (wisdom figures) in every age—Christian, Buddhist, Hindu, Sufi, Jewish, etc.—have always known that beyond the space/time order as we see it, there is this Eternal Reality, and the mystical experience has described it in every age. Nicholas of Cusa, a Christian mystic, said in his *Vision of God*:

> I have learned that the place wherein you are found unveiled is girt round with the coincidence of contradictories, and this is the wall of Paradise wherein you abide! The door is guarded by the most proud spirit of reason, and unless he be vanquished, the way will not lie open.[3]

In every religion, wisdom leads one intent on the spiritual journey beyond opposites, the "coincidence of contradictions," or "contraries," that keep us from seeing and experiencing the Divine everywhere with that ecstatic recognition of the Presence. For with our "most proud spirit of reason," our rational, analytic, self-centered mind, we judge ourselves as either too hot or too cold; it is either too early or too late to be praying; it is too difficult or boring, and so on. The Bhagavad Gita mentions these opposites: "know that a person of true renunciation is one who craves not nor hates; for one who is above the two contraries soon finds freedom" (v. 3).

In the Christian scriptures we find this discovery of the Presence in so many texts. Jesus was always aware that he and the Father were One: "When they see me, they see you." "I must be about my Father's business." "No one can come to me unless you send them." "I know that you always hear me." In all of these cases, "It's you!"

Jesus truly vanquished the "proud spirit of reason" guarding the wall of Paradise, which is composed of the "coincidence of contradictories," by laying down his life for his friends—moving all enemies into the category of friends—until he was faced with that last temptation, no longer humanly able to experience the "It's you!" of the Father, but only able to utter "My God, my God, why have you abandoned me?"—the greatest of contradictions. Perhaps in our own lives it is the fear of that same agony, the void, or "dark night of the soul," that keeps us from the initial leap, letting go, that would allow us to come to that existential breakthrough, to recognize the divine Presence, the "It's you!" The psalmist tells us to "Be still and know that I am God." This quieting down and being still is the role of meditation. And this is where the Eastern religious traditions have so much to share with us.

In 1963, the Fathers of the Vatican Council astounded the Roman Catholic Church and the world by stating that Roman Catholics are to

> . . . reflect attentively on how Christian religious life may be able to assimilate the ascetic and contemplative traditions whose seeds were sometimes planted by God in ancient cultures prior to the preaching of the Gospel. [*Ad Gentes* #18]

Furthermore, never before had the Church of Rome publicly proclaimed that God's divine truth was also in religions other than Christian:

> The Catholic Church rejects nothing that is true and holy in these religions. She regards with sincere reverence those ways of conduct and of life, those precepts and teachings which, though differing in many respects from the ones she holds and sets forth, nonetheless often reflect a ray of that truth which enlightens all. . . . Indeed, she proclaims and ever must proclaim Christ "the way, the truth and the life" [John 14:6]

in whom all may find the fulness of religious life, in whom God has reconciled all things. . . .

The Church therefore exhorts her [children] that through dialogue and collaboration with the followers of other religions, carried out with prudence and love and in witness to the Christian faith and life, they recognize, preserve and promote the good things, spiritual and moral, as well as the socio-cultural values found among these [people]. [*Nostra Aetate #2*]

We need to mutually share and be enriched by all peoples of all religions everywhere. Pope John Paul II not only led the way for us when he invited representatives of each major world religion to come together to pray for peace at Assisi in 1986, but in his message to the people of Asia, who are all but two percent other than Christian, he said:

The Church wishes to do everything possible to cooperate with other believers in preserving all that is good in these religions and cultures, stressing the things that we hold in common and helping all people to live together as brothers and sisters. The Church of Jesus Christ in this age experiences a profound need to enter into contact and dialogue with all these religions.

In the oldest known book in the world, the Hindu Rig Veda, we read: "[God] is the original form of all forms, so we must see [God's] form in all forms." How different our world would be if we all discovered and enjoyed the divine Presence this way, in everything from the soaring eagle to the tiniest blade of green grass in the valley, and especially in one another, realizing "It is you!"

In summary, we need to be open and eager to encounter the Divine in everything, in everyone. We hesitate because of the fear of the emptiness, darkness, aloneness involved in the process. Meditation is necessary in stilling down and letting go. Other religions, especially those of the East, have ascetical and contemplative practices that we in the West need to assimilate by attentive reflection on this. "Today if you hear the Voice"—see the Form—"harden not your hearts," but recognize, love, praise, and adore the divine Heart who calls to us through the Prophet Isaiah:

You are my witnesses, . . .
My servants whom I have chosen
To know and believe in Me
And to understand that it is I.

[Isaiah 43:10]

THE ROLE OF MEDITATION

God cannot be "seen," as such, with physical eyes. We have to look beyond the outer form and the outer level of consciousness until we recognize the divine Presence: "It's you!" Tagore, an Indian poet laureate, defined sin as "the ignorance that blurs the purity of our consciousness." Sin creates the illusion that we are separate from God. But we are *in* God at all times. "In God we live and move and have our being" (Acts 17:28).

Conversion is turning from this illusion of separateness to the reality of communion. When we believe in separation, we judge, label, condemn, withdraw, take sides, and even go to battle because we stop at the outer form. We rightly feel that such behavior is somehow "diabolical." *Dia-bolus* means put apart. Its opposite is *sym-bolus*, put together. St. James tells us that wars begin in the heart; so too does communion. Conversion means renouncing in our hearts the belief in division and embracing at the center of our being the faith that we are one with God and one with one another. And essential to this whole process is true self-knowledge. Hindus say: "The knowledge that we are Brahman is like a fire which altogether consumes the thick forest of ignorance" (Sankara Acharya, *Crest Jewel of Discrimination*).[4] This is the kind of knowledge that is not gained from books but is received from the Holy Spirit through meditation, being still and knowing God.

Someone once asked the Buddha: "What have you gained through meditation?" The Buddha replied, "Nothing at all." "Then, Blessed One, what good is it?" The Buddha said: "Let me tell you what I have *lost* in meditation: sickness, depression, anger, insecurity, the burden of old age and the fear of death. That is the good of meditation, which leads to Nirvana [extinction of selfish desires and conditioning]."

Meditation, which in the West we call contemplation, is not going anywhere and doing anything, but rather is a way, a stance of life—it is experiencing fully at all times. Contemplative meditation methods aim to take us beyond the outer phenomenon, the things we can see and hear, to the Reality beyond. We are all blessed with a Third Eye that penetrates beyond the outer forms to the divine Presence: "It's you!" These methods take us beyond thought, concept, and image and are known as nonconceptual ways of prayer. But nonconceptual prayer is ordinarily not learned unless it is practiced! Such meditation purifies the heart so that we can see more height, depth, breadth, and length. Meditation cleans the windows of our perception, removing selfishness and ignorance.

Thich Nhat Hanh tells the story of a young Vietnamese girl who was brought to him by her father because he had to go out and find a job. Out of compassion Thich agreed, and the father disappeared before the monk could turn around. So, among many other things, Thich trained the child to stop playing when it was time for his own meditation. When it was time for him to settle down in perfect lotus position on his cushion, it was her turn to quiet down and either take her noon nap or go to sleep for the night. One afternoon she had two friends visit her. He poured them three glasses of carrot juice. The guests enjoyed theirs, but the little girl did not touch hers. After the other two departed Thich called her to him and told her to drink the juice. She looked at it and saw that the liquid, which had been cloudy and unattractive (because she had gotten the bottom of the can), was now all clear. She smiled and said, "Oh, juice imitates grandfather monk!" and then she drank it down and enjoyed it.

Meditation does just that—it stills us and clarifies perception. Both body and mind must first be put into harmony. This is the very function professed by yoga in the Hindu tradition. The Beatitudes tell us that it takes a pure heart to see God. The Mundaka Upanishad says "In a pure mind there shines the light of the Self" (III.1.8). Meister Eckhart, a Western contemplative, describes a pure heart as one that is "unencumbered, unworried, and uncommitted, and does not want its own way in anything, but is rather submerged in the loving will of God, having denied self."

Meditation, in stilling our body and mind, surfaces our encumbrances, worries, and commitments. It is at this very time that we can become exceedingly discouraged, thinking that we are not fit for deeper prayer and inner communion. But in the First Epistle, St. John tells us that we should rather take courage at this crucial point in prayer, for we have within us

"One who is greater than anyone (or anything) in this world." God longs for us to have this deeper communion even now.

Most meditation practices begin by teaching one to focus the mind on one point, either outside—on a candle, stone, breath, etc.—or inside—on the eyebrows, navel, *hara* (abdomen), etc.—while constantly bringing the attention back to one's focal point when necessary. It is usually advised to continue for 20 to 30 minutes. This first effort breaks up the old patterns of the mind with their focus on the self-center. Don't look for nirvana, enlightenment, beatitude, or instant bliss at this point. We are well counseled by Swami Sivananda that "unless the mind is first made strong and brought under complete control, it will not be possible to change its course to the opposite direction."[5] And this is why we must bring it back full center again and again in meditation. Buddhists will tell you the very essence of Buddhism is "taming the mind." Each form of Buddhism then has its own unique way to do this: Zen, Tibetan, Insight, and others.

In explaining the rationale behind sitting meditation and its motivational force, Philip Kapleau lists three aims: "1) development of the power of concentration which once mobilized, enables us to move with perfect freedom and equanimity instantly; 2) satori-awakening, which is the realization of Buddha-nature, not mere devotion or strength of concentration, but the sudden realization that 'I have been complete and perfect from the beginning'; and 3) actualization of the Supreme Way in our daily lives, continuous throughout our entire being and all our activities—that is, with perfect enlightenment we apprehend that our conception of the world as dual and antithetical is false, and upon this realization the world of Oneness, of true harmony and peace, is revealed."[6] Notice that we are back to our "coincidence of contradictories," or opposites once again.

The Christian scriptures say that we are made for God and made in God's own image and likeness. Jesus even affirmed the verse that says, "You are gods." As children we know this, that we are gifted with wonder, awe at life and all that is. We are receptive to the new, delighted by surprises. Jesus at one point had to tell his apostles, "Unless you turn around and become as little children, you cannot enter the Kingdom" (Matt. 18:3). Meditation helps us to stop and turn around, to return to innocence. Meditation is an opportunity to be free of all self-evaluation, because at its best it is pure experience with no questioning, no judging, no comparing, no competition.

All this is head work, and the head must be put into the heart during meditation.

But we are so often tempted to give up. The practice is so boring, since there is nothing at all for the senses to do. It is difficult for us to welcome an experience that is non-self-reflective, because we are so good at self-reflection! In meditation we are forced to realize that we are only who we are in the *now*, in this present moment. This is the only place where God is, where grace is. We tend to analyze, criticize, plan—and thus miss the grace of the present moment, Reality Itself. There is a time for these activities, but it is not during the sacred moments set apart for special Presence.

In the Zen meditation tradition they list four levels of motivation, or determination in sitting that might well serve as a checklist for us: 1) with neither faith in Zen Buddhism nor even a cursory understanding of it, one hears about the practice and decides to sit with a meditation group (however, they warn you not to discount the vast spiritual significance of even this much effort); 2) one desires to improve one's physical or mental health; 3) one has faith in the reality of the enlightenment experience, but the resolve to attain it is not yet awakened; and 4) one has the determination to realize the True Self, knowing that others have done so; and, convinced that attainment is possible, one comes with open mind and heart, ready to follow instruction.[7]

The practice of meditation gives us discipline and gradually changes our lives. If during our meditation time we return to the focal point, to the center some fifty times, we have trained the mind that much. Meditation continuously unveils our false, selfish self and surfaces the true meaning in our lives. We are eventually changed radically, but not necessarily during the time of meditation. In Zen they insist that one's practice is going on *always*, not just while sitting on the cushion: it is "continuous throughout our entire being and in all our activities." We hear in this the echo of the first and greatest commandment, to love God with all our heart and all our soul and all our strength. And in the Bhagavad Gita (VI.10 ff) the actual practice of meditation is nicely spelled out, concluding with the promise that one who meditates will "see the Self in the self and find contentment therein" (v. 20).

In the Christian tradition there are the teachings from *The Cloud of Unknowing*,[8] the Jesus Prayer in *The Way of the Pilgrim*,[9] and a profusion of books on how to meditate. However, meditation cannot be learned without practice. From Ruysbroeck we learn that "The one who wants to understand the Mystery must turn to face towards the Eternal light in the depths of one's own spirit, where the hidden truth reveals itself without intermediary."

THE ROLE OF MEMORY

Another one of the ways we reach the Transcendent and discover the divine Presence is through the gift of memory. Louis Dupré, in his *Transcendent Selfhood*,[10] calls memory "the gateway to the soul's ground where God and self coincide," because our memories contain the mind's latent knowledge both of ourselves and of God. Memory is the very road to our inner center where every encounter with God takes place. Therefore, it is important for us to travel this road awake, attuned, and attentive.

The sacred scriptures of most of the world's religions are full of the "Mirabilia Dei," recognition and praise of the wonderful works of God. The Christian liturgy places such praises on worshippers' lips constantly throughout the year. Hindu mythology recounts over and over the wonderful deeds of Hari, the loving Lord, and great reward is promised to those who gather to listen to such stories told and retold.

Memory never just copies the past but constitutes it as past by breathing new life into it. Memory also gives an intimate quality to the past, allowing it to surpass the external events as we perceived, or perhaps failed to perceive them at the time. Memory brings the event into our own intimate focus, into our very own subjective life. It allows us not only to discover "It's you!"—the divine Presence here and now—but to uncover, recover, that unbroken, abiding, loving Presence in and to our lives from the beginning.

Jews, Christians, and Muslims pray to "you," saying:

It was you who created my inmost self, and put me together in my mother's womb . . . You know me through and through, from having watched my bones take shape when I was being formed in secret, knitted together in the limbo of the womb. [Psalm 139:13,15]

On this road of memory it is necessary for us to retrace with the Eternal the road thus traveled. "As a parent carries a little child, so I have carried you to this very place where you are" (Deut. 1:31), God assures us. At times we are led directly down this road. This is what happened to Nathaniel when Jesus told him he had seen him under the fig tree. Nathaniel had a real inner explosion: the existential breakthrough, "It's you!" But we each need to walk back with our God on this path of memory in our own lives, and the lives of our families and communities, even if there is no apparent need for healing memories. We need to allow the divine Presence to reveal itself as always having been with us, loving us. We need to see differently, beyond our original perceptions, into the Reality.

The healing of memories happens more often than we realize. Unpleasant memories need congruence and coherence. It is new coherence of memories that cures, and this is often achieved by mythic models. Jesus was adept at creating mythic models and offering them to us: the Prodigal's Father, the Good Samaritan, and others. St. Basil spoke of the psychic forces at play in our encounter with God that lead to a profound transformation of our very character and way of being. This is our memory as it lies open and reaches deeply into our dynamic unconscious. While others can help us and encourage us on the road, no one can undergo the journey for us. We must touch into our own sacred personal past known truly only to the Self.

Memory has a double function and thereby leads us to a double awareness. While it is true that memory makes us aware of the constant destruction of events as they come and go, and therefore of the continuous passage of the self into nothingness, it is also memory that retains the remembered self in which the religious mind arrives at the "still point," where the passing comes to rest and, as Dupré says, the past is forever preserved. Filled with Upanishadic wisdom and fire, Swami Abhishiktananda said, in his own poetic form:

> Shiva is the one who sets us free from the passing moment by bringing us into the Eternal Present. For the truth is that Being is always present. The origins do not belong to a past that has been left behind but to one here and now. And the Further Shore is already possessed.[11]

Retreat directors often refer to this as "dynamic memory"—this returning to the past with a faith so alive that it brings us to a celebration of the divine Presence and love in our lives. Such religious recollection will bring about a conversion in us, by way of the past toward a more interior self no longer subject to the passing of time, because it abides in the "Eternal Present."

Time is *our* creation. God is not in time but only in the Now! It is said that only in the completeness of the past does the present attain final significance. Perhaps this throws a new light on an understanding of Purgatory and the important role of memory in the Now of our lives. Memory can be a channel for purgation here and now!

We are brought into being by Creative Love as "capacities for God," made uniquely like God. Because the memory contains the mind's latent knowledge both of itself and of God, we have from the beginning an undeveloped sense, a memory of our own goodness and of being totally loved. We are precious to God, in whose image and likeness we are. We have "played before" the Creator, who delighted in us.

But early on we began to receive messages from others that we were "not OK," even that we were not loved. Those caregivers who should be the first to awaken this latent knowledge in us often give just the opposite message. Yet something in us knows that this doesn't ring true. And we are face to face with the antithetical, dual world, the "coincidence of contradictories" once more.

In the Zen Buddhist tradition, it is said that there are three essential reasons for sitting, for meditation practice. First, there is *strong faith*, firmly and deeply rooted in the Buddha's enlightenment experience. The heart of that experience was the Buddha's absolute assurance that human nature— and all existence—is intrinsically whole, flawless, omnipotent, perfect. (Somehow, this says volumes in the light of Jesus' Resurrection experience, his Baptism, and the events on Mount Tabor.) Then, there is equally *strong doubt*, doubt as to why the individual and the world appear so imperfect, so full of anxiety, strife, and suffering, when in fact one's deeper faith confirms exactly the opposite. This doubt produces restlessness, for the longer one fails to find the answer, the greater the energy and perseverance generated in trying to attain it. Finally, there is a *strong determination to overcome this doubt*, backed with overwhelming energy and intent. For the practitioner it is a *strong resolve to discover and experience the reality of this enlightened mind for oneself*. This resoluteness arises from the exigency of dispelling the contradiction between what is believed in faith and what appears to be the exact opposite.[12]

In this we hear another echo of our innate knowledge of our own truth and goodness, and we sense the Presence behind the Wall of Paradise. On the other hand we also experience the ignorance that causes us to lose our memory of who we truly are, a loss likened in some traditions to "losing one's very self."

> Being deluded, one loses all memory. All memory being lost, there is lost the knowledge of the Atman, the divine Self. The loss of this knowledge is called by the wise "losing one's own Self." [Srimad Bhagavatam IV.3][13]

When we forget our true identity and are unaware that we truly are the beloved, then we must kill and lie and cheat in an attempt to have "first place," to gain some artificial status in lieu of the real one.

Asking the question "Who am I?" was the central spiritual practice taught by Ramana Maharshi, a much loved Hindu saint of our own times. He suggested that we not try to answer the question but just let it arise from the depths of our being. By this "self-inquiry" he brought many to enlightenment. The question, no doubt, takes us down the road of memory to the inner center where our encounters with the Divine take place, where in Christ, our radical unity "shines forth": beloved, anointed one, precious, image and likeness, the apple of God's eye, divine.

Other religious traditions and practices can throw so much light on our path. To help us remember who we really are, many Hindu saints have set the example of attaining the Godhead through repetition of the holy Name: Narada, Tukaram Valmiki, Mirabai, and others. Constant repetition of the Divine Name has a strong influence on the mind, calling it to itself, to its own reality. Therefore Swami Sivananda urged his disciples to "repeat the Name throughout the day mentally . . . to repeat the Name with every breath."[14]

As we come face to face with one another, with all others, let us remember who we truly are, who the other truly is: "It's you!" Jesus begged us to remember him by doing what he did, by laying down our lives for one another, and not just when we stand before stone and wooden altars. The celebration of the Eucharist can teach, feed, and energize one to enter ever more continuously and consciously into Christ's death/resurrection experience by having "this mind in you" (Phil. 2:5). We have been given the gift of inner wisdom by the Spirit of Jesus. But where is it? Down in the ocean of our unconscious, always there, always waiting to help us remember: remember who we are, who others are, Who the great Other is. It is to regain this memory, to experience this *existential breakthrough*, that we meditate.

The Eternal Current of Self-awareness is ever flowing within you. It is your Spiritual Heart; ever abide in That by diving within. That is peace profound. I leave you there.

Swami Chittananda

NOTES

1. Adapted from W. J. Wilkins, *Hindu Mythology* (Delhi: Indological Book House, 1988), pp. 134–144.

2. Philip Kapleau, *The Three Pillars of Zen* (Boston: Beacon, 1967), p. 46.

3. Nicholas of Cusa, *The Vision of God*, trans. Emma Gurney Salter (London: Dent; New York: Dutton, 1906), pp. 43–44.

4. Sankara Acharya, *Crest Jewel of Discrimination*, tr. Swami Prabhavananda & Christopher Isherwood (Hollywood: Vedanta Press, 1947), p. 105.

5. Swami Sivananda, *Yoga Sadhana: Perennial Diary of the Saint and Sage of Rishikesh*, ed. Vandana and Ishpriya Mataji (Jaiharikhal: Jeevan Dhara Ashram, 1987).

6. Kapleau, *Pillars of Zen*, pp. 48–49.

7. Ibid., p. 61.

8. *The Cloud of Unknowing*, edited by James Walsh (Mahwah, NJ: Paulist Press, 1981).

9. Gordon R. Dickson, *The Way of the Pilgrim* (New York: Ace Books, 1988).

10. Louis Dupré, *Transcendent Selfhood: The Rediscovery of the Inner Life* (New York: Seabury, 1976), p. 78.

11. Swami Abhishiktananda, *The Further Shore* (Delhi: ISPCK, 1975, 1984), p. 119.

12. Kapleau, *Pillars of Zen*, pp. 58–59.

13. *The Wisdom of God* (Srimad Bhagavatam), tr. Swami Prabhavananda (Hollywood: Vedanta Press, 1943), p. 77.

14. Sivananda, *Yoga Sadhana: Perennial Diary*, 9 June.

Meditative Technologies: Theological Ecumenism

Thomas Keating

Thomas Keating, O.S.C.O., another board member of MID, has been active for years in reviving the Christian contemplative tradition. Open Mind, Open Heart[1] is but one among Father Keating's many widely read and often reprinted publications. In 1984, he inspired the establishment of Contemplative Outreach, whose services are now available in nearly forty regions across the United States and in several other countries to provide support and a sense of community for those committed to the contemplative life in the world and for the practice of centering prayer. He has been deeply involved in drawing together teacher-practitioners of various spiritual paths for meditation and sharing. Here he tells about this group of teachers, the Snowmass Ecumenical Conference, their experiences and some of their conclusions about "how they are one." Keating discusses the point that there are important differences in various paths, so one must be careful about lifting a practice out of its cultural and creedal setting and trying to transplant it to another. His essay speaks of analogs between Christianity and Eastern religions, of Guru and "lineage" in the risen presence of Christ in the sacraments. He also details the characteristic Christian spiritual energy in which the Christian practitioner needs to become more deeply rooted, while advancing in the learning and sharing of conversation with other spiritualities.

—ʬ—

As a member of a community of Cistercian monks since 1944, I have had the rare opportunity to absorb the contemplative tradition of Christianity within the context of monastic practice and experience. Most Christians remain almost totally unaware of the spiritual potential contained in their own tradition. Some have turned to the East in the hope of finding a teaching and practice that would satisfy their hunger for spiritual experience. My own exposure to Eastern methods of meditation began in the 1960s. They have expanded my understanding of the mystery of Christ and the message of the Gospel. Moreover, they mirror aspects of Christian mysticism overlooked in recent centuries. The contemplative dimension of life is present in all the great religions; it is the common heart of the human family.

"In our time," Pope John XXIII said on his deathbed, "we should emphasize what unites rather than what divides." The Second Vatican Council explicitly recognized the values of the non-Christian religions and the work of the Spirit in them revealing various aspects of the mystery of God. The aspects of Eastern spirituality that could be of special value to Christianity today are: the experience of nonduality, the illusory nature of our subjective worldview, the importance of contemplation as the source of action, and the practice of techniques that help to integrate the mind and body.

In reference to the last point, Cardinal Ratzinger in his *Letter to the Bishops of the Catholic Church on some Aspects of Christian Meditation*,[2] manifests significant concerns. While the *Letter* encourages the practice of contemplative prayer, especially the cataphatic approach of St. Ignatius Loyola, it devotes most of its attention to contemporary Christian meditative practices that incorporate the methods of Eastern meditation such as Zen and the use of Hindu mantras. The *Letter* does not forbid their use, and after making some cautionary remarks, is careful to make the following clarification: "That does not mean that the genuine practices of meditation that come from the Christian East and from the great non-Christian religions . . . cannot constitute a suitable means of helping the person who prays to come before God with an interior peace even in the midst of external pressures" (#28).

If I understand the *Letter* correctly, its primary concern is the integration of such techniques into the Christian faith. Catholics will be in a better position to accomplish this task if they first rediscover the forgotten richness of contemplative Christianity in both its cataphatic and apophatic manifestations. The transcendent as well as the immanent dimension of the Trinity must be recovered from ancient and medieval Christian sources. In the Middle Ages, *Lectio Divina* as a meditative practice was the way in which these two streams of contemplation were harmoniously integrated, especially by the Cistercian Fathers and the extraordinary women of their tradition.[3]

In our day many Christians have turned to the Eastern religions because the experience of the transcendent is lacking in the various denominations in which they were raised. Many have also turned away from their churches because an overly strict interpretation of their moral teachings was taught to them at an age when they were too young to understand them or to harmonize them with a barely established trust and love of God. As a result, words associated with the Christian religion, such as "sin" and "salvation," have overtones that they cannot endure.

From among these two categories of alienated Christians, significant numbers have been instructed in Eastern meditative techniques that have done them a lot of good. The technique succeeded in interesting them initially because it was presented in terminology that did not bring about a negative reaction. At some point, however, as a result of the more disciplined life-style that these techniques inspired, they became sufficiently open to spiritual values to feel an attraction to return to the faith of their childhood. If someone could show them how the spiritual experience they found in their Eastern method of meditation corresponds to experiences that are also normal for devoted Christians, this would give them the needed encouragement to consider continuing their spiritual journey in the framework of their early religious training.

SNOWMASS ECUMENICAL CONFERENCE

A brief report of an actual experience of an ongoing interreligious dialogue that I facilitated might be helpful to illustrate ecumenical exploration of the similarities and differences in the world religious traditions. In 1984 a group of spiritual teachers from a variety of the world religions—Zen Buddhist, Tibetan Buddhist, Hindu, Jewish, Islamic, Native American, Russian Orthodox, Protestant, and Roman Catholic—were invited to gather at St. Benedict's Monastery, Snowmass, Colorado, to meditate together in silence and to share their personal spiritual journeys, especially those elements in their respective traditions that have proved most helpful to them along the way. We kept no records and published no papers. As our trust and friendship grew, we felt moved to investigate various points where we seemed to be in close agreement. The original points of agreement were reworked during the course of subsequent meetings as we continued to meet for a week each year. Our final list consisted of the following eight points:

1. The world religions bear witness to the experience of Ultimate Reality to which they give various names: Brahman, Allah, Absolute, God, Great Spirit.
2. Ultimate Reality cannot be limited by any name or concept.
3. Ultimate Reality is the ground of infinite potentiality and actuality.
4. Faith is opening, accepting, and responding to Ultimate Reality. In this sense faith precedes every belief system.
5. The potential for human wholeness—or in other frames of reference, enlightenment, salvation, transformation, blessedness, nirvana—is present in every human person.
6. Ultimate Reality may be experienced not only through religious practices but also through nature, art, human relationships, and service to others.
7. As long as the human condition is experienced as separate from Ultimate Reality, it is subject to ignorance and illusion, weakness and suffering.
8. Disciplined practice is essential to the spiritual life; yet spiritual attainment is not the result of one's own efforts, but the ripe fruit of the experience of oneness with Ultimate Reality.

At the annual Conference in May, 1986, we came up with additional points of agreement of a practical nature:

I. Examples of disciplined practice common to us all:

1. Practice of compassion
2. Service to others
3. Practicing moral precepts and virtues

4. Training in meditation techniques and regularity of practice
5. Attention to diet and exercise
6. Fasting and abstinence
7. The use of music and chanting and sacred symbols
8. Practice in awareness (recollection, mindfulness) and living in the present moment
9. Pilgrimage
10. Study of scriptural texts and scriptures

And in some traditions:

11. Relationship with a qualified teacher
12. Repetition of sacred words (mantras, japa)
13. Periods of silence and solitude
14. Movement and dance
15. Formative community

II. It is essential to extend the formal practice of awareness into all the aspects of our life.
III. Humility, gratitude, and a sense of humor are indispensable in the spiritual life.
IV. Prayer is communion with Ultimate Reality, whether It is regarded as personal, impersonal, or beyond them both.

We were surprised and delighted to find so many points of similarity and convergence in our respective paths. Like most people of our time, we originally expected that we would find practically nothing in common. In the years that followed the formation of our points of agreement, we spontaneously and somewhat hesitatingly began to take a closer look at certain points of disagreement. These became our main focus of attention. We found that discussing our points of disagreement increased the bonding of the group even more than discovering our points of agreement. We became more honest in stating frankly what we believed and why, at the same time without making any effort to convince others of our position. We simply presented our understanding as a gift to the group. It is possible, as we continue to meet, that we may move beyond this stage of dialogue and discover an ultimate convergence that transcends our present insights. In any case, the fundamental differences that we discovered in our respective spiritual paths form an important focus of the rest of this essay.

When Christians try to extract one of the physical or psychological disciplines from an Eastern spiritual tradition and introduce it into their own religious practice, the question might be asked: "Can one graft a branch from one kind of fruit tree onto the trunk of another and expect to produce the same fruit as the old trunk?" Biologically, the branch that is grafted onto the old trunk will continue to bear the fruit of its original tree. What effects a graft from an Eastern spiritual tradition may have on one's growth as a Christian seems to be the primary question raised by the *Letter* of Cardinal Ratzinger.

Much work has to be done to make the similarities between the spiritualities of the East and Christianity better known to the average Christian. This will require not only an intensive study of the spiritual disciplines of other religious cultures but above all a firm grasp of our own. A great deal of experience in dialogue is presupposed in order to understand correctly the terms of another religious tradition, as well as the long range effects of a bodily discipline from one tradition on the psyche of a person coming from another.

In the case of the participants in the Snowmass Ecumenical Conference, all were long-term practitioners of their respective spiritual paths, to the point of embodying their own traditions in a remarkable way. Listening to the immense benefits that particular practices had brought to them opened up, for me at least, the deeper meaning of the terminology (often poorly translated) of the various world religions. Academic lectures in which spiritual teachers speak to an audience, but not to each other, have only a limited value in conveying the profound riches of the spiritual teachings of the world religions. To be fully understood, they need to be explained by persons who have most benefited from them and who embody them in their daily lives. Mutual respect and friendship form the door to this level of understanding.

LINEAGE

In the Eastern traditions divine revelation is based on the careful observation of how the spiritual journey unfolds experientially. The essence of the enlightenment process is often referred to by the term *lineage*. Lineage is the original state of enlightenment of the founder or founders of the religion, or one of its outstanding reformers. The lineage is the passing on of the enlightenment experience by way of interior transmission from master to disciple. It has a broad variety of expressions in the East. In Tibetan Buddhism the *tulku* is believed to be the reincarnation of one of the original disciples of Gautama Buddha. In Zen Buddhism the master authenticates the fully enlightened experience of the disciple that then entitles him or her to teach in the name of the tradition. The actual degree of enlightenment transmitted may be more or less advanced, depending on the spiritual attainment of the teacher and the readiness of the disciple.

Lineage then, is the handing on of the fullness of enlightened consciousness after the disciple has passed through the earlier stages of enlightenment. Is there anything similar in Christianity? In the recent Charismatic movement there has sprung up a phenomenon called "resting in the Spirit," which is communication of spiritual experience, though not of a permanent character. It seems to be an initial mystical experience, which suspends the sense faculties just enough so that the recipient sinks to the ground and stays there for a period of time depending on how deep the experience is. However strong it may be, it is always temporary and subject to the flaws of beginners. Mystical experiences that come before one is prepared for them by preliminary disciplines tend to awaken the emotional programs for happiness of the false self, which then transfers its attachments and aversions to the spiritual plane. It is easy to get attached to the pleasant feelings of "resting in the Spirit" or other forms of divine consolation. A few devotees may even become what might be called "resting in the Spirit bums," going from healer to healer in order to enjoy more of the same. This is not the purpose of divine consolation. Most mystical experiences that are dropped into one's life without any disciplined preparation are really "come-ons," or gilt-edged invitations from God to institute a serious practice of prayer and to open oneself to the contemplative dimension of the Gospel.

In the Christian scheme of things, the enlightened transmission of master to disciple is not passed on by a spiritual director as in the Eastern traditions, but instead through the sacraments, especially the Eucharist, in which Christ transmits his consciousness of the Father, insofar as we are prepared to receive it through the practice of virtue and contemplative prayer. In Christianity, contemplative prayer is our "lineage." It is a participation in Christ's experience of the Father, of Ultimate Reality as Abba—that is, the God of infinite concern and love for every living being. The Christian lineage is the Trinitarian life unfolding within our consciousness: union with the Father through Christ, in the Spirit.

SPIRITUAL ENERGY

Whether or not the ultimate experience of God in this life is the same in all the world religions, the spiritual paths to the experience of unity are clearly not the same. Thus the spiritual energy we invoke by way of prayer or practice is important. If we mingle the energies of two distinct traditions, that is, if we take an Eastern discipline and lift it bodily out of its conceptual and ritual background and insert it into the practice of our Christian faith, this may prove valuable in the beginning insofar as it fulfills a need we had that was missing, namely a method of spirituality. But as we deepen our grasp of the technique, we normally require a conceptual background to understand what is happening—e.g., the mutable dynamics of a relationship with a master, the growth of interior freedom, and in some cases the unfolding of spiritual powers in the form of psychic gifts.

In reference to the latter, unless the process of interior purification has laid to rest the emotional programs for happiness of the false self, psychic powers can become the ultimate satisfaction of one's instinctual needs for power, approval, and security. Hence, the need to purify the unconscious is an essential teaching that belongs to all the world religions across the board. Everybody, as every religion and spiritual tradition acknowledges, is afflicted with the human condition, principally the instinctual needs of early childhood, which become all the more demanding in adulthood when they have been denied by the circumstances of that tender age.

Let us suppose that through a particular Eastern practice we begin to experience a certain spiritual attainment. Unless we are thoroughly purified and the dynamics of our unconscious motivation fully unmasked, the false self can allow this attainment to go to our heads. My impression is that the awareness of this danger is not as strong in the East as it is in Christianity where, because of beginning the spiritual quest in a dualistic place, we recognize—at least in theory—that everything we have is God's free gift. This latter principle is very strong among the Christian mystics. They realized that everything they enjoyed, even their desire for God, was sheer gift.

The deeper one moves into any practice, the more one normally needs whatever first produced and now sustains it by way of ritual, theology, metaphysics, and cultural attitudes. If we advance in the use of a particular Eastern practice, there eventually arises the need for a broader conceptual background. A clash of belief systems may then arise, and one may no longer be able to put the two spiritual paths together. Even having greatly benefited from a discipline from the East, at a certain juncture one may have difficulty reconciling aspects of the discipline with a Christian perspective and commitment. We must recognize however, that there are persons who claim to live equally well in two distinct religious worldviews at the same time. For example, they regard themselves as Christian Buddhists, or as Christian Hindus. Abhishiktananda,[4] who struggled for many years to resolve his experience of advaita with his belief in the Trinity, is a classic example.

In the Christian tradition Christ is the Master, the Enlightened One, and the Teacher. The reason is that he has risen from the dead and now dwells in the midst of each Christian community as its living Teacher. Christians encounter his presence when they come together in his name. They celebrate his life, death, and resurrection, and participate in the mystery of his living presence in the Eucharist. It is not enlightenment in general but *his* enlightenment—*his* consciousness of the Father—that is transmitted through the Eucharist. The Eucharist inserts us, every time we receive it, into the Trinitarian relationships, opening us to the inflowing of divine love. Of course, the gift of grace carries with it the responsibility of sharing it with other people in appropriate ways. While we are not empowered to give the transmission, we must help in whatever ways we can to prepare people to receive it. The most important way is to embody the values of the Gospel in our daily lives.

The sense of union with God is of course a highly personal experience, but it is not dualistic in the usual sense of the term, where one envisages oneself as "here" and God as "out there." Rather, Christian transmission is an interpenetration of spirits. In the transforming union, according to the witness of the Christian mystics, this becomes a relationship that involves total self-surrender to God and forgetfulness of self, even of the new self that emerges out of the ruins of the false self in the night of spirit.

CHRISTIAN LOVE, GRACE, AND HUMILITY

The specific spiritual energy of Christianity is the interaction that arises between God and the soul in love. There is no cause and effect relationship between personal effort and attainment—no technique which, if carried out correctly, leads to the desired goal. This is a different situation from the relationship of a master to a disciple who submits to a particular discipline in order to develop the level of consciousness that the master has attained. There is no doubt that there may be a transmission of enlightened consciousness. The point is, what is the nature of the transmission and how is it perceived? In the Christian view of things there is such a strong emphasis on dependence upon God for everything that the importance of personal effort to dispose oneself for the grace of contemplation is sometimes underestimated. In the East, on the other hand, there is such a strong emphasis on method that the recognition that enlightenment is not the result of one's own efforts seems to be almost overlooked.

The attainment of enlightenment in the Eastern traditions may indeed be the result of grace, but it is also possible that the false self may interfere with the action of grace. In actual fact, if the false self has not been thoroughly dismantled in the night of spirit (or its equivalent in the form of tragedy, physical handicap, or prolonged illness heroically endured), the false self is likely to co-opt the enlightenment experience, and the recipient may succumb to spiritual pride.

The authority by which Jesus, while on earth, transmitted his enlightenment—indeed his unity with the Father—was always exercised in the spirit of humble service. As soon as one senses domination by any master, it is time to grab one's hat and coat and depart as fast as possible. If a particular master gives in to self-exaltation (which can happen in partial states of enlightenment), then the master begins to dominate his or her disciples and can seriously damage the very people who originally experienced the greatest benefit from the teaching. When the adulation of disciples goes to the head of any teacher, Christian or any other, he or she may exploit students in one way or another, at times in ways that by every moral standard are a violation of a sacred trust. This is especially the case in cult leaders of whatever kind. I know of no safety valve to forestall such tragedies except the night of the spirit, in which one is convinced by intimate experience that one is capable of every evil. The person emerges from this experience convinced that whatever gifts one has are the sheer gift of God, and must be exercised in complete submission to the divine inspiration.

St. John of the Cross calls contemplation "the science of love." There is an erotic element in divine love, not in the sense of genital energy as such, but in the broader sense of desire. Of course, desire has a selfish element, but the selfishness is gradually purified by the science of love, which vigorously opposes those aspects of our desires, whether conscious or unconscious, that are selfish. That is why God seems to leave every now and then and tests our spirits in different ways. This is chiefly by apparent absences, but also through external trials, so that we can see what God sees as obstacles to total self-surrender and divine union. We can then manifest divine love through acts that are done under the influence of the Spirit rather than our own self-centered, even if secret, motivation.

WORLD RELIGIONS AND WORLD PEACE

The world religions have a special obligation to contribute to the cause of world peace. In the past their confessional differences have led to violence, injustice, and persecution. Each major religious tradition has developed teachings and practices designed to foster the full spiritual development of the human person. These common elements cry out to be recognized as God's gifts to the whole human family and made available to the world community as powerful means of promoting understanding and peace among nations and races. More and more, the world religions will have to give the witness of mutual respect and understanding to the world community if political, ethnic, and nationalistic divisions are to be overcome or at least held in check. While emphasizing our common values and uniting in social action, however, the world religions must at the same time accept their diversity and cherish the integrity of each other's traditional spiritual paths. Genuine dialogue on this level is the catalyst that would facilitate harmony and cooperation on all the other levels of ever-increasing global interaction.

GLOSSARY OF TERMS

1. **Apophatic** (darksome)—resting in God beyond concepts and particular acts, except to maintain a general loving attentiveness to the Divine Presence; the exercise of pure faith.

2. **Cataphatic** (lightsome)—the affective response to symbols, reflection, and the use of reason, imagination, and memory, in order to assimilate the truths of faith.

3. **Contemplative (or mystical) prayer**—the development of one's relationship with Christ to the point of communing beyond words, thoughts, feelings, and the multiplication of particular acts.

4. **Divine Union**—a term describing a single experience of the union of all the faculties in God.

5. **False self**—the self developed to cope with the emotional trauma of early childhood, which seeks happiness by satisfying or repressing the instinctual needs of survival/security, affection/esteem, and power/control, and which bases its self-worth on cultural or group identification.

6. **Human Condition**—an alternative term for describing the consequences of original sin: concupiscence, illusion, and weakness of will.

7. **Lectio Divina**—reading or more exactly, listening to the book we believe to be divinely inspired; the most ancient method of developing the friendship of Christ, using scripture as topics of conversation with Christ.

8. **Method of Contemplative Prayer**—any prayer practice that is deliberately designed to free the mind of excessive dependence on thinking to go to God.

9. **Purification**—an essential part of the process of contemplation through which the dark side of one's personality, one's mixed motivation, and the emotional pain of a lifetime stored in the unconscious are gradually evacuated: the necessary preparation for transforming union and called by St. John of the Cross, "The Dark Nights."

10. **Transformation** (transforming union)—the stable sharing by all dimensions of the human person in God's life and loving presence, rather than a particular experience or set of experiences.

NOTES

1. Thomas Keating, *Open Mind, Open Heart: The Contemplative Dimension of the Gospel* (New York: Continuum, 1994).

2. *Origins*, 19 (30) (28 December 1989), pp. 492–498.

3. E.g., Beatrice of Nazareth, Mechthild of Magdeburg, and Hadewijch of Brabant.

4. James Stuart, *Swami Abhishiktananda: His Life Told Through His Letters* (Delhi: ISPCK, 1989).

Christianity and the Eastern Religions: The Possibility of Mutual Growth

Wayne Teasdale

In this essay Wayne Teasdale explores ways in which Christianity, Hinduism, and Buddhism can benefit one another, noting that the road to such cooperation has been opened to Roman Catholics by the Second Vatican Council and by subsequent papal pronouncements. He suggests that other religions not be regarded by Christians as untrue, as merely natural, or as preparations for the Gospel, but as complementary revelations. As Bede said, "Each [religion] is imperfect in itself, but there is a convergence on a final truth." Relying on the fundamental principle that Reality itself is One, as attested by the experienced unity of our consciousness and memory, we can see multiplicity as a creative expression of this One Foundation. Teasdale explores Bede's revelation that the great world religions are the fruits of unique mystical encounters with the One Reality, then framed by particular cultures, and now capable of completing one another.

—ᴠᴧᴧᴠ—

The world as we know it is changing and rapidly entering a new age. While this is clearly evident in science, technology, politics and economics, it is also true, but less obvious, in the area of religion and spirituality. The religious history of humankind has begun a radically new phase. The old barriers separating Christianity from the Eastern traditions are quickly giving way and East is coming face-to-face with West.

The Roman Catholic Church is playing an important role in this process, for ever since the historic promulgation of *Nostra Aetate*[1] by the Second Vatican Council, the Church's relationship with the religions of the East, notably with Hinduism and Buddhism, has been steadily unfolding. This document placed the Church in a new situation vis-à-vis the other world religions. Previously, it was much less complicated to be Roman Catholic, because there was no need to consider other faith systems. These traditions were regarded with a measure of curiosity, suspicion, condescension, and even open hostility. But with the advent of *Nostra Aetate* everything changed. The faithful were exhorted "to acknowledge, preserve and promote the spiritual and moral goods" of the other traditions,[2] and some theologians even began to think in terms of a more universal theology.[3] Of course, this changing situation has occasioned feelings of considerable uneasiness, anxiety, and confusion among many Christians, which some still feel.

Even though anxieties and doubts remain among certain Roman Catholic Church leaders, theologians, monks and the ordinary faithful, there is widespread interest in the two principal Eastern religions, Hinduism and Buddhism. Since the Council, this interest has received papal support and encouragement. Given the essential mission of the Church of Rome to proclaim the Gospel, however, it is a serious issue as to what this support means in relation to her ultimate intention regarding the other world religions—religions that in the past have been treated as competitors. At the same time, each religious tradition is evolving in relation to every other, and like any organism, a religion grows, acquiring new insights and experiences. This is also true of the Roman Catholic Church's own self-understanding and her conception of her relationship with the Asian traditions, and so by extension and implication, her conception of Christianity as a whole.

In our own century, John XXIII opened the door to exploration by articulating the spiritual right to follow one's own conscience in matters of belief and worship, natural rights given to us by God.[4] This insight was expanded in the conciliar document, *Dignitatis Humanae*,[5] with related implications in *Gaudium et Spes* and *Lumen Gentium*. These conciliar statements, however, were made within a limited context, namely, from the perspective of the Church and her mission of proclaiming the Gospel. Even today this remains the Church's emphasis, for she is ever faithful to her nature and her divine mandate.

This raises a serious problem—a real paradox with which we must struggle: how to reconcile genuine openness, listening, and learning in the dialogical situation, with the evangelical command to preach the Gospel. How do we remain true to our Christian faith in the uniqueness and finality of Christ, while accepting and promoting the spiritual insights, experiences, and values of other traditions? There are no easy answers, but I believe there is a way to accomplish this, and I will try to give a few indications of how it can be done.

Pope Paul VI expressed a clear and strong interest in the other world religions. His door was always open to receive the representatives of these traditions, and he seemed to understand the authenticity of their faith, sensing perhaps the truth in their sacred texts. He often conveyed a profound respect and esteem for these leaders, their religions, and their constituents in the faith. His expressions of respect would seem to have been more than mere polite diplomatic sentiments; he discerned that the experiences, beliefs, and insights of the other world religions had their origin in "thousands of years of searching for God. . . ."[6] And in *Ecclesiam Suam* Paul VI emphasized that the Church must take the initiative in commencing dialogue with others.[7]

Following the example of Paul VI, John Paul II has spoken on many occasions of the need for dialogue with the non-Christian religions. In his historic visit to India in February 1986, he defined his attitude as "a sincere interest in all the religions of India, an interest marked by *genuine respect*, by *attention* to what we have in *common*, by a desire to promote interreligious dialogue and fruitful *collaboration* between people of different faiths."[8] Later in the same year, on October 27, 1986, he convoked the momentous Assisi meeting, where some twenty spiritual leaders gathered for a day of fasting and prayer—a day symbolizing their determination to work together for peace. Again and again he made statements calling for dialogue. For example, on September 9, 1987, in a speech to Christian and Zen monks, the pontiff clearly stated his support for interreligious dialogue of the deepest kind:

> I believe that initiatives which are carried out in this spirit should be promoted and fostered, since we come to know each other better as we humbly tread the path of truth and universal love. . . . Your specific contribution to these initiatives consists not only in maintaining an explicit dialogue, but also in promoting a deep spiritual encounter. . . . May all of you—partners in interreligious dialogue—be encouraged and sustained by the knowledge that your endeavors are supported by the Catholic Church and appreciated by her as significant for strengthening the bonds which unite all people who honestly search for the truth.[9]

Further evidence of the Church's commitment to expand contact and conversations with other religions is the existence of the Vatican Secretariat for Non-Christian Religions, currently under the direction of Francis Cardinal Arinze. With the reorganization of the curia, this department is now called the Pontifical Council for Interreligious Dialogue. Furthermore, originating from a mandate of this secretariat is the work of the European monastic group, Aide-Inter-Monastères (A.I.M.), and its special subdivision, Dialog-Inter-Monastères (D.I.M.), both based in Paris and guided by Dom Pierre de Bethune, O.S.B., their dedicated president. There is also the very significant contribution of the Monastic Interreligious Dialogue,[10] a parallel commission of A.I.M., composed of Benedictines and Cistercians in North America, and directed by its current president Father James Wiseman, O.S.B., who has long experience in the dialogue movement along contemplative lines.

Related to these efforts we may note that Thomas Keating has been personally engaged in the very practical and fascinating work of in-depth dialogue and encounter with Buddhist representatives for some years now at the Naropa Institute in Boulder, Colorado. This institute was established by Tibetan Buddhists who saw the need of meeting with Christians. In time, the institute became a center devoted to dialogue, mutual understanding, and sharing between Christians and Buddhists, especially around the focus of meditative practice; it has made enormous strides far exceeding the modest expectations of its founders, the Christians involved, or the official

Church. This progress, it should be noted, has not been made at the expense of Christianity, nor has it compromised the teachings of the Church.

The Monastic Interreligious Dialogue has sponsored a very imaginative, bold and stimulating monastic exchange—an intermonastic hospitality and dialogue program—between Christian monks and their Tibetan Buddhist counterparts. This has involved a number of lamas coming to America and spending some three to six months touring different monastic centers. During their stays at various monasteries, they give talks, answer questions, lead meditation groups and engage in formal and informal discussions. Reciprocally, American monks and nuns have been hosted in Tibetan monasteries in India and warmly received by the Dalai Lama in Dharamsala. This program has been—and we hope will continue to be—a great success.[11]

Historically, Christianity's attitude has gone through four phases in relation to the other religions. The first one, held for many centuries, asserted the truth of the Christian faith and the untruth of all other religions. This was a view developed in isolation from these great systems and without any real knowledge of their teachings. The second phase emerged toward the eighteenth century; it was based on some actual knowledge of the other traditions. This period viewed other religions as natural, while Christianity was seen as wholly supernatural. Such a view is still common in our time. An outgrowth of this position is the statement that the Eastern religions represent humanity's search for God, while Judaism and Christianity reflect God's revelation to humanity. Although this is true on the historical level, the other traditions that are not part of biblical revelation may participate in a different form of revelation and are products of it. As study progressed in the nineteenth century, a third view developed. In this phase of Christianity's attitude toward the non-Christian faiths, the notion of fulfillment was adopted. In this position, other religions are considered as a preparation for the Christian faith and the Christian revelation is the fulfillment of these traditions, the apex of God's self-disclosure to humanity. Again, this idea has much truth in it and many espouse it today. The fourth attitude is gaining ground in the contemporary encounter between Christianity and the other faiths, especially with Hinduism and Buddhism. In this position, complementarity is defended as the most mature perspective of how the various traditions relate to Christianity and among themselves. Religions are regarded as completing one another. Each tradition has evolved a unique perspective on the one ultimate reality[12] and each has a contribution to make to the whole picture. As Bede Griffiths said, "Each [religion] is imperfect in itself, but there is a convergence on a final truth."[13]

Complementarity is also my own position. The truth of it is grasped more on the level of praxis than of theological debate, and is appreciated by entering into the contemplative dimension. As we sit quietly, prayerfully, in the presence of people of other traditions, there is a mutual discovery of one another's depth. This is the experience of so many engaged in the intermonastic dialogue. Father Bede illustrated this for us when he said, "What we find is that if you're arguing doctrines and so on, you get nowhere, but when you meet in meditation you begin to share your own inner experience [and] you begin to realize an underlying unity behind the religions."[14] Such a way of formulating the relationship allows the inherent genius of each tradition to come forth, without in any way lessening, subordinating or relativizing the uniqueness, role, and ultimacy of Christ. Christ comes as the fulfillment of humanity's spiritual history, but all the genuine religions have valid insights into the human condition and its turbulent history. These insights are not really antagonistic to the Christian claim—though they may at times appear that way—but are basically complementary to it, that is, they complete or enrich our understanding of Christianity, while the Gospel sheds light on and perfects the other religious traditions.

In what follows, I will demonstrate how Christianity, Hinduism, and Buddhism are inwardly related and relatable through an ontological unity and through transcendent experience. This requires a philosophical excursus and a consideration of the three modes of revelation. It should then become clear how the encounter is actually an interior one, an encounter arising out of contemplation. I will then discuss the terms of the connection between the Christian and Hindu faiths, followed by an elaboration of the terms of the encounter between Christianity and the Buddhist Dharma. The final section will be concerned with dialogue itself and will briefly consider its nature, value, and direction.

PHILOSOPHICAL EXCURSUS ON UNITY

It is becoming more and more evident, with the advance of our knowledge, that the universe, our world, our experience, and reality itself are one. Unity is the foundation of the created order and of everything. This becomes clear, I think, if we turn to ourselves and analyze our own consciousness. Doing so, we discover how much depends on the principle of unity, that it is operative in all experience and all states of awareness, for unity is the basis of consciousness itself as an enduring functional identity in time, and presumably in eternity. Unity is the "golden string," the very thread of identity, allowing each successive moment in the stream of moments called life to be related to the center of knowing, to a subject who can claim each experience as one's own.

Unity guards the integrity of memory, and memory, as a product of the unifying principle of life and thought, attests to the essential truth of this unitary ground of experience—that all experience is, in fact, one. If unity were not the basis of consciousness and reality, then memory would be impossible and consciousness would be at best a fragmentary phenomenon, since nothing would unite the moments together and identify them as belonging to the particular knower who is actually doing the knowing. Each moment would slip out of the present, having no association with what preceded or followed it. Conscious moments would arise and then fade into oblivion. Memory thus grounds knowing and identity. This is an example of a unifying power or principle at work in all experience and perception. But this oneness of experience—always relating everything to the knowing subject—is itself the creative result of a deeper ontological unity. This ontological unity runs through and sustains all that is and can be. Here I am referring to a phenomenological given, something easily accessible when we analyze the data of consciousness.

Again, each conscious, intelligent, knowing subject discovers the evidence of the unitary principle in his or her own experience, especially the inner experience of consciousness itself. This principle is the basic presupposition of all our acts of awareness, whether we realize this or not. Because reality is one, we are able to experience it, relate it to ourselves, make it our own, and have an ongoing memory of it, of every instance of contact with it. This is, for each one of us, not a matter of speculation, but the existential facticity of our consciousness and the cognitive environment of our life in the world as rational, moral, and spiritual human beings. The natural order of created being is offered to each one of us as our experience, not as an alien presence imposing itself upon us. Like consciousness itself, with its innumerable moments, reality presents itself to our knowing minds through the agency of the principle of unity. Reality is expounded in our experience under the category of multiplicity, but it holds together as a system. It does so because its deeper ground is one, the ground from which it is manifested.

Multiplicity requires unity as its source and foundation; otherwise nature could not function in an orderly way, coordinating a vast number of elements and relations. Multiplicity is intelligible only because unity is actual, is real; otherwise, there would be utter chaos. Without unity there is no necessity for order in creation, in nature, and in our lives. In addition, experience, in all its forms, is totally unintelligible unless it is rooted in a unitary principle, and is indeed impossible without such a principle at work. Because unity is actual, the realm of multiplicity is possible, existing and operating fairly smoothly; it is possible only as one integrated system of natural reality. Multiplicity is itself the creative expression of an underlying system of the real that is unified.

Modern physics, in its own way, also exemplifies the human quest for ultimate unity, seeking some Grand Unified Theory, trying to reconcile its two basic visions—Relativity and Quantum Mechanics—and raising questions about the role of the observer, who is also a member of the world being observed. Contemporary physics—and its popularizers—is sensitive to the issue of the wholeness of the cosmic reality that it studies. A number of authors have explored these questions; I find the views of Fritjof Capra and of David Bohm especially interesting. Capra, for instance, says:

> Quantum theory has abolished the notion of fundamentally separated objects, has introduced the concept of the participator to replace that of the observer, and may even find it necessary to include human consciousness in its description of the world. It has come to see the universe as an inter-connected web of physical and mental relations whose parts are only defined through their connections to the whole.[15]

It is the whole system that accounts for the existence and intelligibility of the parts, and these parts are fluid, dynamic relations. Relations by definition are interconnections, and so imply the wholeness of which they are parts and to which they are intrinsically bound. David Bohm conveys the importance of the shift to the wholeness model in physics by his appeal to the analogy of the hologram, which he regards as an appropriate metaphor for the cosmic reality in its nature and structure, and so for a new, more mature conception of cosmology. Bohm declares:

> . . . the difference between lens and hologram can play a significant part in the perception of a new order that is relevant for physical law. . . . we might now note the distinction between a lens and a hologram and consider the possibility that physical law should refer primarily to an order of underived wholeness of the content of a description similar to that indicated by the hologram rather than to an order of analysis of such content into separate parts indicated by a lens.[16]

Just as all reality is related in its human or conscious dimension and in its physical or cosmic dimension, since it is essentially and entirely one system, so too is it related and hence one in its spiritual ground. This ground is the source of unity in the cosmic and human domains. Reality is one, and the Source of this reality is always revealing itself in every moment of time and at every point of space; it is calling, constantly inviting the human race and all creation into relationship with itself. This is the dynamic nature of the Source, of the Divine, of God. All of nature, being, and life are revelatory of the mystery just by virtue of existing. Creation has an inner metaphysical thrust toward reflecting its origin. In this way it reveals something of the Source. Each of the great world religions probably derives from an intimate contact with Ultimate Reality. Each has its source in the divine Source, in the ground of being, in ultimate mystery. The one human reality, in contact with Reality itself, has produced the different expressions of the various traditions we call the world religions.

Here it is not a question of the external forms of these traditions; it is not a matter of formal piety, doctrine, ritual, or cult. It is rather a direct kind of experience, a mystical awakening, or an inner illumination that has most likely produced Hinduism, Taoism, Buddhism, Judaism, Christianity, Islam, and the other faiths in their interior core, their irreducible essence. This is what defines them, since a religion is defined by its goal, its end. And it is *that*, in each of them, that is relatable to every other. The goal for every one of them is to return to the Source, for it is this mystical core that is rooted in the Center of Being, reality, truth, and the absolute mystery. It is in their primary experience that the traditions are already one, because they arise from and are rooted in the same level of depth.

The differences in each religious tradition occur because each, in its spiritual experience, represents a particular perspective on the ultimate mystery. Each is the fruit of a unique language, culture, history, and interpretation. The particular interpretation is itself affected by the historical, cultural, and linguistic experience. The different spiritual paths in human history, found in the great world religions, are the creative results of particular civilizations at particular periods coming into contact with the Source, the fontal origin of all mystery, being, life, nature. These encounters of the founders of the traditions have been recorded, and attempts have been made to capture and codify the awareness gained from those contacts. The experiences of the founders were living, dynamic processes of contact, of breakthrough to the transcendent mystery. Each was something *sui generis*, something unrepeatable in precisely the same way or context, or with the same intensity of experiential insight.

Experiences can be similar, but never quite the same, because the exact conditions cannot possibly be replicated. To be more precise, for example, if a thousand people were to have a mystical illumination simultaneously in the same place and under the same conditions, the results no doubt would be a thousand different descriptions of what happened, even though similar elements would be reported. The uniqueness and capacity of each person would conspire to produce a thousand differing accounts of what actually took place. The same is true, by analogy, of the experience of the founders, of their primary intuitions, at the dawn of the world religions. They differ because each originated in the unique awareness of these persons, a uniqueness that has both its peculiar genius and its attendant limitations.

And yet, the primary spiritual experiences do not seem to contradict one another. They are perspectives on the ultimately Real that actually complete one another, or are applicable to a more adequate understanding. The various world traditions are thus complementary to one another and not contradictory, for they are each authentic participations in the one all-embracing ontological mystery, the one system of ultimate meaning and truth. They are internally related to one another by virtue of their participation in the same Reality; each arises out of the same Ground of Unity and all are connected with the same depth-dimension, the very soil of their authenticity. Each is the child of an active process of revelation. What basically distinguishes them, on a theological level, is the distinctive form revelation took in each case. The revelational type accounts for the phenomenal differences, especially as these are filtered through a language and a cultural identity.

FORMS OF REVELATION: THE COSMIC, THE MYSTICAL, AND THE HISTORICAL

The kinds of revelation that occurred are really three ways in which the Divine, the transcendent Reality, has been and is communicated to human consciousness. There is nothing hard and fixed about these categories; they actually overlap in each of the spiritual traditions, but an emphasis on one of the three is characteristic of each particular tradition. For instance, in Hinduism, Buddhism, and Christianity there is a recognition of the cosmic and mystical dimensions of revelation, though they assign different meanings to these dimensions.

Similarly, historical revelation is present in each tradition, but each treats it differently. In Hinduism this historical truth is almost accidental, because of the emphasis on the transcendent truth itself. In Buddhism, revelation does take a historical form in the sense that all enlightenment experiences are transmissions from Shakyamuni's Enlightenment. But it is only in Christianity that history itself becomes the vehicle of Divine Presence. Revelation thus becomes self-consciously historical.

At the heart of all ancient cultures, whether highly developed and organized like Hinduism and Taoism, or less so, as the Australian Aborigines, the tribes of Africa or the North and South American Indians, there is a very deep experience, an original and abiding knowledge of the cosmic unity. This experience enters human life as an encounter with an all-pervading Presence in the natural world. Depending on the culture, it is called by different names: the Spirit, the devas (in India), the angels, the cosmic powers, God, the Brahman, Tao, the Wakan-Tanka of the Dakota Indians, and so on. The cosmos becomes the vehicle of this mysterious Presence and its communication. This Presence is the holy or sacred reality, the sphere of the numinous One. The communication of the mystery of this Presence is what is meant by the Cosmic Revelation. It also signifies the experience of the cosmic unity and its transmission in myth and other sacred forms of writing.

Such is the original mode of revelation. It is based on a sacramental view of nature and the cosmos. Creation is itself the most universal and permanent sacrament of God's Presence, and this is humanity's first experience of revelation; it is always available to us. Its metaphysical principle is essentially the dynamic disclosure of Being, God, and this disclosure comes through the created order. Creation is in this sense revelational and symbolic; it can best be formulated as grounded in an *aletheiatic* approach.[17] Nature, being, life, and human relationships uncover the mystery, the Divine Presence; it unfolds in our midst. Poetry and myth, as forms of intuitive thought, as a kind of symbolic theology, become the method of conveying the vision of the Cosmic Revelation. The Cosmic Revelation is revelation in its natural state. It is in some sense present or is at least understood even in the biblical tradition. St. Paul says, "Ever since God created the world his everlasting power and deity—however invisible— have been there for the mind to see in the things he has made."[18] In this Paul echoes the Book of Wisdom.[19] From this first revelation a covenant was made with all of humanity through Adam. As a matter of fact, in Hebrew the name Adam simply means "humanity," the people made from the earth.

Even Jesus seemed to possess a knowledge of the first or natural revelation. He often used symbols from nature. For example, "Consider the lilies of the field" and "the birds of the air"; "learn a lesson from the fig tree" and "read the signs of the times" are instances of an implicit recognition on his part that the natural world is a source of knowledge and illumination, of cosmic revelation.

Surely this awareness, this nature-mysticism and religion of nature, is the background and basic insight of the Romantic poets and the American Transcendentalists. Many have been brought to the Christian faith through natural revelation. In the life of Bede Griffiths in particular, it was his experience of the Cosmic Revelation coming through nature that awakened him to faith and ultimately led him into the Catholic Church. He describes his wonderful experience of the cosmic mystery:

I liked the silence of the woods and the hills. I felt the sense of a Presence, something undefined and mysterious, which was reflected in the faces of the flowers and the movements of the birds and animals, in the sunlight falling through the leaves and in the sound of running water, in the wind blowing on the hills and the wide expanse of earth and sky.[20]

It is in this primordial revelation as a common human and spiritual experience that a definite connection can be made between the Hindu, Christian, and even Buddhist traditions, when the factor of the cosmic unity revealed in this form of revelation is considered. Both the Hindu and Christian traditions have a strong realization of creation as what can be called theophanic—sacramental and profoundly suggestive of the Divine Mystery. This realization is deeply present in the culture and literature of both traditions. But it has to be recognized that the Hindu tradition, especially in its Vedic period, is one of the clearest examples of the Cosmic Revelation. This is its primary inspiration, and yet in the Vedic revelation itself there is the further discovery that the Divine Presence in nature and being also dwells in the human heart, in the *guha*, the "cave of the heart." The seers gave the name *Brahman* to the Presence in the cosmos, while to the Presence in the heart they gave the name *Atman*; they then proclaimed an identity between them.[21] Thus, the sense of the cosmic unity comes full circle because it explodes in our inner awareness of the mystery. The first revelation then leads into the second, and is in continuity with it; it is really a further development of the first revelation. This is the beginning of an inner way mysticism. So, in Hinduism revelation moved from its original cosmic mode into a more sophisticated mystical mode. Buddhism, however, while almost entirely an inner way mysticism, carries the memory of the cosmic revelation and reexperiences it from the inside.

Mysticism—as well as cosmic mystery—is at the heart of Christianity and its revelation, even though Christian Revelation is of the historical variety. Each type of revelation is ultimately mystical insofar as each one conveys transcendent knowledge. When mysticism is spoken of as a primary source of revelation, it refers to how the transcendent consciousness of mystical planes engenders a particular kind of spiritual tradition. This is certainly true of virtually all the Eastern religions, which have always had a keen appreciation of a commitment to a contemplative meditative discipline.

Of the three sources of revelation—the cosmic order, personal mystical experience, and salvation history—the East has opted for the first two. I have already commented on this somewhat in discussing the Hindu tradition. The spiritual wisdom of both Buddhism and Hinduism, not to mention Jainism, Sikhism, and Sufism, and the shamanistic phenomenon of primitive tribal societies, has evolved out of mystical life. The source of insight, of knowledge and a coherent vision is a direct relationship to Ultimate Reality in the mystery itself, the mystery of the Divine or Transcendent encountered in the depths of interiority beyond the senses, imagination and reason.

At this point, it is necessary to clarify Christian opinions on the status of spiritual experience in the non-Christian religions, especially in the Eastern schools. It has been common for Christians to deny the validity or value of this body of experience, but I believe this is a serious mistake, because there is genuine mystical insight in the other traditions. Such a conviction rests on the intuition of the unity of reality, the accuracy of the threefold source of revelation and the evident wisdom present in Eastern mysticism. Thomas Merton and others have held this conviction, and in one of Merton's most mature writings, he made this very clear:

> It may be remarked . . . that theologians generally regard the spiritual experience of oriental religion as occurring on the natural rather than supernatural level. However, they have often admitted, with Jacques Maritain and Father Garrigou-Lagrange, that truly supernatural and mystical contemplation is certainly possible outside the visible Church, since God is the master of His gifts and wherever there is sincerity and an earnest desire for truth, He will not deny the gifts of His grace. As we grow in knowledge and appreciation of oriental religion we will come to realize the depth and richness of its varied forms of contemplation.[22]

Mystical revelation begins with the experience of unity in and beyond nature. It penetrates through nature to the ground of unity itself, in the One Who is the Source, even God. The mystic is penetrated, saturated and transformed by and in the Divine Presence. Elevated into transcendent consciousness, into an intense awareness of Who God is, the mystic is made to know oneness with God in the grace and intimacy of the indwelling Spirit. Mysticism is the mode of revelation through which the unitary and unifying ground, the very Source, is experienced as absolute Reality, and so is known in the fullest sense possible. It brings with it an equally absolute kind of certitude. For to be embraced by infinite Love Itself takes the person into the realm of ultimate experience, a realm situated far beyond the limited conditions of knowing so characteristic of finite, temporal life.

Transformation is the fruit of mystical revelation; at least this is its goal and normal course. The person becomes intoxicated by divine love and compassion. True charity then becomes more probable, where before charity was tainted by self-interest or confused motives. Mystical life is integrative, since it unifies all the faculties of the soul, allowing a stable focus on God and others in service. It gives true perspective because it grants an insight into the nature of this present existence and eternity. One sees the value of things, and concomitantly, the illusions of society, which consume so much of the precious time and energy of people. These illusions are ultimately useless because they are conceived in selfishness and egoism, and really only amount to distractions.

Mysticism has but one goal: total transformation into love, or deification of the individual and the ecclesial community. In Christian terms, this means entrance into the fullness of Christ. In Hinduism and Buddhism the goal is *moksha*, or liberation from the chains of illusion that bind us to the realm of becoming, of suffering and striving. Liberation happens through the process of enlightenment. Whether understood as liberation or as salvation, mystical life at once frees us from the constraints of mere social expectation and imposes on us a profound and permanent responsibility for others in love and compassion.

The third form of revelation, the historical mode, has the mystical dimension as primary source, but represents the conscious communication of God to humankind. God takes the initiative in historical revelation, entering into relationship with each individual and with the whole human race as the *Dabar Yahweh*, the *Verbum Dei*, the revealed Word of God. In this way, God is related to us both personally and collectively. Historical revelation is a progressive knowledge disclosed to various figures and culminating in the coming of the incarnate Manifestation (John 1:18), who communicates to us a concrete experience and knowledge of what the hidden God, the *Deus absconditus*, is truly like.

The point of this form of revelation is to remove all ambiguity about God's nature and intention toward us. It is a process of divine self-disclosure to the human in its earthly condition, a condition bounded by time and space, and so by history as well. The whole thrust of historical revelation is to confirm what every Christian mystic knows: God is pure, unconditional love within the Trinity and for each person in creation. We are created from love and sanctified in this same love as members of the Incarnate Word. This God, Who is revealed in the life, actions and teachings of the historical Jesus, is much like the father in the parable of the Prodigal Son. The loving Parent doesn't especially care where we've been or what we've done but cares only for us, for our hearts, our attention, our wills—in very truth, for our love.

At the same time, historical revelation includes the mystical mode as the means of its introduction. The experiences of Moses, the patriarchs, the prophets, of Jesus himself, St. Paul, and others, were mystical, for there was a definitive breakthrough to transcendence, or rather, the Transcendent One broke through to the human sphere in the experiences of these people. God sought us in them, and entered into our condition of being in its transitoriness. Historical revelation is constituted by this transcendent relationship to all humanity. Moses' encounter with Yahweh in the burning bush,[23] Isaiah's vision of God in the temple,[24] the call of Jeremiah,[25] Daniel's vision of "the Ancient of Days" and of "the Son of Man,"[26] Jesus' experience of his intimacy with God the Father, especially as recorded in the Gospel of John,[27] the Transfiguration,[28] Paul's experience on the road to Damascus,[29] and the experience of countless saints and mystics throughout Christian history all attest to the indisputable reality of the mystical dimension as central in our very rich and profound tradition. Even those saints who were not imbued with a direct mystical union still had a deep experience of divine grace and the transforming power of God's love.

CHRISTIANITY AND HINDUISM

Having shown the sources of revelation, the generation of the tradition, and so also the authenticity of the different systems that arose from contact with transcendent truth, the way is open to consider the relationship of

Christianity and Hinduism, and then of Christianity with Buddhism. This should help to clarify the concept of complementarity. The preceding discussion points in the direction of the possibility of complementarity by referring to the source of transcendent knowledge—the hallmark of these great spiritual paths. Since each path presumably leads to an authentic experiential awareness of the Source and harmonizes with the same underlying reality, how can their interrelationship not be one of complementarity?

I think it is vital to keep in mind that there is no possibility of a fruitful relationship between the *sanatana dharma*, or the eternal religion—as Hinduism claims to be—and the saving mystery of Christ on the basis of doctrine and belief. Again, on that level there will only be misunderstanding and endless, tedious debate, which is often fruitless and certainly frustrating.

The locus of real encounter is found in the depths of contemplative experience and spiritual wisdom. It is only in that which is deepest in both traditions, in the mystical life of each, that we can hope to locate such an encounter. Christians and Hindus have to meet in their transcendent awareness, from the interior core of subjectivity, in the *guha*, the "cave of the heart," the "fine point of the Spirit," where we are already one. Abhishiktananda, who gave nearly half his life to the search for God in the Hindu-Christian context, said that Upanishadic mysticism brings us to the depths of the Spirit,[30] the same Spirit at the heart of the trinitarian Godhead.

It is in that intensely profound sphere of transcendent consciousness, where the person is united with Ultimate Reality, that the essential mystical insight of each tradition can be recognized. Hinduism and Christianity are connected within the same experience of the mystery of depth—the depths of God's inner being. In the Upanishadic tradition, this experience is often spoken of in terms of advaita, nonduality, the condition of being "not-two," of pure unity beyond distinction, and yet, this has to be understood in a special way. Nonduality is *ekatvam*, utter identification with the "unicity" of being; it is what characterizes the experience as a mystical state. Ekatvam, if correctly understood, suggests something nearer to the Christian experience, certainly similar to Christ's own inner awareness of his oneness with the Father. Actually, nonduality is part of the nature of the Trinity itself in its inward life. Abhishiktananda, for one, was convinced that the

Trinity offers the key to a fuller understanding of the ultimate experience, the Upanishadic experience of advaita, nonduality being a preparation for this birth into the divine fullness. Thus, in ultimate mystical consciousness there is a plunge into nondual being, into pure unity, a oneness in which distinctions seem to disappear.

But, as in the being of the Trinity, the distinctions are permanent although nonduality prevails as the essence of a common nature, so also the ontological difference is maintained in the person's encounter with God although one is in a unitary or advaitic relation to the Source. It is an advaita or unity of consciousness, not a unity of being. Unity in the latter case would annul the metaphysical difference between Creator and creature. Abhishiktananda located the source of this paradox in the Trinity: "The perfect prototype of the complete experience is the mystery of the Blessed Trinity itself, at once a supreme unity in the Spirit, and also the very source of this unity, the mysterious 'face-to-face' of the Father and the Son."[31]

In Hinduism, the term for the deepest state of mystical consciousness— what is regarded as the Godhead itself—is *Saccidananda*. It is a Sanskrit word formed by combining three other words: *sat*, the word for Being, or existence; *cit*, the term for consciousness or knowledge; and *ananda*, the word for bliss or joy. Saccidananda is thus the experience of absolute existence or being, absolute consciousness or knowledge of being, and absolute bliss; it is the total bliss of being absolutely conscious of the fullness of being. Like Nirvana, it is an ultimate level of transcendent awareness, but in the Vedanta, it is also the name for the Godhead.

Abhishiktananda claimed a real ontological continuity between Sacci-dananda and the Trinity. At first he suggested Saccidananda as a kind of stepping-stone to the Trinity,[32] but later he actually seemed to see them both as one. Here is how he put it:

> The experience of Saccidananda carries the soul beyond all merely intellectual knowledge to her very center, to the source of her being. Only there is she able to hear the Word which reveals within the undivided unity and advaita of Saccidananda the very mystery of the Three Persons: in *sat*, the Father, the absolute Beginning and source of being; in *cit*, the Son, the divine Word, the Father's Self-knowledge; in *ananda*, the Spirit of love, Fullness and Bliss without end.[33]

Somehow he experienced the Saccidanandan state of mystical awareness as the door into the deeper, more ultimate reality of the Godhead, the trinitarian communion at the center of the divine mystery. Thus, on this level of depth there appears to be a real possibility of not only reconciliation and an actual, and indeed substantial, relatability of what matters in both traditions in their contemplative theology, but a real convergence as well.

After his awakening, Abhishiktananda lived almost permanently out of a mystical state of consciousness. He knew from personal experience that both Hinduism and Christianity were true in their core mystical insight. He possessed a certitude that both advaita and Trinity were absolute; he also knew that they were somehow one, but he didn't quite know how this was so.[34]

CHRIST AND HINDUISM

In a rather remarkable essay, Raimundo Panikkar speaks of the eventual advent of Christ in the heart of Hinduism. Hindus have had a strong impression of Christ ever since the beginning of the Hindu renaissance in the middle of the nineteenth century. The Gospel also had a powerful impact on Mahatma Gandhi's thought and on his movement for nonviolent reform. That movement was, in a true sense, an application of the social Gospel—especially pertaining to the Sermon on the Mount—of India's struggle for independence and for justice among her own people. Panikkar boldly states: "There are Indian gurus of great and profound spirituality who tell me: 'The final stage in spiritual evolution is the discovery of Christ.' They realize that Christ is the most sublime Epiphany that has ever existed on earth."[35] Panikkar feels that the encounter between Hinduism and Christianity must take place in Christ.[36] His meaning is more on a metaphysical and theological level than on a contemplative one, which is Abhishiktananda's perception. When Panikkar makes his point he has in mind the *theandric* (union of God and humanity) function of Christ, that is, the metaphysical function of Christ as "Lord" as the concrete mediation of the Absolute to the human. This mediating or theandric function exists in all religions to some degree. Panikkar is confident that we can call it "Lord" and even "Christ." It is in this metaphysical function of linking the absolute with the relative, the infinite with the finite, and the eternal with the temporal—a function recognized in Hinduism—that it becomes evident that Christ is already present in some sense in the Hindu dharma.

This "Christ" is the origin and end of all things. Through him all creation comes into existence and then returns to the Source. Through the Logos principle, Christ is present and hidden in the bosom of Hinduism. In a sense, what Panikkar is saying is that through this metaphysical principle an opening is made in Hinduism for the Christ of faith, though the starting point is the Logos function. That is the meeting point on a theological level as he conceives it. Panikkar elaborates:

> The Christ we are speaking of is by no means the monopoly of Christians, or *merely* Jesus of Nazareth. We may be allowed therefore to call Christ that which we consider to be almost by definition the meeting-point, and which at the same time meets the demands of Christian religion. This . . . is Christ: that reality from whom everything has come, in whom everything subsists, to whom everything . . . shall return. He is the embodiment of Divine Grace who leads every man to God. . . . Is not this what Christians call Christ? . . . Hence from the point of view of Christianity, Christ is already present in Hinduism.[37]

The Christ to which Panikkar refers is not, in this context, the Jesus of the Gospel, but a certain *theological* principle performing a *metaphysical* task in the structure of the *cosmic* reality. Again, it is the Logos function, and Panikkar places the emphasis here because it is a universally recognized insight in the various world religions. One can almost say that where theology fails in dialogue, perhaps logic and metaphysics can open the door to unity by developing parallel insights.

In the Vedantic tradition, and really going back to the dawn of this system, the Logos principle is identified with the mysterious divine figure called the *Purusha*. This is the Supreme Person, the primordial, universal, cosmic Person.[38] The Purusha is not a human being, but purely divine and is the archetype or exemplar of all human persons and all creation. It is the third element in the Hindu Trinity: Brahman, Atman, and Purusha. Purusha is the personal dimension of supreme reality, of the Brahman, and is one with Brahman and Atman.

—ᴠᴵᴵⱽ—

Panikkar remarks that this "Person" in the Upanishads is " . . . the inner Man who is also Lord of all. . . ."[39] But the Purusha is not the Atman, for the Purusha is the universal, archetypal human being. Thus the Purusha is not quite the Self. We may also note that Purusha in Indian thought is coterminous with the tradition, and is found in its first instance in the Veda.[40]

Bede Griffiths, who considered the Purushatic doctrine an important point of departure in the development of an Indian Christology, outlined the metaphysical function of the Purusha—much like Panikkar—and this included the Logos principle. He maintained that "Purusha is the cosmic person who contains the whole creation in himself and also transcends it. He is the spiritual principle which unites body and soul, matter and conscious intelligence, in the unity of a transcendent consciousness."[41]

The Purusha, however, is not only a metaphysical principle; it is also, like Christ, the way to immortality. There is thus a soteriological (salvation through Christ) aspect to the Purusha's function. It is through the Purusha that we come to know God, or the transcendent Brahman, just as we come to know the inaccessible Father in Christ, in the Son. The Svetasvatara Upanishad says that we must be united to the Purusha, for the Supreme Person is the Lord of immortality who leads us to the ineffable Brahman. By knowing Brahman we achieve immortality ourselves.[42] This is how the Upanishad expresses it:

> I have come to know that mighty Person [the Purusha], golden like the sun, beyond the darkness, by knowing whom one transcends death; there is no other path for reaching the goal.[43]

This is the One known in meditation, in the hiddenness of prayer, known to us through its own mighty self-revelation. Such is the path to the knowledge of the Cosmic Person.

Is Purusha the Logos as understood in the Christian comprehension of the term? Is it the Christ, the Son, the Second Person of the Trinity? These are difficult issues to work with, and they would need considerable research, debate, and prayer to resolve. But since the Logos dimension exists in Hinduism, it is a natural point of common ground in associating the Christian faith and the Hindu dharma on the theological/philosophical level in dialogue. A case can be made for Purusha fulfilling a similar function in Vedantic theology as the Logos does in (Hellenistic) Christian theology. Furthermore, it can be argued rather strongly that both the Purushatic and Saccidanandan intuitions emerge out of mystical consciousness. And since I believe that all genuine mystical awareness originates from the same ontological unity, there is some chance that they both reflect similar—if not precisely the same—realities in the Christian tradition, namely, Christ as the Word or Logos (Purusha) and the Blessed Trinity (Saccidananda). More than this would be speculation.

As this line of approach indicates, we must constantly bear in mind the deeper level of the meeting of these two faith systems—the domain of the mystical, where encounter in depth must—and indeed does—take place, and where we are beyond the merely speculative questions of theology and comparative spirituality. In that domain we may, in the same contemplative subtlety, associate the intuitive breakthrough to Saccidananda, the culmination of the advaitic revelation, and the revelation in the Christian soul of the Trinity. As Jules Monchanin believed, this revelation is the essence of Christian mysticism in which the distinction between God and the soul remains, because it is founded upon the distinctions among the very Persons of the Trinity Itself. We share in the trinitarian interrelationship, but we are not ourselves *it*.[44]

Finally, Abhishiktananda, speaking about the enormous task of the Church in India, warned us that it is only on this contemplative plane, from the mystical life, that the Church can ever hope to enter into a fruitful dialogue with India, and so to make any real progress there. The Church has to actualize her own contemplative understanding of the faith, to renew and spread it; she must live out of those depths " . . . where the authentic spiritual life of India is lived. . . ."[45] When this happens—and the dialogue in contemplative depth leads to mutual understanding and possibly even to existential convergence in some areas in an interior way—something truly wonderful will surface: "A kind of osmosis will have taken place in their souls (Hindus and Christians) between the Hindu experience of the depths of the Self and the Christian experience of the depths of the Heart of Christ."[46] It is along these lines that some sort of mutual growth and cross-fertilization will take place.

CHRISTIANITY AND BUDDHISM

Trying to relate the Christian and Buddhist paths of spirituality presents many difficulties and is fraught with paradox.[47] How can one relate a theistic faith with an apparently atheistic one? How is a complementary relationship possible? How are they compatible? I believe that I can answer these questions, but three observations on Buddhism may help to clarify these issues.

First, the Buddha never denied the existence and reality of God. When asked about God, he silently held up a lotus flower and smiled. This is the famous "silence of the Buddha," even though this story itself is regarded as a later Mahayanist text. The question is: why was the story added? Why this particular gesture? Curiously, this is a positive gesture or hint with respect to the Buddha's attitude toward God.

In the Hindu context of the Buddha's life—a context with which he would have been intimately familiar—the lotus flower had a very special significance. From the time of the Upanishads it has always symbolized the inner discipline of meditation as the way into a knowledge of the hidden Presence, the divine indwelling of the Atman in the *guba*, the "cave of the heart." When the Buddha raised the lotus and smiled, was he not saying, "Meditate, and you will discover the Presence"? This gesture and symbol would have been perfectly intelligible to his Hindu audience of the time, and so not require explanation. By the same token, it would be an ambiguous gesture to subsequent non-Indian Buddhist generations who lacked his original cultural/religious milieu with its Vedic background— who even lacked an adequate commentary on the symbol and the gesture. But, properly understood—and regardless of whether it is historically accurate—the story does shed light on the issue of theism in Buddhist self-understanding.

Second, what are we to make of the story in the Buddha's life in which Brahma, God the Creator, appeared to Shakyamuni after his enlightenment under the Bo Tree, instructing him to teach his doctrine? This came somewhat after the awakening, when Gautama had resolved to remain silent because he assumed that no one would understand his teaching. If this is just another pious legend or embellishment, why is it that subsequent Buddhist apologists left it intact? Why was it included in his biography, and what purpose did it serve? Put another way, would Prince Siddhartha, the Awakened One, have been "a Buddhist" in our understanding of this term today—a religious man without a God? What then is the significance of this intervention of Brahma at the crucial moment of his life and of the birth of the whole Buddhist tradition? Surely this story is inconsistent with the seeming "atheism" of the later development of the tradition.

Third, the highly mystical experience in Buddhism—the goal of life and the liberation itself—is Nirvana, and it is a state described as essentially *shunyata*, emptiness. But emptiness, or Nirvana, is also and simultaneously fullness, or pleroma. According to Lama Govinda, shunyata is both plenum and void, both emptiness—"no-thingness"—and form, or creativity—form-giving.[48] The way Buddhists talk about Nirvana reminds us of the way that some Christian mystics—notably Eckhart and Ruysbroeck—talk about the Godhead. Edward Conze, among others, drew attention to this fascinating parallel when he put the matter this way: "When we compare the attributes of the Godhead as they are understood by the more mystical tradition of Christian thought, with those of Nirvana, we find almost no difference at all."[49] This issue is something that deserves to be thoroughly explored by Christian scholars and their Buddhist counterparts.

The dialogue between Buddhists and Christians is at once both promising and very problematic. Actually, the state of things is very subtle. For instance, there have been a number of surprises from Buddhists on the issue of theism in the course of years of dialogue at the Naropa Institute. An atmosphere of openness, keen interest, intense listening, and genuine kindness characterizes the relationship of the two traditions at this center. There is a palpable sense that Tibetan Buddhism is flexible enough to grow in its own knowledge of ultimate truth, that it is capable of learning from the Christian tradition, as the latter is able to learn from it and from other Buddhist schools.

THE BODHISATTVA AND CHRIST

Struggling with the question of whether and/or how these two great systems of faith relate or are connected on a concrete level has led to the present insight on the Bodhisattva ideal and Christ, an understanding of their similarity to some extent. Both traditions can find serious common ground on this point of spiritual pragmatism. The Bodhisattva path developed out of Mahayana Buddhism, the "Great Vehicle School," in the first century of the common era. While Theravada Buddhism emphasized enlightenment, liberation, and the ideal of the *Arhat* (the one who seeks these), the Mahayana branch stressed service to all sentient beings in the attempt to achieve enlightenment for all. The Bodhisattva, upon assuming this path, takes a vow not to enter the ultimate Nirvana until all sentient beings enter first. Simply put, the Bodhisattva undertakes self-sacrifice for the sake of others. The term itself literally means one whose very being (sattva) is enlightenment (bodhi) and can be interpreted to mean "one who has the courage to tread the way of the awakened state." Historically, it can be conjectured that the evolution of this ideal in Mahayana Buddhism reflects the indirect influence of Christ on the Dharma, the way of the Buddha. Prior to Christ the notion of the Bodhisattva did not exist in Buddhism—a faith system that antedated the coming of Jesus by some five centuries.

There is a very unusual Christian thinker who has been published anonymously but who is thought to be Valentin Tomberg (a Russian emigré to Paris). This person argues along these lines, and is convinced of the influence of Christianity on Buddhism. In a spellbinding and epochal work on Christian Hermeticism, the author makes this rather suggestive remark:

> When the Gospel was preached by the light of day in the countries around the Mediterranean, the nocturnal rays of the Gospel effected a profound transformation of Buddhism. There the ideal of individual liberation by entering the state of *nirvana* gave way to the ideal of renouncing *nirvana* for the work of mercy towards suffering humanity: The ideal of *mahayana* . . . then had its resplendent ascent to the heaven of Asia's moral values.[50]

The Bodhisattva aspiration leads to *bodhicitta*—enlightened consciousness, Wisdom-heart, loving-kindness—and does so by practicing the Four Immeasurable Thoughts: 1) Loving-kindness, 2) Compassion, 3) Joy, and 4) Impartiality. There is no limit put on this bodhicitta, this compassion and joy, and there is no discrimination in the practice of loving-kindness. All are served equally; no one is denied care and attention. Imagine what would happen to the world if everyone were to embrace the Four Immeasurable Thoughts!

The classic text of the Bodhisattva path was written by the great eighth century Buddhist master Shantideva, who was from the monastic university of Nalanda in northern India. He wrote the *Bodhisattvacharyavatara* in verse, and it has been translated as *A Guide to the Bodhisattva's Way of Life*.[51] In Mahayana Buddhism, especially among Tibetan Buddhists, this is a highly revered text—a sacred teaching absolutely indispensable to practice. What is striking about this work is its resonance with the Gospel, its soteriological orientation. It has a deeply Christian sense to it, underscoring sacrificial service to others, compassion, and selflessness. As an example of verses that illustrate these qualities:

> May I be the doctor and the medicine. And may I be the nurse for all sick beings in the world until everyone is healed. . . .

> I become an inexhaustible treasure for those who are poor and destitute; may I turn into all things they could need and may these be placed close beside them.

> Without any sense of loss I shall give up my body and enjoyments as well as all my virtues of the three times for the sake of benefiting all.[52]

The Bodhisattva is able to develop loving compassion because of having *prajña*, or transcendent knowledge. This is a direct understanding of the illusory nature of the ego—that the ego is insubstantial, unreal. This liberating knowledge allows the Bodhisattva to let go—one becomes open, sensitive, and spontaneously generous and joyful.[53] Eventually such a one becomes, like the Buddha, a *Tathagata*, one who has gone to the absolute and ultimate Reality, who experiences all reality *as it is*.[54]

Thus grounded and rooted in the Transcendent, the Bodhisattva is able to be committed to the practice of the six virtues, the six transcendental activities. They are called the *paramitas*, from the words *param*, which means "other shore" or "other side of the river," and *ita*, which signifies "having arrived." These are the virtuous activities appropriate to the enlightened state, the condition of being aware of the ultimate state of being, the nirvanic life, the "further shore," in the language of the Indian tradition.

These paramitas not only characterize those who "have arrived," but are ideals held before those who are striving and seeking. They aim at an expanded view and understanding that transcends the ego and facilitates spontaneous compassion and loving-kindness. They are "transcendental generosity, discipline, patience, energy, meditation, and knowledge."[55]

Transcendental generosity requires utter openness. Chogyam Trungpa, the Tibetan teacher who founded the Naropa Institute, says, "Your action must be completely open, completely naked," and completely selfless.[56]

The Bodhisattva's action flows spontaneously because of this openness and freedom from rigidity. The spontaneity is also aided by the Bodhisattva's patience. One who has no expectations can be patient and so can enter into the pattern of each situation, doing what is required.[57] The Bodhisattva has a special "energy" that comes from spiritual discipline. This is *virya*, the energy of joy itself. In every situation the Bodhisattva discerns and brings joy. One who has thus "arrived" is able to enjoy life, to live it fully and mindfully. Even those still on the way find that wisdom and compassion increase in them and radiate from their lives and actions. Being completely awake means being enthusiastic about life, full of the energy of joy.[58]

The paramita of *dhyana* is meditation, and this is essentially awareness; it is the basis of the Bodhisattva's state of being "awake." On the "further shore" we are simply awake to life situations as they are. We are "particularly aware of the continuity of meditation with generosity, morality, patience and energy. There is a continual feeling of [being] 'awake.'"[59]

And finally, knowledge, *prajña*, the sixth paramita, refers to transcendental intelligence, which is what permits wise discrimination and dissolves all hesitations and doubts. The prefix *pra* is "super," and the root *jña* means "knowing"—thus, "super-knowing," or "super-knowledge." It is an all-seeing knowledge, a "complete, accurate knowledge which sees everything."[60]

When this ideal is applied to Christ, there is, I believe, a very significant point of convergence, a truly common connection between the two traditions. Lama Govinda himself mentions the similarity of Christ's teaching on enemies to the attitude of a Bodhisattva. He says: "Every true Buddhist who hears . . . [Christ's] words will be convinced that he who spoke them was one of the great Bodhisattvas, one of the enlightened helpers of humanity. . . ."[61] But is not Jesus the supreme example of the Bodhisattva? The Bodhisattva is the embodiment of *bodhicitta*, loving-kindness and compassion, but Christ *is* loving-kindness, *is* love itself enfleshed in a sacrificial act of self-giving for others. He is the perfection of compassion, a compassion that has been transformed into love, that has involved itself intimately in the human condition. In Shantideva's terms, he did not hesitate "to give up his body,"[62] and present his life as a sacrifice for broken and sinful humanity.

Like the Bodhisattva's, Christ's actions were guided by spiritual wisdom. His perfect love was directed in its application by an equally perfect knowledge, a "super-knowledge," a *prajña;* it was a transcendental knowing that understood the human condition and his place in redeeming it. He was able to give generously out of his openness and fluid perception of what was required in each situation. Christ's redemptive sacrifice had in mind the transformation of humanity's darkness, negativity, and sin, the altering of the consequences of these things, and the spiritual liberation or salvation of each member of the human race. Also, Jesus acted from the heart of divine love itself, and not simply from compassion. This love was and is vulnerable and directly engaged in the human situation, urging the world to further growth, not merely sharing the joys and sorrows of things as they are.

Jesus' way of dealing with human suffering was different from that of Gautama the Buddha. The Buddha's approach was like that of a doctor; he gave a diagnosis of the human condition, finding suffering to be at the center of it, and like any good doctor, he prescribed a remedy. He recommended that we overcome suffering by transcending its causes through his program outlined in the Eight-fold Path, the Four Noble Truths being the diagnosis. Jesus, however, did not advocate a program of escape from suffering and the more subtle existential anxiety of life. Rather, he demonstrated how essential human suffering—symbolized by the Cross—is to the process of redemption, spiritual maturity and continuous growth in genuine love. Christ transmuted suffering by his loving act of acceptance, which squarely faced suffering and the causes of it, taking upon himself its consequences. In this he was acting from a transcendental awareness, for he was acting from the wisdom of the Father.

These are the reasons I believe that Jesus is the perfect Bodhisattva, *the* Bodhisattva, and that the saints are Christian Bodhisattvas. So we have two versions of the Bodhisattva ideal—one Buddhist, the other Christian—but

I feel it is an ideal in which the two traditions have some solid common ground for mutual exploration.

NO-SELF, CHRIST, AND THE TRINITY

Another point of contact between the Buddhist dharma and the Christian faith is the Buddhist notion of "no-self" and Christ's inner awareness of his relationship with the Father in their bond of love called the Holy Spirit. Here I have avoided the very complicated comparison of the Buddhist *Trikaya*[63] doctrine with the Trinitarian vision, because it is too difficult an issue to consider effectively in this limited space, and also because I believe the "no-self" doctrine is a good lead into some further common ground.

One of the critical issues that apparently divides Buddhism from all the other world religions, and especially from Christianity, is its insistence on the nonreality of the self, the "I" of consciousness, its point of identity. Buddhism is firm in its denial of a role to a fixed point of identity, such as a substantial center of knowing that can be regarded as a real self. It claims that there is nothing supporting the "I," no self, no real person. Instead, the self is regarded as a grand gesture and a pretense at separate existence; it is a dualistic projection. There is no substance-like entity giving identity to human consciousness, nor is there any real nature individuated in the beings we call persons. Selfhood is a phantom concept upholding the illusion of autonomous existence through the focal structure of the ego. What exists behind the staging and props of consciousness are tendencies and habits; these are the residues of previous lives, but there is no enduring subject to which they belong.

What is interesting in this respect is that Christ never claimed a reality to selfhood, and never spoke in terms of a substantial identity behind the ego. He did not see selfhood in those terms, and he never referred to anything that fits the description of the substance category in Western thought. Instead, he spoke about the necessity of "losing yourself" as the very condition for "finding yourself."

The transcendence of self and all self-preoccupation is the constant recommendation of each mystical tradition—something emphasized by every Christian mystic and saint without exception. Jesus does not reveal a God who is "the self" in the rigid sense of the substance doctrine of Greek essentialistic metaphysics. He reveals God as pure relation within an undivided unity. God is not a static Self but a dynamic interrelationship, or, put another way, God's selfhood *is* interrelationship, an inner communion of being. Now what is actually communicated in this divine interrelationship and communion is Presence itself; it is also conscious and intelligent. This Presence is life; it is the energy of the Spirit and it is also love; it is likewise wisdom or supreme knowledge. Presence is the inner consciousness of divine knowing and God's own self-understanding. Ultimately, enlightenment is the awareness of and participation in this interrelationship in communion, in Presence, at the very heart of God: *that* is transcendent consciousness. God's being *is* intercommunion and intercommunication, since it is mutual indwelling; it is an interpenetration of the three Persons united in the one Being. God's selfhood is the mystery of pure interaction, a self-contained exchange of conscious Presence in the intimacy of an eternal act of identity. God, as Trinity, is the communion of knowledge and love. God's triune selfhood is not dualistic, because differentiation here is based on unity, a unity that knows itself in the distinction of relations. "I know the Father and the Father knows me," says Christ, and this signifies the intimate knowledge of relationship in an identity established in communion.

Each of the three Persons is a conscious relation to the other two, and each enjoys self-knowledge in the others. What is again known is the Presence of love, which arises out of the act of identity found in interrelationship; it is at once the nature of identity and the fruit of it. The function of the three relations we call Persons is the simple but infinitely profound act of eternally working out God's inner being and self-awareness. Identity is constituted in this relationship, in communion, where what is being related—the mutual Presence of a living love—is communicated, nourished, and then expanded outwards in the creative process of sharing with creatures.

God, as Trinity, is a community of mutually shared Presence, and this Presence is what is meant by the Holy Spirit. The Spirit is the very nature of what is being communicated eternally in the act of a total relationship existing between the Father and the Son, or between the Source and the Logos. God is always renewing the Divine Being in the act of threefold identity. This act is the inner metaphysical, indeed mystical secret of how God subsists in the Godhead. It is in this subtle sense that one can speak of God's selfhood which is "no-self," but not nothing; it means no fixed substance-nature, other than the intense dynamism of the threefold communion. God is this dynamic "self"-relation, and *relation is the moving affirmation of being*, which always bears fruit in the total reality of the divine identity.

This approach to me seems consistent with the Buddhist doctrine, while at the same time it remains completely true to Christian faith. To say that God's self is relationship, or communion, is to say that God's "self" is love. And this is not terribly different from saying that the essence of Buddhahood is loving-kindness, or compassion, not the illusory existence of a static substance that is called a nature and supposedly constitutes a self. Although there is no self in this old Greek and Scholastic sense—an abiding subject defined through a substantial nature—there *is* a self in the much deeper sense of the Presence of love. Doesn't St. John tell us that "God is love," and didn't Jesus prove this to us in his life and passion? It remains then for Christians and Buddhists to educate each other on the ultimate nature of this love and that compassion.

THE NATURE OF TRUE DIALOGUE

Finally, I want to consider briefly the practical level of complementarity, the associating of the Christian, Hindu, and Buddhist faiths in the context of depth-encounter and in active cooperation for humanity. I call this dialogue "practical" because its thrust is existential encounter and collaboration, rather than formal or academic conversations about the different positions. Certainly the academic dimension plays a critical role, but I am convinced that it is more in the way of preparation for the deeper, more interesting work of encounter. This is not to denigrate the value of the scholarly dimension of interreligious exchange, but only to emphasize the direction in which we must go in order to achieve the kinds of breakthroughs that will serve our future.

The deepest form of dialogue is not with words. Again, it is the common experience of so many engaged in interreligious dialogue[64] that really little can be achieved on the level of doctrine and belief. Doctrines (the domain of words and concepts) always occasion serious differences, misunderstandings and precious little agreement. But when Christians, Buddhists, and Hindus meet in silence and meditation, there is usually a deep experience of union and communion transcending the divisions that conceptualization brings. There is a discovery of that place of depth from which the various paths have arisen. This is the quality and degree of dialogical life pursued, for instance, by Buddhists and Christians at the Naropa Institute, and it has proved to be one of the best and most fruitful methods of interreligious exchange to date.

Meeting in the quiet of prayer, a mutual understanding unfolds. With this comes an openness to the others and the spiritual authenticity of their traditions. There can then be a fruitful sharing of the contemplative teaching present in these three great ways. As this process continues and matures over time, profound trust and a greater willingness to learn from one another develops. The competitiveness of the past dissipates and is replaced by love and the subtle realization of complementarity—how the paths mutually complete one another. Each has a unique experience of Ultimate Reality, and these experiences have an incomparable value for the human race and for a more adequate understanding of Truth. It is out of this fruitful type of openness and depth that cooperation on the urgent concerns of humanity emerges.

In 1982 Abbot Thomas Keating, a spiritual teacher and leader in the dialogue movement, joined with others to formulate the "Guidelines for Interreligious Understanding." These are eight highly nuanced and carefully crafted principles that developed out of their practical experience in dialogical encounters. The first six guidelines attest to the validity of the transcendent experience of the various traditions, which go by so many names. The seventh guideline deals with differences, and carefully says that the differences, "should be presented as facts that distinguish [the religions], not as points of superiority." Guideline eight is the most detailed and is concerned with the principles defining the moral responsibility of the religions in the domains of peace, hunger, politics, ecology, morality, social life, and spirituality, and has three subdivisions to it. Section (a) deals with the issue of peace and the responsibility of the religions to encourage nonviolent, peaceful means to settle disputes and conflicts. Section (b) urges the world religions to promote equal treatment by governments of each religious tradition. Finally, section (c) summarizes the whole scope of the principles on which the religions should unite and which they should selflessly labor to implement. This section accents the practical cooperation that originates in the profound encounters in silence and meditation:[65]

> The world religions should work for the practical acceptance of the dignity of the human person; a more equitable distribution of material goods and of opportunities for human development; the cause of human rights, especially the right to choose and practice one's own religion or no religion; the solidarity and harmony of the human family; the stewardship of the earth and its resources; the renewal of their respective spiritual traditions; and interreligious understanding through dialogue.[66]

Naturally, this list is not exhaustive, but it does include the most important areas, and it indicates the very real responsibility the religions have to unite their efforts in the work of improving the global and human situation. This practical collaboration may well be the crucible for the dialogue movement, for here the habit of cooperation on common concerns creates the environment for mutual trust, openness, and listening that will have an impact on the level of spiritual practice and the deeper encounters in silence and prayer. Up the road of history in the next few centuries the traditions, through their representatives, will come to appreciate and assimilate the great treasures of wisdom and spiritual insight in each of the paths. Then we will lock hands together across the barriers of millennia that have separated us into competing camps, dissolve all the obstacles, and finally realize our oneness, actualizing it universally in society. We will have direct experience of the complementary relationship that binds us together toward the Ultimate Mystery.

If the Christian Church can maintain an attitude of openness, a willingness to learn and to share, she may well be the ultimate beneficiary of the encounter, since she will have deposited these moral and spiritual treasures in her own heart, as she once did with Greek and Roman thought. There, in the bosom of the Church, they will be fruitful and become part of a new expression of her vision, a fresh theological statement that will be genuinely catholic because it will be built on the collective, universal wisdom of humankind and vivified by the supreme wisdom of the Gospel. The Christian faith will then be at home with all learning and, speaking all languages and addressing all concerns, it will communicate the message of Christ to the heart of the other traditions, thus opening a whole new horizon for humankind. But those of us at the dawn of this movement must live with the paradoxes, the doubts and the hope.

NOTES

1. *Nostra Aetate*, "Declaration on the Relationship of the Church to Non-Christian Religions," *The Documents of Vatican II*, ed. Walter Abbott, S.J. (New York: Guild, 1966), cf. pp. 660–668.

2. *Nostra Aetate*, n. 2.

3. For example, see *Towards a Theology of Religions*, by Heinz Schlette, *Quaestionis Disputatae* 14 (London: Burns & Oates, 1966). An important work on this subject, in the Indian context, is Thomas Emprayil's *The Emerging Theology of Religions* (Rewa, India: Vincentian Publications, 1980). The earliest known work on religious pluralism and reconciliation was by Nicholas of Cusa, a cardinal. The publication of his *De Pace Fidei* at the time of the Fall of Constantinople in 1453 sought to encourage peace between the Church and Islam.

4. Pope John XXIII, *Pacem in Terris*, n. 14.

5. *Dignitatis Humanae*, "Declaration on Religious Freedom," Abbott; cf. pp. 675ff.

6. Pope Paul VI, *Evangelii Nuntiandi*, n. 53.

7. Pope Paul VI, *Ecclesiam Suam*, n. 72. A large section of this encyclical is concerned with dialogue.

8. *The Pope Speaks to India* (Bombay: St. Paul Publications, 1986), p. 13, my emphasis.

9. "Discourse of the Pope to Zen and Christian Monks," *Bulletin* (Secretariatus Pro non Christianis), vol. 23/1, no. 67, 1988, pp. 5–6. An address given to Christian and Zen monks participating in "The Third East-West Spiritual Exchange."

10. Formerly called the North American Board for East-West Dialogue. It publishes a free newsletter three times a year; it presents condensed articles, documents, news, interviews, book reviews and listings of significant events, retreats and workshops, and can be obtained by writing to: *MID Bulletin* Abbey of Gethsemani, 3642 Monks Road, Trappist, KY 40051–6102. (Materials for publication should be sent to: Father James Conner, O.C.S.O., Editor, *MID Bulletin*, Abbey of Assumption, Route 5, Box 1056, Ava, MO 65608–9142.) Also, both A.I.M. and the Council for Interreligious Dialogue publish journals. The former is called *A.I.M. Monastic Bulletin* (English Edition), which can be ordered by writing to U.S. National Center for A.I.M., Benedictine Convent of Perpetual Adoration, 8300 Morganford Rd., St. Louis, MO 63123. The Vatican publication can be subscribed to by writing: *Bulletin*, Pontifical Council for Interreligious Dialogue, Vatican City, Europe.

11. It is no exaggeration to say that the Tibetan Buddhists are as enthusiastic as we are about the new relationship, that they view this relationship as extremely important, and

that in all this they understand our joint responsibility to the rest of humanity. For a very valuable book on Naropa, containing the views of the various leaders of the movement there and geared especially to the level of practice, see *Speaking of Silence: Christians and Buddhists on the Contemplative Way*, ed. Susan Walker (Mahwah: Paulist Press, 1987).

12. For this useful sketch I am indebted to Bede Griffiths, who acquired this understanding in conversations with Aloysius Pieris, a Sri Lankan theologian. Father Bede outlined these positions in a lecture to the Theosophical Society in Wheaton on August 25, 1983. The lecture is entitled "The Interface between Christianity and Other Faiths," and is available on cassette from The Theosophical Society, P.O. Box 270, Wheaton IL 60189–0270. Complementarity has also been embraced by Raimundo Panikkar, Thomas Keating, David Steindl-Rast, to name a few. For a good study of this whole issue, see Gavin D'Costa's *Theology and Religious Pluralism: The Challenge of Other Religions* (Oxford: Blackwell, 1986). Professor D'Costa uses different terms in the debate: "exclusivism," "inclusivism," and "pluralism." Complementarity would be similar to, or consonant with, pluralism. The inclusivist paradigm is the one Karl Rahner defends, and it underlies his proposal of the "anonymous Christian." D'Costa's book develops these positions in the context of Christ and God's universal salvific will. Another significant work that attempts to put the case for pluralism is *The Myth of Christian Uniqueness*, eds. John Hick and Paul Knitter (Maryknoll, NY: Orbis, 1987).

13. Griffiths, lecture "The Interface between Christianity and Other Faiths."

14. Ibid.

15. Fritjof Capra, *The Tao of Physics* (Berkeley: Shambhala, 1975), p. 142.

16. David Bohm, *Wholeness and the Implicate Order* (London: Routledge & Kegan Paul, 1980), p. 147. For a similar view in biology, on the principle of form, see Rupert Sheldrake's *A New Science of Life: The Hypothesis of Formative Causation* (Los Angeles: J. P. Tarcher, 1981); in psychology there is the radically pioneering work of Ken Wilber. See especially his *The Atman Project: A Transpersonal View of Human Development* (Wheaton, IL: Quest Books, 1980).

17. *Aletheia*, from the Greek: Truth (lit., "not-forgetting"). Martin Heidegger uses it as a pivotal term in his metaphysics to mean "unfolding, uncovering."

18. Romans 1:20.

19. Wisdom 13:1–9.

20. Bede Griffiths, *The Golden String: An Autobiography*, p. 28.

21. This unity is expressed in the first *mahavakya*, or "great saying" of the Upanishads: "This self (Atman) is Brahman" (*ayam atma brahma*, Mandukya Upan. 2). There are four mahavakyas altogether. The other three are: (2) "Brahman is consciousness" (*prajñanam brahma*, Aitareya Upan. 5.3); (3) "Thou art That" (*tat tvam asi*, Chandogya Upan. 6.8.7); and (4) "I am Brahman" (*aham brahmasmiti*, Brihadaranyaka Upan. 1.4.10).

22. Thomas Merton, *The Inner Experience*: "Society and the Inner Self" (II), *Cistercian Studies*, vol. 18, no. 2 (1983), p. 133.

23. Exodus 3:1–6, 14.

24. Isaiah 6:1–5.

25. Jeremiah 1:4–10.

26. Daniel 7:9–14.

27. John 17:21–26.

28. Matthew 17:1–8; Mark 9:2–8; Luke 9:28–36.

29. Acts 9:3–9.

30. Abhishiktananda, *Hindu-Christian Meeting Point* (Delhi. ISPCK, 1969), p. 89. For an in-depth study of the relation of the two traditions, see my *Towards a Christian Vedanta: The Encounter of Hinduism and Christianity According to Bede Griffiths* (Bangalore: Asian Trading Co., 1987, obtainable from Philosophers' Exchange, 3425 Forest Lane, Pfafftown, NC 27040.)

31. Abhishiktananda, *Hindu-Christian Meeting Point*, p. 58.

32. Abhishiktananda, *Saccidananda: A Christian Approach to Advaitic Experience* (Delhi: IS-PCK, 1984 rev.), p. 228, Appendix 3. This is a translation of the Introduction to the old French edition, *Ermites du Saccidananda. Sagesse hindou, mystique chrétienne* (Paris: Casterman, 1956).

33. Ibid., p. 178.

34. This was told to me by Father Murray Rogers, an Anglican priest, who was a long-time personal friend of Abhishiktananda's—someone in whom he could confide. Murray Rogers founded Jyoti Niketan Ashram in the state of Uttar Pradesh in the north of India, a place where Abhishiktananda felt at home. There are some good secondary works on Abhishiktananda: M. M. Davy's *Henri Le Saux, Swami Abhishiktananda: le Passeur de deux rives* (Paris: Cerf, 1981), is a sound biography. *Swami Abhishiktananda: The Man and His Teachings*, ed. Vandana (Delhi: ISPCK, 1986), is a slim collection of papers by his friends and disciples. Also Odette Baumer-Despeigne's "The Spiritual Journey of Henri Le Saux-Abhishiktananda," *Cistercian Studies*, vol. 18, no. 4 (1983), is an inspiring talk that she gave to the "East-West Monastic Symposium" at Holyoke, MA in November 1980. The most powerful presentation to date, however, is a video of his spiritual transformation. It was produced in French but has an English version. Titled *Swamiji: Interior Journey*, it can be obtained for $20 by writing to Brother John, Ojai Foundation, P.O. Box 1620, Ojai CA 93020.

35. Raimundo Panikkar, "Hinduism and Christ," in *In Spirit and in Truth: Essays Dedicated to Father Ignatius Hirudayam, S.J.*, ed. Ignatius Viyagappa, S.J. (Madras: Aikiya Alayam, 1985), p. 115.

36. Raimundo Panikkar, *The Unknown Christ of Hinduism: Towards an Ecumenical Christophany* (Maryknoll: Orbis, 1981, rev.), p. 115.

37. Ibid., p. 49.

38. Chandogya Upanishad 8.12.3.

39. Raimundo Panikkar, *The Vedic Experience (Mantramanjari): An Anthology of the Vedas for Modern Man and Contemporary Celebration* (Pondicherry: All India Books, 1983), p. 729.

40. Rig-Veda X.90. For other descriptions, see Mundaka Upanishad 2.1.2 and Svetasvatara Upanishad 1.8 and 5.5–6.

41. Bede Griffiths, *The Marriage of East and West*, pp. 70–71.

42. Svetasvatara Upanishad 3.7.

43. Ibid., 3.8. This was a favorite passage of Abhishiktananda's.

44. "The Quest of the Absolute," in *In Quest of the Absolute: The Life and Works of Jules Monchanin*, ed. and trans. J. G. Weber (Kalamazoo: Cistercian Publications, 1977), p. 131. See also J. Monchanin, *Ecrits spirituels* (Paris: Centurion, 1965) and Joseph Mattam, *Land of the Trinity: A Study of Modern Christian Approaches to Hinduism* (Bangalore: Theological Publications in India, 1975). The latter has a valuable section on Monchanin and R. C. Zaehner.

45. Abhishiktananda, *Hindu-Christian Meeting Point*, p. 110.

46. Ibid., p. 111.

47. For an excellent article on this issue, which discusses it in terms of the language barrier between the two traditions, see Aloysius Pieris' "Christianity in a Core-to-Core Dialogue with Buddhism," *East Asian Pastoral Review*, vol. 25, no. 1 (1988). An earlier article of Fr. Pieris' presents an overview of the dialogical situation of the Church in Asia. See "Western Christianity and the Eastern Religions," *Cistercian Studies*, vol. 15, no. 1 (1980), and (part two) vol. 17, no. 3 (1982).

48. Lama Anagarika Govinda, *Creative Meditation and Multi-Dimensional Consciousness* (Wheaton IL: Quest Books, 1978), p. 105.

49. Edward Conze, *Buddhism: Its Essence and Development* (New York: Harper & Row, 1959), p. 39. For a good treatment of Nirvana, see Ananda Coomaraswamy's work, *Buddha and the Gospel of Buddhism* (New York: Harper & Row, 1916 & 1965), "Nibbana," pp. 115–126.

50. Anonymous, *Meditations on the Tarot: A Journey into Christian Hermeticism*, trans. Robert Powell (Amity NY: Amity House, 1985), p. 102. Of course, the author does not offer any real evidence for this view, but it seems plausible. Obviously there had to be contact in some form or other between Christians and Buddhists at that time due to trade. It is also a well-known fact that a Buddhist community existed in Alexandria as early as the first century C.E. After conceiving the possibility of linking the two traditions on this level, I discovered a valuable book, *The Christ and the Bodhisattva*, eds. Donald Lopez and Steven Rockefeller (Albany: SUNY, 1987). This work contains papers from a symposium, but none of the articles actually compares Christ with the Bodhisattva.

51. Shantideva, *A Guide to the Bodhisattva's Way of Life*, trans. Stephen Batchelor (Dharamsala: Library of Tibetan Works and Archives, 1979). The best commentary on this crucial work is by the Tibetan master, Geshe Kelsang Gyatso, *Meaningful to Behold: View, Meditation and Action in Mahayana Buddhism: An Oral Commentary to Shantideva's A Guide to the Bodhisattva's Way of Life*, trans. Tenzin Norbu and ed. Jonathan Landaw (Cumbria, UK: Wisdom Pub., 1980).

52. Shantideva, *A Guide to the Bodhisattva's Way of Life*, Chap. III.8, 10 & 11, pp. 30–31.

53. Chogyam Trungpa, *Cutting Through Spiritual Materialism*, eds. John Baker and Marvin Casper (Boston: Shambhala, 1973), p. 168.

54. The *Tathagata* refers to the Buddha in his ultimate reality; the *Dharmakaya* means the body of ultimate reality. It is found in the Mahayanan text, the *Prajñaparamita Sutra*, or the *Sutra of the Perfect Wisdom of the Heart*.

55. Chogyam Trungpa, *Cutting Through Spiritual Materialism*, p. 170.

56. Ibid., p. 172.

57. Ibid., p. 174.

58. Ibid., pp. 175–177.

59. Ibid., p. 177.

60. Ibid., p. 178.

61. Lama Anagarika Govinda, *Creative Meditation and Multi-Dimensional Consciousness*, p. 144.

62. Shantideva, *A Guide to the Bodhisattva's Way of Life*, Ch. III.11, p. 31.

63. The Trikaya doctrine elaborates the notion of the threefold body of the Buddha: the *Nirmanakaya* or earthly body, the *Sambhogyakaya* or heavenly body, and the *Dharmakaya* or body of ultimate reality (cf. no. 54 above). Both the Trikayan and Trinitarian doctrines are approaches to the perennial problem of the mediation of the transcendent, absolute and eternal to the finite, relative and temporal. It would thus be appropriate to explore the connection. Two articles are significant to supply background: Ruben Habito's "The Trikaya Doctrine in Buddhism," and "Trikaya and Trinity: The Mediation of the Absolute," by J. C. Cleary, both of which appear in *Buddhist-Christian Studies*, vol. 6 (1986), Univ. of Hawaii.

64. A classical work on this subject is Raimundo Panikkar's *The Intra-Religious Dialogue* (Ramsey NJ: Paulist, 1978).

65. See *Speaking of Silence* (no. 11 above), pp. 127–29. Abbot Thomas formulated these with fourteen other spiritual masters, each representing a world religion. These "Guidelines" were the fruit of years of discussion by Abbot Thomas' group, the Snowmass Conference.

66. Ibid.

Poems from Jonah: The New Story, Poem #28

Albert J. LaChance

The sense of the various religions being culturally diverse expressions of real contact with the one Source is expressed musically in Albert LaChance's "Poem #28," from his epic, Jonah. This poet is also a Christian ecological thinker who has studied with Matthew Fox and Thomas Berry. He has applied the famous "Twelve Steps" (of Alcoholics Anonymous) to an ecological therapy in his book, Greenspirit, *and has joined John E. Carroll in editing* Embracing Earth: Catholic Approaches to Ecology. Jonah *describes a spiritual journey from despair through death, resurrection, and a vision of a new cosmology, synthesizing insights from Joseph Campbell and Thomas Berry within a poetry inspired by T. S. Eliot. Poem #28, from the section "The New Story," represents Earth as giving different names to Great Heart, as the different cultures and significant individuals appear in evolution.*

JONAH

The New Story: Poem #28

Great Mother Planet brought forth a daughter-people
priestess—children for Herself, natural, wholly,
whose dance was sunlaughter and moonsong and starrain,
a people whose feet prayed the dust prayer, whose skins bathed
in wetgrace, breathers of spiritfires, their bodies are
her soils, their breath, her winds; Her womb pulse is their blood.

Earth named Great Heart: WAKAN-TANKA

And Great Mother Planet birthed a sage so keen
that fables hold, he was born an elder, who
at the frontier of his exile wrote his book: "The mind
of Great Heart is like a bellows, breathing galaxies
of mind-dust into being, with the sun and his planet
who groans in birthing the wisdom of the myriad things."

Earth named Great Heart: TAO

There was born of Great Mother Planet a people
so astounded at the Presence as to name thousands
of gods and goddesses, which in unison could
proclaim not the least hint of that Luminosity,
a people so pregnant with memory and hope
that a million lifetimes seemed less significant than dew.

Earth named Great Heart: BRAHMAN

Great Mother Planet delivered a man so
confident that the human heart throbbed at the core
of creation, and rippled through the home, the city,
the nation, the earth, and the galaxy, as to dream
of cultures to tabernacle the Luminous,
making humans partners with earth and with the universe.

Earth named Great Heart: SINCERITY

And there was born of Great Mother Planet, a prince
of such compassion for the whole agonizing tribe,
that he would nullify all the gods and goddesses known,
that the One Love unknown could be felt shivering through
atoms, molecules, cells, hearts, nations, planets and stars,
in the one tremendous Song that could still the suffering.

Earth named Great Heart: MIND

Great Mother Planet brought forth a people
of the Original Journey burning with fires
of prophecy, pregnant with the seed of Great Heart,
a people born to be the son, who parted the sea,
ate bread of the skies, a nation of patriarchs, prophets
and priests, who would dare to call Great Heart, "Father."

Earth named Great Heart: YAHWEH

And there was born of the Oneness of Great Heart
with the Blessed Virgin Earth, a son who sucked the body
and blood of the planet from the breasts of a woman,
a Son, Father of his Mother, born bloody and writhing,
and who died bloody and writhing to accomplish what
even He despaired of doing until He died and did.

Earth named Great Heart: JESUS

Great Mother Planet gave birth to a man aglow
with the miseries of so many missing fathers, that he
would plead for years in the cave of desperation,
beseeching Great Heart for fathering, and when the fire
of the Origin, suffused the cave of the Earth-womb,
he announced One Love in a scream whose ripples tremble still.

Earth named Great Heart: ALLAH

New Possibilities for Interreligious Dialogue

Paul Knitter

Paul Knitter is a member of the Theology Department at Xavier University in Cincinnati and is General Editor of Orbis Books' Faith Meets Faith *series. In this piece he continues the considerations of interreligious dialogue, and gives us a glimpse of a new field of study, the theology of religions. This field is a response to contemporary theological feelings that, in the global village that is quickly taking shape, we human beings need a way of understanding—with genuine respect, acceptance, and love—our relations to one another as members of diverse traditional cultures. Distinguishing his position from previous models of exclusivism (non-Christians are excluded from salvation) and inclusivism (other religions find their fulfillment in Christianity, and good people, even if not Christian, are saved by Christ), he recommends pluralism, and also offers guidelines for dialogue. Knitter develops the theme that pluralism recognizes the equal rights of all religions to be listened to with respect—subject to subsequent evaluation—on the basis that each has its own validity and may have something not previously known to other traditions that they can learn from. He summarizes that in any case, the criterion to be used by Christians in judging if they are "with Jesus" is whether they follow his example and act in love towards their neighbors.*

I. The New Theological Perspective on Religious Pluralism

The following remarks, coming from a Christian theologian, are geared toward Christians, in that I hope to convince my fellow believers that there are really new possibilities for Christian dialogue with other religions. I hope, however, that my thoughts will also be of interest, and perhaps even of help, to followers of other religious paths.

My thesis in what follows is that there are new perspectives and models for Christian conversation with other faiths. Although they are *really new* in the sense explained below, they are not *totally new* in Christian consciousness and belief. Totally new would mean something utterly different and therefore in opposition to what Christians have felt and practiced through the centuries. What I propose is in continuity with Christian tradition and carries on the spirit and intent of Christianity. However, my approach does represent a really new stage in the evolution of Christian attitudes toward other faiths and toward its own. There are Christians who may be disturbed by some of these ideas, for these ways of thinking are a departure from some orthodox thinking of the past; yet this disturbance need not last. I believe that the new model can still be a faithful way of continuing to live out the Gospel, a new way of living the old message.

Need for a New Model

Why is there a need for a new Christian approach to other religions? Many Christians are finding themselves drawn toward the realization that there must be a change in Christian attitudes toward followers of other religious paths. The first reason for this need to redefine the Christian position towards other faiths has to do with the Gospel and with what is the heart of the Christian Good News. The first commandment of Christ to Christians is *not* a "missionary mandate" to go forth and make disciples of all nations, but is, of course, to love one's neighbors. Many people feel that there is a certain clash between this commandment and the missionary mandate. Previous attitudes towards and ways of approaching other faiths have not allowed Christians to properly love their non-Christian neighbors. What, after all, does love mean, but to respect someone, to honor them, to really listen with an authentic openness to what they are saying? In the past, some Christian attitudes towards other believers and the seeming need to make them disciples of Christ have not enabled this kind of love. Can we really love others when we are convinced that our truth is better than theirs, or that they are inferior to us in what they hold to be true and sacred? For many Christians, therefore, the missionary mandate and the commandment to love one's neighbor have been mutually exclusive.

The second reason many Christians feel that past attitudes toward other religions are not adequate today comes not from the Gospel but from the contemporary world. This is a world that many have called a "global village"—where we can know and talk to each other and have possibilities for cooperation in a way that has never existed before. But our world is not only a global village. It is also a threatened, endangered village; it is a world that, in a variety of ways, seems intent on destroying itself against its very will.

There is the threat of socioeconomic injustice—often built on sexist and classist injustice—that is causing so much poverty and oppression, and thus so much unrest among the community of nations. There is the threat of ecological oppression that is destroying the very source of life. And there is the nuclear threat—the horrifying reality that human beings have created and multiplied the kinds of weapons that could bring about something humanity was previously incapable of: humanocide. These real threats of socioeconomic injustice, ecological oppression, and nuclear devastation are realities in our world that call for a response, for a new solution, for a new world order and way of living together among nations and cultures. But if such a new world order is ever to be created—if such a conversion in our way of understanding and living with each other is ever to take place—the world religions will have to make a significant contribution to global change.

Humanity today needs the kind of vision and energy that can come especially, if not exclusively, from these religions. In all the living faiths one can find, in an amazing variety of forms and expressions, a vision of unity among human beings. One can also hear a call to find one's fulfillment, not by living centripetally, or in sole concern for oneself, but centrifugally, in a relationship of love, compassion, and respect with others. But if the world religions are going to make this contribution to saving our threatened world village, they're going to have to listen and work with each other as never before. This means that new ways and new models for dialogue and cooperation are needed. Many Christians feel that the old ways of viewing other faiths do not promote the kind of dialogue that will bring salvation for the modern world.

This new model for interreligious dialogue that will be *really* but not *totally* new for Christians, and that will meet the needs of our contemporary civilization is what some theologians call a "pluralist model." To fully explore and understand this concept, it will help to elucidate the previous models or attitudes that this new one seeks to correct and fulfill.

PREVIOUS MODELS FOR INTERRELIGIOUS DIALOGUE

For most of its existence, Christianity has looked upon other faiths with an attitude of exclusivism, the attitude that because there is truth and grace and salvation only in Christ and Christianity, other religions have little validity—*extra ecclesiam nulla salus*—"outside the church, no salvation." However that dictum may have originally been understood, it captured the way Christians felt about other faiths and motivated their determination to go forth and preach the Gospel. Missionary work meant saving souls from hell. Although there were notable exceptions, this model was part of the fabric of Christianity from the fifth to the sixteenth or seventeenth centuries.

However, with the discovery of the New World, new questions about and new attitudes toward the vast world outside of Christianity began to develop. An inclusivist model began to take shape. People questioned whether a loving God could ship off to hell those millions of souls who, through no fault of their own, had never heard of Jesus. As a reaction to this conundrum, the Council of Trent in the sixteenth century developed the concept of baptism of desire—that one can be saved by doing good and following one's own conscience.

This new view was developed through the centuries, especially by my own teacher, Karl Rahner, and by the second Vatican Council, which for the first time in Roman Catholic Church history officially recognized the value of other religions. In general, the World Council of Churches also now endorses a new, inclusivist model.

How does the Roman Catholic inclusivist model regard other believers? It states that there is truth and goodness in and through other religions, and that therefore we not only can, but we *must* dialogue with them; Christians can learn from other religions. However, it also states that because the fullness of God's revelation or the final Word of God resides in Jesus Christ and is passed on in the Christian community, because there is only one savior, because all of God's activity in the world stems from and is directed toward the God-man Jesus—all other religions have to be fulfilled, or included within Christianity. The truth or goodness found within other religions is, as the Church Fathers and the Second Vatican Council put it, a *praeparatio evangelica*—a "preparation for the Gospel." The other religions are thus to find their fulfillment by being "included" in Christianity.

This inclusivist model expresses the common opinion or prevalent attitude of most mainline Catholic and Protestant theologians today. Still, there are a growing number of theologians—and an even greater number of Christian laity—who feel that even this so-called positive or liberal model is inadequate. In different ways they are proposing or trying to work out what might be called a "plurality" approach to other faiths. Essentially, this approach is one that recognizes the possible validity of other faiths independently of Christianity, which really means that Christianity may have to consider itself "one among many." In other words, there may be other religions that are carrying out as important a role in the history of humanity as Christianity.

Although this new model is still being worked out by theologians, it has already been rejected by some Christians as contradicting the very essence of Christianity. Thus, at this juncture it is important to make clear what this pluralist model does and doesn't mean. With such clarifications, I hope it will be evident that while the pluralist model represents something *genuinely new*, it does not embody a *totally new* turn in Christian beliefs. Indeed, for many Christians it represents not just a valid, but a necessary evolution in Christian belief and practice—an evolution that is necessary if Christians are truly to remain faithful to the Gospel values of Jesus.

A PLURALIST VIEW OF OTHER RELIGIONS AND OF CHRISTIANITY

The first hallmark of the pluralist model is to accord "equal rights" to all religions. This means that all religious believers enter the forum of dialogue with the same rights to speak their minds and make their claims to truth, and it means that other religions have the duty to listen to what they are saying. To claim the equal rights of all religions, however, does not mean that all religions are equal in value or have the same essential meaning. The pluralist model does not claim a common essence within all religions, or include the concept that their differences don't make a difference. Most Christian pluralists that I am aware of want to maintain the bewildering differences among the religions; they also want to seek out ways of not only understanding the beliefs of other traditions but also of evaluating or judging the value of these beliefs. Pluralism does not mean relativism.

To recognize the equal rights of other religions is also to recognize the *possibility* that these religions have a validity of their own, independently of Christianity and of Jesus Christ. In other words, their validity or truth does not consist of being a preparation for Christ or for the Church. By embracing this possibility, one is really saying that other religions do not have to find their final fulfillment in Christianity. But to admit to the proposition that other religions have a value in themselves is also to admit that there may be truth in other religions that has not been revealed to humankind through Jesus Christ. There may be more truth about God or the Ultimate, or about human nature and how we are to live, than has been made known in Jesus Christ. *If this is so*, then Christians can learn of such truth only in dialogue. *Whether it is so* can also be learned only in this way.

There are deep, perhaps unsettling, christological implications in what I have just said. For many Christians these implications constitute one of the most threatening aspects of the new pluralist theology of religions. To attempt to remove some of these threats, let me first state what the Christian pluralists are not saying about Jesus: they are not proclaiming that Jesus is one among many, in the sense that there are really no differences between Jesus and the Buddha or Krishna or Mohammad. Jesus is not simply "one of the boys"; the archetypal religious figures of history, like the religions, are not all the same. Nor are the pluralists suggesting that the revelation and salvation made available in Jesus Christ are only for Christians. In the pluralist model, Jesus and his Gospel retain universal relevance. The missionary mandate remains. Pluralists, in other words, are not questioning whether Jesus is *a* universal savior; they are questioning whether he is the *only* universal savior.

The pluralists *are* asserting that although Christians can and must continue to affirm that Jesus of Nazareth effectively and universally reveals the Mystery of God, they cannot claim that he exhausts that Mystery. While Jesus is certainly a window by which we can and must look out onto the universe of Divine Mystery, there may be other windows. To say that he is totally divine does not mean that he bears the totality of Divinity. He "defines but does not confine God," as John A. T. Robinson has said.[1] More precisely, he describes but does not prescribe the ever-living, self-communicating Mystery of God.

Therefore, Christians must be open to the possibility that the Buddha or Mohammad or the seers of the Upanishads have a message that, though very different from that of Jesus, may be as "universally relevant" as that of Jesus' message. This means that Christians must also be open to the possibility of really learning something new, something important, from the Buddha or from other traditions. Both Jesus and the Buddha may, therefore, be unique—but with a complementary uniqueness. The missionary mandate then also assumes a complementary character; the purpose of missions becomes to go forth not only to teach all nations but to learn from all nations in order that we may all be better disciples of the truth.

Today, Christians are being called upon to carry out their discipleship of Jesus in a more demanding and more exciting way: they must be as fully committed to Christ as they are genuinely open to other religions. But is this psychologically possible? Can we be fully committed to our own Savior and authentically open to others? I believe that it is possible. It might work in a similar way to a good marriage: my particular all-embracing love for my spouse, as it deepens and matures and grows secure, opens the way for me to have more healthy relationships with other persons in whom I find much to appreciate and emulate.

Actually, this transformation is what naturally results from knowing and being committed to Jesus Christ: the God who is known through Jesus Christ is the God who persistently calls one to greater truth, greater challenges—the God who is always transforming us. To know the God of Jesus is to have the security and the courage to follow the Spirit wherever she might lead—even when she leads us to truth other than what we have found in Jesus. John Cobb puts this idea even more emphatically: "In faithfulness to Christ, I must be prepared to give up even faithfulness to Christ."[2] In other words, the more we know Christ, the more we are able and eager to learn from others. A good Christian, then, is a good pluralist.

—ψ—

BIBLICAL BASIS FOR PLURALISM

One might ask, however, whether such an understanding of the uniqueness and meaning of Christ is not contrary to the biblical witness about him. I do not believe that this is so. In fact, as strange as it may sound, many of the theologians who are proposing a new pluralist theology of other religions are doing so in the name of the Bible—that is, as a means of being more faithful to what they hold to be the spirit and the deeper meaning of the scriptural witness. There are at least three ways in which these theologians claim that the Bible *not only allows but requires* a more pluralistic, positive view of other believers.

1) A number of theologians ground their pluralistic turn by emphasizing what seems to be a fairly well established hermeneutical principle for New Testament Christology—that the titles and images given to Jesus by the early Christian communities are better understood as literary/symbolic rather than as literal/definitive attempts to say who Jesus was for them. In other words, images such as Son of God, Word of God, Lord, Messiah, and Savior are to be interpreted as doxological or confessional expressions of personal and community experience of this man and his message and as exhortations to follow him, rather than as definitive, propositional statements about his nature or ontological status in the universe. This is the position taken by John Hick in his well known, but often poorly understood appeal to accept and live the incarnation as myth.[3] Rosemary Ruether and other theologians engaged in Jewish-Christian dialogue also follow this symbolic/poetic interpretation of New Testament images of Jesus when they suggest that his Messiahship places him not in the absolute center of history, but on a leading edge—as a paradigm of the future, along with other paradigms.[4]

With this literary/symbolic reading of New Testament Christology, Christians can enter the interreligious dialogue with clear claims of what God has *really* done in Jesus without having to insist that God has done it *only* in Jesus. In firmly proclaiming Jesus as incarnate Son or Messiah, one is also open to the possibility of other incarnate Sons/Daughters, or of other Messiahs.

2) Among many pluralist theologians there is a general preference for Johannine Logos/Wisdom Christology over Pauline Paschal Christologies. In other words, they find both basis and imperative for dialogue in locating

the particularity of Jesus within the universality of God's self-revelation, rather than in locating God's universality within the particularity of the historical Jesus. They choose the Wisdom trajectory, which sees Jesus as a concrete, historical, normative manifestation of what God has been doing and is doing, from the beginning and everywhere, in preference to the Easter trajectory which, as it has been understood, identifies the historical ministry/death/resurrection of Jesus as the starting point or source of what God intends to do universally. In other words, with Wisdom/Logos Christologies, Christians can affirm what *really* has happened in Jesus without claiming that it happened *only* there. Hence we have Panikkar's trenchant and sobering axiom that while Christians can affirm that Jesus is the Christ, they cannot so easily announce that the Christ is Jesus.[5] Interestingly, the theologians who are offering the boldest interpretations of traditional Logos Christology are from the East, such as Stanley Samartha of India, Aloysius Pieris of Sri Lanka, and Seiichi Yagi of Japan,[6] and are blending their Christologies with Hindu and Buddhist images and experience.

3) Another avenue to a pluralist reading of the New Testament witness follows a linguistic approach. This approach recognizes the clear, undeniable presence of "one and only," exclusive, normative claims made about Jesus in the New Testament. The statement that "There is no other name given to humankind by which we can be saved than the name of Jesus Christ" (Acts 12:4), is perhaps the most thunderous example. But pluralist theologians ask, what kind of language is this? What is its purpose or nature?

To broadly summarize the possible meaning of this exclusivist language, they suggest that given the lack of historical consciousness in the early community of Jesus' followers, given their threatened minority status, given the apocalyptic mentality that expected all to be over soon—their absolutist language about Jesus can be considered part of the historically conditioned medium by which they wanted to deliver their central message about him. Simplifying, we might say that in their historical circumstances, in order to announce that God had *really* acted in Jesus, they also had to say that God has acted *only* in Jesus. Today, however, we can hold onto the same central message of "really" without insisting on the medium of "only."

This possibility is all the more likely in light of the nature of the New Testament "one and only" language descriptive of Jesus. It is confessional language, or what Krister Stendahl has called "love language," rather than philosophical, dogmatic, apologetic language. Lovers naturally use "one and only" language about their partners—but they do so to affirm their partners and to express their commitments, not to make philosophical claims or to denigrate others. "No other name" was meant primarily to affirm Jesus, not to rule out the Buddha.[7]

II. PLURALIST GUIDELINES FOR DIALOGUE

This, then, is the new pluralist perspective for interreligious dialogue. Granting its validity, which for many Christians is still open to question, what kind of concrete guidelines might it provide for a conversation between Christians and followers of other religious paths? I have formulated four such guidelines. In explaining them, I hope not only to facilitate dialogue among religions but also to provide further reasons why the pluralist model is both valid and urgent for all religious believers. My hope is that other religions will adopt similar pluralist models and guidelines.

ABSOLUTE COMMITMENT TO RELATIVE TRUTH

The pluralist model for understanding religious dialogue calls for the participants to embrace a paradox. (Here followers of Eastern paths should have an advantage over Christians.) Dialogue can and must be based on an absolute commitment to truths or understandings that we recognize as relative and limited. This means, first of all, that if dialogue is going to be at all fruitful, the participants have to have something meaningful to say to each other—something clear, something strong, something they are committed to.

For example, for Buddhists and Christians to dialogue with each other, they must make truth claims to each other. In other words, I have to tell my Buddhist friends not only what I hold to as a Christian but also why I think it would be worthwhile for them to hold to it as well. Because of my devotion to Christianity, I do this with passion and a desire to convince them of the worthiness of my position. I don't want to "convert them," since that is an unfavorable word in dialogical circles, but I do want them to agree with me, and I think they want me to want that. This is what I mean by being "absolutely" committed to one's own truth. But at the same time, this absolute commitment recognizes that one's knowledge or grasp of what one is committed to is limited, not the final word—that is, nonabsolute. The reality to which we are committed, as well as the degree of our personal commitment (faith), remains absolute; but the knowledge of the reality (beliefs) ever remains limited, relative, changing.

Thus we confront a paradox: religious experience has a decisiveness about it—it calls forth our full commitment, it engages us. And yet, religious experience also tells us that our knowledge of what we are committed to, like all historical knowledge, is limited. So, we are fully committed to it, and at the same time we are ready to adjust, clarify, correct, and even abandon that commitment insofar as our knowledge or grasp of what we are committed to is adjusted, clarified, corrected. Is that psychologically possible? Some would say it is not. I feel that this is not only possible but necessary.

THE PRESUMED TRUTH OF THE OTHER'S EXPERIENCE AND CLAIMS

A second guideline made possible and required by the pluralist model for interreligious dialogue calls for the participants to enter into the conversation with the presumption that what they are going to hear from the other side is true. Why do I emphasize this? First, out of common sense. All of us can recognize, I suspect, that we don't really listen with open ears and an open heart to another person unless we trust that the person has something worthwhile or something true to tell us. This is why Raimundo Panikkar, a pioneer of interreligious dialogue, has insisted through the years that the first step in the conversation with believers from a different religious path is to believe in the truth of their religion. Otherwise, we won't be able to hear them at all. Thus, in the Buddhist/Christian dialogue a Christian, in a limited but real sense, has to *become* a Buddhist (and, of course, vice versa).

To believe that what those of other religious paths are saying or living is true is not only necessary for the first step of dialogue, it is also required of us if we are to enter authentically into the deeper dialogical process. That process has been described as an effort to "pass over" to the world of experience, feeling, and practice of another faith. Dialogue is possible only when we enter into the very heart of another religion. "Passing over" is a process by which we let our hearts take the lead as we allow our imagination the freedom to feel and follow the symbols of the other faith, wherever they may lead us. We abandon ourselves to the stories and symbols and worldview of the other and we open ourselves to whatever new feelings and insights might show themselves to us. As David Tracy has suggested, dialogue becomes a game that we do not play but that plays us.[8] But if this game is going to be played—if our passing over is going to reveal anything to us—we have to believe in the truth of the other believers.

Such belief calls for great trust, for we don't know how the game is going to play us or what we are passing over to. What's going to happen when, in Gandhi's terms, we experiment with the truth of Hinduism? What changes will be required of us? We don't know. We *must* trust. And this is where Christians should be well prepared. The God revealed in Jesus Christ is the God who said that there is always more to the divine Mystery than what we already know; it is the God who eschatologically leads us into the future of ever greater realization of truth; it is the God who provides us with the security to follow wherever the Spirit might lead us. Of course, it is also possible that after we presume the truth in the other path, after we pass over to it, we discover that, at least for us, there is no truth to be discovered. But even for that to happen, we must begin the dialogue with the expectation and trust that God has something to tell us through the life and witness of our fellow believers.

DIALOGUE BASED ON THE DISTINCTION BETWEEN FAITH AND BELIEF

A third guideline that can help us handle the risks and the trust that are required of us in opening ourselves to the truth of our spiritual partners is that we bear in mind the difficult, yet so important, distinction between faith and beliefs. Because many Christians do not realize this distinction, they find dialogue especially difficult. They identify beliefs with faith, and that, really, is a form of idolatry.

Faith is the personal experience of revelation or enlightenment. It is the experience of grasping or being grasped by the Ultimate, by the Mystery of God, and is an experience whose content is as real and transforming of one's life as it is ambiguous and more than we can ever say or know. Simply put, faith is religious experience.

Beliefs are the necessary, but always inadequate, expressions of that experience. I say "necessary" because I am a Christian; Buddhists might feel differently. Within Christian experience and tradition, based as it is on the "Word" of God, words and symbols and doctrines have played an integral role in gathering and holding the Christian community together and in enabling it to be genuinely involved in the world.

So Christians hold that "speaking" (doctrine) and "acting" (ethics) are part of their experience of the God of Jesus Christ. But while they have been good at insisting how important words are, they have been delinquent in recognizing how limiting such words are. This is where we must emphasize the distinction between faith and beliefs. As important as beliefs may be, they can never be identified with the experience or the content of faith. No belief is absolute or the one and only way of expressing faith. No belief is immune to change and clarification and correction.

Fortunately, as Bernard Lonergan has pointed out, the distinction between faith and beliefs can be an immense help to interreligious dialogue. To open ourselves to other beliefs and symbol-systems, to feel our own beliefs challenged, to take on new beliefs or even to let go of old ones—all this does not necessarily mean that we have harmed or lessened our faith. On the contrary, through the clarification and expansion of our belief that comes through the encounter with another religious path we can deepen and strengthen our faith. As has so often been the case, Christians can become better—that is, more "faith-filled"—Christians through dialogue with another's faith.

THE PRIORITY OF ORTHOPRAXIS OVER ORTHODOXY

But aren't there limits to how far one can go in changing or adjusting one's beliefs? Isn't there a point where there is so great a change that one loses one's previous way of "experience"—that is, one's faith? Isn't it possible that in the "transformation" that can occur in religious dialogue, one may let go of the "core" or the "defining characteristics" of one's own religion? There are no easy answers to such important questions. But perhaps a fourth guideline, which is provided by liberation theologians and emphasizes the important of orthopraxis over orthodoxy, can help.

Liberation theologians stress that fidelity to what it means to be a Christian, fidelity to following Jesus Christ, is primarily (though not exclusively) a matter of "right action" rather than of "right belief." The heart of Christianity and of being a faithful Christian is, in other words, much more a matter of what we do than of what we say. Naturally, we hope that there is conformity between our words and our lives, and that our words are ways of enabling us to live more consistently and committedly. Still, the final measure of whether we are "with him or against him" will be decided not by our adherence to precisely formulated doctrine but by the way we have lived our lives in following the example of Jesus' life. Jesus implied this, I think, when he clearly stated that it is not those who proclaim him "Lord, Lord!" that will enter the Kingdom, but instead those who *do the will* of God (Matt. 7:21–23). What Jesus stated here was mirrored in his own life. As Jon Sobrino has pointed out, if we read the Gospels carefully, we will see that what was most important for Jesus was not that people belonged to a group of his followers (his church!), nor was it that they recognized him as the only Lord or the final prophet, nor even that they explicitly came to a belief in God as Abba. What was primarily important for Christ was that people committed themselves to and worked for what he called the Kingdom of God.

What this means is brought out in the parable of the sheep and goats at the final judgment: those who are saved are those who, even when they didn't know about Jesus, fed the hungry and clothed the naked and visited those in prison. In other words, commitment to the Kingdom of God means believing in and working for a world in which human beings can live together in love and justice and cooperation. What was most important for Jesus was that people commit themselves to trying to bring about such a society in this world and in the next.

Here, then, Christians have the final criterion for deciding whether a particular new belief or practice that results from dialogue is "still Christian" or not, and whether it is faithful to the Scriptures and tradition. Does it still enable and encourage the "orthopraxis" of following Jesus and working for the Kingdom? If it does—even though it may appear new and contrary to traditional words—it can still be judged to be an evolution, rather than an aberration, of Christian tradition. For example, say that through the dialogue with Buddhism or Hinduism, Christians find themselves embracing a suprapersonal, or an "empty" image of God, or perhaps they come to an understanding of Christ that no longer insists on his superiority or finality over other religious figures. Would such new "beliefs" be continuous with Christian belief? The way of deciding that question would not be to measure their cognitional meaning against the "meaning" of previous doctrines and to see whether they are "orthodox." It would be, rather, to investigate whether such new beliefs still enable Christians to commit themselves to following the example of Jesus and to working for the Kingdom of love and justice. The final criterion, in other words, would be whether those new beliefs are orthopraxic.

SPEAKING, LISTENING, UNDERSTANDING, ACTING

If religious persons of any tradition follow guidelines similar to those that have just been suggested, I believe that they will find themselves doing two things, and as a result, achieving two things: First, they will be *speaking* to each other out of their own convictions in an open, honest, perhaps passionate, way. And second, they will be *listening* to each other with a genuine openness that will enable them not just to grasp each other's ideas but also to pass over into each other's lives. By doing this, they should find that they are *understanding* and *appreciating* each other as Christians or Buddhists or Hindus with a clarity and a challenge that perhaps is new. From this understanding and appreciation, those of differing religious paths may find themselves called to *act together* in transforming the world and relieving its suffering. From speaking and listening openly, from understanding more deeply, peoples of diverse traditions can find themselves *together* in greater harmony with God, with Brahman, with their Buddha nature—with the Fullness that is empty and the Emptiness that is full.

NOTES

1. John A. T. Robinson, *Truth Is Two-Eyed* (Philadelphia: Westminster, 1980), pp. 125–127.

2. John B. Cobb, Jr., "The Meaning of Pluralism for Christian Self-Understanding," in *Religious Pluralism*, ed. Leroy S. Rouner (Notre Dame Univ. Press, 1984), p. 175.

3. John Hick, *God and the Universe of Faiths* (New York: St. Martin's Press, 1973), pp. 120–147.

4. Rosemary Radford Ruether, *To Change the World: Christology and Cultural Criticism* (New York: Crossroad, 1981), pp. 31-43; and John T. Pawlikowski, *Christ in the Light of the Christian-Jewish Dialogue* (New York: Paulist, 1982), pp. 108–135.

5. Raimundo Panikkar, *The Unknown Christ of Hinduism* (Maryknoll: Orbis, 1981), p. 14.

6. Stanley J. Samartha, "The Cross and the Rainbow: Christ in a Multi-Religious Culture"; Aloysius Pieris, "Jesus and Buddha: Mediators of Liberation"; and Seiichi Yagi, "'I' in the

Words of Jesus," in *The Myth of Christian Uniqueness: Toward a Pluralistic Theology of Religions*, ed. John Hick and Paul F. Knitter (Maryknoll: Orbis, 1987).

7. See the following in two articles in *The Myth of Christian Uniqueness*: John Hick, "The Non-Absoluteness of Christianity," and Paul F. Knitter, "Toward a Liberation Theology of Religions." See also Robinson, *Truth Is Two-Eyed*, pp. 105–112; Peggy Starkey, "Biblical Faith and the Challenge of Religious Pluralism," *International Review of Missions* 71 (1982), 68–74; Krister Stendahl, "Notes on Three Bible Studies," in *Christ's Lordship and Religious Pluralism*, ed. Gerald H. Anderson and Thomas F. Stransky (Maryknoll: Orbis, 1981), pp. 14–15.

8. David Tracy, *Plurality and Ambiguity: Hermeneutics, Religion, Hope* (New York: Harper & Row, 1987).

Abandonment to God: Jean-Pierre de Caussade and the Bhagavad Gita

Robert L. Fastiggi

Robert Fastiggi is a member of the Department of Religious Studies, St. Edward's University in Austin, and is personally active in the dialogue movement in Texas. His article provides an example of how two different traditions can speak together about love. Beginning with an appreciation of Dom Bede's Christian commentary on the Bhagavad Gita, River of Compassion, he develops the parallels between the Gita and the Christian classic, Abandonment to Divine Providence, by the eighteenth century Jesuit, Jean-Pierre de Caussade. The parallels that he finds are detachment from desire, surrender of heart, mind, and will to God, experience of peace and bliss, and awareness of divine omnipresence and glory. Fastiggi presents both the Gita and Caussade as revealing the deep mysteries of God in terms of an interpersonal relationship of total love and self-giving—of God to human beings and of human beings to God.*

One of the creative tensions in Hinduism is the concept of God as Impersonal Absolute versus the concept of God as Personal. In the Bhagavad Gita (written c. 400–200 B.C.E.), the concept of God as personal, loving and compassionate is emphasized. It is not surprising, therefore, that many scholars and spiritual writers have found in the Bhagavad Gita a rich source of comparison with Christian spirituality.

A definite similarity between the image of Krishna in the Gita and the image of Christ in the New Testament has been observed. We need only compare the words of Krishna with the words of Jesus in the Gospel of John. For example, in the Hindu text, Krishna says: "but those who commune with Me in love's devotion (*bhajanti bhaktya*) [abide] in Me, and I in them" (9:29).[1] In the Christian text, Jesus says: "On that day you will realize that I am in my Father and you are in Me and I in you" (John 14:20).

HINDU BHAKTI AND CHRISTIAN DEVOTION

The recognition of a definite similarity between the path of bhakti proclaimed in the Gita and the path of love enjoined in the New Testament should not cause us to ignore the differences that exist between the two religious worldviews with which we are dealing. The Gita emerges out of a Hindu tradition that had already achieved speculative maturity on metaphysical and spiritual matters. The New Testament, though, emerges out of a Jewish worldview that was only beginning to incorporate certain elements of the Greco-Roman philosophy. Thus, while it is possible to do a thorough comparison of the Bhagavad Gita with parallel texts from the New Testament, it is probably better for Christians to read the Gita from the viewpoint of the whole Christian mystical tradition. Certainly, Christian mysticism has its roots in scripture, but a Christian commentary on the Gita is best achieved when the great mystical writers are also considered.

This is precisely what Father Bede Griffiths did in his sensitive and thoughtful book, *River of Compassion: A Christian Commentary on the Bhagavad Gita*. Not only does Bede show parallels between the Gita and scriptural writers, such as St. John and St. Paul, but he also draws upon Christian contemplatives and theologians, such as St. Bonaventure, St. Thomas Aquinas, Julian of Norwich, Meister Eckhart, and St. Ignatius Loyola. The breadth of the *River of Compassion* is also demonstrated by reference to Greek, Buddhist, and Taoist sources.

As Bede shows in his commentary, one of the great parallels between the message of the Gita and the message of Christianity is the emphasis on the complete love and devotion to God. This path of love is called bhakti within the Hindu tradition. In discussing the line of the Gita that reads: "Offer in thy heart all thy works to Me, and see Me as the end of thy love" (18:57), Bede observes:

> We now come to the climax of the *Gita's* teaching on the love of God.
> This is the way of *bhakti;* the whole mind is fixed on God all the time and
> one surrenders everything to Him and does everything as an offering to
> Him. It is a total self-surrender.[2]

In reading the phrase, "total self-surrender," a great spiritual classic immediately comes to mind, the *Abandonment to Divine Providence* by Jean-Pierre de Caussade (1675–1751),[3] an eighteenth-century Jesuit and spiritual guide. *Abandonment to Divine Providence* is actually a collection of various letters and lectures Caussade directed towards some French nuns of the Visitation Order. Caussade's spiritual instructions were saved and cherished by the Visitation nuns, and were eventually handed over to a Jesuit named Henri Ramière who edited and published them in a small book over one hundred years after the death of the author (1861).

In spite of the differing religious and cultural contexts of these two writings, the spiritual paths enjoined by both Caussade and the Bhagavad Gita are remarkably similar. Four definite movements of the spirit can be traced in each text: 1) A disciplined detachment from all selfish desires; 2) A complete surrender of the heart, mind, and will to God; 3) The experience of peacefulness and beatitude, once surrender to God takes place; 4) A sense of divine omnipresence and glory. Although these spiritual movements are not always understood or presented in a sequential manner in either text, they still deserve individual attention.

DETACHMENT FROM DESIRE

The Bhagavad Gita was written within a few centuries after the beginnings of Buddhism.[4] One of the central teachings of Buddhism is that suffering is the result of attachments and desires. The message of the Gita can be understood as a response to the same problem perceived by Buddhism but with a different solution. Whereas Buddhism teaches the Noble Eightfold Path as a means of detachment from desires and cravings, the Gita offers detachment from selfish desires by means of attachment to the person of God. Thus, Krishna tells Arjuna: "Cast all your works on Me, your thoughts [withdrawn] in what pertains to self; have neither hope nor thought that 'This is mine': Cast off this fever! Fight!" (3:30).

The spiritual logic working here is simple but profound. Human beings are easy prey to all types of "vain hopes and selfish thoughts." This is the same as what the Buddhists have already said. However, the devotee offers up all of his or her works to God and rests the mind on God alone. Absolute surrender to God frees one from the bonds of attachment and leads to union with God. Speaking of the true devotee, Krishna says: "[His] self detached from contacts with the outside world, in the Self he finds his joy, [his] self in Brahman integrated by spiritual exercise (*brahma-yoga yukt'atma*), he finds unfailing joy" (5:21). Such freedom results when attachment to God leads to detachment from the transient pleasures of life. Devotion to God, therefore, achieves the same goal for which the Buddhists so diligently labor: namely, detachment from selfish desires and the realization of bliss. The words of Krishna are so clear in this regard: "Attach your mind to Me; engaging [still] in spiritual exercise put your trust in Me" (7:1). The person who puts total trust in the Blessed Lord experiences inner peace and "from attachment freed, steadfast and resolute remains unchanged in failure and success . . ." (18:26).

Caussade's counsel regarding attachments to created things follows the same wisdom of both Buddhism and the Gita. As he writes, "If we wish to enjoy an abundance of blessings we have only one thing to do: purify our hearts by emptying them of all desire for created things and surrender ourselves wholly to God."[5] Caussade, like the Gita, sees absolute devotion and submission to God as the sure path to liberation and beatitude. His instruction on this matter is quite lucid:

> How fortunate we are if we understand God's loving strictness and eagerly cooperate with it. We rise above all that passes away and repose in the unchanging and the infinite, and no longer put our trust in created things, but have dealings with them only when God wills it. God sees that we are empty of all our own desires and unable to make our own choice. We are dead and buried in complete indifference. When God in all his fullness comes and fills our hearts, he casts over all created things an annihilating shadow which blots out all their differences and variety. So these creatures lack all power to accomplish anything and we feel no attraction for them, for the majesty of God fills our hearts to overflowing. Dwelling in God, we are dead to all things, and all things are dead to us.[6]

The spiritual logic of Caussade is quite direct: we must detach ourselves from created things in order that God may fill our hearts and minds with his all-pervasive presence. This state of detachment and abandonment, therefore, is the pure state of mind needed for the experience of God in each moment. As Caussade explains: "This annihilation of all creatures and then their restoration to serve the designs of God, ensures that in each moment God is both himself and all things for us. For at each moment our hearts are at peace in God and completely abandoned to all creation. Therefore each of these moments contains all things."[7]

Both the Gita and Caussade demand a total detachment from selfish desires. As long as we are attached to the fruits of our actions, we remain in bondage. So much is clear in the Gita: "The integrated man, renouncing the fruit of works, gains an abiding peace: the man not integrated, whose works are prompted by desire, being attached to fruits, is bound" (5:12). In a similar way, Caussade tells how those who are abandoned to God experience serenity in any circumstance. "Whatever the world offers them is nothing. They judge all things by God's standards. If he takes from them their powers of thought and speech, their books, their food, their friends, their health, and even their life itself, it means no more to them than if he did the exact opposite. They love all he does and find his activity always sanctifying."[8]

—\\\\\//—

COMPLETE SURRENDER TO GOD

In the Bhagavad Gita, there is a clear affirmation of love as the supreme path to the Godhead. Krishna tells Arjuna: "Indeed, it is only by love [*bhaktya*] that I can be known and seen in such a form as I really am, O Arjuna, and it is only by love that one may enter into Me" (11:54). The effect of this love of God is salvation or liberation (*moksha*). The devotee is liberated from the bondage of selfish desire because his or her thoughts are fixed entirely upon God.

There is a twofold movement in the process of salvation: the movement of the devotee towards God and the movement of God towards the devotee in grace. The two, though, work together. Krishna is willing to respond to any gesture of love on the part of the devotee. As we read, "Be it a leaf or a flower or fruit or water that a zealous soul may offer Me with love's devotion, that do I [willingly] accept, for it was love that made the Offering" (9:26). The true devotee ultimately dedicates all actions toward God as an expression of love. Krishna gives Arjuna the instruction, "Whatever you do, whatever you eat, whatever you offer in sacrifice or give away in alms, whatever penance you may perform, offer it up to Me" (9:27). The result of this supreme devotion is harmony of soul and intimacy with God. Krishna says: "On Me your mind, for Me your loving devotion, unto Me your sacrifice, to Me your prostrations; now that you have thus integrated self, your striving bent on Me, to Me you will [surely] come" (9:34).

The Gita also makes it clear that Krishna reaches out in compassion towards suffering humanity. In chapter ten, Krishna says, "Out of compassion for these same men [all] darkness born of ignorance I dispel with wisdom's shining lamp . . ." (10:11). Then in chapter eighteen Krishna reveals: "Thinking on Me, you will surmount all dangers by my grace" (18:58). Krishna calls upon those who suffer to seek refuge in him: "Give up all things of law, turn to Me, your only refuge, [for] I will deliver you from all evils; have no care" (18:66).

We see that the Gita makes clear the double movement of humanity reaching out towards God in devotion and God reaching out towards humanity in love. Krishna summarizes this point very well: "Bear Me in mind, love Me and worship Me, sacrifice, prostrate yourself to Me: so will you come to Me, I promise you truly, for you are dear to Me" (18:65).

—\|//—

Caussade likewise expresses the need for complete devotion to God. In a moment of self-revelation, Caussade tells God: "All I want to do is love you and devote myself to the duties of each moment, and so allow you to act on me as you wish."[9] In many ways the spirituality of Caussade is very simply stated. As he writes: "The essence of spirituality is contained in this phrase: 'complete and utter abandonment to the will of God.' By that I mean we should never think of ourselves but be continually occupied with loving and obeying him."[10]

Caussade believes the expression of this total abandonment to God is found in both active loyalty to the duties of our state of life and passive loyalty to whatever God wills for us. This attitude is summed up in this way: "We must be active in all that the present moment demands of us, but in everything else remain passive and abandoned and do nothing, but peacefully await the promptings of God."[11]

THE EXPERIENCE OF PEACE AND BEATITUDE

The practice of bhakti and abandonment to God results in a deep sense of peacefulness and blessedness. It is the peace that the world cannot give. It is the peace of knowing that God loves us and wishes what is best for us. It is the peace that sees God in all things and all things in God. Krishna describes the peaceful person as the one who has "cast off [all] attachment to the fruit of works, ever content, on none dependent . . ." (4:20). Whereas passions and desires cloud the mind and lead the soul into chaos, detachment brings forth a feeling of blessedness and joy. Krishna reveals the secret: "For upon this athlete of the spirit whose mind is stilled the highest joy descends: [all] passion laid to rest, free from [all] stain, Brahman he becomes" (6:27).

Caussade is moved by the same sense of joy. When we let go of our own will and our own selfishness, God becomes our constant source of joy. As we read, "We find all our joy in fulfilling God's pleasure—his happiness, his glory and the fact that he is our great and only delight. Once we have this foundation, all we need to do is to spend our lives rejoicing that God is God and being so wholly abandoned to his will that we are quite indifferent as to what use he makes of our activities."[12] This is a profound psychological as well as spiritual truth. Self-forgetfulness brings forth a sense of peace and a reduction of needless anxiety. Living in total abandonment to the will of God produces a freedom and protection from the oppressive "whips and scorns of time." Even setbacks and annoyances of life can be peacefully endured by the person abandoned to God. As Caussade counsels:

> My friends, you lack nothing. You would be very ashamed if you knew what the experiences you call setbacks, upheavals, disturbances, and tedious annoyances really are. You will realize that your complaints about them are nothing more nor less than blasphemies—though this never occurs to you. Nothing happens to you except by the will of God, and yet his beloved children curse it because they do not know it for what it is.[13]

THE SENSE OF DIVINE OMNIPRESENCE AND GLORY

In both these writings, there is communicated a profound sense of the divine omnipresence. In the Bhagavad Gita, Arjuna addresses Krishna in the most exalted language: "You are the Primal God, Primal Person (*adidevah, purusah puranas*), You of this universe the last prop-and-resting place, You are the knower and what is to be known, [You our] highest home, O You whose forms are infinite, by You the whole universe was spun" (11:38).

Arjuna is blessed because Krishna tells him that his glory is not seen by all (7:25). What is it then that enables a person to see God? In part, it is due to an individual's willingness to concentrate the entire heart, mind, and soul on God. In part, it is also due to the grace of revelation that provides glimpses of the celestial glory of the divine. Thus, in chapter eleven, Krishna undergoes a transformation that enables Arjuna to see "the whole [wide] universe in One, converged, there in the body of the God of gods, yet divided in multiplicity" (11:13).

The Bhagavad Gita is filled with many powerful expressions of divine omnipresence and glory. Krishna says: "I am the Self established in the heart of all contingent beings" (10:20). "And what is the seed of all contingent beings, that too am I. No being is there, whether moving or unmoving, that exists or could exist apart from Me" (10:39). Krishna elsewhere reveals that "the splendour centered in the sun which bathes the whole world in light, [the splendour] in the moon and fire—know that it [all] is mine" (15:12).

Krishna tells Arjuna that he penetrates the earth and sustains all beings with his strength (15:13), and that he transcends "the perishable" and is more exalted than "The Imperishable Itself" and thus he is extolled as "the Person [All] Sublime (*purusottamah*)" (15:18).

All of these expressions point to the mystery of divine transcendence and divine immanence. The Bhagavad Gita is able to join these metaphysical concepts to the religious exercise of devotion, love, and service to God. Although the knowledge of the universal spirit (Brahman) is present in the Gita, it is clearly superseded by loving devotion to Krishna as a personal God who transcends even the Imperishable which is "the highest Brahman" (8:3). Indeed, for the Gita, love is the lamp of knowledge. To love God is to know God. The words of Krishna express this with power and eloquence: "Do works for Me, make Me your highest goal, be loyal-in-love to Me, cut off all [other] attachments, have no hatred for any being at all: for all who do thus shall come to Me" (11:55).

However, when one lives with complete devotion to God, the knowledge of God as the "Supreme Person" is also gained. This superior knowledge, by its very nature, gives rise to intimate love with God. Thus, knowledge unites with love, and love gives birth to knowledge. As Krishna reveals: "Whoever thus knows Me, unconfused, as the Person [All-] Sublime, knows all and [knowing all] communes with Me with all his being, all his love" (15:19).

Caussade echoes the same theme. Faith and total abandonment to the divine will are the keys that unlock the treasures of God's presence that are to be found everywhere.

> Faith transforms the earth into paradise. By it our hearts are raised with joy of our nearness to heaven. Every moment reveals God to us. Faith is our light in this life. . . . Faith unlocks God's treasury. It is the key to all of the vastness of his wisdom. The hollowness of all created things is disclosed by faith, and it is by faith that God makes his presence plain. Faith tears aside the veil so that we can see everlasting truth.[14]

The beauty of Caussade's spirituality is that it discloses God's presence in the midst of everyday experience, in "the sacrament of the present moment."[15] Like the Gita, Caussade sees love as the true path to the knowledge of God. As he writes: "For those who abandon themselves to it,

God's love contains every good thing, and if you long for it with all your heart and soul, it will be yours. All God asks for is love, and if you search for this kingdom where God alone rules, you can be quite sure you will find it."[16] Abandonment to God is simultaneously an act of faith, hope, and love. It is the sure path to the knowledge of God, and it is the sure path to salvation. Abandonment to God, as taught by Caussade, appears to be a Christian parallel to Hindu bhakti, the complete surrender of the soul to God in love.

CONCLUSION

In this age of scholarship and cross-cultural fertilization, it is sometimes important to be called back to the most fundamental aspirations of the human heart. Both the Bhagavad Gita and *Abandonment to Divine Providence* lay open the simplicity and the beauty of the heart clinging to God in love. The realization that God is the source of all reality and the source of all life moves the human heart into a posture of dependence upon divine grace. Both the Gita and Caussade express this need for total surrender to God in love.

While the similarities between the two texts appear compelling, it is important to note a few possible differences. Caussade believes in God's omnipresence, but it is not entirely clear whether his Christian theism is the equivalent of the panentheism or "cosmotheism" of the Gita. Since the Gita is such a rich and complex text, it is open to numerous interpretations within the various schools of Hindu thought. R. C. Zaehner believes that it is the school of Ramanuja, known as *visistadvaita* (qualified nondualism) that "probably comes nearest to the mind of the author of the Gita."[17] If this is true, then we would have to say that Caussade's sense of divine omnipresence differs from that of the Gita since he would always maintain an ontological difference between God and the created order. If there is a Christian thinker who approaches Ramanuja's sense of panentheism it would be Caussade's fellow Jesuit, Pierre Teilhard de Chardin (1881–1955), who might have been influenced by Caussade.[18]

Caussade's sense of the "sacrament of the present moment" is probably best interpreted as the recognition of the divine will or divine providence in all things. However, there are passages that do suggest a cosmic presence of the divine. For example, Caussade tells us that "God's activity runs through the universe. It wells up and around and penetrates every created being. Where they are, there it also is."[19] No doubt Teilhard could find nourishment for his concept of the "Cosmic Christ" in passages like these, along with his readings of certain passages of Paul and Greek Patristic sources.

Ultimately, it may be impossible to decide whether Caussade's sense of the divine omnipresence is the same as that of the Gita. Historically, Christianity has tended to stress the radical difference between the Creator and creation while incorporating mystical traditions that sometimes move in the directions of pantheism and occasionally monism. Hinduism, on the other hand, has always had a stronger tendency toward nondualism and pantheism but has also been able to incorporate the school of Madhva that emphasizes the difference between God and the phenomenal order.

Another possible difference between Caussade and the Gita is in their understanding of the nature and purpose of detachment. The language of the Gita reflects a highly developed yogic system that had been nurtured and practiced for centuries within India. Caussade's language of detachment also reflects the historical tradition of Christian asceticism, especially in terms of the three stages of purgation, illumination, and union. But is Hindu detachment the equivalent of Christian purgation? Certainly, both are intended as means for purifying the mind and the will of any obstacles that stand in the way of spiritual illumination.

However, Hinduism has always had a more negative view of the worth of the phenomenal world, and *moksha* has usually been understood as a release from the conditioned realm of phenomenal existence. Christianity, on the other hand, is a tradition with a greater affirmation of the importance of the temporal order and has always placed its hope in the renewal and transformation of creation rather than a release from it.

To be sure, the history of Christian asceticism can give us many models of men and women who live in the world but are not of it. Yet, at first glance, it is not certain whether the example of Arjuna going into battle, detached from the concern of whom he might kill, is a model that a Christian could uncritically embrace. While Caussade speaks of the importance of fulfilling the duty of one's state of life, he also speaks about the importance of active loyalty to the will of God. For the Christian, therefore, the question must always be asked whether any given course of action is in harmony with the will of God.

In this regard, however, it can be argued that Arjuna is also practicing "active loyalty" to the will of God by performing the dharma required by his state in life. The intervention of Lord Krishna onto the scene of battle enables Arjuna to accept the righteousness of his action while abandoning the fruits of what he does to the divine will. The message of Krishna also gives Arjuna a transcendent confidence in the indestructible quality of the persons he might be obliged to kill. In the final analysis, the Hindu and Christian expressions of detachment from the fruits of one's actions, as well as their respective ideas of active loyalty to the will of God are not really that different.

While some possible differences may exist, we must admit that the similarities between Caussade and the Gita are remarkable. Both of them deal with the question of how one can achieve peace and serenity in the midst of trials and struggles. The psychological root of pain is found by both authors in the selfish attachments to desires and material things. They both acknowledge God as a benevolent personality who has a deep and abiding love for the human person. For both of them, it is the awesome power and beauty of divine love that lifts the individual out of the conditioned realm of sin and pain and into the transcendent state of intimacy with God.

This complete and utter abandonment of the soul to the will of God is understood as the royal path of Christian love and the sweet fragrance of Hindu bhakti.[20] It is as if the author of the Gita and J. P. de Caussade are kindred souls who write centuries and continents apart, but somehow they come to cross paths in the spiritual geography of love and devotion to God.

NOTES

1. R. C. Zaehner, *The Bhagavad-Gita with a Commentary Based on the Original Sources* (London: Oxford University Press, 1969), p. 77. Since all my citations from the Gita are taken from Zaehner's translation, the remaining citations will simply be indicated by chapter and verse. In a few cases (5:21 and 11:54), Zaehner's translation has been slightly altered in consideration of the original text and after comparison with other translations.

2. Bede Griffiths, *River of Compassion: A Christian Commentary on the Bhagavad Gita*, p. 319.

3. J. P. de Caussade, *Abandonment to Divine Providence*, trans. by John Beevers (New York, 1975).

4. Ibid., in Introduction, p. 7.

5. Caussade, *Abandonment to Divine Providence*, p. 68.

6. Ibid., p. 75.

7. Ibid.

8. Ibid., p. 61.

9. Ibid., p. 58.

10. Ibid., p. 73.

11. Ibid., p. 79.

12. Ibid., p. 72.

13. Ibid., pp. 46–47.

14. Ibid., p. 37.

15. Ibid., p. 24.

16. Ibid., p. 114.

17. Zaehner, *The Bhagavad-Gita*, p. 8.

18. See Thomas M. King, S.J., "Teilhard, Evil and Providence," in *Teilhard Studies* 21 (Spring/Summer, 1989). At times, the panentheism of Christian writers such as Teilhard comes very near the "qualified nondualism" of Hindu thinkers such as Ramanuja. Traditionally, however, the Christian doctrine of creation forces a recognition of the ontological distinction between the uncreated and eternal being of God and the created and dependent mode of being enjoyed by created reality. It would seem that a strict pantheism would not be possible for Christians who accept the uncreated/created distinction. However, panentheism, which recognizes God's omnipresence in creatures (since God is the source of their being and the power that sustains them), is perfectly acceptable for Christians. On the level of poetic expression, the panentheism of Hindus such as Ramanuja seems identical to the panentheism of Christian mysticism. The difference would be found in the underlying metaphysical models of the two traditions. Hinduism tends toward an emanationist metaphysical model while Christianity tends toward a creationist model. On the level of experience, the two traditions appear very close to each other. It is in the subsequent metaphysical reflections that differences tend to appear.

19. Caussade, *Abandonment*, pp. 25–26.

20. It is worth noting that Zaehner sees a similarity between bhakti and the Christian love characterized by the "holy indifference" (*sainte indifférence*) of St. Francis de Sales. Caussade certainly stands in this Salesian tradition, though he prefers the term *abandonment* over *indifference*. See Zaehner, p. 285.

Multireligious Experience and the Study of Mysticism

Judson B. Trapnell

Judson B. Trapnell, like Teasdale, wrote his Ph.D. dissertation (1993) on Father Bede, entitled "Bede Griffiths' Theory of Religious Symbol and Practice of Dialogue: Toward Interreligious Understanding." He develops the theme that cultural change is dynamically related to individual transformation. Trapnell sees Father Bede as resembling Augustine and other key figures in the history of cultures who, having lost confidence in the values with which they were brought up, sought to transform the cultural vision through their own life processes. He notes that the result of this quest is that such figures become incarnate paradigms of the cultural transformation, of the passage to a new age. The present essay is one of the fruits of this line of research, exploring the question of whether there is a mystical common ground from which those of diverse traditions can constructively relate themselves to their colleagues in other traditions. Trapnell feels that individuals who in their own lives enter another culture from the mystical common ground can become agents of transformation for both cultures.

J n one of his last articles Father Bede Griffiths expressed his vision of possibilities for interreligious dialogue as follows:

> We are in a position now to be open to all the religious traditions of the world, being aware of their limitations but also, most importantly, realising their unity in the depth-dimension which underlies them all; and that, of course, is the mystical dimension.[1]

This vision of the dialogue among religions arose both from Griffiths' examination of the mystical texts of numerous traditions and from his own experience in meditation—both of which, in turn, were affected by his life among different cultures and religions in India. This dual method enabled him to integrate a rational discernment of differences and an intuitive recognition of convergence, balancing analysis, and synthesis. Ever careful to distinguish his vision from a facile syncretism that neglects or underestimates the importance of differences among the religions, Griffiths once described the different levels of the cross-cultural study of religions in this way:

> I often use the illustration of the fingers and the palm of the hand. Buddhism, Hinduism, Islam, Judaism, and Christianity are all separate in one sense. But as you move toward the source in any tradition, the interrelatedness begins to grow. As one might say, we meet in the cave of the heart. When we arrive in the center, we realize the underlying unity behind the traditions. But I'm suspicious of attempts to mix them on the outer level.[2]

In distinguishing different levels of comparison, Griffiths believed that he charted a practicable course for the Christian community to follow in its dialogue with other traditions.

Appealing as Griffiths' vision of interreligious dialogue might be for some, his position would raise significant objections from a number of contemporary philosophers of religion. Steven Katz, for example, has strongly criticized any attempts to establish common elements or common ground in the cross-cultural study of mysticism. Such attempts, he argues, overlook or inadequately account for the irreducibly conditioned and private character of all mystical experience.[3] Because mystical experience, like all experience, is shaped by preexisting mental constructs and is never free of all such conditioning, Katz asserts that the idea of a "pure" or "unmediated" experience as the common ground for all mystical traditions is invalid. Further, he contends that such experiences do not provide evidence for the verification of truth claims about the relationship among the various religions because they are not subject to the accepted modern criterion of objectivity, i.e., intersubjective or public demonstrability.[4]

Katz is not alone in raising philosophical objections to attempts to articulate common ground for the religions on the basis of mystical experience that supposedly transcends all cultural and religious conditioning.[5] As one who upholds the mediated or "constructed" character of mystical experience, Katz distances himself from the so-called perennialists who claim that there is a unity underlying the various religions that is transcendent, beyond doctrines and symbols and who believe that this truth can only be verified finally through mystical experience.[6] Katz responds that such experiences are the fulfillment of beliefs and expectations that have conditioned and thereby biased the experiencer and so do not constitute innocent, unbiased realizations of an independent truth. At stake in the constructivist/perennialist debate is the validity of using mysticism as a significant and reliable rubric under which to conduct interreligious dialogue. If Katz is correct in his critique of past tendencies in the cross-cultural study of mysticism, then statements such as Griffiths' above may be misleading for the task of dialogue and even unintelligible for his contemporary audience. There is a conflict of viewpoints here, the exploration of which reveals much about one's assumptions of how and what human beings may know.

Donald Evans, for instance, challenges Katz directly on the application of strict constructivist principles to mystical experience:

> [U]nlike Katz, I think that mystics may be able to settle among themselves what academics cannot. Perhaps only by becoming a mystic can one come to verify the claim that pure consciousness is possible. And perhaps a mystic can then tell, intuitively, whether someone is in the same state. Katz, as an academic, is not in a position to dictate what mystics can or cannot do.[7]

The present article follows up on Evans' suggestion that mystics may know "intuitively" what academics cannot prove rationally regarding unmediated mystical experience ("pure consciousness"), and explores more explicitly the claim made by some mystics that such an experience represents common ground for dialogue among the various religions.[8]

Among mystics, the most intriguing examples to investigate regarding the related possibilities of unmediated experience and the intuitive knowledge of interreligious truths are those who have consciously exposed themselves to more than one religious symbol system, opening themselves to what Raimundo Panikkar has called "multireligious experience." In indirect reference to his own life, Panikkar describes the experience of the explorer of different religious traditions in this way:

> He starts by making a real, heartfelt, unselfish effort—a bold and hazardous one—to understand the belief, the world, the archetypes, the culture, the mythical and conceptual background, the emotional and historical associations of his fellows from the inside. In short, he attempts an existential incarnation of himself into another world—which obviously involves prayer, initiation, study and worship. He does this not by way of trial but rather with a spirit of faith in a truth that transcends us and a goodness that upholds us when we truly love our neighbor. . . .[9]

The number of such explorers among Christians from Western countries has increased in recent decades as churches have assumed increasingly open attitudes toward other religions. A thorough study of the impact of multireligious experience upon the cross-cultural analysis of mystical experience would take into account the lives and writings of Mateo Ricci in China (d. 1610), Roberto de Nobili in India (d. 1656), and Charles de Foucauld in North Africa (d. 1916). Contemporary examples to be studied would include William Johnston and Hugo Enomiya Lassale in Japan, and Jules Monchanin, Henri Le Saux (Abhishiktananda), and Bede Griffiths in India.

This article draws upon the multireligious experience of Bede Griffiths to discuss the potential implications of such experience for the cross-cultural study of mystical experience. To narrow the vast field of inquiry opened through a philosophical study of mysticism, the following questions will be addressed: How did Griffiths' understanding of other religious traditions evolve in relation to his own maturing multireligious and mystical experience? What were Griffiths' own conclusions regarding the role of mediating factors in such experience and the question of whether such factors can ever be transcended to allow intuition of a common mystical ground for the many religions? What are the implications of multireligious experiences like Griffiths' for the cross-cultural study of mysticism, especially regarding the strict constructivist model articulated by contemporaries such as Katz?

At the outset, three key terms must be defined: *mediation, intuition,* and *mystical experience.* As a psychological dynamic, *mediation* has been defined as "the interposition of one or more ideas or acts between an initial stimulus or idea and a given end result whose genesis is under investigation."[10] The result of such an investigation is thus an indirect or mediate rather than immediate knowledge of an event or object, given the instrumental role that ideas that are already in the mind play.[11] In modern philosophical works *intuition* is understood as an "immediate apprehension of an object by the mind without the intervention of the reasoning process."[12] The term thus signifies a kind of knowing that happens in the knower through non-inferential means, that is, not through relating perceptions and concepts, but through what Aquinas called a "connaturality" between the knower and its object.[13] Finally, a *mystical experience* is a conscious encounter with what is felt as a sacred or divine reality, an encounter that exceeds the limits of human comprehension.[14] While all experience frustrates full description through concepts and language, mystical experience by definition discloses a depth and breadth of reality that is incommensurate with human capacities, an unknowability that goes beyond that of human and natural mysteries.

While carefully crafted, such definitions nevertheless reveal my own sympathy toward the possibilities of immediate knowledge and intuitive experience, mystical experiences being the most bewildering and thus most humbling examples for a scholar to examine with concepts and language.

BEDE GRIFFITHS' MULTIRELIGIOUS EXPERIENCE

The details of Griffiths' life both before and after his emigration to India in 1955 as a forty-eight year-old Benedictine priest have been published in both autobiographical and biographical forms.[15] A brief description of the multireligious character of his experience since 1955, however, will contextualize his own conclusions regarding the constructed nature of mystical experience and the relationship among the religions.

A significant degree of empathy with and openness to Indian cultures and religions characterizes Griffiths' early writings from his new country, attitudes nurtured even before his departure from England by his reading of scriptures like the Bhagavad Gita, by his meeting of Westerners who had begun the study of yoga, and by his own early, formative experience of a divine presence in nature and in the soul. The impact of his first years of encountering the Indian "sense of the sacred" through village life and the "contemplative dimension of existence" through Hindu symbology forced Griffiths, in the words of Henri de Lubac to Jules Monchanin, "to rethink everything in terms of theology, and to rethink theology in terms of mysticism."[16]

After an unsuccessful attempt to begin a monastic foundation along traditional Benedictine lines in Bangalore, Griffiths joined a Cistercian priest from Belgium, Francis Mahieu, to form Kurishumala Ashram in 1958, a monastic community structured after an Indian spiritual model. While at Kurishumala Griffiths received initiation into sannyasa, an Indian tradition of renunciation that symbolizes a complete detachment from the world of appearances. Taking on a new Sanskrit name and wearing the orange kavi robes, the sannyasin represents that which transcends all religious symbols and customs even while participating freely, if desired, in religious observances. Griffiths also deepened his study of Indian scriptures and philosophy, finding both an affinity and an incompatibility with Vedantins such as Sankara, Ramanuja, and Madhva as well as with the more devotional schools within Hinduism. The two contemporaries most influential upon Griffiths' life and thought were Mohandas Gandhi and Aurobindo Ghose. On the impact of the latter upon his thinking, Griffiths said, "For many years I studied his writings—they have a profound influence. I found him nearer to the Christian idea than any other Hindu writer, and so his doctrine became almost a part of my own thinking."[17]

With increasing depths of personal commitment, Griffiths engaged in interreligious dialogue through meetings and discussions with other Christians, which sometimes included representatives of other religions. Simultaneously, a dialogue took place within him between what he characterized as the two "halves" of his soul, the rational (associated with Western culture and Christianity) and the intuitive (corresponding to Indian culture and Hinduism).[18] In order to foster both dimensions of dialogue, external and internal, Griffiths studied yoga at Kurishumala Ashram, both as a tradition of spiritual practice and as a philosophy. He became especially interested in kundalini yoga, with its holistic understanding of and attending to the physical and psychological, as well as the spiritual dimensions of the person. It is apparent from Griffiths' later writings how thoroughly he assimilated the language and techniques of this Indian system into his own spiritual practice, especially his use of a Christian form of meditation—the Jesus Prayer—that he began in 1940.[19]

After ten years at Kurishumala Ashram, in 1968 Griffiths accepted the call to revive and become the spiritual guide of the Christian ashram begun by Fathers Monchanin and Le Saux in 1950. Griffiths took the opportunity to shape the life of Saccidananda Ashram—or Shantivanam as it is now more frequently known—more fully along the lines of an Indian ashram, by setting the times of individual meditation rather than corporate liturgy as the foundation of the community's practice. He also engaged the ashram in a fuller assimilation of Indian religious traditions into its Catholic worship, incorporating Sanskrit chanting and readings from non-Christian scriptures into each meeting for prayer. Once approved by the bishop, an Indian rite of the Mass was used at Shantivanam, one that included some of the symbols and gestures associated with the Hindu *puja*. Even when traveling abroad, it was this type of worship that Griffiths preferred because of its integration of what he calls the primordial or cosmic revelation with the Judaeo-Christian. To the end of his life, Griffiths often began his public lectures with a Sanskrit chant due to its powerful symbolic capacity to evoke interior silence.

While remaining a devout Catholic monk and priest throughout his life, Griffiths undertook the exposure to and immersion in another religious tradition characteristic of multireligious experience. As will be seen, this experience opened him simultaneously to the spiritual riches of his own tradition and to the profound value of non-Christian religions. While glimpsing both the diversity and the unity of the numerous religions through such experience, he remained to the end a staunch critic of a facile syncretism and an energetic upholder of the unique contribution that each religion—including Christianity—can make to the transformation of the individual and the world as a whole.[20]

MULTIRELIGIOUS EXPERIENCE, MYSTICAL LIFE, AND VIEW OF NON-CHRISTIAN RELIGIONS

In the context of discussing both the constructed nature of mystical experience and the verification of interreligious truths, two questions are raised by Griffiths' multireligious experience. First, what were the effects of this deepening multireligious experience upon Griffiths' own mystical life, especially upon his understanding and experience of God as a Reality or Mystery that was revealed through his meditation? Second, what was the relationship between his maturing mystical experience and his ongoing evaluation of non-Christian religions?

In Indian culture and religions Griffiths found reflected the other, intuitive "half" of his soul, a part of himself that had been relatively under-nourished within Western culture and by Western Christianity.[21] He was particularly impressed by the practical understanding of the spiritual life preserved for millenia in India, including techniques, long neglected in the West, for stilling the mind and body for meditation. In contrast, the West had emphasized refinements of theology, generating subtle and precise theoretical understandings of the divine nature and its relationship to creation, from which he believed Indian thought could benefit.[22] Especially with the move to Shantivanam and the increased attention to meditation and to diverse symbolizations of God, Griffiths' writings disclose the impact of deepening mystical experience, the direct encounter of what he called the Reality or the Mystery toward which the symbols of all religions point.[23] A further significant transition in his spiritual growth occurred as an effect of the stroke he suffered at his ashram in 1990. Crowning his gradual opening to the intuitive side of himself through Indian culture and spirituality, "a psychological breakthrough to the feminine" took place, radically rebalancing his psyche and deepening his intimacy with the divine mystery as an interpersonal communion in love.[24] Thus, through his multireligious experience, Griffiths came to a fuller experiential knowledge of the mystery that Christianity symbolizes as the Trinity.

A chronological reading of Griffiths' writings reveals a close relationship between the stages of development in his mystical life and his positions on the status of non-Christian religions.[25] At the time of his emigration to India, Griffiths endorsed what has come to be known as the "fulfillment theory," according to which the numerous non-Christian traditions are understood as providential means through which God has prepared humankind for the revelation of Jesus Christ, a revelation that in turn fulfills all other religions.[26] While some rethinking of this position appears to have been prompted by his first years of encountering the religions of India, there is a particularly strong correspondence after his move to Shantivanam between his deepening insights about the divine mystery experienced in meditation and his emboldened claims about "the one spirit of all religion."[27] This correspondence is clearly apparent in passages like the following:

> In meditation I can become aware of the ground of my being. . . . I can get beyond all these outer forms of things in time and space and discover the Ground from which they spring. I can know the Father, the Origin, the source, beyond being and not-being, the One "without second". . . .
>
> In each tradition the one divine Reality, the one eternal Truth, is present, but it is hidden under symbols. . . . Always the divine Mystery is hidden under a veil, but each revelation (or "unveiling") unveils some aspect of the one Truth, or, if you like, the veil becomes thinner at a certain point. . . .
>
> It is not by word or thought but by meditation on the Mystery that we can pierce the veil. This is where all human reason fails. All these words, Brahman, Nirvana, Allah, Yahweh, Christ, are meaningless to those who cannot get beyond their reason and allow the divine Mystery to shine through its symbol. . . .
>
> It is this "mystery of Christ" which lies at the heart of the gospels and of all the evolution of Christianity. . . . And this Mystery when known in its ultimate ground is one with the mystery of Brahman, Nirvana, Tao, Yahweh, Allah. It is the one Truth, the one Word. . . .[28]

Thus around the time of this move to Shantivanam, one may note in his writings on other religions a shift from a fulfillment theory to one of "complementarity."[29] According to Griffiths, this latter theory presents each religion as revealing a unique aspect of the one Truth, aspects that when compared to one another are not contradictory but complementary, like the different colors within white light.[30] Beneath this level of understanding of the uniqueness of each tradition, however, one may discover at "the deepest level" a "fundamental unity" or point of convergence of the various religions.[31] It is significant that he uses a specifically mystical metaphor from the Upanishads to portray at what level of human experience such a convergence may be recognized—"the cave of the heart."[32]

THE MYSTICAL REALIZATION OF THE FUNDAMENTAL UNITY OF RELIGIONS

Two related consequences of Griffiths' multireligious experience have been identified: first, the deepening of his mystical life through opening to his feminine, intuitive side, and second, his discovery of a fundamental unity or convergence underlying the various religions. The constructivist critique of mystical experience raises the important question, however, of just what exactly is the relationship between these two consequences. Did Griffiths innocently realize the unity of religions through a deepening mystical sensitivity? Or, had he undergone a subtle reconditioning in India, such that his mystical praxis led to the fulfillment of different expectations than those he brought with him? To address this issue of the source of Griffiths' interreligious claims would demand an in-depth treatment of his intellectual and spiritual journey, and even then a final resolution would probably be elusive. However, for discussing the relationship between mystical experience and interreligious truths, Griffiths' own statements about the constructed nature of mystical experience are highly illuminating.

In an article written almost ten years after the move to Shantivanam, Griffiths speaks directly to the issue of the mediated nature of mystical experience. His discussion rests upon a distinction between "two elements in mystical experience," one that is unconditioned and another that is conditioned: "Though the object of mystical experience is the unconditioned and though the mystical experience itself is ineffable, yet the divine reality (the unconditioned) is experienced in a conditioned being."[33] Griffiths makes clear that the mystic's conditioning through culture and language affects not only the report of the experience, but also the experience itself, and that therefore one cannot claim that the mystical experiences found in the various traditions are the same—a point with which Katz strongly agrees.[34] What can be claimed to be one in all such experiences is the Reality encountered, the unconditioned:

> The mystical experience . . . in each religion is an experience of God (the unconditioned) in the Spirit, that is, beyond image and thought, but in each religion the experience is conditioned by the images and thought patterns through which the experience is reached and necessarily seeks expression through those same images and thought patterns.[35]

According to Griffiths, it is "the unconditioned" that each mystic encounters in "the cave of the heart," and that therefore constitutes the Reality toward which the various traditions point through their symbols and in which they converge. Griffiths' position is thus similar to what Michael Stoeber has called a "moderate constructivism," in which expectations shape but do not limit mystical experience, and in which spiritual knowledge is accumulated gradually as a result of "a dynamic interchange between the Real and the mystic," one that is informed by concepts in the mind.[36]

The philosopher might ask the mystic, such as Griffiths, how do you *know* that there is a common "unconditioned" element in all mystical experiences that is the point upon which all religions converge? Griffiths responds in at least two different ways, one drawing upon cross-cultural analysis and the other appealing to a traditional anthropology that is in turn based upon Christian scripture and theological tradition, and most fundamentally, upon an intuitive experience.

Griffiths states his qualified agreement with the constructivist view of mystical experience in a letter as follows:

> I would agree with Steven Katz that mystical experience is always conditioned by the individual's subjectivity and also by the cultural environment (Hindu, Buddhist, etc.). But I believe that it also transcends such conditioning and this is shown in the extraordinary agreement among Hindu, Buddhist, Muslim, and Christian mystics as to the nature of ultimate reality and how it is to be known.[37]

In his 1990 text, *A New Vision of Reality: Western Science, Eastern Mysticism and Christian Faith*, Griffiths draws specifically from Hindu scriptures, mostly the Upanishads and the Bhagavad Gita, as well as Sankara, Mahayana Buddhist philosopher Nagarjuna, and Muslim seer Ibn al Arabi to document this "extraordinary agreement." Griffiths concludes that through interpreting the "original" mystical experiences at the foundation of their traditions "in the light of rational, conceptual thought," these philosophers have each come to recognize and describe a Reality beyond all images and concepts.[38] While the languages used to describe this Reality as well as the specific means for experiencing it may be quite diverse (the conditioning element), Griffiths argues that reasoned inquiry will also disclose close parallels at these linguistic and practical levels as well.[39]

Griffiths' claim for an unconditioned element within all mystical experience rests not only upon a reasoned comparison of mystic philosophers but also upon an anthropology derived from St. Paul, for which he found parallels in other philosophical and religious traditions. According to Griffiths, in addition to the aspects of the individual that are conditioned by one's education and culture (body—*soma*, and soul or mind—*psyche*), there is a dimension of the human being that is not touched by such factors, the spirit or *pneuma* "which transcends both the mind and the senses and is in contact with the transcendent reality itself."[40] Through his comparative studies Griffiths finds analogous terms for spirit in Indian philosophy (*atman*, *buddhi*). It is this tridimensionality of the individual that allows Griffiths to state paradoxically that mystical experience is both unconditioned and conditioned, or unmediated and mediated. Mystical experience is thus defined as an opening or transparency of the psychophysiological organism to the point of the spirit, a self-transcendence where one is in "communion with the universal spirit" or "spirit of God."[41]

Griffiths' multireligious exploration and use of a Pauline anthropology support further conclusions about the type of knowing that may occur in mystical experience. In his Christian commentary on the Bhagavad Gita, Griffiths draws a distinction between faith and wisdom.[42] Faith is the reflection of the divine light or truth in the rational mind and so is a degree of knowledge dependent upon concepts, images, and language; in short, faith is a culture-specific way of knowing the truth. Wisdom, on the other hand, is reached "when we rise . . . above all these images and concepts and awaken to truth itself."[43] This deeper knowledge is a knowing in the spirit, beyond body and mind, beyond concepts, images, and language, beyond culture, and is strikingly similar to what Hindus mean by *jñana* and Buddhists by *prajña*. Griffiths labels this type of knowledge intuitive, as distinguished from rational:

> [T]here is a mode of experience which transcends both body and soul, an experience of the Spirit, which is not merely rational and so dependent on the senses, but intuitive—a direct insight which comes not from the soul and its faculties but from the Spirit himself, the absolute, which is present in the ground of the soul of everyman and reveals itself to those who seek him.[44]

For Griffiths, knowledge of the fundamental unity of religions in their convergence upon the unconditioned Spirit is thus not just a conclusion from cross-cultural studies; it is a mystical intuition born of his multireligious experience.[45]

Can the "universal wisdom" intuited through mystical experience be expressed at all, potentially confirming its cross-cultural character? Griffiths believed that there is a "perennial philosophy" founded in this knowledge of truth in the spirit and revealed diversely in the great scriptures of the various religions.[46] Central to this philosophy is the principle of the transcendent unity of religions. To discern such a universal wisdom demands both an openness to the "transcendent truth" and "a certain detachment from our own culture and religion."[47] For Griffiths, multireligious experience has nurtured both mystical openness and cultural/religious detachment through self-transcendence—an awareness of the union of human spirit and divine Spirit that is beyond all conditioning, as well as an appreciation of how diversely the "transcendent truth" has been expressed in various cultural and religious contexts.

Griffiths was equally clear, however, that any articulation of the wisdom that is reached in the "cave of the heart" and that is common to all traditions can only be an approximation, an attempt to capture in words a mystery that goes beyond all words.[48] Words can point one in the direction of, but cannot capture the fullness of, what is known by the mystic in the spirit. The same principle may be applied to the terms of his anthropology. Body-mind-spirit is simply a metaphor for the mystery of the human person. It can be used to point to and illuminate experience but must itself be recognized as a limited vehicle of understanding used by a particular culture, though one that has resonances within other cultural systems.

—ᴟᴟ—

POSSIBLE CONSTRUCTIVIST OBJECTIONS TO GRIFFITHS' INTERPRETATION

How would a strict constructivist interpret what is going on in the multireligious experience out of which emerge Griffiths' conclusions about the fundamental unity of religions? Katz specifically discusses the claim, at least implicit in Griffiths' writings, that spiritual ascesis, including the practice of yoga, enables one to transcend one's conditioning. (Note that Griffiths should not be included among those perennial philosophers criticized by Katz for believing that such self-transcendence brings about a "universal common mystical experience" or "pure consciousness *per se* achieved by these various, common mystical practices"[49]) Katz writes: "Properly understood, yoga . . . is *not* an *un*conditioning or *de*conditioning of consciousness, but rather it is a *re*conditioning of consciousness, i.e., a substituting of one form of conditioned and/or contextual consciousness for another."[50] In other words, the practical side of Griffiths' multireligious experience, e.g., his experience of transcendence through the Jesus Prayer, yogic disciplines, and a variety of cultural/religious symbols, does not bring the openness and detachment he claims but rather cultivates a different set of expectations that in turn condition his spiritual experiences. Such expectations could have been internalized from Hinduism and from the writings of other Christian sannyasins with similar multireligious experience, such as Abhishiktananda.

According to a strict constructivist critique, Griffiths also brings changing expectations to the theoretical side of his multireligious experience, e.g., his study of different scriptures and mystical philosophers. Rather than finding confirmation for a fulfillment theory of religions as he did in England, Griffiths later recognizes a relationship among the religions closer to that found among the Hindus around him and the perennial philosophers he has studied. Thus Katz would be likely to reject Griffiths' claim that strong agreement exists between the mystical philosophies of different religions as evidence for their fundamental unity. For Katz, not only do the differences among reported experiences integral to such philosophies outbalance the similarities, but there is no legitimate way to establish that such similarities reflect common experiential rather than doctrinal elements.[51]

How would a strict constructivist handle the other primary way in which Griffiths supports the possibility of an unconditioned or unmediated element in mystical experience, the existence in the human of a spirit that both transcends body and mind and is in touch with or open to the divine Reality or Spirit? While Katz merely assumes that the concept of unmediated experience is self-contradictory,[52] others have attempted to explain why this is so. John Hick, for example, has argued that all experiences, including "unitive intuitions of ultimate reality," are in some way shaped by culturally instilled concepts; all experience is "experiencing-as."[53] Ian Barbour, making an even stronger claim for the constructed nature of all experience, describes the experiential process as "interpreting-as."[54] Further, Jerry Gill argues that context and relationship are constitutive of all human experience, including the mystical.[55] In other words, according to these constructivists, if something like a spirit exists in the human, it is in such inseparable relation to the body and mind as not to escape their limiting or conditioning effects. If such a spirit is identifiable as belonging to a particular individual, then it is limited, conditioned, and therefore must serve as a mediating factor in any experience of a reality that is by definition unlimited and unconditioned. In short, it is fallacious, according to these philosophers, to claim that there is something unconditioned or unlimited in the individual.

Supporting the theory that all human experience is mediated is the need to render mystical experience continuous with ordinary experience.[56] A variety of motivations contribute to this felt need for continuity: to retrieve mystical experience from its otherworldly status as accessible only to the few; to make such experiences subject to the same principles of verifiability that apply to other ways of knowing; and to ground and control the frequent focus of interreligious dialogue upon such experiences. In addition to the quality of mediatedness, intentionality is often cited as another characteristic of all human experience, including the mystical. That is, all experience intends an object.[57] Commenting on phenomenologists such as Brentano and Husserl, Gill points out that this intentional quality of all experience further supports the constructivist view:

> Our consciousness is always consciousness *of* some concrete aspect of the world, of some particular aspect whose reality for us is constituted by our intentional activity in relation to it. This intentionality is clearly a mediational factor which undercuts the possibility of unmediated experi-

ence. The vectorial character of consciousness gives it thrust or flow that provides the ever-present and necessary interpretive framework within which all experience is possible and understood.[58]

Thus, when a mystic says that she or he experiences God, the grammatical intentionality must be seen as indicative of a similar structure in the experience itself, with the condition that the intended object is to some degree shaped by the context of the experiencer.[59]

If all experience is interpreted, mediated, and intentional, then either the human spirit does not exist in a nondual relation to the divine Spirit as Griffiths has claimed, but rather is an inseparable part of the mediating subject, or the type of mystical intuitions that he and other mystics have described are not experiences in the technical sense, but are a deep communion of spirit with Spirit beyond the dynamics in consciousness usually identified as experience. Suggestive here is Louis Dupré's interpretation of Christian mystical union as a "unitive state of being" entailing a radical change in consciousness rather than an experience *per se*.[60] Intellectual visions as described by sixteenth-century Spanish mystics, for example, seem to contradict the conventional understanding of how knowledge is gained by a subject encountering an object. "Where knower and known are substantially united, that union no longer allows for subject-object oppositions such as determine ordinary epistemic processes. The mind functions here in a different mode of being-with reality, rather than of reflecting upon it."[61]

For Stephen Bernhardt, neither the theory that all experiences are intentional (such a theory is reductionistic, he says), nor the caveat that mystical experiences are not really experiences at all is satisfactory for disclosing what the mystic undergoes. He thus proposes that the notion of experience be expanded to include "all events had by conscious beings," consciousness itself eluding any "single, nontrivial definition" including intentionality.[62] Like Dupré, Bernhardt implies that consciousness itself may be transformed into nonordinary states, including one in which a clear distinction between subject and object is not found. In order to describe a nonintentional state of consciousness, however, the mystic often must rely upon expressions that grammatically suggest intentionality, e.g., "I experienced God."[63] He thus disagrees with phenomenologists and some constructivists who claim that intentional grammar necessarily reveals an intentional structure in experience. Bernhardt concludes:

> What the mystic needs is a language for experience which carries no dualistic implications. Much of their language may be seen . . . as an attempt to develop or push toward such syntax. Expressions like "merges with," "is engulfed by," "like a drop becoming the ocean," and so on, may be thus construed.[64]

It is interesting to note that Griffiths felt the grammatical problem of dualistic language to describe mystical experiences of nonduality, and was "pushed toward" a solution by means of his multireligious experience, especially his study and experience of what Hindus mean by advaita.

The strict constructivist would thus reject Griffiths' methods for establishing the fundamental unity of religions, both the cross-cultural comparison of mystical philosophies and the translation of intuitive insights through the spirit into a universal wisdom—methods that would identify Griffiths as a perennialist for most philosophers, although he upholds the constructed nature of mystical experience to a significant degree.[65] The epistemological principles on each side that underlie this disagreement seem irreconcilable; there is a fundamental conflict in viewpoints about how and what human beings may be said to know. Is mystical knowledge a meaningful concept or not? Some of the responses to Katz's articles, such as Bernhardt's and Michael Stoeber's mentioned above, seek to resolve this impasse between strict constructivist and perennialist epistemologies by arguing in part that one's frame of reference for epistemological issues may change as consciousness is transformed through spiritual practice and divine grace. Short of undergoing such transformation oneself, what seems necessary in order to see alternative solutions is to listen openly as well as critically to what mystics such as Griffiths have to say, while understanding that their views spring from a depth of multireligious experience that few have had and that therefore may stretch one's standards of intelligibility. This article will conclude with one such attempt.

ANOTHER WAY OF KNOWING

· It is through Griffiths' multireligious exploration of the mystery of non-duality that he suggests a resolution to the impasse reached in comparing strict constructivist and perennialist interpretations of mystical intuitions of the fundamental unity of religions. For the strict constructivist, no experiential evidence nor agreement among mystical texts can substantiate the claim that the various religions share a mystical ground. The argument supporting this position is clear: Due to the conditioned, mediated, intentional, and private nature of mystical experience, no verification of claims from such experience, such as the unity of religions, is possible. Religious and mystical pluralism is irreducible. In contrast, the perennialist argues that the fundamental unity of the religions is self-evident through intuitive, immediate experience. Pluralism is the conclusion of the mind that limits itself to only a narrow range of experience. Through a life of interreligious and intercultural dialogue, Griffiths sought to resolve this epistemological impasse both theoretically and experientially.

While Griffiths often emphasized what the West has to learn from the East, including an intuitive way of experiencing, the true fruit of his multireligious exploration was the conviction that a mutual discovery and even a "marriage" must take place between East and West—an interrelationship in which each cultural group would learn from and complement the other. In his writing as in his life he sought to define and relate the characteristics of this complementary relationship, e.g., rational and intuitive, masculine and feminine, individualistic and nondual. He sought to affirm the value of each point of view but also to describe its limitations. Thus he argued that the material results of the Western emphasis upon the rational mind are valuable but also have fostered an overemphasis upon the individual and the reality of this world. The spiritual gifts received through the East's emphasis upon the intuitive mind are also of great value but are easily misinterpreted to support a denial of the value of the individual and of this world. In the spiritual realm as well, Western religions have followed paths that affirm the ultimate existence of the individual, while Eastern spiritualities have tended to portray the ultimate insignificance of the individual in relation to ultimate reality. Griffiths' goal was to experience and articulate the integration of these cultural, religious, and spiritual tendencies. The key symbol for this integration, as it dawned within him in his later years, is nonduality.

Informed by his theological and mystical exploration of the Christian Trinity, Griffiths interpreted the relationship between the individual and God as nondual, as "not-one" and "not-two," as neither a plurality nor a simple unity. Just as the divine nature is love, as symbolized by the Christian Trinity of three persons in communion, so also the soul's relationship to God is a loving communion in which each partner is both one with and distinct from the other.[66] Any doctrine or spiritual path that emphasizes either unity or plurality is incomplete. From his study of the scriptures of various Eastern and Western traditions, Griffiths eventually concluded that, while each religion has dualistic elements within it that promote a radical distinction between the soul and ultimate reality, "Every religion goes beyond dualism through its mystical tradition."[67] Significant for the constructivist/perennialist debate on the nature of mystical experience is Griffiths' additional conclusion that "Meditation is the only way to go beyond dualism. As long as you think rationally you will have a dualistic attitude. But when you stop the mind, you discover the unifying principle behind everything."[68] Griffiths also concluded that there are different degrees of realization of nonduality, including one in which all distinctions are lost in the oneness of the ultimate reality. He argued, however, that this monistic viewpoint is not the final truth. In many traditions as well as in Christianity he found support for his own conviction and experience that ultimately all distinctions exist in relationship within the divine mystery. Again, it was primarily Griffiths' own meditative path as informed by religious scriptures and mystical philosophies that led him to this deeper realization of nonduality as "unity in relationship."[69]

Griffiths thus would not be surprised that the empiricist philosopher who takes reason as the only arbiter of truth would be unable to justify claims made from an entirely different style of thinking. Meditation for him constitutes the most complete expression of a different capacity of the mind, one approximated by various other types of nonrational ways of knowing, such as sensation, emotion, and poetic imagination.[70] While reason distinguishes coexisting elements, intuition grasps wholeness or existence itself.[71] Intuitive knowledge, of which meditation is the purest form, is based in a different style of mind and thus has different criteria for verification. While Griffiths did not work out what these criteria for intuitive and mystical knowledge might be, he was deeply interested in those who attempted such clarification.[72] Thus Griffiths' claim concerning the fundamental unity of religions points not only to a sacred mystery beyond images and concepts, but perhaps more importantly to a common way of intuitive or mystical knowing that is very different from that achieved by what he and others call dualistic thinking, i.e., a subject knowing an object.[73]

Griffiths found exponents of intuitive knowing in the West, such as William Wordsworth, Samuel Taylor Coleridge, and Jacques and Raissa Maritain. However, his experience of the nondualistic mind did not flower fully until he encountered India and Hinduism. This consequence of his multireligious experience has important implications for Western philosophy and for East-West studies in general. One important implication of Griffiths' multireligious experience for the cross-cultural study of mysticism can be viewed as an invitation to others to pursue such a path. Griffiths' example of immersing himself in different cultures and religions, each with their own unique approaches to knowledge, invites the Western philosopher to open to ways of knowing other than reasoned inquiry in order to explore what Griffiths discovered as the other half of the soul. Only after having appropriated the experience of "intuitive knowing" through sensory, aesthetic, and especially meditative modes will the philosopher, like Sankara, Nagarjuna, and Ibn al Arabi in the past, be qualified to analyze such experience through reason. Griffiths, then, invites us to mystery, to unknowing, to "being-with reality" (Dupré), with the promise that what has appeared before as irreducible diversity will gradually appear as a plurality within a deeper unity.

A second implication thus arises from Griffiths' own mystical intuitions and cross-cultural study as a thesis to be tested. On the basis of his own realization of nonduality through multireligious experience, Griffiths believed that he could recognize in many traditions a similar understanding of plurality within unity at their mystical sources. Regarding Hinduism for example, he concurred with those who, like Sara Grant and Richard De Smet, have argued that Sankara has been misinterpreted. Rather than meaning that this world, the individual, and the personal God are purely illusory, Sankara actually stated the more subtle truth that apart from

Brahman, from God, all diversity is unreal. Griffiths believed that he found similar principles of plurality in unity in other Indian schools of philosophy such as Saiva Siddhanta and Kashmir Saivism, and in the teachings of Sri Aurobindo. One of Griffiths' final projects, entitled *Universal Wisdom: A Journey Through the Sacred Wisdom of the World,* was an attempt to point to a direction for future research into his thesis that each tradition has reached toward a similar mystical understanding of nonduality, however diversely symbolized.

A third implication of Griffiths' multireligious experience follows as another thesis, this one already being explored by other so-called dialogue theologians. This thesis—that for him appears to have been confirmed by his own intuitive experience—presents the various religions as not only unique and therefore plural, but also as in intricate relationship to one another within a greater wholeness.[74] Robley Whitson and Paul Knitter have described a similar thesis as "unitive pluralism."[75] Developing the narrower claim of a transcendent unity for the religions, Griffiths believed that while that which unites the diverse traditions is indeed a mystery— the divine mystery—the diverse elements are not merely in a plural but in an interdependent relation to one another. As a model for this unitive pluralism, or what he preferred to call unity in relationship, Griffiths uses the Platonic theory of ideas, especially as adapted by Christian theologians such as Maximus the Confessor, in which all diversity is said to exist in God, like ideas in the divine mind.[76] More enduringly, however, Griffiths felt deep affinity with the vision of unity in relationship expressed in John's Gospel (17:21), a vision of the love that unites the soul and God while necessarily maintaining all distinctions, that same love that unites the vast diversity of creation with its creator.

A final implication of Griffiths' multireligious experience is a practical one. In order to enrich one's ways of knowing to include the intuitive, and in order to appreciate how it is that the various religions are related to one another both as mystical paths and as symbol systems, one must undergo self-transcendence, a going beyond familiar habits of thinking, which is powerfully evoked through the encounter of cultures and religions other than one's own. While multireligious experience for many may not be possible to the degree that Griffiths lived it, the openness to others and detachment from one's own cultural and religious biases are. In a mysterious way that illuminates how all humans are indeed interrelated within a greater wholeness, the lives of those who have experienced self-transcendence through a variety of symbol systems affect us all. Narrow-mindedness and attachment to a particular worldview are shaken thereby. One is opened to the interreligious and intercultural dialogue that may easily take place through a sensitive participation in one's own religion and culture.

Is Griffiths' multireligious experience typical? Are the implications of his experience for the cross-cultural study of mysticism generalizable as lessons from all multireligious explorers? One cannot say without further extensive research. What is apparent from a review of these lives is that the limited picture of reconditioning suggested by Katz's article and strict constructivists does not do justice to the transformation that takes place in those who dare to open to truth through persons and symbols outside their tradition and culture. Multireligious experience clearly enhances the "dynamic interchange between the Real and the mystic" (Stoeber). Griffiths knew both the costs and the gifts of multireligious experience. He knew as well that such experience transforms those clinging fearfully to the distinctions that separate person from person, and tradition from tradition:

> [W]e ourselves have to meditate and open ourselves to the transcendent reality. If we only work on the rational plane we are not going to make any real advance. We have to be open to the transcendent in the depth of our hearts and that is where we meet. When the Jew, the Christian, the Moslem, the Hindu and the Buddhist open themselves in prayer, in meditation, to the transcendent mystery, going beyond the word, beyond thought, simply opening themselves to the light, to the truth, to reality, then the meeting takes place. That is where humanity will be united. Only through transcendence can we find unity.[77]

NOTES

1. Bede Griffiths, "The New Consciousness" (1993), p. 70.

2. Bede Griffiths, "Benedictine Ashram: An Experiment in Hindu-Christian Community," interview by Fred Rohe and Ty Koontz (California, 1984), *The Laughing Man* 5, no. 3, p. 37.

—⚜—

3. Steven T. Katz, ed., *Mysticism and Philosophical Analysis* (New York: Oxford University Press, 1978) and *Mysticism and Religious Traditions* (New York: Oxford University Press, 1983).

4. Katz, *Mysticism and Philosophical Analysis*, pp. 22, 26.

5. Cf. Jerry H. Gill, "Mysticism and Meditation," *Faith and Philosophy* 1 (January 1984), pp. 111–121; and John Hick, *An Interpretation of Religion: Human Responses to the Transcendent* (New Haven: Yale University Press, 1989).

6. Evelyn Underhill, *Mysticism: A Study in the Nature and Development of Man's Spiritual Consciousness* (New York: E. P. Dutton, 1961); M. Frithjof Schuon, *The Transcendent Unity of Religions* (Wheaton, IL: Theosophical Publishing House, 1984); Seyyed Hossein Nasr, *Knowledge and the Sacred* (New York: Crossroad, 1981), pp. 280–308.

7. Donald Evans, "Can Philosophers Limit What Mystics Can Do? A Critique of Steven Katz," *Religious Studies* 25, no. 1 (1989), p. 56.

8. Cf. Price, James Robertson, "The Objectivity of Mystical Truth Claims," *The Thomist* 49 (1985), pp. 81–98; Robert K. C. Forman, ed., *The Problem of Pure Consciousness* (New York: Oxford University Press, 1990); Michael Stoeber, "Constructivist Epistemologies of Mysticism: A Critique and a Revision," *Religious Studies* 28, no. 1 (March 1992), pp. 107–116.

9. Raimundo Panikkar, *The Intrareligious Dialogue* (New York: Paulist Press, 1978), p. 12.

10. *The Compact Oxford English Dictionary*, p. 1056.

11. Cf. Bernard Lonergan, *Method in Theology* (New York: Seabury, 1972), p. 28.

12. *The Compact Oxford English Dictionary*, p. 872.

13. *Summa Theologiae* II-II, q. 45, a. 2; Jacques Maritain, *Creative Intuition in Art and Poetry* (New York: Pantheon Books, 1953).

14. Evelyn Underhill, *Mysticism*, pp. 90–91; William James, *The Varieties of Religious Experience: A Study in Human Nature* (New York: Collier Books, 1961), p. 399; Rudolph Otto, *The Idea of the Holy*, trans. by John W. Harvey (New York: Oxford University Press, 1958), p. 22.

15. Bede Griffiths, *The Golden String: An Autobiography* (1954); idem, *Christ in India: Essays Towards a Hindu-Christian Dialogue* (1966), pp. 7–37; idem, *The Marriage of East and West: A Sequel to the Golden String* (1982), pp. 7–45; Kathryn Spink, *A Sense of the Sacred: A Biography of Bede Griffiths* (Maryknoll, NY: Orbis Books, 1989).

16. Bede Griffiths, *Christ in India*, p. 21; idem, *The Marriage of East and West*, p. 10; idem, "The Mystical Tradition in Indian Theology" (1982), p. 159; Jules Monchanin, *In Quest of the Absolute: The Life and Works of Jules Monchanin*, ed. & trans. Joseph G. Weber (Kalamazoo: Cistercian Publications, 1977), p. 25.

17. "Father Bede Griffiths," interview by Malcolm Tillis, Shantivanam, India, 27 January 1981, pp. 119–126.

18. Griffiths, *Marriage of East and West*, p. 8.

19. Bede Griffiths, *The New Creation in Christ: Christian Meditation and Community* (1992), pp. 33–36.

20. Bede Griffiths, "The One Mystery" (1974), p. 233; idem, "Mission Is Dialogue: An Interview with Bede Griffiths" (January 1981), pp. 47–49; idem, "On Poverty and Simplicity: Views of a Post-Industrial Christian Sage," interview by Renée Weber (Fall 1983), p. 25.

21. Griffiths, *Marriage of East and West*, pp. 7–8.

22. Griffiths, *Christ in India*, pp. 15–16, 173–175.

23. Bede Griffiths, *Return to the Center* (1976), p. 71; idem, *Marriage of East and West*, p. 25.

24. Griffiths, *New Creation in Christ*, p. 103.

25. Judson Trapnell, "Bede Griffiths' Theory of Religious Symbol and Practice of Dialogue: Towards Interreligious Understanding," Ph.D. diss. (1993), chaps. 3–5.

26. Bede Griffiths, "Catholicism To-day" (1950), pp. 11–16; idem, *The Golden String*, pp. 176–177.

27. Griffiths, *Return to the Center*, pp. 71–75; idem, *Vedanta and Christian Faith* (1991), p. 163.

28. Griffiths, *Return to the Center*, pp. 36, 71, 73, 74; cf. idem, *Marriage of East and West*, p. 25.

29. Jesu Rajan, *Bede Griffiths and Sannyasa* (1989), pp. 246–247.

30. Bede Griffiths, *River of Compassion: A Christian Commentary on the Bhagavad Gita* (1987), p. 290.

31. Griffiths, "On Poverty and Simplicity," p. 25; cf. Wayne Teasdale, *Toward a Christian Vedanta: The Encounter of Hinduism and Christianity according to Bede Griffiths* (1987), pp. 128–129.

32. Griffiths, "Benedictine Ashram," p. 37.

33. Bede Griffiths, "The Mystical Dimension in Theology" (1977), pp. 242–243.

34. Katz, *Mysticism and Philosophical Analysis*, p. 27.

35. Griffiths, "Mystical Dimension in Theology," p. 243.

36. Stoeber, "Constructivist Epistemologies of Mysticism" pp. 113–114.

37. Bede Griffiths, letter to the author, May, 1988.

38. Bede Griffiths, *A New Vision of Reality: Western Science, Eastern Mysticism and Christian Faith*, ed. Felicity Edwards (1990), pp. 268, 245–246.

39. Cf. Stoeber, "Constructivist Epistemologies of Mysticism," p. 112.

40. Griffiths, "Mystical Dimension in Theology," p. 231; cf. idem, *Marriage of East and West*, p. 58; 1 Thessalonians 5:23.

41. Griffiths, *Marriage of East and West*, p. 58; cf. p. 167.

42. Griffiths, *River of Compassion*, pp. 289–290.

43. Ibid., p. 290.

44. Griffiths, *Marriage of East and West*, p. 101.

45. Griffiths, *Return to Center*, pp. 71, 73; idem, *Marriage of East and West*, pp. 167–169.

46. Bede Griffiths, *Universal Wisdom: A Journey Through the Sacred Wisdom of the World*, ed.. Roland Ropers (San Francisco: HarperCollins, 1994), pp. 8–9.

47. Ibid., p. 10.

48. Griffiths, *Return to Center*, p. 71; idem, *Marriage of East and West*, p. 102.

49. Katz, *Mysticism and Philosophical Analysis*, p. 57.

50. Ibid.

51. Ibid., pp. 24–25.

52. Ibid., p. 26.

53. Hick, *An Interpretation of Religion*, p. 295.

54. Ian Barbour, *Myths, Models and Paradigms* (San Francisco: Harper San Francisco, 1974), pp. 51–56.

55. Gill, "Mysticism and Meditation," pp. 111–114.

56. Ibid., p. 120; cf. Suzanne Langer, *Philosophy in a New Key: A Study in the Symbolism of Reason, Rite and Art* (Cambridge: Harvard University Press, 1942), pp. 90–100.

57. Katz, *Mysticism and Philosophical Analysis*, pp. 63–64.

58. Gill, "Mysticism and Meditation," p. 113; cf. Karl Rahner, *Foundations of Christian Faith: An Introduction to the Idea of Christianity* (New York: Crossroad, 1986), pp. 31–35.

59. Katz, *Mysticism and Philosophical Analysis*, p. 64.

60. Louis Dupré, "The Christian Experience of Mystical Union," *The Journal of Religion* 69, no. 1 (1989), pp. 3–5.

61. Ibid., p. 5.

62. Forman, *The Problem of Pure Consciousness*, p. 233.

63. Ibid., pp. 221–223.

64. Ibid., p. 223.

65. Cf. Teasdale, *Toward a Christian Vedanta*, p. 57.

66. Griffiths, *New Creation in Christ*, pp. 49, 68–69.

67. Ibid., p. 50.

68. Ibid.

69. Griffiths, "On Poverty and Simplicity," p. 27; idem, *River of Compassion*, p. 126; idem, *Vedanta and Christian Faith*, p. 141.

70. Griffiths, *Marriage of East and West*, pp. 150–171.

71. Griffiths, *New Vision of Reality*, p. 100; idem, *Vedanta and Christian Faith*, pp. 150–152; cf. Ken Wilber, *The Spectrum of Consciousness* (Wheaton, IL: Theosophical Publishing House, 1977), p. 43.

72. Ken Wilber, *Eye to Eye: The Quest for the New Paradigm*, expanded edition (Boston: Shambhala, 1990); Michael von Brück, *The Unity of Reality: God, God-Experience, and Meditation in the Hindu-Christian Dialogue*, tr. James V. Zeitz (New York: Paulist Press, 1991), pp. 58–64, 174–182.

73. Griffiths, *Return to the Center*, pp. 24–25; idem, *New Vision of Reality*, pp. 140, 143, 182, 244, 251.

74. Griffiths, *New Vision of Reality*, p. 286.

75. Robley Edward Whitson, *The Coming Convergence of World Religions* (New York: Newman Press, 1971); Paul Knitter, *No Other Name? A Critical Survey of Christian Attitudes Toward the World Religions* (Maryknoll, New York: Orbis Books, 1985).

76. Bede Griffiths, "A Meditation on the Mystery of the Trinity" (Christmas 1986), p. 72.

77. Bede Griffiths, "Transcending Dualism: An Eastern Approach to the Semitic Religions" (1985), p. 87.

Christ and the Buddha Embracing

Michael von Brück

Michael von Brück is author of The Unity of Reality *(1991),[1] which deals with God-experience and meditation in the Hindu-Christian dialogue. He is on the Evangelical Theological faculty of the University of Munich and is also a Lutheran Pastor. Having taught for some years in India, he became a friend of Dom Bede's, and together with his family was a frequent visitor at Saccidananda. He also translated the Bhagavad Gita into German with an edited/annotated version of Father Bede's* Commentary. *Von Brück is keenly aware of how the encounter of religions involves a change in consciousness that can have an effect on how global social problems are addressed. Pointing out that conservatism, nationalism, and intellectual and religious/existential decay block interreligious dialogue, he urges that we must build new relationships on the level of spirituality. As an example, he cites the "Ecumenical Center for Meditation and Encounter" in Germany, where various traditional practices are taught to thousands of people, who then return home to join local practice groups located throughout the country. Out of this background, von Brück recommends that local/regional spiritual encounter experiences are needed, as well as those that represent the global aspect of our unity in diversity. Furthermore, he feels that these exchanges should base themselves on the present experience of the people actually communicating, rather than on theoretical or dogmatic views, their history or their traditions.*

I. Homage

Events change the course of life when, due to historical circumstance, the time is ripe for the generation of a situation into which towering creative figures say their empowering word and actualize their hope-giving action. The pioneers of interreligious encounter and communion in India—Jules Monchanin, Swami Abhishiktananda, and Bede Griffiths—have been such figures. Bede Griffiths was able to build on the work of his two predecessors, but his own creative contribution really was to enlarge the community of communion-seekers to include the world of science and his Buddhist colleagues. It was during the last fifteen years of his life that Shantivanam became a place where scientists and Buddhist meditation masters, especially from the Tibetan tradition, met frequently.

Though firmly rooted in Hinduism by his reading of the Vedic texts and the Upanishadic wisdom, Bede Griffiths' approach to the plurality of historical Indian spiritual traditions remained unbiased: He considered Gautama Shakyamuni—the Buddha—to be one of the greatest sages, and the Buddha's modern day disciples from Tibet, Japan, Sri Lanka, and Western countries impressed him very much. The sacramental view of reality in Buddhist Tantrayana resonated with his own experience: Bede's spiritual goal was to integrate all aspects of life into one great poem of spiritual transparency. He strove to combine the arts and the formless, silent meditation, the sublimity of chanting, stillness, and dynamism (as expressed in the Avatamsaka Sutra), complete beyondness and the colors of life, and—especially during the last months of his life—the fatherly and the motherly aspects of the Divine. Therefore, it seems appropriate to continue Father Bede's vision of a Hindu-Christian communion with an integration of the Buddhist-Christian encounter, so that all three traditions may gather in the ecstasy of silence under the tree of Awakening.

The Buddhist-Christian dialogue has a long and exciting history, extending for more than one hundred years. In Sri Lanka, Japan, America, Germany, and other places, disciples of both traditions have been active in trying to understand and benefit from each other by clarifying their patterns of living and thinking in the light of each other's traditions. I would like to share here only a few of the many existential insights that have resulted from this dialogue, starting with a revealing story that highlights the humility necessary for any encounter and communion between human beings themselves and between humans and God—a spontaneous humility that Father Bede radiated more than anything else:

> A Christian missionary met a Buddhist Zen-master in Japan, and they talked about Jesus. The Zen-master acknowledged that Jesus was certainly a great man; however, the missionary insisted that he was the greatest person of all humankind. To this statement, the Zen-master then replied: "Well, perhaps the greatest." After some time the missionary asked, "Don't you believe like me that Jesus was the Son of God?" The Zen-master's answer was, "If you want to express his spiritual greatness in this way—well, perhaps he was the Son of God." The missionary left this encounter, but around the corner he met Jesus on the street. "Lord," he said, "I have managed to get this pagan Buddhist to acknowledge your divine nature. I am sure that the next time we meet I will be able to baptize him." Jesus replied, "And what good did this do for you except inflate your Christian ego?"

Cross-cultural encounters such as this one are a result of our modern civilization. In our global society today there is certainly increasing interreligious discourse—not only the Zen-master and the missionary are meeting!

The tendency towards religious pluralism, and the pluralization of values as well as life-styles, historically started with the Enlightenment in Europe and with the American Revolution. Since the end of nineteenth-century colonialism, other cultures—especially some Asian and Islamic ones—have become self-aware. Christian theologians now realize that the "otherness" of foreign traditions, indeed, possessing a different religious identity from Christianity, is not an evil to be eradicated, but instead might actually be a gift of God. These "other" religions are part of the created God-given world; they may even be penetrated by the presence of the Holy Spirit (for in Trinitarian terms, the Creator and the work of the Spirit cannot actually be separated), and God might even speak to Christians through the language and images of other religions. People of these traditions then become not objects of our missionary zeal but fellow subjects under the providence of God.

—⟋⟍—

Religions *are* different. The religions' answers to the human predicament often do clash with one another. There are then the inevitable conflicts—some avoidable, because they reflect human egotism and power-struggles, others not avoidable, because contradictory attitudes to life and politics lead to controversies. A Christian tenet, as well as the presupposition for democracy and a more peaceful international scene, dictates that conflicts be solved nonviolently. Understanding is required for this to occur, and understanding is now being sought in dialogue. In fact, there is a dialogical imperative for this to occur. In 1993, the centenary of the World Parliament of Religions was celebrated in Chicago; there, people of all religions started to embrace each other's differences—to rejoice in these differences as being enriching, to learn from each other and to cooperate in the spiritual, social, and political field. Some of us, and certainly all those who have been inspired by Bede Griffiths, seem to have made a quantum leap from centuries of hostility to a new attitude of mutual understanding. We now realize that peace among religions is a requirement for world peace.

However, it is difficult really to determine the result of all of this encounter and dialogue—is real progress occurring, or do seeming gains quickly fade after each conference? Are isolationist and exclusivist or fundamentalist tendencies really prevailing? To answer these questions, we need a clear analysis of the present social, political, as well as intellectual condition of interreligious encounter. Also, unless we have at least a vague idea of an endpoint and an ultimate goal, it is difficult to determine whether any specific path is actually appropriate or not. Therefore, more than anything else, it is now necessary to obtain a sober and truthful analysis of the present state of interreligious affairs.

II. ANALYSIS

I am not able to give a comprehensive analysis here (or elsewhere!), but I would like to show how this might be achieved. There is a worldwide intellectual community struggling in the field of interreligious understanding, hermeneutics, and praxis. Of course, interreligious encounter is not new for Christianity—for example, consider the second-century theologians, and Nicolas of Cusa, Matteo Ricci, and others. But since 1893 (the year of the first World Parliament of Religions in Chicago) the movement towards interreligious cooperation has become stronger for many reasons.

First, in order even to instigate analysis of interreligious dialogue, one must consider the very structure of the dialogue itself. What do we mean and intend when we enter into dialogue? Each tradition has to work out a clear understanding in accordance with its basic tenets. Christians call this a "theology of religions," which is different from the analytic "comparative religion." It does not suffice to proclaim a pragmatic position to work out a "world ethos" independent of the specific credal structure of a given religion, for the details as well as the motivating forces are important in any given situation that calls for ethical discernment. Rather, internal reflection in each tradition must lead to the presentation and development of the reasons for dialogue: Whether I am an *inclusivist* or a *pluralist* (I do not mention the *exclusivistic* position since it cannot be a basis for dialogue), dialogical communion with the "other" is possible only when I recognize this other as a potential source for my truth and salvation, or at least for my understanding of these. The other must be accepted as a possible medium for my transformation (metanoia), or conversion of my life to God. Whether one really does or doesn't make this transformation is tested during fruitful dialogue.

As long as I am convinced that I have to "win over" the other into my camp, to my way of thinking (proselytization), there can be no genuine dialogue. This is not to say that partners in dialogue should not defend the views and ways of their own traditions. They must do this, in order to prevent dialogue from becoming stagnant and boring. In dialogical encounter, one should witness to the truth that is experienced in one's own specifically unique way—and this really is "mission" as genuine witness, to use traditional terms. But when actual productive dialogue does occur, it is more of a spontaneous occurrence than a strategy, because if one intentionally tries to force results, the whole process may become artificial. On the other hand, those who engage in interreligious discussion need to be open to accept the truth that they might receive, mediated by their dialogical partner. "Mission" is not an enterprise to "get people into one's own camp" in order to become more powerful, but it is instead witnessing to truth in the dialogical discourse and allowing transformation to occur when truth really is present. Dialogue is authentic only when it comes from the center of one's own theological convictions.

Right now, however, we seem to be in a painful stalemate in dialogical progress. Few people outside the academic community participate in this kind of exchange and building of communion. Spectacular dialogical events are held from time to time—for example, the Assisi Peace Prayer. But some of the people/religious leaders who participate in these events tend to use them as a chance to show their worldwide social and ecological engagement, while at the same time running their own religious affairs with poor dialogical attitudes towards those in their own socioreligious group who have different ideas and styles of life. The basic question is not whether we need an inclusivistic or a pluralistic theological model (although to advance clear arguments for one or the other is essential as well), but how deeply rooted our commitment to the other *as other* really is.

In addition, there are at least three social trends that increasingly seem to be blocking interreligious dialogue: a) *conservatism*, b) *nationalism*, c) *intellectual and religious-existential decay*. In order to analyze the threads of interreligious dialogue we must realize that dialogue problems are very much embedded in the general state of affairs of our respective cultures.

CONSERVATISM

Conservatism as a concept in and of itself is not necessarily bad. However, it becomes an obstacle to interreligious development when it absolutizes certain forms or relative expressions of religious tradition. Conservatism today is often very much a reaction against the uncertainty and complexity of modern societies; it can be a result of fear—and there is no intellectual argument against fear. What helps defeat fear and its reactionary conservatism is intense spiritual practice. And the new possibilities that are arising in the field of spiritual practice are precisely a fruit of cross-cultural encounters. Therefore, dialogue on the level of spirituality seems to be a promising way to break down the walls of fear and religious reactionary conservatism and to build a new spiritual milieu.

We do not have to push for any specific form for spiritual transformation—prayer, meditation, music, the arts in general—all can express and mediate this change. In each of our own religious traditions we need to emphasize and foster spiritual practice and exchange. Instead of investing so much of our effort in academic studies and religious comparison, as important as these may be, we should put more of our energy and our resources into this new field of "dialogue by spiritual practice." If we do not possess the spiritual discipline to do this, there will be no interreligious future, but instead—almost of sociopsychological necessity—a falling back into all varieties of parochialism.

My own experience of interreligious work and study may reveal one way to accomplish this spiritual transformation. About twenty years ago, the German Jesuit Hugo M. Enomiya-Lassalle started a center for Zen practice in Germany. There, the smiling Buddha and the suffering Christ met and still continue to meet in the serious spiritual practice of their disciples. Later, the center came under the direction of another Roman Catholic priest who had married, and it was thus relocated from a place that was owned by the Roman Catholic Church. Those who were already enrolled as practitioners started an independent society and raised funds for its development. After some time an old abandoned mill was bought and reconstructed to be the new home of this spiritual endeavor. For the past fifteen years this organization has been called the "Ecumenical Center for Meditation and Encounter."

Those who direct the meditation courses come from all walks of life. There are Zen sesshins,[2] yoga, physical therapy, eutony,[3] work with gems, fasting, Tibetan meditation (Kum Nye), Chinese Tai Chi, prayer of the heart from the Eastern Orthodox tradition, reflective meditation on the gospels, etc. People come for a weekend or a week, and upon their return home they usually join practice groups that are part of a growing network all over Germany. Every year we have about three thousand participants in the courses.

Celebration of the Eucharist occurs once a week in the chapel as the central Christian practice, and everything else is built around this. There is a daily silent peace meditation, which is sometimes closed with songs from the Christian Taize community. But the courses offered and their spiritual framework are independent of this practice. Course leaders and participants may join the worship in addition to their own practice (sutra chanting, etc.), or not. Participants include Christians and Jews, and quite a number who have converted to Buddhism or Hinduism. Most of the participants are German middle-class people (because the program is expensive).

The Christians rediscover their Christianity (which most of them had lost) in a much deeper way, and at the same time develop a spirit of total openness to the encounter with other traditions. Interreligious exchange here is neither a theoretical concept, nor a social practice in living together of different communities, but is instead a spiritual experience. Perhaps it is a kind of "laboratory situation," for this experience is different from everyday life insofar as there are no pressures of resisting one another's social and political identities. If we can begin to multiply such "exceptional" situations, we may start to build mutual trust based on inner experience. This is an investment in a more peaceful future, after all.

NATIONALISM

"Nationalism" needs to be distinguished from the search for a national, cultural, and a religious identity that seems to be innate in human beings. In Europe—in the process of the European integration that is now occurring—we are just trying to learn how to balance our local (regional), national, and supranational identities. Neglect of any of these levels might trigger counter-reactions that could possibly be harmful or violent. Nationalism is an absolutization of genuine national identity that kills both regional identity and the identity that is reaching out beyond the national—ultimately to all humankind and even to the cosmos. Human beings have a tendency to cling to a false sense of national identity. However, this is the current state of affairs and the condition under which our efforts for dialogue must begin.

What has been said so far about national identity can also be applied to religious identity. For example, suppose you have an identity as a Buddhist. What does that really mean? On a certain level of identification—especially when you face a Muslim or a Christian—you are a "generic" Buddhist, with all the characteristics that compose "Buddhism." But in your daily life you are a Pure Land, Zen, or Shingon Buddhist, or maybe a Tibetan Buddhist of a certain school. As a Buddhist, you do not speak Pali or Sanskrit, you speak your local language, and all of these cultural hallmarks combine to give you your current religious identity. Living separated from your tradition's religious-cultural roots, you might lose this identity, but you may sense something missing. You may even find ways to compensate for this.

Similarly, you are not just a "Christian," but are Orthodox, Protestant or Catholic, or you identify with a specific denomination. Even as a

Christian, your religion is not abstract "Christianity" but is very much localized, and this shapes your primary religious identity. Most people go to worship and hear sermons, not to be instructed on the globally abstract Christian tenets, but instead to be shaped by narratives that represent a local identity. Immigrants try to build their new regional identity by maintaining ties to a socioreligious group that guarantees the continuity of their original identity. The United States is a good example of this process in action.

I urge the following as a path to interreligious and global cooperation: To counterbalance the religious analog of "nationalism," i.e., the absolutization of the religious identity in Buddhism, Christianity, Hinduism, and other traditions, we need two different emphases—the local-regional identity, and the global identity of one humankind. Often, interreligious exchange takes only the global aspect into account, but in many cases this is too abstract and lacks the warmth and real living relationship that you have in your village, community, or neighborhood. We need to develop a way to engage in religious sharing on the local level.

But here again we meet the problem of fear. The fear that is generated with regard to the problem of upheaval of one's tradition and value system has already been mentioned, and it is only spiritual practice that will overcome and heal this fear. Another malignant source of fear is the possible loss of one's national identity. Europe—and Germany in particular—is an excellent example of just this reaction: There are so many immigrants coming into Europe that irrational fear about this is generated in all strata of society. It is not the case that most of the fearful hold a basic anti-foreigner or anti-other-religions view. They just feel crowded by too many immigrants who represent an unfamiliar culture.

A major reason for the current immigration is economic disaster in Africa, Latin America, Asia, and elsewhere. Unfair and unjust international economics, as well as financial and trading conditions are among the reasons for economic instability, as are also governmental inefficiency, corrupt bureaucracies, and undemocratic power-struggles in the troubled countries. In order to build a sound interreligious future society we need to counter, even undercut if possible, nationalism that is born out of fear of foreigners and foreign control. This will happen only when entire populations of potential migrants are able to find decent living conditions at home.

—\|//—

This kind of societal change requires a transformation of the international economic and financial order. The Judeo-Christian insistence on justice is not satisfied merely by acts of false charity—only giving when it is convenient from our superfluous wealth. Our spiritual tradition requires our fundamental concern for the welfare of all, without partiality or preference—a difficult but most important aspect of our human and interreligious relations. Solving these problems, actually, is intrinsically connected with our search for interreligious peace.

Our religious identity is not simple or static. We live with different identities depending upon the context of our lives, and these identities can and do change. An interreligious identity of our future is not a substitute for our other identities, but is an additional dimension that informs and changes these, while not replacing them. Having said this, I want to add emphatically that the level of interreligious identity that can be mediated by spiritual practice has influence on our local and regional identities, and we must make conscious efforts to link these different identity levels. However, we must also realize that they are not the same and should not be confused. To embrace a Muslim or a Hindu or a Buddhist at an interreligious conference, as a result of the radiation of a certain appealing intellectual and spiritual climate, is something completely different from embracing a Muslim or a Hindu or a Buddhist in our own neighborhoods. This difference is not only due to the divergent aspects and sociopolitical influences that play a role, but it is different insofar as separate levels of identity are being touched upon. The entire concept of identity can benefit from elaboration, and perhaps even from a complete course in intercultural psychology and learning. However, here it is important to understand that in order to build lasting interreligious cooperation and friendship without provoking new tensions, we have to keep in mind these differing levels of identity and act from this level of understanding.

What would be a specifically Christian contribution to understanding the search for identity in a situation of interreligious communication and communion? Christian faith is rooted in the *unconditional* love of God that is revealed in Jesus Christ in a unique way. This love extends to the whole cosmos in space and time, and perhaps embraces even more than that. Unconditionality implies that love cannot be limited spatially or temporally, nor can it depend on the condition of knowing this. Faith as trust in God's unconditional love, therefore, is a pure gift of the loving God. In Christian theology, God is conceived in Trinitarian dynamics so that God's actions *ad extra* are indivisible (*opera trinitatis ad extra indivisa sunt*). Consequently, the very act of reconciliation is present in creation and in the free presence of the spirit everywhere and at all times, not only implicitly but also explicitly. What follows is that human beings in all their languages, religions, circumstances of life, and attitudes of consciousness are being reached by God's reconciling presence.

Religions are and remain different. They organize their varied experiences in differing symbol systems and languages. Yet, languages and religions can also be learned. How far one can really travel the path of another tradition depends on many factors, such as one's personal biography and hermeneutical awareness. In any case, this process of experiences and learning is not easy, for it requires one to make an effort and to change. Such experiences are occurring to everyone who lives with people of other languages or other religious traditions. When such a person returns to one's own home or ground, she or he is not the same person anymore: patterns of thinking, values, judgments, and religious perceptions have changed. Thus, in our highly pluralistic living conditions, where Buddhists, Christians, Hindus, and other traditions mix freely, one sees that there are different possibilities and interpretations of one's life. In relating to the other we change ourselves. This is precisely the history of all religions that have developed in encounter with others. For the last hundred years Christianity has been changing while in contact with Hindu and Buddhist cultures and other traditions, and a similar process could also be described for Buddhism, Islam, Judaism, and other religions. The pioneers of interreligious dialogue and experience such as Bede Griffiths have made deliberate efforts to make these processes conscious and integrative.

Here, an important point of criticism that has been raised against the inculturation theology in India—as practiced by Abhishiktananda, Bede Griffiths, and others—needs to be clarified. In the past—and in some ways even more so today—Europe and America have had a history of exploitation of other cultures in terms of their material as well as human resources. The question has been raised whether interreligious dialogue is just another means to exploit non-European and non-American cultures in a spiritual way, insofar as their religious traditions are now being made available to us. This is a tremendous danger, indeed, that can be avoided only when we, as partners in dialogue, do not stand immovable in our own "lofty" traditions, and when other religions are considered not as objects of our mission or even subjects of our enrichment, but real partners. The notion of partnership, which we know from psychology, can be applied here: In partnership, both partners change inasmuch as both travel a common path. They learn from each other, take from each other, but also give to each other. Only the process of mutual giving and receiving can prevent one from dominating and depriving the other psychologically, materially, and also spiritually. This is the concept of a partnership in identity.

Buddhism, Christianity, Hinduism, and other religious traditions are rooted in different cultures or origins. What we know as Catholic, Protestant, or Orthodox Christianity, or as Mahayana, Theravada, Tantrayana Buddhism—in other words, the confessional plurality—is a reflection of these diverse roots and influences. Current religions would have disappeared long ago if their identity was truly fixed and they could not integrate new aspects. A spiritual movement, a culture or religion can assimilate what corresponds with it, what somehow does not throw off this movement from its own center or its own axis. This can, from time to time, imply dramatic changes in basic attitudes, in terms of a rediscovery of the original impetus or experience of a given religion. A religious tradition, however, must dissimilate what does not correspond with it. For instance, in Christian faith basic human unequality, injustice, and human sacrifices (there are certainly modern forms of destruction of human beings!) must be excluded because they would categorically contradict the experience of the presence of God in all creatures.

Each tradition forms a unique identity, and yet can integrate others. This is precisely what happens today worldwide. Religions are in a fundamental crisis in facing secularism and an economized culture into which the world is developing. This is occurring in India, Japan, Europe, and America. All religions, therefore, face the question of what their unique and important contribution for humanity really is. They are called not just to legitimize or strengthen their religious institutions, but to offer selfless service to human beings on the basis of their original impulses.

Religious identity is not static, and various identities can contain each other. In religious idiom, we recognize that regardless of identity, we all are children and creatures of one God. Such a statement relativizes traditional religious identities through which different cultures have been held apart. The present emergent understanding and practice of the concept of one humanity has no parallel in the previous history of humankind. It will continue to emerge, even if certain institutions, because of their interests in mere power, are struggling against these developments.

To summarize, in the present partnership of religions on all levels of human expression and formation, a common identity is emerging in our respective traditions that has not previously been recognized, and therefore we have no former model to draw upon. Bede Griffiths, Abhishiktananda, Enomiya-Lassalle, and others have become important mediators of building a model of mutually inclusive identities.

INTELLECTUAL AND RELIGIOUS DECAY

Due to many different factors that are at work, and not just in industrialized societies, we can observe both an increase in the number of people participating in various educational systems and at the same time a decrease of what in the West could be called the "humanistic values," due to consumerism and an egocentric individualism. The broader educational system is very selective concerning the type of knowledge and education it mediates. What is nearly totally lacking is training in intercultural communication. This training would require a more careful attempt to relate the assumptions and underlying myths of a culture to the present-day problems, patterns of thought, and behavior of people; for without clearly understanding what motivates your own thinking and action you cannot meaningfully relate to other and different value systems and behavioral patterns. This is one of the reasons for the need to deepen the practice and understanding of one's own tradition in order to be fit for interreligious dialogue.

Therefore, a nonsectarian religious education is probably one of the most pressing needs for increasing interreligious cooperation and cross-cultural understanding. By "nonsectarian" I mean an unbiased (as much as possible) appreciation of all that is meaningful in different religious traditions. Even more, the scholarly task of discerning the meaningful from the meaningless or even dangerous aspects of an appropriate interreligious hermeneutics in our religious traditions needs to be given special emphasis.

However, I do not know how to persuade "those in charge" (at UNESCO level or wherever) to embark on such a difficult path.

III. PROJECTIONS

CREATIVE IMAGINATION

To envisage "Christ and the Buddha embracing each other" requires much more than a scholarly approach to the problems of interreligious dialogue. An intellectual (linguistic, historical, methodological) analysis describes and relates patterns of the past in order to construct a present. The future, however, is not the business of the scholar. It requires the artist, the poet, and the mystic visionary to see what is already there to be seen and to project images as guiding principles for possible ways to a transformed future. From a scholarly or theological perspective, we need to discern the theological and the comparative-methodological problem.

First, let's examine the theological issue: In order to appreciate other religions as theologically meaningful, we need to acknowledge that God speaks to us through other religions. This can be interpreted in different ways, but it rules out an exclusivistic position that says salvation comes only through Christ as *we* know him, historically mediated through the church(es). Such a position is strange, anyway, because it would exclude most of humankind *ante* and *post Christum natum*—Abraham's faith, after all, is valid. If God shows universal saving will in Christ, this intention cannot be particularized historically. So we have to opt for an *inclusivistic* position (there is salvation outside of Christianity, but it is mediated through Christ in unknown ways) or a *pluralistic* position (God has given many answers and speaks different salvation languages). I do not want to argue the advantages and disadvantages of the various positions here. It is enough to state that there is salvation outside the Christian Church, while at the same time recognizing that not everything that other religions say and have said is necessarily true for Christians.

The second issue is methodological: getting to know the other without the bias of *my* tradition and *my* language. Is it possible to take a third position in order to judge both my own and the other's position? I cannot escape altogether: I think and speak always in my "language." But I can look at my processes of thinking, tradition, language and religion critically, i.e., I can use the tools of my spiritual path in order to reflect and to distance myself from the presuppositions of my own religion. In other words, I can realize that my tradition and language are limited and not universal. The point of comparison is not an already fixed tenet informed by my traditional way of thinking and prejudice, but is the dialogical discourse in the actual encounter of people of different traditions itself. If the other partner enters into the encounter on the same basis, creative development for both is possible. There are many examples of this "mutual transformation" (for example, John Cobb) that lead us deeper into the mystery of the sources of our respective traditions. In other words, our interreligious concern needs more visionary and poetic impulses. The poet might be informed by an academic study of historical patterns and paradigms, and this would be the ideal case, because it helps to distinguish visionary quality from escapist fantasy. Bede Griffiths' life was lived as a wonderful integration of poetic and theological expression.

An example of this interreligious integration is *Buddha and Jesus*,[4] by Carrin Dunne (a poet who is also a scholar in religious studies). This booklet contains Dunne's imagined talks between these two masters. She does not claim some sort of "historical proof," but projects the basic impulses from these two human beings and their traditions into the field of reference of our present-day questions. The result is a very touching drama that reflects the questioning heart of a contemporary secularized (or not yet secularized) man or woman who lives in doubt of his or her own and humankind's future. For this sort of dialogue to be successful, a creative translation of our respective traditions is called for, not just a repetitive pattern that perpetuates what we believe to have been the glorious past. For instance:

> Gotama argues that Jesus should not direct attention to his divinity but to the divine nature of his disciples, for to accept their own divine nature would be much easier than to accept another person's claim. Jesus answers that it is precisely because it is more difficult that it should be the starting point for religious practice. Gotama recognizes: "Not being in the grip of another's illusion of self, one is quicker to perceive another's shortcomings and biases than one's own."[5]

The point of interreligious encounter is not to demonstrate that one religion is correct and another is not, or to assert that all religions really say the same thing. The point is to encourage each other to true practice, which requires everyone to go beyond ego, beyond the common religious claims of true pronouncements, established identities, etc. This is why it is the mystic who is the archetype of a person who is able to reach out to people of other faiths and identities. Conceptual clarification is important for hermeneutical awareness, and without this awareness we could not understand the other in its otherness, which again would deprive us of the real experience of learning and change. But beyond clarification is the communion in a mystery beyond the ego. The pioneers of dialogue, among them Bede Griffiths, are the genuine witnesses to this mystery.

THE HERMENEUTICAL PROBLEM

Again, much has been written and said about the hermeneutical problem, and the process of clarification is still going on. I do not think that any methods to solve it have been totally satisfactory so far, and I, of course, don't have an answer either. The basic problem can be stated as: How do we really understand the other, without imposing our own structure of language, meaning and psychology on it, so that it still remains the other, yet at the same time allows us to understand it? This understanding, of course, means that it is not the other any more, for understanding is an act of integration.

Recently, one of the most thorough attempts at resolution in this field was published in Germany by Perry Schmidt-Leukel: *Listening to the Lion's Roar: Towards a Hermeneutics of a Christian Understanding of the Buddhist Message of Salvation.*[6] After discussing (and mostly dismissing for good reasons) so many hermeneutic attempts of the past and present, the author suggests that we have to start with the basic human experiences (such as suffering, death and relationship), because they can be found in all traditions, yet they stand in a specific hierarchy that is different in Buddhism and Christianity. Whereas Buddhism takes off from the experience of impermanence and suffering, Christianity starts with the experience of personal (and person-making) relationships. All other concepts of God/the Ultimate, the religious path, the understanding of the human situation, etc., are derived from this basic concept. Such a hermeneutic attempt sounds well grounded, and it is not the first time that this has been suggested. The problem is, however, that even these basic experiences of the human being are mediated by our particular religious background. They are not experienced as independent of the conditions shaped by the history and language of their respective traditions.

Therefore, I suggest that the hermeneutic basis for interreligious communication is not in the past, it is not the search for an original historical pattern or whatever, but it *is* in the present. Precisely in this moment where I speak, and a follower of another tradition with a different mother-tongue listens, or instead, where she or he speaks and I listen ("speaking" in the sense of an all-comprehensive communication, not just by words), the field of communication is created and the proper hermeneutics are worked out by trial and error in this very process of communication, not before it. In interreligious communication and communion we do not rehearse the past and present it to the outsider, but together we create a new situation that is informed and conditioned by different pasts. We do not find out "as it really has been" and relate these *bruta facta* to each other, but we are much more imaginative, and the rules for the process are being formed in the process itself. The motivations of each partner and for entering the process might be different in each case, but via *communication* gradually there emerges *communion*, fragile and not ultimate, but again and again undertaken as part of the cosmic play of mutuality and interrelationship that we can observe on all levels of the evolution of reality.

A CALL FOR HUMILITY

What I have been saying so far could be put into more philosophical (and precise) or even mythic language. But the problem is that we easily and readily identify with "our" philosophic/traditional parlance, are proud of our heritage and regard interreligious communication as an opportunity for self-staging. Interreligious endeavor, however, more than anything else requires humility in face of the ever greater mystery; it requires honesty in facing my (and my tradition's) real state of affairs in the past and present, and a kind of awe in the presence of that which I do not yet, or cannot, understand.

We may say that this is the way of the cross or *kenosis*, or a mutual conditioning envisaged by the concept of *pratityasamutpada* that helps us to overcome clinging to our own substantialist concepts—or deconstructed symbols, as the Buddhists would call it; we might also call it an act of total and unconditional surrender (Islam). However, more important than the name is that the concept really becomes an attitude that shapes our lives, including our interreligious relations and interpretations, as these have to do with our spiritual level of development.

The ways of silence and engaged love, of communion in psychologically manageable groups, are building blocks for an interreligious future none of us is able to project. We do not need a call for more (and better) institutions; we do not need to speculate on whether religions (and languages) will merge or stay apart, whether learning from each other and mutual transformation touches the identity of the present religious traditions in such a way that they disappear or that they become even more self-aware. After all, all our religions have appeared in time, changed in time, and they may disappear or transform in time. We do not know and do not need to know.

All that is required is honesty, simplicity, and an integrated approach (perhaps similar to Gandhi's model) to shape pathways for an interreligious concern that are genuine (measured according to the basic insights of our respective traditions) and helpful (measured according to the present-day real liberative impulse in a holistic sense). What is required is that we recognize our different identities, which are always "soft," flexible, in the making, relational. I have called this the process of building identity in partnership. This, again, is possible only on the basis of a strong and unconditional faith in God/the Ultimate Good, which supports us even if we fail, or better yet: precisely in our failures and errors.

NOTES

1. Michael von Brück, *The Unity of Reality: God, God Experience & Meditation in the Hindu-Christian Dialogue*, trans. by James V. Zeitz (Mahwah, NJ: Paulist Press, 1991).

2. A *sesshin* ("meeting in the depth of consciousness") is a traditionally structured week-long Zen retreat with eight to ten hours of formal sitting-meditation (zazen) each day, and frequent interviews with the teacher.

3. *Eutony* is a psychosomatic practice of muscle tension and relaxation with focused awareness.

4. Carrin Dunne, *Buddha and Jesus* (New York: Templegate, 1975).

5. Ibid., p. 64.

6. Perry Schmidt-Leukel, *Den Löwen brüllen hören: Zur Hermeneutik eines christlichen Verständnisses der buddhistischen Heilsbotschaft* (*Listening to the Lion's Roar: Towards a Hermeneutics of a Christian Understanding of the Buddhist Message of Salvation*), (Schöningh: Paderborn, 1992). •

Part Three:

Spirituality of the Future—
Experiencing Wholeness

God as Feminine: Experiencing Wholeness

Felicity Edwards[1]

With Felicity Edwards' contribution, we turn to Dom Bede's concern for wedding the "masculine" and "feminine" aspects of human consciousness. Edwards teaches systematic theology in the Department of Divinity, Rhodes University, South Africa and has long been committed to feminist issues. She has a Presbyterian and Anglican religious background. Edwards was connected with Father Bede not only as a friend, but also as an editor of some of his works. She, like several other contributors, sees him as embodying, through his own experience, the new cultural ideals, which he embraced by a process of integration of the remarkable spiritual growth that he underwent in the last months of his life—a result of his opening to the feminine.

In this piece she tells us something about that last phase of Dom Bede's life, noting that the Christian religion has generally limited itself by excluding or neglecting feminine images of God that are actually available in its own tradition. She believes that if gender oppression—which belongs not to the order of creation but to the order of sin and fallenness—could be eradicated from the Church, this would set a strong foundation for release from all other forms of social oppression. Edwards argues for a sense of wholeness, in which the masculine/feminine polarity will be preserved as a creative tension that promotes humanization, without subordinating either energy to the other. In Dom Bede she sees an example of such "holistic feminism."

When Dom Bede Griffiths first went to India in 1955, he wrote to a friend that one of the impulses drawing him there was that he "wanted to discover the other half of [his] soul."[2] By this he meant that he sensed that in India he would discover for himself both the intuitive dimension of human experience and also what we know as the "feminine." Having been brought up in the West where masculine consciousness, patriarchy, and the rational functioning of the mind are generally dominant, Father Bede was deeply aware of the need to discover this intuitive and feminine "other half," and so to integrate on the one hand the rational and the intuitive, and on the other, the masculine and the feminine, in what he referred to as "the marriage of East and West."[3]

While he continued to experience this as a personal quest, Father Bede was developing a growing awareness of the transpersonal implications of this integration. At the level of sheer survival the materialistic, technocratic and dualistically inclined West needs the contemplative wisdom and sense of interconnectedness experienced in the East. Conversely, to an extent, at least, the East could do with some of the less aggressive and more positively nature-friendly strategies being developed in Western technology. But at the evolutionary level, Father Bede came increasingly to realize that it is only with the integration of the polarities of rational and intuitive, and masculine and feminine, that transcendence of both is possible. This is an immense challenge, for it makes retrieval of the intuitive and of the feminine—and of their integration with the rational and the masculine—a task of major evolutionary import. Further, Father Bede was increasingly aware that the actualization of such integration within one's own person is part of the integrative process on the cosmic scale. He was very fond of the metaphor of the hologram—brought to his attention by quantum physicist David Bohm—which suggests the nature of the interconnectedness that exists between the parts and the whole, such that any transformation in the part affects the whole, for the whole is enfolded in each of the parts.

Back in 1955, one of the first things Father Bede did on arrival in India was to visit the eighth-century Cave Temple on the Island of Elephanta, off Bombay. That this is a cave temple is itself significant, for the temple space is, as it were, hewn from the body of Mother Earth and the temple sculptures cut from the living rock. There in the deepest part of the ancient cave, mysterious, immense and high above you as you approach, is the great figure of Shiva Maheshvara, the Great God. Here Shiva is represented with three faces, one representing his creative aspect, one his power of dissolution, while in the center facing you the face of Shiva is in deep contemplation, symbolizing the moment by moment divine upholding and sustaining of the universe. Shiva is understood as the all-pervading consciousness whose form is knowledge, and is particularly the union and resolution of opposites. Here the figure is absolutely peaceful, "infinitely distant yet infinitely near, solemn, benign, gentle and majestic."[4]

Father Bede had the experience in this temple of recognizing, carved in stone, what it was that he had come to India to find. He wrote that "here engraved in stone one could encounter that hidden depth of existence, springing from the depth of nature and the unconscious, penetrating all human existence and going beyond into the mystery of the infinite and the eternal, not as something remote and inaccessible, but as something almost tangible, engraved in this stone."[5] Also in the same temple, on the right as you enter, is another figure of the Lord Shiva, this time as Shiva Ardhanarishvara. One side of the figure is masculine and the other side feminine—male and female in androgynous completeness. This figure is complementary to the other of Shiva in his creative, destructive and contemplative aspects. Experienced together, the sense arises of having to be in some way both masculine and feminine and yet also of having to go beyond masculinity and femininity—beyond the cosmic process.

Father Bede was always saying, "You must go beyond." This is perhaps the first of his great teachings on the practicalities of the spiritual life. A second principle he espoused was that in order to "go beyond," one must find and feel and identify with that which one is to go beyond. In other words, there is no way that one's materiality, sexuality, and psychology can be bypassed. The third principle that he insisted upon was that whatever is being transcended is not to be rejected or repressed or repudiated, but rather is to be integrated. Integration of the stages of experience is the key to personal spiritual growth and to cosmic evolution. In this great process nothing is lost.

Throughout his long life and profound experience in India, Father Bede was penetrating ever more deeply into the divine mystery that was drawing him, and yet until the events of January 1990 seemed to conspire to change this, his masculine side clearly predominated. On the 25th of that month, while meditating in the early morning, he suffered a stroke. He said that it felt to him like a blow, coming from the left, and that it hit him on the left side of the head with such violence that his vision became "blurred like a television screen before it is focussed." It was not until a week later that he became fully conscious and began to interpret the change that had taken place in his awareness. He wrote, "It was really that I had died to the ego, I think. The ego mind, and also maybe the discriminative mind that separates and divides, all seemed to have gone. Everything was flowing into everything else, and I had a sense of unity behind it all."[6]

At that point Father Bede thought he was going to die. Feeling that he was, in fact, ready to let go of everything, he prepared himself, said the appropriate prayers, and waited for this to happen. As he told this story, he would smile in a most engaging way as he said simply, "Nothing happened, you know." But following this profound experience something extremely important occurred. As he put it, he had a strong impulse "to surrender to the Mother." And so he made this surrender, and as he did so waves of overwhelming love flowed into him and through him. As he said, "It was a wonderful experience." He was being overwhelmed by love.[7] When I asked him, "Father, what does the Mother mean to you as you look back to what happened?" he replied that the Mother meant his own femininity, his mother, Mother Earth, motherhood, and the whole feminine principle generally. The Mother meant as well the Virgin Mary to whom he prayed, but also, he said, "the Black Madonna came through," which was for him an important link with the earth and the Earth Mother.

Interpreting together the experiences of the stroke and that of surrendering to the Mother, he saw them as a breakthrough both to the feminine, and to the intuitive, nondual level of awareness. The fact that he felt the blow on the left side of his head he felt was a link with the symbolism of the left as representing the feminine. But he also had the sense that the left brain, which is understood to correspond to rational as opposed to intuitive functioning, was being knocked out, while the right brain and its intuitive faculty was being opened up. Speaking of it later he said that this new way of experiencing reality had continued ever since. It was not that the left brain was incapacitated completely; in this transformation the left brain keeps going but the right brain is in control. This is not the repudiation of the left-brain and of rationality but rather the integration of rationality into the greater capacity of intuitive awareness.

Most importantly, Father Bede spoke of how there came with his transformation the sense of advaita, of nonduality, and how for him this persistent sense of nondual awareness was such that, although people and things were experienced as flowing into one another in their underlying interconnectedness, the differences and distinctions between them remained, contained in the unity. "I've never lost the sense," he said, "that all the diversities are contained in the one." He stressed that "it is extremely important, when we go to a deeper level of consciousness, that we should not lose the diversity and the individuality of people and things, but on the contrary, the diversity and the multiplicity are taken up into the unity." And here he linked this further with the underlying experience in the great religious traditions—the experience of the Hindu, Buddhist, Taoist, Sufi, and Christian mystics. He said that the more deeply you penetrate these traditions, the more you realize that this understanding of nonduality, of distinction in unity, has been the great discovery. Beyond the rational mind with all its dualisms, light and darkness, black and white, conscious and unconscious, male and female, all these distinctions are there but they are contained within a unity, a wholeness, that transcends them all.

How different this is from our usual theological language! All too often language about God has been taken as if it is meant to be literal. The haggling about whether God is male or female or both is a direct result of such inappropriate literalism. An alternative way of considering this is discussed further on. It is important to be aware that the heartfelt cry of feminists for the recognition of femininity in God is genuine and is the result of 1) the one-sided masculinization of God that has held sway so destructively for so long, and 2) the gross and totally unjust oppression of women that is linked with both the conceptualization of God as male and the androcentricity of society and culture. Not only do women need to be liberated, there is also the need to liberate "God" from the all-too-Babylonian captivity of male exclusivism.

The urgency to reexamine the doctrine of God from a feminist perspective has emerged in correlation with the urgency to free women for the attainment of full human potential and to reevaluate our understanding of the feminine principle. In both cases I am advocating an holistic perspective that understands liberation as the soteriological (salvational) aspect of that great gathering of all things into unity in Christ of which Paul speaks in Ephesians 1:10. This is the goal or *telos* of the cosmic process and it includes affirmation and celebration of both femininity and masculinity, of both humankind and God. To deny or undervalue any element in that quaternary is not only to court impoverishment but to deny the purpose of human life. And so I am personally working towards, and here will argue for, a wholeness that means *inter alia* the dynamic inter-relating, balancing and integrating of complementary principles and polarities, not the domination of one over the other. Such wholeness includes healed relations between entities unnaturally separated and seemingly opposed. Among these polarities are included not only male/female and masculine/feminine but also mind(spirit)/body, grace/nature and God/humankind.

SEXUAL POLARITY AND GOD

In any particular context the current doctrine of God reflects the human search for ultimate reality, ultimate meaning and ultimate wholeness. Human sexuality is intimately implicated in that search. Human beings are in progress towards God and towards the fullness of human life. As developments proceed these turn out to be mutually interrelated such that progress in one is progress in the other.

The basis of polarity between femininity and masculinity lies in both genetic constitution and cultural conditioning. The polarity between the sexes is good, necessary, and irreducible. Each person is called to be fully human and also fully her or his sex. The order is: first a person, then a female (in the genetic biological sense), then feminine. Femininity concerns how we understand the essence of femaleness; femininity undergirds and sustains what it is to be female. In a man the same order pertains: first a person, then male, then masculine. Masculine and feminine poles are of equal weight and value.[8]

We need to be aware that sexual polarity is not only inter-personal but intra-personal. Biologically, no one is exclusively either male or female. Every male has at the level of his body, physiology and so on, a degree of femaleness and at the level of his personality a degree of femininity. Similarly every female has in her body elements of maleness (including in various levels, testosterone, one of the main male hormones), and in her personality, elements of masculinity. The sexual polarities contain one another holistically, as do the yin and yang of Chinese metaphysics. In permeating each individual person sexual polarity is an invitation to integration.

In the history of human development there are characteristics that have come to be associated with femininity and another different set associated with masculinity. Concerning these sets of characteristics there is much confusion and cross-argumentation. I suggest that two crucial points must be clarified here or else we slip from holistic feminism into one or other unbalanced view: 1) The characteristics correctly associated with femininity are *not* negative and humanly undesirable, as neither are most of the male-valued attributes listed by Broverman and others.[9] 2) The feminine characteristics that are more naturally developed in women on the ground of their female sexual constitution, and that are rightly associated with femininity, are *human* characteristics that need to be developed in both men and women if they are to be fully integrated human persons. Correlatively, masculine characteristics, that is, those attributes appropriately associated with maleness, are similarly *human* characteristics and must not be regarded as the sole prerogative of those who are biologically male.

To be fully integrated persons, women need to contact, and allow to develop, characteristics traditionally regarded as masculine, which include initiating, asserting, ordering, incisive logical rational reflection, leadership, and so on. Conversely, the characteristics appropriately associated with masculinity are not the negatives of the genuinely feminine ones. Feminine characteristics include intuitive wisdom, sensitivity, love, openness, warmth, receptivity, concreteness, nurturing, compassion, patiently waiting, relating and so on.[10] This is a list not of weaknesses but of strengths— pertinent strengths—that need to be accessed and developed by those who are biologically male in order that they may reach full actualization as human persons. For instance, in addition to their own natural strengths, men need also to be receptive, supportive, intuitive, and warm, while women need also to be initiating, at home in the world of abstract logical thought, and so on.

It cannot be emphasized strongly enough that what has gone so tragically wrong is the negative assessment of femininity in contrast to the high value that has been placed on maleness in society, culture, and church. It is about that and the ramifications of its oppressive outworkings that all feminists are angry, and rightly so. Holistic feminism insists that in the polar opposites of masculinity and femininity, one is not the negative of the other; both polar opposites are equal, positive, and mutually complementary and each is incomplete without the other. Moreover, as I later elaborate, it is through our sexuality that we move not only towards our human polar opposite but also towards psychological wholeness, ecclesial wholeness, and towards God.

THE NEED FOR SYMBOLS AND THEIR LIMITATIONS

The One we call God is ultimately ineffable, totally other than humankind and far beyond comprehension by the human mind. On that the Scriptures, patristic theology, the reformers, and most of our theological contemporaries are in one way or another agreed. We gain access to God both ontically and noetically through Jesus Christ our Lord, in the Holy Spirit, knowing God as God gives Self-knowledge. This vital access that we have to God involves the use of symbols and images that necessarily derive from intramundane experience, from realities and relationships such as the personal, familial, social, political, and so on, and from the deep hidden areas of the human psyche.

A symbol typifies, represents, suggests, or recalls something other than it, either by functioning analogically or metaphorically, or by association in fact or thought.[11] Symbols and images do not usually come singly but in constellations and take their meaning at least in part from the context in which they function. Language itself is symbolic; words are not things but function ostensively in pointing away from themselves to the realities they signify. In correctly using symbols of whatever kind, the understanding or consciousness must pass beyond the symbol to the reality symbolized.

Such transcendence of the symbol is necessary if we are not to take the symbol literally and, having thus misused it, fail to gain access to the reality symbolized.

On the one hand, then, we cannot really know God as God is. For this knowledge, we have to "unknow," to transcend the known aspects of all our symbols, to fragment the images, to enter into the "Cloud of Unknowing." It was the apophatic tradition in the Eastern Christian Church that most clearly recognized this, and we can learn much (and should do so as a matter of priority) from the hesychasm that relates to God in the light beyond images and in the silence beyond verbalization. In theology this corresponds to the *via negativa*, or negative way, where to predicate anything of God is to do so only in terms of negatives (infinite, eternal, incomprehensible, invisible, immortal, and so on). It is immediately recognizable that quite a considerable component of our present doctrine of God works in this way, recognizing ontically the otherness of God and noetically God's unknowability.

On the other hand, there is very much that can be said positively of God (the *via affirmativa*), for not only is God the One of thick darkness and incomprehensible mystery, but also God is Self-revealing. The Scriptures are full of positive symbols and images of God. The most basic is *person*, and it is here that sexual polarity and sexual language are immediately implicit. God is Self-revealing personally to persons. We relate to God personally as persons. Love is ultimate personal relationship in the dynamic mutuality of self-giving. Our doctrine of God is trinitarian in positing that God is love within God's very being: love given and received within the mutuality of the Godhead. In God's Self-giving to us through Christ and in the Holy Spirit, we are able to live, as it were, in the overflow of God's divine love, receiving and giving forth that love. Correlative to this is the transformation into God's image, which is our destiny in Christ, and the transformation of the cosmos that is consequent on our liberation.[12] There is nothing new in this. It is basic biblical doctrine. But it has to be said here because it is precisely in this symbolism of God as "person" and "personal" that, as assets accrue (it is good to think of God in personal terms), so problems and distortions arise. A whole range of misleading implications can arise from the symbolism of God as person. You could say, speaking anthropomorphically, that being misunderstood was a risk God took.

FEMININE SYMBOLS FOR GOD AND THE CHURCH

Krister Stendahl, when he was dean of Harvard Divinity School, said in an address in 1973, "The masculinity of God, and of God-language, is a cultural and linguistic accident."[13] Is this going too far, or not far enough? The history of the development of the doctrine of God in relation to femininity raises complex hermeneutic issues. In this discussion I am closely following Rosemary Ruether's historical summary[14] and am much indebted to her for her clarity and perspicacity.

The most basic symbol for God in both Testaments is Father. God was experienced as the Father of Israel, undoubtedly in a male role, and Israel was God's son, the symbolism being taken from relationships within the human family. At once the influence of the contemporary culture comes through. Israel was a patriarchal society. The covenant was made with the males of Israel, with circumcision the great sign of the covenant. Women in this culture were included marginally and were, generally speaking, considered more as property of the males along with their other possessions, servants, cattle, and so on. One of the reasons for the subordination of women in Israel was that women in tribal and early agricultural societies were in general segregated, subjugated, and hedged around with all manner of taboos and rituals connected with uncleanness thought to derive from female sexuality, menstruation and childbirth,[15] and much of this attitude and practice came over into Hebrew social structure.

Important here was the cultural conflict between the worship of Yahweh and the fertility religion of the Canaanites that continued to be practiced after the conquest and settlement. In common with the surrounding nations of the ancient Near East, Canaanite religion involved the worship of a goddess, in this case Anath, as well as a god-king, Baal, who between them were responsible, among other things, for the active renewal and fertility of the land, the crops, the livestock, and society. Yahwism was uncompromisingly opposed to all such "nature-religion." In another context Ruether suggests, "The OT [Old Testament] rejection of female symbols for God, and perhaps also of female religious leaders, probably had something to do with this struggle against Canaanite religion with its powerful goddess figures and its female-dominated ceremonies of worship."[16] So culturally and cultically the pendulum swung the other way towards male symbolism for God and male-dominated ceremonies of worship. Yahweh was the God of history who championed his people in battle, and also the God of nature (replacing the Baalim) who renewed the land or withheld his renewing power in the face of Israel's not infrequent disobedience. Intermarriage (though forbidden) between Israelites and non-Israelites reinforced the constant temptation to slip into worship of the local gods. Jeremiah speaks of the women of Jerusalem baking ritual cakes for the "queen of heaven," the goddess Ashtoreth, who was believed to have had more power than Yahweh to avert disaster.[17]

Another image of God in the Old Testament changes the symbolism, perhaps the result of God drawing Israel into closer relationship. Yahweh was seen as betrothing himself to Israel; she (Israel) was the bride or spouse of Yahweh and he her faithful husband who loved her and sought her out even when she was unfaithful to him. When the relationship between God and Israel was seen as a marriage, Israel's unfaithfulness, that is, her withdrawing her love from Yahweh and worshipping other gods, was seen as harlotry.[18] In this symbolism Israel as a whole is experienced as feminine and Yahweh as male and masculine, but here also his tender, self-giving love, and care for Israel is a characteristic that is basically feminine and is essential for any deeply intimate relationship between each and every lover or husband and his beloved. This symbolism of tender, intimate marriage is carried further and expressed more explicitly in the Song of Songs, with its sensual imagery and delight in the pleasures of sexual love. It is the allegory of love between Yahweh the lover and Israel the beloved. To this day this symbolism remains perhaps the most adequate and appropriate for the relationship between God and his beloved, which is you and me.

There is an interesting development in the Wisdom Literature of Judaism where another dimension of feminine symbolism for God emerges. There, wisdom (*Sophia*) was seen as the female personification of God, parallel perhaps to the very masculine symbol of the divine Logos that came into Judaism from Hellenistic philosophy, reinforcing the understanding of the creative and revelatory Word of God already strong in the Old Testament. The Logos is the divine "son"; wisdom is a divine "daughter." This feminine wisdom symbolism may again have come in from Israel's neighbors: it may also be evidence of the necessity to recognize the feminine in God. In Egypt the goddess Isis was spoken of as the embodiment of wisdom. The

Babylonian goddess Ishtar was the bringer of wisdom from the gods to humanity. In Egypt *Maat*, or divine justice, was a feminine being, daughter of the sun-god, expressive of divine wisdom in ordering and governing the world. In chapter eight of Proverbs, wisdom is the agent of God in creation and in continually ordering and governing the world, and also in bringing those who accept her back to communion with God. There is then a striking coincidence of roles between the feminine wisdom of the Wisdom Literature and the masculine Logos of John 1:1–8. In the apocryphal Wisdom of Solomon the language about wisdom becomes more mystical and the figure is undoubtedly feminine.[19]

Another very fascinating feminine symbol for God in the Old Testament is the shekinah or "presence," the presence of God on earth.[20] The divine presence as feminine became joined in later rabbinic thinking with the biblical tradition that speaks of Israel as the wife or bride of God.[21] In the plight of the exile, God was understood to have been separated from his people Israel. But God's shekinah, his divine presence and his beloved spouse, accompanies Israel into exile, like a sorrowing mother going with her children after they have been estranged from their father. The exile, then, can in this sense be considered a separation of God from himself, the estrangement of God from his own shekinah or presence. I suggest that this is highly appropriate symbolism in terms of which to talk about the suffering of God, in contradistinction to the still commonly prevailing idea of the impassibility of God inherited from classical Hellenism. In rabbinic thought the return of Israel would mean the overcoming of this estrangement. But of course final return, reconciliation, and consummation are eschatological; compare Revelation 21:2 where, at the end of history, the Church, the holy city, descends from heaven as a bride to be united with her husband. Jürgen Moltmann significantly uses this feminine symbolism of the shekinah in the development of his doctrine of the Trinity.[22]

It seems, then, that while the notion of a goddess was systematically suppressed in Israel, the feminine principle reasserted itself in various ways. In relation to Israel, the covenant community itself could be seen as the bride of Yahweh and hence Israel could be seen as a mother who mediates the commands of God to the "sons" of Israel, her children. And in relation to God, if God is to be spoken of in personal terms, there is no way in which feminine characteristics can fail to be predicated of God. For example, masculine power untempered by feminine compassion would be something quite other than the power of God experienced by God's people.

The dichotomy between nature and grace that was an integral part of Reformed theology accentuated the activity of God against the passivity of nature. It thus accentuated the maleness of God and the femininity not only of nature but of persons, reinforcing the hierarchy, God-male-female.

Linked in with this grace/nature dichotomy was the theologically correct and necessary doctrine of justification by Christ alone, by faith alone, by grace alone, which raises—particularly for those in the Reformed tradition—the crucial question of how to proceed with, and in light of, our justification of this. It is the question of sanctification and of ethics. The tendency, then, was to dichotomize human response to God's grace into a "spiritual," dependent, individualistic, "feminine" relationship with God as against "masculine" activity in the secular world. The Church thus became relegated to the private sphere and played a supportive, feminine role, being taken out of the male roles of power and activity.[23]

Also, while being theologically correct and necessary, the doctrine of God creating *ex nihilo*, out of nothing, reinforces the symbolism of God as male, creating from outside. A. R. Peacocke, who is a molecular biologist as well as a theologian, suggests that we can perhaps help to redress the balance between the stress on the externality of God's creative act and the feminine aspects of God's creativity by taking into account the analogy of woman's contribution in creating *in utero* a new being. This could be seen as an analogy of God creating the world within herself. God creates a world that is, in principle and origin, other than himself/herself but creates it, the world, within himself/herself.[24] This is very like Tillich's symbolism of God as "the ground of being"; and Tillich himself saw that this was a feminine rather than masculine symbol for God. In Peacocke's symbolism God is the divine matrix, the ground of all the possibilities of creation, which is both a very feminine understanding of God's creativity and is itself an immensely exciting concept. Relating to God as the ground or field of all possibilities enables one to relate existentially to God in moment-to-moment awareness of God's continuous creativity.[25]

God, as far as I am aware, is never directly called in Scripture the mother of Israel, but there is a reference to precisely this relationship in Deuteronomy 32:18. Significantly, this text has been mistranslated in the

Jerusalem Bible (1966 ed.), in what can only be a sexist hermeneutic gaffe. The translation reads, "You forget the Rock who begot you, unmindful now of the God who fathered you." The word in the first line of the parallelism translated "begot" is the word *yalad*, for which "begot" is a possible translation, but the word is more usually used in relation to a woman giving birth, where it means to bear or to bring forth a child. But the word translated "fathered" in the second line is *chul*, which is cognate with *chil* and means pain, sorrow or pang. The literal meaning of *chul* is "to writhe about" and is used for a mother bringing forth a child with difficulty. In this case the text is speaking to Israel of "God who brought you forth with difficulty," which is a good way of putting it. By the shift in image from female to male this sense of the anguish of God's struggle to bring Israel to birth is eliminated and the poignancy of the passage diminished.

There is a word frequently used in the Old Testament for God's tender compassion for humanity that again brings out femininity. The word is *rachamim* (an intensive plural) and it comes from the noun *racham*, which means "uterus." *Rachamim* refers to the uniquely tender love that a mother has for her newborn child—again symbolism poignant in its femininity.[26]

In the eleventh century St. Anselm addressed prayers to "Jesus our Mother," and Julian of Norwich, that great woman mystic of the fourteenth century, attributed motherhood to both God and Christ: "Jesus Christ who doeth good against evil, is our very Mother . . . As truly as God is our Father, so truly is God our Mother."[27]

Another example of the use of feminine terms to embody the concept of God in the Old Testament is the word *ruach* for God's Spirit, which is a feminine noun (as it is also in Aramaic, the language that Jesus spoke). This might both express and reinforce the experience of the femininity of God's presence. The Spirit is the "Go-Between-God,"[28] the relationship-maker; and relationship-seeking is a feminine characteristic, as contrasted with masculine isolation-independence seeking.[29] Against this is the fact that in Greek, and therefore in the New Testament, the word for Spirit is *pneuma*, which is a neuter noun.

Having reviewed some of the symbols and images for God, both masculine and feminine, it must be made clear that theologically we cannot divide the persons of the Trinity into male and female, for the important reason that the divine persons are *homoousios*, of the same substance.[30] This further

—ᴡᴡ—

highlights the fact that no symbols and images for God can be put forth as if they were a matter of logic. And ultimately, all have to be transcended.

FEMININITY, MASCULINITY, AND WHOLENESS

The above discussion traced the polar opposites of femininity and masculinity within each person as well as between persons, and it was proposed that for various reasons, men and women need to contact, and allow to develop, both sets of characteristics.

In inter-personal relations the paradigm is that sexual maturity leads to marriage or partnering where female and male, masculine and feminine, complement one another. But that, I contend, is not the ultimate goal of sexuality. Over and above the outer marriage or partnership between a man and a woman (or quite apart from it in the case of celibacy), an intra-personal or interior marriage has to take place between the masculine and feminine elements within the one person. In Jungian terminology, this is the culmination of the integration of a woman's *animus* with her femininity and with the rest of her psyche, and of a man's *anima* with his masculinity and with the rest of his psyche. There is a sense in which exterior marriage is for the sake of interior marriage, as Father Bede himself emphasized.[31] The process by which this interior marriage takes place is different in men and in women, and is why the attempt to reduce maleness and femaleness to the common denominator of their conflated characteristics is misguided and misleading. Individuation is a dynamic balance in which the polarities in the union are retained and integrated, not a static uniformity that merely cancels out the differences.

This interior integration is the basis of the humanization of both men and women, and holistic feminism regards this as being a deeper goal of sexuality than male-female sexual relations. Yet there is a more ultimate stage of humanization that involves the union of the more ultimate "opposites," humanity and God. Humanity cannot be fully human unless it is united with God and permeated by God. The process here as Jung probed it is that a woman's *animus* can lead her to her inner world, her soul (psyche), her self,[32] while the ultimate stage is, as Thomas Merton frequently pointed out, that one's deepest self or center must be transcended unto God who is beyond but also permeates all that is.[33] Similarly a man's *anima* leads him "to the path of wholeness and spiritual development."[34] It is sadly to the discredit of the institutional Church that, because of the Church's fear of both sexuality and the human psyche, it gives so little encouragement to travelers on this inner journey towards wholeness and God.

The ecclesia, the Church, should be the context *par excellence* in which humanization reaches its zenith. In the New Testament, symbolism and ways of relating to God that were developed in the Old Testament converge and focus on the person of Christ, the Son of the Father who is not other than God. In Jesus "the perfect man" (Eph. 4:13)—the paradigm of manhood—we may posit perfect integration of the opposites in his person. His maleness and masculinity are not in doubt. He certainly showed aspects of femininity; above all love (balanced with the more masculine truth), and including, for instance, being tenderly compassionate, mediating, relating, "being with" (Emmanuel means "God with us"), waiting upon God, being utterly receptive of God. Certainly he nurtures his people, feeding us on his own body.

The Church as a whole may be seen as the Body of Christ receiving her life from him, and as the bride of Christ in reciprocal love relationship with him—striking feminine symbolism! The image of the body is not static and homogeneous, but dynamic and organic, for it is made up of mutually supportive and interfunctioning parts. The parts function together in their contribution to the whole. Paul's symbolism in Ephesians is particularly central in leading us to develop an understanding of male and female, masculine and feminine roles in the Church in their appropriate mutual interrelationship. The Church (*ekklesia*—feminine noun) is the Body of Christ (Eph. 4:13) and the principle is love, where the members are to be rooted and grounded in love (Eph. 4:16), each part "adding its own strength" (Eph. 4:16, Jerusalem Bible [JB]). The way Paul puts it is so appropriate: 1) that the separate parts work together each "according to its function" (Eph. 4:16), 2) under Christ the head (Eph. 4:16), which means both under his control and finding unity in him, 3) making a "unity in the work of service" (Eph. 4:13), which is an integration into unity, and 4) with at least part of the aim being that of becoming "mature people" (Eph. 4:13, Good News Bible [GNB]), "fully mature with the fulness of Christ himself" (Eph. 4:13 JB).

In a pattern of whole and balanced rather than male-dominated ministry, the presence of women working alongside men both complements their masculine contribution and assists them in the development of their own femininity, and also facilitates their becoming more whole, integrated persons and therefore more, rather than less, efficient in ministry. And similarly, *mutatis mutandis*, with women. For characteristics previously acknowledged as "feminine," particularly those of nurturing, being accepting, being warm and preeminently being loving, are indispensable in anybody's ministry— and woe to the male minister or priest who lacks them. The "masculine" characteristics of incisive logical, rational, reflective thought, ordering, initiating, asserting, and so on need *mutatis mutandis* to be added to woman's feminine characteristics to enable her to be effective in her service. In terms of the tendency to polarity between truth and love, females can teach truth-oriented males to be more loving; males can teach love-oriented females to be more concerned with the truth.

This can be seen as being a valid and practical interpretation of Paul in the fourth chapter of Ephesians, where he speaks of the contribution of truth and love and of each part adding its own appropriate component to be built by Christ into holistic maturity. "If we live by the truth and in love, we shall grow in all ways into Christ, who is the head by whom the whole body is filled and joined together, every joint adding its own strength, for each separate part to work according to its function. So the body grows until it has built itself up in love" (Eph. 4:15ff JB). It is significant that this interpretation deemphasizes the domination of one part or group or office or sex over another; all are to work together under "Christ, who is the head." In Paul's interpretation, each would use the appropriate energy, masculine or feminine, to motivate and enhance the energy of the other. Each would use her or his power to raise and build the other up. I suggest that the famous passage in the fifth chapter of Ephesians that tends to be used in certain circles in the contemporary Church to resubordinate women all over again should be read in the light of Ephesians, chapter four, with its beautiful balance of humanizing complementarity.

It is necessary for this holistic feminism to assert, over against all attempts to subordinate women on biblical grounds, that subordination of women to men is not of the order of creation but is most definitely part of the fallenness of creation. Yahweh's pronouncement to the woman in

Genesis 3:6 is, "Your yearning shall be for your husband, yet he will lord it over you" (JB). That is the *fallen* state of affairs. "Being one in union with Christ Jesus" (Gal. 3:28) does not mean that there is no difference between men and women (v. 27) (which is the *reductio ad absurdum* interpretation some people are using to deflect the real meaning of the text). It means rather that *both* male "lording it" and female acceptance of subordination are done away with. This is the soteriological correlate of the new understanding of the lordship of God suggested in the penultimate section of this article.

Since the Church is the Body of Christ and since his work is complete (cf. the emphasis on the finished work of Christ in the Reformation), the Church already has its wholeness, its *telaiōsis*, complete in him, and so its task now is to actualize that wholeness in its historical existence. The purpose of what Paul said in Ephesians about the building up of the body to wholeness is "to fill the whole universe with his [God's] presence" (Eph. 4:10 GNB; cf. the divine *shekinah*). Christologically, what immediately springs to mind here is that we need to reemphasize the Irenaean understanding of incarnation, in which redemption in Christ is the reunion of all things unnaturally separated, the healing of all estrangements and alienations and the restoration of all things (*ta panta*) to God, as in Ephesians 1:10, Colossians 1:17, 20, and Romans 8:21ff. The alternative, the position that Irenaeus was theologically countering in his own pastoral situation, is the Gnostic, Marcionite separation of creation and redemption, which in the Church today appears in the frequent and insidious separation of spirituality from praxis. When this happens it can easily lead to the fatal dichotomy between political activism and individualistic pietism. This is all too evident in some parts of the contemporary ecumene, when what is needed for healing and wholeness is the integration of "contemplation in action" and "activity in obedience" (perhaps along the lines suggested by Thomas Merton). It may well be that because contemplation has so largely dropped out of our experience we cannot get either the praxis or the necessary balance between being active and being passive right. Since the alienation between male and female over the years has provided the paradigm relationship of oppressor/oppressed, it would be highly significant if the Church took deliberate action to "get it right" between male and female in its membership. Not only would this be one less dimension of alienation in our societies, but it could be a positive contribution to the liberation required on both sides of all societies' oppressed/oppressor separatedness.

It has been pointed out by Clinebell that the major nurturing movement these days, led mostly by men because they have the training and the expertise, is the ecology movement. These men value and are using "their feminine side, the nurturing, caring, preserving, creating qualities."[35] It is ecology that sees creation as a whole in relation to its parts and the parts in relation to the whole, emphasizing constantly the mutual interrelatedness of events, parts and whole. Holistic feminism is all set to work with an ecclesial ecology (or ecological ecclesiology!) centering on the dynamics of this interrelatedness within the body, and extending to its obviously cosmic implications. Interdependence and mutuality between man and woman (which are better words than equality, because they are dynamic rather than static) would then, among other interpretations, mean at the level of the community sharing the load, sharing the responsibility (the answer-ability to God), sharing the leadership, each in the appropriate way, and envisaging the goal as filling the whole universe with God's presence (Eph. 4:10).

Both "Both/And" and "Neither/Nor" in the Doctrine of God

The suggestion is often made these days that we should desexualize our doctrine of God and get "new more inclusive ways of describing the indescribable."[36] I am very much in favor of getting new ways of speaking of God as long as we do not think we can ever "describe" that Ultimate Reality. On the other hand, the strategy of desexualization of our language about God would be a serious mistake because, as in a similar way that we relate to each other as persons through our masculinity and femininity, so God relates to us in the Spirit in and through the masculinity and femininity that make up our personhood. Sexual symbols are so alive for us today that we devalue them at our peril.[37] So what we have to do is not to abandon the symbols but retain them and use them correctly. Human relationships would not get very far if they were desexualized; we are sexual beings and all we do in a sense partakes of our sexuality.[38] We cannot relate to each other without our bodies and our sexual and psychological makeup. But we *also* relate to each other *beyond* our sexuality. We transcend our sexuality, without denying it, in authentic, *personal* relationship. Indeed, our sexuality is only properly being used insofar as it is also being transcended.[39] So in relationship with God, we need the anthropomorphic symbolism of masculinity and femininity, but we also need overall consciousness of the ultimate inadequacy of both sets of symbols. God is neither masculine nor feminine. In our relationship with God we have the symbols as means of existential, psychological and ontic access, but we have also to transcend the symbols in mutual (if asymmetrical) relationship with God in the Spirit. So the furthest that we can go is to say that, in our relationship with and speech about God, it is a case of *"both both/and and neither/nor"*; **both** *masculine and feminine symbols* **and** *neither masculine nor feminine symbols*. This incorporates the apophatic tradition as well as the affirmative way and assures positive proclamation of the Good News while guarding against misuse of it.

An example might help. If one of the essential characteristics of femininity is waiting, is not God waiting for us? Is not this, perhaps, of the essence of the *feminine* principle in God? But God is also taking the initiative in actively seeking us out, as the doctrine of the incarnation and much of the teaching of Jesus affirms. Is not this, perhaps, of the essence of the *masculine* principle in God? We relate to God as Father, but we also experience God's caring, nurturing, tender love (very feminine). And so it is that God waits for us dynamically, not passively. And so it could go on, the masculinity and femininity complementing each other and giving us, as it were, something to hook our minds on to, which is necessary given that we have minds that have to hook on to something. But all the time the reality of God far transcends all human symbols. Our relationship with God is in fact prior to, and undergirds, our knowing. If we can relate to God in this way, I believe we will be going a long way both towards "letting God be God," which was one of the essential principles of the Reformation, and towards letting ourselves be fully human, which is our destiny in union with Christ.

HOLISTIC FEMINISM AND GOD

The God of holistic feminism is the liberator, not a tribal, national, or sectarian god who frees by exclusion, by separation, by apartness, but God the Lord who frees and unites. This is good news about liberation, God and us.

First, liberation is an evangelical promise, not a threat. Second, as long as anyone remains oppressed, liberation is incomplete because liberation as it is in Christ is for all; in particular, it is the freeing of the oppressor as much as of the oppressed. Third, liberation means renewal of the whole person of both oppressor and oppressed. This includes all that has been said above about integration and it means that in order to actualize their liberation, women, and any other previously oppressed people, have to think and behave and be as those who have been liberated in Christ—and the practicalities of that are not easy to achieve when the history of the acceptance of oppression is long and deeply inculcated into the very structures of femininity. Fourth, on the one hand, those who subjugate, subordinate and oppress are doing as much harm to themselves as to those they hold back, both positively in their active impeding of progress and negatively in what they miss by not receiving what the other has to give. Oppressors are losers. On the other hand, if women who up to now have been held in one kind of subjugation or another are being set free for the possibilities of abundant life, it cannot be emphasized strongly enough that it is not only for their benefit but for the benefit of all human persons and the structures they devise and work with. Liberation, then, is to be seen as an holistic process within which the present feminist movement is playing an indispensable role. "Liberation is experienced when people are one again, one with each other, one with nature and one with God."[40] In the liberty that unites there is that "free access to each other which people find in the love that binds them and in the joy they find in one another."[41]

Further, God's lordship is understood in a new way. The God who so holistically liberates and unites is the God whose Son said, "No longer do I call you servants, for the servant does not know what his master is doing; but I have called you friends, for all that I have heard from my Father I have made known to you" (John 15:15). This kind of freedom "only becomes possible when people know themselves in God and God in them."[42] It is through the same liberating knowledge of God in us and of us in God that God wants in us the "boldness and confidence of friends who share his rule with him."[43] This reflects a new understanding of God's lordship that is not as traditional monarchial monotheism would have it, a lordship "which legitimizes dependency, helplessness and servitude," but a lordship "which overcomes all supremacy and subjection."[44] In such a community of believers that "is not only in fellowship *with* God but in God too,"[45] subordination and servitude are replaced by the mutual service of those who love one another.

Finally, in and through this God who so liberates and unites there is a rediscovery of genuine mysticism. Dorothee Sölle characterizes this as 1) "based on experience, not authority" and 2) speaking of "a God whose essence is *not* independence, might and domination."[46] Third, she emphasizes that "mysticism helps us to learn the great surrender," that is, the surrender of the "I," the self.[47] It is in this *cognitio Dei experimentalis* (experiential knowledge of God) that we come to know that the God who is experienced as within and the God who is experienced as transcendent are one, God in us and we in God, and action is balanced, inspired, and supported by contemplation. For Moltmann this is a "new 'direct' relationship with God" in freedom,[48] in which arises "the process of maturing through experiences that are continually new."[49] It is to this God, this experience and this maturing that holistic feminism is an open invitation.

I believe that Father Bede can be seen as an exemplar of such holistic feminism, leading to genuine mysticism. Soon after his eighty-seventh birthday, Father Bede had another stroke, followed by an additional very serious one about a month later, on January 24th, 1993. Physically he was weak and in the process of his final decline but his mystical, intuitive awareness was radiantly alive. When he was asked the question, "Who is the Mother for you now?" his response was, "It is too deep for words. She is the background to everything." He was also identifying with the *ajata*, the Unborn One, or rather the One who has gone so far beyond that it is as if she or he were one with the ground of all things. At this stage, intellectual explanations were not what Father Bede was concerned with and I do not want to risk overinterpreting him. But it feels right, and would be entirely consistent with what he had been explaining so carefully prior to his final illness, that what was likely happening was that he was in some sense experiencing both the ground of all things, which he had identified as the Mother, and also himself, in his transcended but still-present masculinity and femininity, one in that ground, in the mystery of the nonduality of divine love.

NOTES

1. Much of the material in this article is an edited extract from my work, "God from a Feminist Perspective," in *Sexism and Feminism in Theological Perspective*, ed. W. S. Vorster (Pretoria: University of South Africa Press, 1984).

2. B. Griffiths, *The Marriage of East and West* (1982), p. 8.

3. Ibid.

4. Ibid., p. 10.

5. Ibid.

6. B. Griffiths, *The New Creation in Christ* (1992), p. 103.

7. Cf. ibid.

8. J. A. Sanford, *The Invisible Partners* (New York: Paulist, 1980), p. 108.

9. I. K. Broverman, et. al., "Sex-role Stereotypes and Clinical Judgements of Mental Health," *Journal of Consulting and Clinical Psychology* 34 (1970), pp. 1–7.

10. E. S. Fiorenza, "Feminist Theology as a Critical Theology of Liberation," *TS* 36 (1975), p. 615.

11. Cf. F. W. Dillistone, *Christianity and Symbolism* (London: Collins, 1955).

12. Cf. Rm. 8:18ff.

13. K. Stendahl, "Enrichment or Threat? When the Eves Come Marching In," in A. L. Hagemann (ed), *Sexist Religion and Women in the Church: No More Silence!* (New York: Association, 1974), pp. 117–123.

14. R. R. Ruether, *Liberation Theology* (New York: Paulist, 1972); idem, "Mary: The Feminine Face of the Church," *Enquiry* 9 (1976), pp. 1–38.

15. Cf. Ruether, *Liberation Theology*, pp. 96ff.

16. Ruether, "Mary: The Feminine Face of the Church," p. 5.

17. Jer. 7:18; cf. Ruether, "Mary: The Feminine Face," p. 6.

18. Cf. Hos. 1–3.

19. Cf. Wisdom of Solomon, 7:25–27 and 8:2.

20. Cf. Ex. 40:34–38, Num. 9:15–23.

21. Cf., e.g., Hos. 2:19–20.

22. J. Moltmann, *The Trinity and the Kingdom of God* (London: SCM, 1981).

23. Ruether, "Mary: The Feminine Face," p. 32.

24. A. R. Peacocke, *Creation and the World of Science* (Oxford: Clarendon, 1979), p. 142.

25. Cf. Col 1:17 and Heb. 1:3.

26. Examples are: Is. 63:7; Ps. 77:9, 79:8, & 119:77; Zech. 1:16; and Neh. 9:28.

27. J. Walsh, *The Revelation of Divine Love of Julian of Norwich* (New York: Harper & Row, 1961), p. 167.

28. J. V. Taylor, *The Go-Between God* (London: SCM, 1972).

29. Cf. P. Teilhard de Chardin, *Human Energy* (London: Collins, 1969), p. 74.

30. Cf. G. H. Tavard, "Sexist Language in Theology?" *TS* 36, pp. 700–724.

31. Griffiths, *Marriage of East and West*.

32. Sanford, *Invisible Partners*, pp. 75–77.

33. Cf. J. J. Higgins, *Thomas Merton on Prayer* (New York: Doubleday, 1975).

34. Sanford, *Invisible Partners*, p. 72.

35. C. H. Clinebell, *Meet Me in the Middle: On Becoming Human Together* (New York: Harper, 1973).

36. C. Miller & K. Swift, *Words and Women: Language and the Sexes* (London: Penguin, 1976), p. 98 & Ch. 5ff.

37. Sanford, *Invisible Partners*, p. 92.

38. H. Thielicke, *The Ethics of Sex* (London: James Clark, 1964).

39. Cf. F. Edwards, "Designing a Theology of Sexuality," in T. D. Verryn, ed., *Church and Marriage in Modern Africa* (Pretoria: Ecumenical Research Unit, 1975), pp. 51–81.

40. Moltmann, *Trinity and Kingdom*, p. 216.

41. Ibid., p. 220.

42. Ibid.

43. Ibid., p. 221.

44. Ibid., p. 192.

45. Ibid., p. 202; his italics.

46. D. Sölle, "Mysticism, Liberation and the Names of God: A Feminist Reflection," *Christianity and Crisis* 41 (1981), pp. 179-185; her italics.

47. Ibid., pp. 179, 184.

48. Moltmann, *Trinity and Kingdom*, p. 220.

49. Ibid., p. 222.

The One and the Many: Communitarian Nondualism

Beatrice Bruteau

My own background, which forms a basis for my spiritual approach, is in science and philosophy, and in Vedanta and Roman Catholicism. My publications, here and in India, express a spirituality integrated from these sources and include books on Aurobindo and Teilhard de Chardin. What We Can Learn from the East *and* The Easter Mysteries *(both 1995), are my most recent publications.[1]*

I met Father Bede at an MID meeting in 1983 and was received as an Oblate by him in 1991, having carried on an extensive correspondence in the meantime. I seek to contribute to Dom Bede's hopes for renewal in contemplative life and for new forms of monasticism by participating in the ecumenical Schola Contemplationis, and in a local monastic community founded for this purpose.

Holism and the preservation of differentiation in the heart of Unity appear as themes in my own piece, where I endeavor to resolve the tension that the Saccidananda gurus felt between Trinitarianism and nondualism. The essay offered here develops a metaphysics of reconciliation of the One and the Many through what I call the "I-I relation" between persons who, in love, simultaneously differentiate and unite themselves. The Ultimate Reality is presented as such a nondual community, and the cosmos is conceived as its expression, securing a ground for the ecological values so important to our future.

Jt seems that mystics all over the world in all the various traditions come to similar conclusions. Asking "What is the Ultimate Reality?" and "Who am I?" they eventually undergo spiritual experiences in which they find that there is no distinction between the seeker and the Sought, that specifying a difference between the two is something that is no longer possible or can be given meaning. Ways of characterizing the Reality have been abandoned, ways of characterizing the self have been stripped away. The mystics then say that they have become—or have discovered that they always were—one with the Ultimate Reality. Nearly always—in fact, it seems to be a good test for the genuineness of the experience—such people now refuse to acknowledge any separation between themselves and others. They exert themselves for the benefit of others as we ordinary people do for ourselves, and they devote themselves to the welfare of friend or stranger or enemy with equal vigor.

What has happened to them? What have they seen? They are clearly operating out of a meaning-context that transcends the one in common usage in this world. Can we offer a model of the structure of Reality that will on the one hand allow us access to the mystics' *experience*—of the "nondifference" between themselves and the Ultimate—and on the other hand allow us to realize their *behavior*—expressive of self-giving love to all? This model must also explain why not all of us yet see what the mystics see, and how we can come to see it.

There have been various myths and models created in different times and places around the world and appearing among the various peoples of the earth to explain, to teach, and to celebrate this supreme experience of human beings. What follows is another such model that perhaps suggests a way of reconciling some disparate features of previous ones. Perhaps it also can be found congenial with the most significant source of images of Reality in our modern world—the natural sciences.

I will not undertake to discuss the model in terms of its relations to existing traditions, including the scientific. The main lines of those relations will most likely be apparent to the informed reader. In any case, the most important thing for a spiritual model to do, whether it is in strict continuity with previous efforts or not, is to help ordinary people make sense of their ordinary daily lives, which nevertheless include a spiritual depth dimension of which no one is deprived. This is what I hope to accomplish.

THE ONE AND THE MANY

The basic problem in representing the Reality to ourselves is typified by the two outstanding features of the mystics' transformed lives mentioned above: They claim an experience of "oneness" with the Ultimate, and they energetically go out in love to all others. Clearly the mystic has not concluded from this experience of oneness that other beings do not exist—their experience is not of solipsism. Rather, it is the reverse: The transfigured personality has a heightened sense of the reality of other persons—and of other living, and even nonliving, beings—that seems to arise out of the revelation of oneness and out of the liberation from exclusive concern with oneself. What kind of "oneness" is this, then? And how does it transform the "otherness" of others? Has something happened to the mystics' conception of selfhood?

Another way of putting the problem is this: Each of us is urged to undertake spiritual practices in the hope of attaining the mystical experience of oneness. But when we have reached this realization of oneness, where is "each" of us? Do we not each experience the oneness? And are there not many of us, all realizing oneness?

It is not satisfactory, it seems to me, to say that the "many" are illusory, an error of perception or judgment. Nor is it satisfactory to say that the "oneness" is illusory or imperfect or partial. To me, such arguments seem to sacrifice the empirical reality of the mystics' lives to theoretical tidiness in a system of abstract concepts. Experience is what we *really* have; models of explanation or interpretation must be in service to experience and judged by it, not the other way around. At the same time, we must keep in mind that a transformation is involved: The experience itself shifts; those who have not "seen" come to "see."

My way of dealing with this dilemma is to try to find another way of conceiving "oneness" and "manyness" themselves, so that they are not exclusive of each other. Usually, we think that manyness implies that beings *are* exclusive of each other: this one is unambiguously *not* that one. What makes them exclude another? We can tell them apart because this one has some feature that the other one lacks. It is the *not-having* that gives each being its claim to separate and definable being. This negation determines the separate being to be what it is.

But this is looking at the situation from the outside, from the point of view of someone who is none of the beings concerned, who looks *at* them. What happens when I am one of the beings? I think we do the same thing: We pretend to look at ourselves as if at some outside being, in the same way that we regard "other" beings. And so I see that "I" have certain qualities that distinguish "me" from all others and establish me in my own reality. Thus, we identify our reality with this set of distinguishing qualities, and it is the habit of identifying ourselves in this way that produces fear and disorientation as we approach mystical experience: We find our "qualities" slipping away, and consequently we do not know who we are anymore—at least in the way we *used* to know who we are! So we feel that we are falling into emptiness, losing ourselves.

On the other hand, as long as we do not live in mystical realization it seems perfectly obvious to us that we must protect our "qualities" in order to sustain our being. Survival, self-defense—these are fundamental principles of living. And this, paradoxically, leads to all the selfishness and consequent greed and cruelty that we denounce, while at the same time we rationalize and justify them (for our "self-esteem," for our "national interest," for "corporate solvency"), even while suffering from their grave consequences.

But suppose that instead of looking at my "I" this way—from the outside, as if it were an inert *object*—I experience existing from the inside, as being a living *subject*. Experienced this way, I am not a collection of qualities but an *activity*. (However, we must guard against looking at the activity, conceptualizing it, and again endowing it with distinguishing qualities.) When we do this, we experience ourselves in "real time," not as abstractions, not as something confined by concepts or fixed in a given definition and character. From the very fact that we are living activity, we are not defined or definable. What is usually called "change" from the point of view of fixed characteristics—the moving from one definition or description to another—here has dissolved all the fixed points; only the flow itself is real. These fixed points are abstractions, artificially frozen stills that are unreal as soon as they are snapped. In real time I experience living, existing itself, "in the first person," as *I*—by being/doing it, not by reflecting on it—"in the third person," as an *it*—talking about it, describing it.

If "manyness" has been realized by defining beings that are outside one another by virtue of their mutual negation of each other's combination of qualities, is "manyness" still there if I do not perceive/conceive myself in this way? If there is no difference between us (if you don't have what I lack and vice versa), then do we all not collapse into identity? That would follow only in a scheme in which the sole reality that any of us can claim is vested in our possessed qualities, in our descriptions. If our reality is instead our activity of actually living in real time—something experienced from the inside, not looked at from the outside, then "collapse into identity" is not the only alternative to "difference." We can be nondifferent (because not defined) and still be ourselves (the subjects who are actually existing), because our reality is our act of existing.

We can indicate "manyness" by a different kind of "difference." To make the idea clearer and easier to understand, I will define a specific terminology for it. Let *differentiation* be the general term, and *difference* and *distinction* be species of it. *Difference* is established by the assertion that I am my description and my description excludes your description: I am I because I am not-you, and you are you because you are not-I. This is *mutual negation*, and it suggests that we define *distinction* in terms of *mutual affirmation*. Could our act of being, of living in real time, experiencing ourselves from the inside, be an act of affirming another? This other, of course, would also be an act of subjective living in the same real time. It would be necessary to avoid turning that other subject into an object—abstracting it from the act of living in real time—by looking *at* it in terms of defining qualities attributed to it.

But if our act of living could be also an act of affirming the act of living of the "other," then we would establish our distinction without creating or referring to any difference between us. It is especially interesting that such an act simultaneously establishes "oneness" for us, a oneness that does not contradict or abridge our "manyness," and also establishes the "manyness" that in turn does not prevent the "oneness."

—⚬—

The Person According to Daniel Walsh

To explain this idea further, I need to establish the notion of *person* as different from *nature*. I learned this distinction from the philosopher, Daniel Clark Walsh—although I have added my own interpretation and further development onto his original doctrine.[2]

A *nature* is a certain form of being; it answers the question, "What is it?" The nature can be specified, defined; it can be multiplied—many beings may have the same nature. The nature channels the activities of the being in relation to the other natures in its environment. A single instance of a nature is an "individual." The nature and the individual are contingent, nonnecessary, therefore created beings.

The *person*, by contrast, is formless. Walsh terms it a "subsistent relation."[3] It answers the question, "Who is it?" rather than "What is it?" Having no form, person cannot be specified, cannot be defined or described; it has no character or qualities. When we talk about it, we make it sound as though person is a "kind" of being, but that is due to the structure of our language and is not really accurate. There are many persons, but they are not instances of a "kind." Persons are absolutely unique. Being neither the same nor different (in our definition of "different"), they are simply incomparable.

At this point it is important to distinguish explicitly between *person* and *personality*. Personality is the aspect of our human nature that we describe in terms of basic attitudes and interests, and patterns of reaction and relation. Personality, unlike the person, has form and can be described. It is what we inquire into by means of astrology, enneagrams and Myers-Briggs Type Indicators. We identify ourselves as personalities when we acknowledge certain descriptions of ourselves rather than others: we are Fire signs rather than Water, number 2s rather than 5s, ESTJs rather than INFPs. Personality is a sort of stained glass window through which the light of the person shines, or it is a costume that the person wears. In the model I am proposing here, personality is definitely *not* our ultimate and true self. It is *not* the person. As between the concepts of *person* and *nature*, personality belongs on the side of nature.

The *person*, on the other hand, can be called the unborn and the immortal. It is not the medium or instrumentality by means of which, or through which, one acts—as the nature is—but it is the primordial *acting* one. Thus

I am not a human nature that "has" a person; I am a person who "has" a human nature. The human nature is contingent, it is born and it dies, but as Walsh says—and I agree—the person is not contingent.[4] He also says that the person arises *in God* as a noncontingent subsisting relation with the ultimate ground of being, Who is foundational Person—or actually, Persons, because the Person-God must be a complex unity, or community. Person, Walsh says, arises in the intuition God has of Godself. Its arising is not an act of "choice," as the creation of natures is. In Walsh's metaphysical division, *persons* originate directly in God's *being*, while *natures* are created by the exercise of God's *will*.[5]

The person has this special relation to God because "God is Love." This is the starting point, says Walsh, and the choice of starting point is all important.[6] If God is Love, then God must be the relational activity of loving. To be a person, in Walsh's view, is to be an act of loving that is a subsisting relation. And that is what God *is*—Personal act(s) of Loving. All such acts of loving are persons and arise within the Divine Being. Perhaps the most startling thing that Walsh has said is: "Love is so intense that it expresses itself as the Trinity. The Trinity is not God; the Trinity is the first expression of Love, who is God."[7]

Walsh distinguishes the Persons of the Trinity from those persons subsequently gifted with angelic and human (perhaps other?) natures, by calling the Trinity the "first effusion of God's love," and the rest of the persons the "second effusion." But all persons are transcendental relations, "more or less co-extensive with being," because they are not limited by association with a nature.[8] This is a very interesting remark and can help us to understand how love makes possible that mutual affirmation by which persons can be distinct (not "different") within a nondual community.

Those who speak of the nondual mystical realization often represent it as an "impersonal" experience. The Divine Reality from which one is nondifferent is not experienced as a "personal God"—that is, one with name and form, a finitized expression of the Ultimate. That being so, one does not have the usual dialogical relation with the Deity—that relation of self and other. More generally, then, the impersonal character of the nondual realization may be said to be a collapse of the I-other perception.

But why does the I-other, or subject-object, relation collapse? I think it is because it is based on *natures*, that is, on different qualities possessed by the self and the other, including even the qualities of being the "knower" and being the "known." If one defines oneself—and consequently others—in this way, by the nature, there must come a time in the development of the mystical life when that definition breaks down. And if such definition was what one meant by "personal"—one's own collection of descriptive attributes that make one visible to oneself and others—then of course the experience of the collapse will be perceived as being "impersonal." The relation itself, like the ones related, was contingent, capable of dissolution—of nonbeing—and it came to dissolution.

Person, however, in Walsh's sense, is noncontingent and not defined. It is not a collection of attributes; it is not limited by a nature. It is not a personality. It is transcendental and coextensive with being. It is not capable of collapse, but is embedded in Absolute Being itself and cannot *not* be.

But when such a person relates to another person, do they not by this relation limit each other—the one as active, the other as passive, the one as knower/lover, the other as known/loved? It is this subject/object dualism that *mutual affirmation* is intended to overcome. Some help in comprehending this is obtained from Walsh's declaration that all persons are transcendental relations to God/Love. But it is also necessary to consider carefully exactly what is going on in *love*. This is a subject that I discuss more fully in the next section, where I suggest that the nondual realization is precisely *personal*—in Walsh's and my sense of the term—although still "impersonal," as being beyond finite description and "difference."

As a preparation for this discussion of love, I want now to add to Walsh's discussion of person a stress on dynamic imagery in our appreciation of what it means to be a person. I believe that if any of us "centers in" to the person that we are, we will find that we are not a thing, a substance or a static being, but an activity, a process, a flow. We are not, however, a "changing." We correctly sense that *we*—the deep self—are somehow above change. We are the ones who observe and judge concerning changes. The closer we get to the center of our being, to the person, the more clearly we see that we transcend change—because we transcend the "things" that are capable of change.

The concept of "change" arose because we thought of things as fixed in certain states, with certain descriptions. When the descriptions became "different," we then understood that the "things" had "changed," but we had a difficult time explaining how the things had passed from one description to another. Aristotle's substance/accident model, for instance, is an attempt to deal with this problem. However, Walsh's person is not a substance possessed of accidents. To follow his thought, we have to keep reminding ourselves of this, because we are so used to thinking in those Aristotelian terms. Walsh says that the person is an eternal subsistent relation to God. My addition of dynamic imagery describes the person as the undefinable *wholeness* of *flowing activity* of which the apparent "substances" are arbitrarily frozen slices, or snapshots.

Fixity is an abstraction from the fundamental dynamism of reality. It is these arbitrary abstractions that give their subjects their characteristic descriptions, definitions, limitations, mutual exclusion, mutual negation— each one being not-another. A world conceived as consisting of such frozen bits of the flowing Whole can correctly be said to be an illusion. Only abstractions can have definitions, can be set over against one another, can be "different." Dualism persists as long as—and only as long as—one sees the world, sees one's experience, as relations between such abstractions, which relations themselves are also abstractions, limited by definitions, contingent, and illusory.

It takes a kind of metanoia, a fundamental reorientation of the mind, to see the primary reality as not the "things"—with respect to which motion is a transition between two descriptions of the things—but rather as the motion itself, with respect to which the things are cross-sections, or abstractions. This metanoia is a second moment in the reorientation that began with shifting from looking at ourselves from the outside to experiencing our existence directly from the inside.

We are moving toward the perspective in which, instead of seeing defined, separated, localized being as primary, we see transcendental being— undefined, undivided, nonlocal—as primary. This is the view that in my opinion will enable us to see that the mystical experience of nondifference, or nondualism, is precisely an inter-*personal* experience, and conversely that all interpersonal relations must be nondual.

Dualism essentially involves being aware of something from which, in some way, one is excluded. But if the person is a transcendental relation— "more or less co-extensive with being," as Walsh says—and has no description or definition, then it is hard to see on what ground a person could be excluded from another person. This is why the mystics speak of "interpenetrating" that with which they are one, of being "coincident," or better, "confluent." They say that they are "in" the "other" and the "other" is "in" them. (Of course, what is meant is not "otherness" in the way we usually construct otherness by exclusion. We do not have a suitable word for this relation.)

Again, metanoia is needed to shift from seeing everything as *outside* ourselves, to seeing persons as precisely those beings who are *inside* one another—to seeing that being *inside* is normal, "the norm" of being, not something miraculous. It is the appearance of exclusion, of being outside, that is abnormal, secondary, or even illusory. Once we give up projecting onto persons our abstractions and definitions that imply mutual negation and exclusion, we may be able to see that the relation of person to person may be nondual, and that a community of transcendental, mutually indwelling, confluent persons would still be a nondual reality.

Bede Griffiths also said that "person is essentially being-in-relationship," that "there is no such thing as an isolated person," and that "each person is totally transparent to every other."[9] In addition, he said that the "Godhead is a communion of persons," and that "humanity [is] a web of interpersonal interrelationships." And yet, we feel very strongly that we are ourselves, profoundly and firmly centered in our own self-being, primarily the self-being of intentional activities: knowing, willing, appreciating, and so on. We are not easily convinced that we are only an intersection in some huge context. When we learn to go into our center and coincide consciously with the deep reality that we are as persons, we experience ourselves as *originating actions* and attitudes, not merely re-acting to outside stimuli or relaying activities as a link in a chain.

I have termed these originating actions the exercise of "creative freedom," as contrasted with "choice freedom."[10] *Choice freedom* is applied to situations of contingency, in which things could be one way or another, in which there are alternatives. It is not a perfect freedom, for the environment initiates and limits the action, setting up the alternatives and putting pressure on the agent to make a choice among them. Since it involves contingency, choice freedom is exercised through the mediation of *natures* and concerns the relations among the various natures, with their respective definitions and descriptions.

Creative freedom, on the other hand, is exercised directly by *persons* and can be present in situations in which the concept of "choice" has no meaningful application. In Walsh's scheme, for instance, natures would originate from God by choice freedom, while persons would originate in God by creative freedom. Creative freedom is perfect freedom: it has no dependence on an environment; it is not even restricted to dealing only with contingent items, with alternatives. It originates everything it does immediately and unconditionally from itself. This is why I have termed it "creative" freedom: It creates out of nothing, out of emptiness, with no prologue, no past, no needed goal to be attained, and no context except the one that comes into existence with its own action.

Creative freedom is not only the origin of persons but it is the characteristic act of persons. It is what we sense in ourselves when we feel bound to declare ourselves as origin, as source, as the beginning of our own action. It is the foundation of "responsibility," which we usually discuss in terms of being justly praised or blamed for our actions. The deeper meaning, I suspect, is our sense that the action is ours, it originated in us, we brought it into being, created it. We know, even if only dimly, that we are essentially *authors*—*authoritative* agents who act *authentically* from ourselves. And we know this by direct experience; it is not known through something else, or by reflection. It is self-luminous. It is our sense of our own personal presence.

Nevertheless, at the same time we also feel moved to affirm with Dom Bede that "we are all connected with one another at the deepest centre of our being."[11] How can we account for both these experiences in a unifying model of ourselves—and of God and of the rest of the world?

The first step, I am proposing, is to have a clear sense of what it is to be a *person*, as a self-luminous center of original intentional activity, transcendent of all description and thus of all difference from other beings. The Walshian doctrine on *person*, as distinct from *nature*, is important for this understanding, for it is essential that we not confuse the two. As Karlfried Graf Dürckheim says:

> Today the time has come . . . to recognize that the center of the living, suffering, searching, loving—in short, real human being is something "unconditioned, superhuman, overpowering" . . . that the core of the human being is something that transcends his natural state of personality

as conditioned by the world . . . that transcends the ego's capacity for understanding and the horizon of its world view. . . . But just this is our own proper, most profound essence.[12]

If dualism is essentially some kind of exclusion based on difference or mutual negations among properties, attributes, or descriptions, then persons, who have no descriptions and do not negate or exclude others, must escape dualism. But by doing this they do not forfeit their central sense of being present, being aware, being appreciative or blissful. This is their self-luminosity. Moreover, persons do not only escape dualism, they positively destroy it by their characteristic personal dynamic. The discussion of creative freedom lays a foundation for this claim, and I have already indicated that the clue to the whole puzzle lies in the reality of Love. This theme must now be developed in order to further the argument that persons—not natures, which includes personalities—are able to maintain a certain kind of "plurality" or "manyness" without falling into the exclusionism of dualism. Indeed, I will argue that persons must exist as distinct interweaving dynamic centers of creative freedom and love that necessarily constitute a perfect union, a nondual community, a *communitarian nondualism*.

MUTUAL KENOTIC AGAPE AS COMMUNITARIAN NONDUALISM

Daniel Walsh said that the key to a true metaphysics is to start with love: God is Love, Ultimate Reality is Love. But Love is Persons, and persons are lovers. Because loving is the way *it* is, persons have to be the way *they* are—that is, both multiple and united.

The love that is spoken of here is called *agape*, that is, a love that wills the well-being of the beloved, as distinguished from *eros*, which seeks the good of the lover. Agape is an ecstatic movement; it is a going forth of the lover. It is an act of giving. It is, in fact, an act of self-emptying: thus, *kenotic* agape. The intention of the lover is to pour out all that one is into the beloved and thus to unite with the beloved. For this reason, there must be (at least) two *persons*. And yet they are not "different." Neither is defined by possession of a set of descriptions unmatched by the other.

But can we not argue that the lover is *defined* by this act of loving and is thus made "different" from the beloved, the one who is loved? It would seem so, except that the whole intention of this loving is precisely to eliminate any difference between the two. Loving is the willing that there be no difference between the lovers, no exclusion, no private properties. The sharing of a single life—in incarnational metaphor, to become "one body"—is the characteristic goal of love.

There is a well-known story of a lover who knocks at the door of the beloved but is not admitted so long as the beloved's question, "Who is there?" is answered by any word indicating difference. Only when the lover replies, "Your own self," is the door opened. Paradoxically, what the lover gives most to the beloved is just what we might argue separates them, namely the act of loving the beloved; for it is this act that is most central to the *selfhood* of the lover and therefore what the lover most intends to *give* to the beloved.

I would like to note at this point that this whole situation is a good example of how difficult it is for us to talk about this sort of experience using our usual concepts and rules for discussing it. However, we can be more successful if we remember that we do have the *experience*. On that level, we know what we are talking about. The concept system and language are supposed to convey that experience, to remind us of the experience itself. We would be turning things upside down if we were to conclude that the experience is impossible and does not happen because we cannot make the concepts and words relate to one another without inconsistency or paradox. Our method of analyzing and ordering our experiences must not be allowed to judge the experience itself. Analysis must fit itself to experience and not the other way around.

From this point of view, striving for an analysis that fits experience, consider what the lover intends when willing union with the beloved. The beloved is also a *person*, that is, a lover. The beloved also is engaged in loving yet other persons. Therefore, when the lover wills to unite with the beloved, the lover is actually willing to unite with the beloved in loving these additional persons. Thus the community of love is (at least) three.

Notice that the *ecstatic* intention of the lover—the going *out* from oneself—would not be satisfied if the beloved did not love still other persons but merely loved the lover in return. The completeness of the self-donation insists on proving itself—fully manifesting itself—by uniting to a love that does *not* revert to the lover. The lover wills to be totally stripped of possessive love, to have nothing left, to be given to the beloved absolutely unconditionally. This is the creative freedom of the act. Of course, by this act the lover does not cease to exist, but continues the activity of living/loving, which now consists of joining the beloved in the beloved's own living/loving. When the beloved in turn loves yet another person, it is with the same intention, to give all unconditionally, and thus to join *that* person in loving still further persons.

This could go on indefinitely. But to demonstrate my conception of the nondual community, suppose that the third person's central activity, with which our "second person" (the beloved) wills to unite, is the act of loving the first person mentioned (the lover). Thus we come full circle. However, at each stage the one loving wills to unite with the one loved by loving whomever else that one loves, without condition. Even when the second person loves the first, it is through the mediation of the third, and thus the purity of the ecstatic intention is preserved. It is not a case of "I will love you if you will love me," or "I love you because you love me," or "I love you" equals "I want you to love me." Instead, it is always a case of "I love you . . ." without any "if" or "because" or desire for oneself. If the fullness of love is the will to this complete abnegation of self-seeking, then a community of at least three is required. The paradigm also shows that to demonstrate the principle, no more than three are required.

I have said that the love of one person for another may be mediated through a preceding love, but this idea needs clarification. When love in union is perfect, when the first person is thoroughly united with the second person in the latter's act of loving the third, then the first person also acts with authenticity—from the personal origin, with creative freedom—in loving the third person. The first person does not in effect say to the third person, "I love you only because the second person loves you; if it weren't for that, I wouldn't care anything about you; it is only for the second person's sake that I love you." This would be very imperfect love and would not constitute uniting with the second person at all. The only way to *unite* with a person is to do—*as* oneself and *from* oneself, as one's *own* action—the same thing that the beloved is doing.

And, of course, the love circle also flows in the opposite direction, with the second person loving the first person by joining the first's love for the third. Or, it could begin with the third and move in either or both directions. In reality, in a love community, all these processes are going on simultaneously. There is no first, no beginning; I only used this in my explanation to clarify the unconditionality and totality of the ecstatic movement, and to show why there must be a *multiplicity* of persons in order for there to be *persons* at all. And yet, the persons are all *one;* they all unite with one another when love is complete. Each one dwells in each other one, joining in that one's most central activity of loving still further ones, joining by loving from one's own center, as one's own authentic act. Thus, the loving simultaneously establishes *each one* as an originating lover and *the community* as a unity in which there is no difference, no exclusion, no private possession of a characteristic not shared with all the others.

THE "I-I" RELATION

To examine the concept of "joining" further, I need to explain what I call the "I-I" relation[13] in order to defend the claim that this constitutes a genuine case of nondualism. The explanation will make use of the grammatical sense of "first person" (I, we), "second person" (you), and "third person" (he, she, it, they) to distinguish three ways of relating to others.

In the first way of relating, I observe, think *about,* talk *about* the other; in other words, I speak of the other in the "third person," saying "it," "he/she" or "they." I am clearly the subject and the other is clearly the object of my consideration. This object is either physically absent, or even if physically present, is still absent from the conversation, spoken about as if it were not there. Its own subjectivity is not recognized or acknowledged by me. I alone am the subject. This is our usual relation to inanimate objects, and it is our position with regard to human beings who are not present or are not parties to the conversation. To get a concrete sense of the subjective absence of the other, imagine the situation of two people talking about a third individual who is present but is not mentally on the same level as they are—perhaps a child, or someone retarded or senile. They will talk *about* that individual as though she or he is not there—is cut out of the circle of personal exchange between the speakers. The individual's subjective presence is not acknowledged, not engaged. The world of her or his subjective reality and that of the speakers do not overlap.

In the second way of my relating to another, I speak *to* the other person, speak in the "second person," not *about* them. We are all familiar with the sense of shifting our orientation when we have been talking about someone, and that person then joins our group and must be addressed directly. To change from saying "she" to saying "you" is a big change; the whole dynamic of the situation is completely reorganized. What has happened in this case is that the subjective presence of the other is now acknowledged and engaged. Although we are still acting *toward* the other and imaging the other as the recipient of our action—in that sense we are "subject" and "object"—we can also feel the presence of the other as another *subject*, one who in turn acts toward us, to whose action we are recipient, with respect to whose subjective activity we are the object. We have conceptual knowledge about this situation, but in the actual conversation we are focused on being existentially present in the engagement of the other's subjective presence. Our intentional dynamic is absorbed in the *to*, or *toward*, not reflecting on the *about*. In sighted people, this engagement is usually accompanied by looking directly into each other's eyes. This is a metaphor of the experience of engagement, a sense of a partial penetration into the other's personal reality. One gets some sense of the reality of the other as a subject in her or his own right, not merely an object of my knowledge or action. Some realization develops that this other person feels inside just the way I do, in other words has a sense of being, of being *her*self or *him*self, even as I immediately experience being *my*self.

This is the beginning of realization of the *person* world. If the engagement with the other is friendly, the minimal form of the interpersonal dynamic is that we expect benefit from the encounter. We may be willing to give something in order to obtain this benefit in exchange. But at some point, as the sense of the other's subjective actuality (reality, presence, and active mode of being) grows, sympathy appears: the ability to *feel together with*, or parallel to, the other person. This is based on the recognition that the other is a person, has the same kind of interior reflexive selfhood that I myself have.

—\ﾘﾘ/—

At first, this realization is clothed in the same garments with which we cover our own persons—pains and pleasures, desires and fears. As I have felt these, so I can imagine the other person feeling them. The next step is that I may occasionally wish, want, hope, will that the other person have experiences that I regard as favorable and therefore believe that the other will also find favorable. Part of my dynamic toward the other is now an attempt to feel for the other the way that person feels for herself or himself in the various circumstances of life. When I do this, I distract part of my intentional energy from the concern that favorable experiences attend *me*, and devote that liberated energy to the will that good fortune grace the other. And since I am trying to look at reality and feel it from the other's own point of view, what I am trying to do is to live inside the other's reality.

When any of us first starts to do this, we in a way repeat the arrangement of the "I-her/him" relation: we try to feel the other's feelings, but in the *absence* of the other. We initially neglect the subjective presence of the other in our imaginative development of the parallel to our own interior experience. But the distraction of our energy from concern for our own welfare is nevertheless real. Our friendly feelings for the other shift from the expectation that we will receive benefits to the desire that the other be benefited, and even to the willingness to expend ourselves in order to accomplish that end. This distraction of our energies from concern with ourselves actually has the paradoxical effect of deepening our own sense of personal being, our sense of active presence, of existential reality, of independence from the circumstances of life. The more we devote personal intentional energies toward the other, the more power of being we seem to have and the more we experience ourselves as *persons* in the Walshian sense—as transcending our natures and the favorable or unfavorable circumstances that affect those natures.

This level of development prepares us for the third way of relating to the other—in the "first person." On the one hand, the more I become involved in desiring the well-being of the other person, the more I want really to know that other, to understand, to share the other's life, to be admitted to the inner secrets so that I may will their success. This leads to my practicing of sympathy with the other actually *present*, to trying to feel the other's feelings directly, not merely feeling a parallel to them devised from my own experiences. I am now trying to enter directly into the other's subjective presence, not to *confront* it by looking *into* the other's eyes, but to *flow together with* it, to join its own dynamic, by looking *out* through the other's eyes. I no longer address her or him as "you," but instead join my "I" to her or his "I."

But on the other hand, as I have progressed in this practice and come to experience myself as a transcendent person, so I must know the other is also a transcendent person. The scaffolding, so to speak, of our relationship—by means of interest in the advantageous circumstances first of my life and then of her or his life—falls away. That person is no more dependent on circumstances than I am myself. Her or his interior being is as indescribable as my own, equally transcendent of nature. Not being a *nature*, she or he cannot be an "object" for me as a "subject." There is nothing there that can be conceived and known. Just as I cannot "know" myself but can only "be" myself, so I cannot know another person but only existentially join that one's actuality. This is not a deprivation of knowledge; on the contrary, knowing itself is merely an impoverished substitute for being. But this "being" is conscious, self-luminous, an "I."

In this "I-I" relation, there is no exclusion. First, the persons do not desire to exclude anything about themselves from each other. They try to open themselves up to each other, try to enter into each other's inner self. Second, since they are *persons*, there are no properties, attributes, or other possessions for them to sequester. They cannot be defined and cannot be "different" from one another. They *are* their existential actuality as persons, whose characteristic dynamic is this devotion of positive intentional energy to other persons.

Persons are given from their origin in Ultimate Reality, God/Love, as necessarily plural, as many. Each person is a unique source of agape authenticity, and actuality. And yet they are one. And yet *therefore* they are one; for the whole intent of this relation is to coincide with—to *flow together with*—the other until there is nothing about either that is not present in both. No person is "environment" or "object" for another. Every person is immediately "subject" for every other—not just acknowledged subject but subjectively experienced subject, by virtue of the confluence of their intentional dynamisms. Germane to the total understanding of unity with the other, Robert E. Carter, incorporating the ideas of Nishida Kitaro,[14] very neatly says, "To truly empathize is to enter into the deep self of the other, . . . such that he, she, or it arises as a *self* within one's own place of appearance." Carter also cites Keiji Nishitani as calling this "circuminsessional interpenetration,"[15] and Robert S. Hartman as writing of "compenetration."[16]

This presence of the other as a self with oneself is something that can be experienced only by persons with respect to other persons; it is not possible for natures. Therefore we should not imagine it as being accomplished by human personalities. We must transcend the "human nature" aspect and center in the person in order to glimpse how this can be. Natures exclude one another by their definitions. Persons include one another by their dynamic intentions. Since there is no definition and no one is an "object," it is really not correct to speak of an "other." There is rather a . . . what? a "second self"? But this is just what the mystics have said—no dualism, no "other"! And yet, because of the agape, neither is it correct to say that they are only "one." Both unity and plurality must be preserved.

In the "I-I" relation, each of us experiences this union of our personal lives. I can no longer say that your experience is not my experience, because we both share it. Nevertheless, you have experience as yours subjectively and I have it as mine subjectively. Or, even better, you are it and I am it; you are the whole of it, and I am the whole of it; we do not exclude each other and we do not divide up the reality we share. This is what I call *communitarian nondualism*.

KENOTIC AGAPE

The secret to this metaphysical mystery is, of course, the kenotic agape. It is the one principle that grounds both differentiation and union simultaneously. It can be spoken of in terms of both *emptiness* and *emptying*.

Persons are "empty." They have no definitions or properties—nothing can be predicated of them. As the mystics say, they are "naked." They have no location. They are extratemporal. Realizing ourselves in this way, wakefully coinciding with such existence, we attain access to agape. Perfect agape is not possible so long as we identify ourselves with a nature. All natures are needy and dependent on their environments for the support of their continuing operations. They are obliged, by the first law of being—all being strives to continue in being—to will their own maintenance. They cannot devote all their energies to concern for others.

Persons, however, are not contingent. Free—by virtue of their *emptiness*—of the urgency of protecting their own existence, they verify their reality precisely by kenotic agape, by *emptying* themselves into one another. This is their essential dynamic, the "doing," or process, or motion, or activity that is *who* they are. It is what makes them to be as they are. And so, the more persons practice the art of kenotic agape, the more they are, and the more they are *themselves*, their central *who*.

There is a famous maxim that says, in effect: "If you try to hoard your life, you will lose it; but if you are willing to pour out your life for another, then you will not only survive but maximize your living." It is interesting to notice that this is the rule for all *persons*—even Divine Persons must live by it. It is only by emptying Themselves into one another in agape that Divine Persons are *persons*. So when this maxim is confided to us, we are being told the secret of Divine Life, with the implication that we are capable of it, that it is the life for us, the truth about our own real being.

This total self-gift is the Fundamental Being-Dynamic, the "Ground of Being." And because of being self-gift of person to persons, the Fundamental Being-Dynamic has to be a Community—of mutual self-emptying love, of kenotic agape. This is what establishes the subject-subject coinherence of the "I-I" relation—the interpersonal circuminsession—of that Ultimate Reality.

THE INNUMERABLE COMMUNITY

I previously mentioned that the minimum number for (the explication of) this Community is three. But there is no reason why there could not be more, even infinitely more. But, of course, persons cannot really be "counted," because they have no form. Countables have to have some quality in common by which they constitute a "set"; then they must have distinguishing features by which the individual items can be told apart; and finally, they must have an ordering principle by which we can know when we have already counted a particular item so we don't count it again. But *persons* fulfill none of these conditions. As Thomas Aquinas said of the angels, persons cannot be counted. They constitute an *innumerable community*.[17]

In view of the way mystics report the nondual experience, what I propose as a metaphysical model for *What Is*, is a vast innumerable *Person-Community*, all the persons indwelling all the others so that there is no exclusion and no subject/object polarity. The persons are not ranked or graded or classified or specified in any way. For instance, persons are not categorized as human, angelic, or divine. However, to speak of Divine Persons, as I just did above, is to engage in myth-making that reveals the highest truth about personhood itself. Having explained personhood by means of the myth, as if we were speaking of something other than ourselves, we must then say, "But we ourselves, at our heart, our central reality, we *are* That."[18] That is the revelation, the enlightenment, the enormity that, we say, requires nothing less than divine grace to be believed.

"God," in this context, then, is the dynamic of the Community. Daniel Walsh made a daring statement by saying, "The Trinity is not God. The Trinity is the first effusion of Love, which is God." It is the Dynamic Nothingness Itself that is fundamental, that is "God." Raimundo Panikkar has also suggested that "God" is the "pure relationship" among things.[19] But we must not set up a dualism between "God" the dynamic relation and "we" the persons so related. "We" are that dynamic, as already explained; as persons, we are nothing but the kenotic agape we actually intend toward one another and by which we indwell one another.

This Community is perfectly nondual, for there is nothing outside it, and there is nothing outside any person-"member" of it. Each person perfectly indwells every other person and so *is* the entire Community, as well as all the kenotic agape intentions and relations in the way that was previously set forth under the image of "joining."

Since even I find this a rather outrageous and frightening doctrine, it seems important to repeat two fundamental points here. The first is that this is being said only of *persons*, not of *natures*, therefore not of human personalities. To the extent, then, that we experience ourselves and identify with our human nature and our human personalities, we will not verify these statements; they will not be true of us. The second point is that in thinking about this, we must approach it from the inside, from the subject side, by way of intuition, by way of doing/experiencing it, rather than by trying to conceptualize it as if we were viewing it from the outside. It is true that the model is mediated through concepts, but it must be remembered that all models are only pointing the way and giving suggestions of what to attend to as we center into our existential sense of being *person*.

Nevertheless, we have to emphasize that we *are* "this way" in our depth reality, right now, whether we realize it or not. This is not intended as a description of some condition into which we may pass later on. Our constant talk about "enlightenment," "mystical union," "beatific vision," in conjunction with our usual daily experience of identifying with the contingent circumstances of human nature and its environments, does tend to make us think that there are two different states, the state we are in now—ignorance, or sin, or fallenness, or whatever we may call it—and the state we look forward to being in—illumined, saved, restored, and so forth. But again, this dualism must be both rejected and explained in such a way that the rejection does not constitute another kind of dualism.

First, we must insist that we are persons, noncontingent acts of kenotic agape, in a Community of perfect mutual indwelling. When we experience ourselves, no matter how conditioned, the fundamental self that is having that experience is the *person*. We already are "in enlightenment," in that sense—we just don't know it! In other words, we don't know that the pure dimensionless undefined "I" is this noncontingent, universally present reality. We always experience it clothed with various conditions and forms, and also limited in space and time and to certain states and other descriptions. When all those are removed, it is evident that this pure *person* is what we are—have been—all along. But even when those conditions are not removed, this is still what we really are. As the sadhu called "Harilal" in Swami Abhishiktananda's *The Secret of Arunachala* said, "The fundamental obstacle to realization is precisely the notion that this realization is still awaited."[20]

But what about all these conditions and states and forms and descriptions? How do they fit into the picture? In the model I am proposing, the finite worlds, whatever and however many they may be, are creative expressions of the Person-Community. Perhaps we may speak of them as phenomenalizations of the Person-Community. The Person-Community acts as an artist, revealing or showing itself in the guise of various forms. As with any artwork, the form both conceals the transcendent and inexpressible artist and yet somehow also reveals the expressing artist.

I liken this phenomenalization to artwork primarily in order to respond to the question of motivation: Why create the universe(s)? Ultimately, of course, there can be no purpose—that is, no purpose outside the Creator and the created themselves. The finite worlds are not utilities, not means to some end other than and beyond themselves. In this sense, they are perfect in themselves, just as they are. The Creator does not exactly "need" them, and yet, such is the pressure of agape that the Creating-Community does spontaneously create them.

It is again a case of self-emptying, the characteristic of the Fundamental Dynamic. Infinitude does not cling to being only infinite, formless, but empties itself and takes on form, becoming finite. This is, it seems to me, best imaged as a work/play of loving art: a spontaneous, authentic, or original activity of self-expression of its Creator, who cannot help being present in it and even as it. I like to image it as a song or dance, so that the artwork is in no way separate from the artist but actually *is* the artist in the activity of creating.

But there may be another interesting answer to the motivational question. Perhaps the artwork does have a kind of "purpose." Perhaps it is an externalization of the Person-World in finitude, in which difference makes possible complexity of organization, and complexity makes possible emergent consciousness. And perhaps this emergent consciousness, born of finitude itself, evolves to the stage where it becomes aware—realizes— that it *is* the phenomenalization of the absolute Person-Community. The Person-Community would now have two versions of its awareness of itself: the interior, infinite, formless version and the exterior, finite, formed version. Since these are two possible ways for Being to be, and we must affirm that Being will be in every possible way, can we not also say that the Fundamental Dynamic presses to realize Itself so?

We need to notice that in order to go into finitude, it is necessary to accept limitation. This includes limitation on consciousness itself, on awareness of who one is and how one relates to others. Finitude means construction by means of differences and exclusions. The finite are precisely those who effectively say to one another, "I am not you"—those who mutually negate one another.

This is one way of putting the difference between persons and natures: the natures—including our personalities—are established in their essences by mutual negation, and the persons are established in their existential dynamic by mutual affirmation, or kenotic agape. Persons sustain and express their being by self-giving; finite beings strive to sustain and increase their being by self-defense and accumulation.

Nevertheless, the finite beings, because of their inherent neediness and their definition by reference to one another, always exist in a system, in a community, in a network of dynamic relationships. As George Seielstad points out in his book, *At the Heart of the Web*, we can't have just one organism: living is a community activity, a vast complicated traffic in foodstuffs and wastes, as well as homesites, travel patterns, weather systems, and various other conditions for carrying on the activities of living.[21] In this respect, even from the simplest beginnings, finite beings are an image of the Person-Community. Community—different ways of differentiating, relating, and uniting the many—seems to be the fundamental characteristic of all Being.

I suggest that the Person-Community finitizes itself and thus becomes the finite world. I could have said that it embodies itself, or even incarnates itself. These seem to be the two great principles of all Being: being both One and Many by being Agape-Community, and being both Infinite and Finite by phenomenalizing and realizing. Both are instances of kenosis, of self-emptying. The Persons empty themselves into one another as the unity of their Community, and the Infinite (formless) Community empties itself of its formlessness and takes on form, including form in space and time, experiencing impermanence and radical relativity and contingency, coming to be and ceasing to be. But in the midst of this impermanence, because of the complexity of the dynamic relations, consciousness emerges with reflexivity and self-reference, which compound the complexity to the point where the consciousness can empty itself of all its attachments to itself as finite and realize itself as the original Formlessness. Nondualism is verified even between the Finite and the Infinite, and I will return to this point later.

But what we all want to know is where *we* fit into the general scheme. My answer is that we are members of the Person-Community who have become incarnate as human beings on earth. As such, we have two types or levels or versions of consciousness or awareness. As Persons, of course, we have to be fully and perfectly aware and cannot be unaware. But as incarnate in the conditions of finitude, we have only limited consciousness, the kind of consciousness that emerges from the activities of our bodies, especially our brains.

It is with this latter consciousness that we tend to identify; that is usually what we mean when we say "we." Even when we talk about the transcendent awareness, we tend to speak of it as though it were something else, not really ourselves. We project it and deify it. When we finally attain to realization of our rootedness in it, the former self-identification disappears and we speak either of "union with God" or of "self-realization," or of "enlightenment." But prior to that realization, we experience ourselves as limited.

THE MYSTICAL ROSE

I sometimes image our situation this way: Suppose that each empirical consciousness is a single petal of a great flower, such as a lotus or a rose. Out at the tips it is clear that the petals are separate; they do not overlap or even touch. But as they approach the center of the flower, they overlap more and more with a greater number of other petals, until at the center (of this imaginary flower) they totally overlap with every other petal. I call this image "The Mystical Rose" and try to explain various concepts in reference to it.

In ordinary daily life what we call "myself" is a reflexive loop of consciousness—a consciousness of being conscious as a self. Our usual, or unenlightened consciousness does not take in the whole petal that we actually are, but is confined—by a "short circuit" of our reflexivity—to the tip of the petal, where it appears that we are separate, individual beings. I call this "tip consciousness."

In tip consciousness we experience being outside of one another, over against one another, in need of one another, and potentially hostile to one another. Finitude is very much in evidence and the need for self-defense is paramount. This is not surprising, because the matter-energy-space-time universe is necessarily structured this way. Concern for self-maintenance and self-growth is almost a definition of finitude, given the general laws of Being: to continue being and to be more in every way. All the levels of complex organization of matter/energy have operated on that basis from the very beginning, garnering to themselves electrons (if trying to complete an atom), atoms (if trying to form a molecule), ready-made smaller molecules (if assembling a megamolecule), and so on. Every organization seizes from the environment whatever it can to sustain, complete, enlarge, enhance, and duplicate its own kind of organization. Our initial consciousness of ourselves in these terms and possessed of these drives is perfectly natural. A finite world probably cannot be made in any other way.

Of course, the organizations also eject unwanted or waste materials and energy, which can be (to a certain extent) picked up and used by other organizations. So universal and interwoven is this practice that we could say that the total biota on planet Earth constitutes a sort of gigantic symbiosis of mutualism, enabling one another to continue the maintenance, growth, and reproductive behaviors that we call "living."

A materials/energy/information exchange structure of this sort is called a "system," and it has a certain unity of its own. In fact, the various suborganizations form *within* the system; they cannot exist prior to the system. The whole community has to arise and grow together, its various components dependent on one another. The one and the many coexist as the whole. At some point, our consciousness becomes aware of this systematic aspect of our finite existence. I believe that on some level (or levels) we are always aware of it, but our reflexive consciousness just doesn't bring it to explicit, or rational, consciousness. We live in terms of the great symbiosis, but we don't often think about it or discuss it.

Feelings for other human beings, especially genetic relatives, and feelings for the environment, in particular those parts of it on which we are most obviously dependent, gradually emerge into reflexive consciousness. As we ratify these awarenesses and feelings, the loop of our self-consciousness begins to include more of our petal and may even reach portions where it overlaps other petals and begins to share their consciousness. True sympathy and unselfish friendship are one sign of this; perhaps certain psychic experiences are another—such as when we are mysteriously aware of an event or trauma affecting an absent relative.

I interpret these "sym-pathies"—these feeling-together events and attitudes—as real consciousness-sharing. According to the Rose model, it is not uncanny that we can feel sympathy in these ways for a being who is not our self, or who is at some physical distance from us. Rather, it is not telling the whole truth (but only part of it) to say that the other is "not our self" or that the other's consciousness is "distant" from us. This is the usefulness of the rose petal image of "overlapping." We do indwell one another and share one another's lives. It is not strange that we should know what is in another's consciousness, because that consciousness is actually shared to some degree between us; it is "my" consciousness as well as "yours."

At deeper levels of the overlapping petals, we find those aspects of consciousness that we more thoroughly share with even greater numbers of people. Are they archetypes of the "collective unconscious" perhaps? They are almost surely basic values of moral life, and they certainly include forms of interpretation of sensory data, such as our intuitions of space and time, and the categories of the understanding. When reflexivity takes in yet more of the petal, we become conscious of sharing with even greater numbers of people, other living beings, and even inanimate things. Sympathy expands; that is, the sense of "self" expands. The motivation to protect, defend, acquire goods for, enable to develop and grow, is extended to more and more beings as being part of my own being, members of what I am now willing to count as my own embodiment.[22]

According to the image of the Rose, we are always overlapping with each other to all these various degrees, but as incarnate beings we are initially unmindful of most of this. "Spiritual development" is the growth of reflexive consciousness of all this unconscious material, the emergence of awareness of deep sharing. It culminates in *center consciousness*, where all the petals completely overlap, which we recognize as "cosmic conscious-ness" in its embodied aspect and as "mystical union" in its transcendent aspect.

If something like this should be true, then what do we, or should we, mean when we say "I"? One of the most important points I want to make is that it is precisely our sense of what we mean by "I" that shifts during this process of increasing consciousness. This is why we cannot make fixed statements about what "I" can or cannot do. Statements that are true at one level or one stage of spiritual development may not be true at later stages. The whole passage from religious dualism to mystical nondualism is involved in these considerations. The I-consciousness that identifies strictly with the created nature and embodiment will genuinely experience its relation to Ultimate Reality quite differently from the I-consciousness of the central person. People at different stages will make very different statements about how Reality is structured—and each of them will be giving voice to a true state of affairs. There is no single answer to what "I" am. It changes as "I" grow.

At first limited to the tight short circuit of the reflexive consciousness in the tip of the petal, my "I" gradually extends to take in more and more of "my" petal, which inevitably includes more and more of "your" petals because of the overlapping. When I say "I," therefore, I come to mean more and more of the Whole. I gradually recognize more and more beings as "my relatives," and I identify myself with whatever happens to even the least of them. This expansion of the self is what "overcomes the world" of the finite, while at the same time assuming the whole of finite reality into this universal "I" consciousness. I return, as it were, into the Infinite, taking finitude with me. I remember who I am, that I am unlimited personal being totally outpouring into all the rest of you, as you in turn are doing. We are all one, in our infinitude and in our finitude and as between our infinitude and our finitude.

HOLY WHOLENESS

The Cosmic Community of forms is the phenomenalization of the formless Person Community. The Infinite has thoroughly expressed itself in the finite so that the finite may come full circle to "remembrance" of itself as being the Infinite so expressing itself. Finitization necessarily requires "forgetfulness" of infinitude, but evolution of complexity restores the remembrance of it through the gradual growth of self-consciousness and sympathy.

To clarify this concept, I call my luminous self-awareness as Person *Consciousness 1* and the mentality that develops as an emergent phenomenon from neural activity *Consciousness 2*. Consciousness 1 is the formless spiritual reality of the person. Consciousness 2 is bodily consciousness, the consciousness that is contingent upon material circumstances, that varies with genetic inheritance (species, size of brain, any abnormalities), experience, physical shock (it can be rendered dysfunctional by a blow to the head), chemical environment (drugs, anesthesia), disease, and even normal rhythmic states (sleep, dream).

We ordinarily identify ourselves as our Consciousness 2. Spiritual traditions tell us that we are really Consciousness 1 and indicate to us various practices by which we can shift our felt sense of personal identity from Consciousness 2 to Consciousness 1. When this happens, then the finite, or phenomenalized being has in some way matched Infinite Being, or—in mythic terms—has discovered itself as a Child of God.

Divine Incarnation is perfected at this point, for the Person who has phenomenalized has now returned to full awareness of being that Person-who-has-phenomenalized. Both the infinite and the finite aspects are fully present and united. This is the perfect or complete state, superior to either the infinite alone or the finite alone and superior to a dualism of infinite and finite. The activity of phenomenalization is the activity of self-emptying. The Formless empty themselves of their formlessness and take form. But the "return" movement is no less a self-emptying, for Consciousness 2 must divest itself of all the forms with which it is accustomed to identify itself, empty itself of all claim to be something of itself, and thus discover itself as the revelation in finitude of Consciousness 1.

This mutual emptying into one another of the infinite and the finite is their mutual indwelling and constitutes the *wholeness* of Reality. Mythically, this has more than once been represented as a relation of Parent and Child, in which the Child comes forth from the Parent, grows up to be an image of the Parent and finally matches the Parent by doing the essentially parental thing: self-emptying into another. The Child then is *in* the Parent and the Parent *in* the Child in such a way that one cannot ask to be shown the one apart from the other. The phenomenalization/realization cycle is the ultimate nondualism of the total Subject (Person Community) and total Object (Cosmic Community).

It is this nondual, but internally complex, Wholeness that is Reality. When we analyze it into various polarities, we make abstractions from its reality; we do something artificial. The Person Community of absolute being is not a separate domain from the Cosmic Community of phenomena, although it does transcend the latter. Nevertheless, it is from the very heart of the Person Community's own interiority that the movement of phenomenalization issues, and it is the very heart of the Person Community's own interiority that is expressed and exposed by the phenomenalization: it is what is thereby *shown forth*. We may say that it is exteriorized, or "birthed."

Thus, the phenomena are never anything but the exteriorization of that absolute interiority. And the phenomenal beings of the Cosmic Community, expressing the interrelated energies of their external beings, eventually develop an interiority that becomes sufficiently intense as interiority to realize itself as Person Community. The effect, as we might say, of intense interiority is exteriorization; and the effect of intense exteriority is interiorization. The inside is the outside is the inside. If we take a cross-section of this Wholeness anywhere, in the local slice it will appear that there are distinct poles of inside and outside, of interiority of absolute and exteriority of phenomenon, but in reality it will not be so, for in the Wholeness they mutually indwell one another.

Some of these cross-sections and polarizations are useful, though, for we do have to make distinctions and judgments in order to carry out the functions of the finite world and to express the transcendence of the Person world. The trouble is that we usually have elevated these functional utilities into eternal verities and have believed that Reality is actually divided into the Divine and the created, the created being subdivided into really different kinds of beings.

However, when we look closely, we see that any being is a system of movements, of communication with its fellows, who are its "environment." The whole Cosmic Community is made up of these systemic movements of intercommunication. There are no isolated or independent objects in actuality; to picture them so is to make an abstraction. There is only the endless interrelationship of communication.

Physicist David Bohm, like a number of other scholars, has found the hologram a convenient metaphor for a new perspective on the natural world, seeing the world as "an order of undivided wholeness . . . rather than an order of analysis of . . . content into separate parts. . . ." Like the hologram, each tiny portion of physical reality contains information about the whole of the reality that relates to it. "A *total order* is contained, in some *implicit* sense, in each region of space and time. . . . each region contains a total structure 'enfolded' within it."[23] When "unfolded," the implicate order appears to our observation as "a set of recurrent and relatively stable elements that are *outside* of each other."[24] But "the relationships constituting the fundamental law are between the enfolded structures that interweave and inter-penetrate each other, throughout the whole of space, rather than between the abstracted and separated forms that are manifest to the senses (and to our instruments)."[25] The metaphoric "hologram" is really a "holomovement" because of the fundamental dynamism of reality. "*What is* is the holomovement, and . . . everything is to be explained in terms of forms derived from this holomovement."[26]

It is hard for us to think this way, because we are used to thinking in terms of fundamental separated finite beings that are first real in themselves, as static substances, and then interrelate with one another and perhaps experience change or motion. Like David Bohm, I call such a view an abstraction, or "cross-section" of the Wholeness of the intercommunicating processes of the Cosmos. This Whole is originally and fundamentally dynamic, neither only one nor only many, full of sharing, but having no real separations. And at the same time, all this cosmic intercommunication is itself the exteriorization of the intercommunion of the Person Community. There is *communitarian nondualism* within the Person Community, within the Cosmic Community, and between the Person Community and the Cosmic Community. That entire consideration constitutes what I regard as the Holy Wholeness of Reality.

To experience this Wholeness, we have to abandon object-viewing and enter into subject-presence. This is also connected with shifting more and more from mere reactions of choice freedom to authentic original actions of creative freedom and the profound ecstasy of the "I-I" relation. This shift enables us to realize ourselves as simultaneously the formless Person and the form of some particular finite being in dynamic interrelation with all the rest. As Consciousness 1 we are ever-free and perfect, and as Consciousness 2 we are evolving and maturing toward fuller realization of our transcendent reality. There is no contradiction in this. It is precisely *because* we are Consciousness 1, whose creative free act is ever self-emptying, that we are the becoming of Consciousness 2. And because that self-emptying is so complete, our phenomenal becoming is totally permeated by the interiority of the Absolute. Viewed from the outside, as if we were only analyzing objects in terms of concepts, this would be a paradox, a contradiction, or nonsensical. But experienced on the inside, as subject, it is an immediately grasped whole that is self-luminous.

The dynamism of self-sharing is the secret of Being on every level. I said earlier that the mystery of the whole of Reality, of the Divine Community no less than of our phenomenal communities, lies in this: If we try to hold onto our lives, keep them for ourselves alone, we will destroy ourselves, whereas if we will pour ourselves into others, we will expand in life without limit. This is not only a moral ideal but an ontological principle—this is how Being is structured. It is why the Person Community is rooted in kenotic agape, why it gives itself without stint to the Cosmic Community, why the Cosmic Community is made up of matter/energy exchanges and ultimately of Consciousness 2 self-gifts. It is why those who have learned to situate themselves in subject-presence rather than in object-comparison—that is to say, the mystics—both experience oneness with the Ultimate or Absolute, and energetically go out in love and service to all phenomenal beings.

We do not all experience this yet because we are trapped in "tip consciousness," the short circuit of reflexivity produced by the forgetting of our transcendent selfhood—necessary fault though that is, since it is the condition for finite embodiment and the eventual blossoming of the realizing mystic consciousness. Our embodied consciousness has to evolve. It is not "wrong" for us to have limited consciousness at this time. That is all part of what is going on—our embodied consciousness is growing. We can help it grow more as we learn something of the total scheme of things, or we can at least find a myth-model that makes sense of our lives at this time.

The mystics tell us that when we do come into full realization, we will still give ourselves to the phenomenal: We will not consider that "liberation," our own peace and happiness in the realm of eternity, is something to be clung to, but will renounce this liberation and engage in selfless action in the finite world. To live in nondualism is to do everyday acts in full knowledge, to be both supremely transcendent and quite ordinary.

ECOLOGICAL ETHICS

In this nondualistic perspective, ethics as ecology is seen as a branch of cosmology. Ecology is perhaps the most general expression of the ethical imperative, for it speaks for the value of the Whole. The cosmos has evolved to the level where it includes ethically competent consciousnesses, and now the growing edge of the cosmos is in our consciousness. By "our" I mean at least human beings on Earth, but also any other consciousnesses that ought to be included in such a designation, whether here or on other planets. But I also must mean that we count as our extended selves the rest of the cosmic expression. Our sense of *wholeness* is what is growing; our sense of the values included in that sense of wholeness is our ecological ethics. This is the arena of significant cosmic action today.

This perspective does not claim that Earth and human beings are the center of the cosmos in some pre-Copernican sense, but it does claim that a certain spiritual value marginalized at the time the great astronomical (and later the biological evolutionary) discoveries were made is now restored: We are at the center, we are included in the center, because we are *acting centrally*. It is not a question of a spatial center, or a largeness, or brightness center, or a question of a special creation for human beings that separates us from the rest of the cosmos. We are rather at the functional center of the whole cosmos; we are at its *meaning* center. This "center" is where efforts are "coming to a head"—an "encephalization" center, to use Teilhard's word. It may well be scattered in space, but it is nevertheless *together*: it is *we*.

Thus, we are not "lost in space," in a vast alien universe that "rolls impotently on." We are the *"crème de la crème"* of the cosmos, the "apple of its eye." We are that mode of functioning of the cosmos in which it is struggling to become conscious of itself. The whole cosmos is striving to become awake, aware of its Buddha-nature. "The whole creation has been groaning, *laboring together* until now . . . longing for the revealing of the children of God" (Rom. 8:19 & 22). Every move we make is part of this common labor. Nothing is insignificant, nothing is wasted, nothing can be hidden. Everything is knitted in and has its consequences.

The cosmos is a system on the edge of chaos. This means that while any local event may be strictly deterministic in its matter and energy relations, the interrelations of local events are so multitudinous and so complex and so dependent on one another that the progress of the whole—its state at any future time—cannot be predicted. An amusing example of this is the "Butterfly Effect." A butterfly off the coast of Brazil flutters its wings, disturbing the air molecules in its vicinity. Each of these molecules communicates a version of the disturbance—that is, its own original state, plus the change it has now undergone—to its neighbors, who in turn transmit their adjusted characteristics, and so on. These local characteristics accumulate as temperature, wind velocity, and humidity; then currents develop, clouds form, winds begin to whirl, and a storm moves up the coast and ultimately evolves into a weather system that traverses a continent. The moral is twofold: We may not be able to foresee what the consequences of even a very small act may be, but that act will have consequences. There is nothing so small that it has no effects, no meaning, no significance.

As no action takes place in a vacuum but always in a community, so no-one's act is buried under an avalanche of statistics or is just one of a crowd. Everyone makes a significant contribution to the common effort. Everyone is a "butterfly" initiating some chain of events, as well as an adaptor and relay unit of chains begun elsewhere. Every single thing we do, say (by whatever kind of language), think, or feel is literally knit—woven—into the fabric of the evolving world. This is a community effort and enterprise. And the communications themselves—the net of interrelationships—is what this fabric consists of. It is the Seamless Garment of God.

No one can tell what form this Garment will take in the future. It is in principle unpredictable. But even chaotic systems have "attractors," focal points or patterns around which their various values throng. *Organization as community* is, I believe, the attractor for this cosmos. That form is always present, no matter how primitive the universe, no matter how evolved. Community is unity and plurality, shared being and differentiation, complexity and consciousness.

My thesis is that the theme of the functioning of the Whole is this: The formless Person Community is endeavoring, in an artistic and birthgiving way, to express itself in the finite. The whole of cosmic evolution—as the Cosmic Community—is this enterprise.

The fruitful stage of the enterprise comes when the Cosmos Community becomes conscious enough to realize that it *is* the self-expression of the Person Community. And this realization itself is a community event, even though it appears to show here and there in the lives of individuals. *Bringing the cosmos as such to self-realization is the goal of the phenomenalization*—not the escape of individuals from the cosmic projection. The whole cosmic event has been ecological from its inception, and it must be ecological in its culmination.

As our awareness of what we are trying to do—to express the values of divinity in the forms of finitude—becomes clearer to us, so do ethical considerations more and more constitute the domain of this birth-struggle. And the ethical rule itself is communitarian: we must behave in such a manner that the community flourishes.

This means that individual self-development must be protected and nurtured, for the wholeness is the interrelations of the individuals, and those interrelations—if the community is advancing toward greater self-realization—must come increasingly out of creative freedom. Maturity and integration, self-reliance and authenticity, are essential to the ethical growth of the embodied community. "Community" and "individual" are not a pair of opposites in this model. In the wholeness generated by kenotic agape, community is precisely the mutual indwelling of the individuals, the fulfillment of individual self-presence, subjectivity, and original creative action.

THE EVOLUTION OF EVIL

Ethical evolution takes the curious form of an increased sensitivity to evil. Attitudes and actions that have been unconsciously, or even consciously, accepted as natural and matter of course—dominating weaker people, despoiling and/or enslaving foreigners—gradually come to be seen as unacceptable human behavior. Little by little we become conscious that other people—of whatever gender, race, wealth, or culture—have exactly the same rights as ourselves, as our own group. Failure to respect these rights is transgression, evil.

The struggle with evil is a middle stage between unconsciousness, in which such acts are regarded as merely natural and therefore right, and full consciousness, in which the sense of wholeness is so vivid that transgression becomes impossible. In the middle we struggle to dilate our sense of community, to enlarge our "we." The evolution of the sense of evil is an effort to become more conscious, to appreciate what is really going on in this world, who we are and what we are doing. It is paradoxical because the more progress we make in becoming conscious, sensitive, awake, the more "evil" there is in the world. This happens because we discover more

instances of attitudes and actions that we formerly thought acceptable—
maybe even heroic—to be transgressions against the rights of others. As we
recognize and acknowledge these rights, those "others" are brought within
the bounds of our "we."

It is, of course, like all evolutionary developments, a slow business,
with many ups and downs. Dim awareness of the rights of others contends
against entrenched habits of protecting a narrow sense of self-interest.
Partly we want to wake up, and partly we want to reject the sharpened and
enlarged consciousness and remain within the familiar limits. It is hard to
face the fact that our greed and cruelty and lust for power grow out of the
basic insecurity of a too-small self-identification. All our efforts to secure
this poor self by dominating others and accumulating goods for ourselves
come to nought, because the small self still feels inadequate. We think we
can overcome this inadequacy by obtaining external wealth, power, and
pleasure for the small self. It is often a long time before we realize that the
thing to do is to enlarge the self.

To enlarge the self is to realize that we are essentially community. This
community includes not only all the human beings, but other living creatures and even the entire cosmos, for the human is functionally embedded
in—systemically integrated into—the cosmos as a whole. Human existence
is dependent on practically everything else in the whole universe being
exactly the way it is, down to the location of a suitable star for one's
planet on the cool edge of a galaxy, to the spacing out of the galaxies
for gravitational balance, to the setting of the great cosmic parameters
at just the values they happen to have so that atoms may form and stars
coalesce.[27] On the planet itself we are finding out just how interwoven
are the mixture of gases in the atmosphere, the chlorophyll-bearing plants,
the bacteria, and many other systems, including our own domestic and
industrial behaviors.[28]

Thus, the current concern for the ecology of our planet is integral to
the view I am proposing and the communitarian ethical rule of so behaving
that the whole community may flourish. In this regard, too, what we had
formerly taken for granted as our (human) right to "utilize" the resources
of the planet may now have to be reassessed in terms of the rights of other
creatures and the continued health of the entire system on which we are
all dependent.

THE TRINITARIAN LIFE-CYCLE

I began by saying that the problem we face in trying to make sense of our lives is putting together unity and multiplicity, not only so as to preserve them both without reducing either to the other, but so as to reveal them as enhancing one another instead of appearing as alternatives. I have proposed *kenotic agape* as the principle that achieves this and I have suggested that it is the foundation of *communitarian nondualism*.

Kenotic agape, I said, is originally the life principle of the transcendent, infinite, formless Person-Community, the way in which the innumerable Persons of that Community relate to one another within the Community. It is also the way in which that Community as a whole expresses itself, exteriorizes itself, phenomenalizes itself, as the Cosmos-Community. There is nondualism within the Person-Community and between the Person-Community and the Cosmos-Community.

My final point is that the Cosmos-Community itself evolves toward fuller realization of kenotic agape within its own community and thus comes to realization of itself as the self-expression of the Person-Community. The more the Cosmos-Community evolves toward self-realization, the more the Person-Community succeeds in incarnating itself as the Cosmos-Community with the fullness of the divine values, so that the fullness of the Godhead can dwell in the Cosmos corporally.

This self-realization on the part of the Cosmos-Community is also a communitarian nondualistic reality, for it consists precisely of realizing that there is no separation among any of the members of the Cosmos-Community and no separation between the Cosmos-Community and the Person-Community. Furthermore, this consciousness tends to rise within the Cosmos-Community as such, as a global phenomenon, something that comes in "the fullness of time." It is the initiating, or christening, Event. It is the connection to the beginning, to the Formless, and is again done by self-emptying, both with regard to the relation of the formed to the Formless and regarding the relations of the formed among themselves.

Cosmic Self-Realization is the summary and consummation of the whole functioning of the Real, which can now be seen to consist of three moments, or a Trinitarian Life-Cycle: first, the fully conscious formless

Person-Community; second, the manifestation of the Person-Community as Cosmos-Community, temporarily hiding its full consciousness in order to become finite; and third (when the embodied consciousness is sufficiently complex and reflexive), the self-realization of the Cosmos-Community *as* the embodiment of Person Community the return to full consciousness as the awakening spirit brings to mind all that was latent in the cosmic self-expression of the Infinite. In mythic language, this might be seen as Parent, Child, and the Holy Self-Realization of their union and mutual indwelling, as the Child mysteriously becomes parent, giving birth to the divine values in the finite order by fulfilling the kenotic agape, and by that action being assumed again into the infinite order.

The mystics tell us that as consciousness grows in the realization of the Holy Wholeness, we will find the mutual penetration of the Absolute and the phenomenal going deeper and deeper. We will also discover, on the one hand, that we are nothing but the exteriorization of the Absolute, that is, the Absolute's own self poured out into the finite, and on the other hand, that there is no Absolute somewhere else, separate and apart from our phenomenal expression. Thus, the Child is only the Parent, exteriorized in love; there is no way to see the Parent as something other and apart from the Child. For the Parent is thoroughly in the Child, and the Child thoroughly in the Parent.

In our daily phenomenal life, this will mean that we will be vividly aware of being the formless Person who is totally kenotic agape, and whose actions in the phenomenal world are rooted in creative freedom and expressed in beauty. This is the divine life in the Wholeness: realization as Absolute, formless Person-Community, the effusion of Love, and realization as relative, formed Cosmos-Community, the unceasing Birth in Beauty.

NOTES

1. Beatrice Bruteau, *What We Can Learn from the East* and *The Easter Mysteries* (New York: Crossroads, 1995).

2. See Robert Imperato, *Merton and Walsh on the Person* (West Palm Beach, FL: Liturgical Publications, 1987), and feature review of same by B. Bruteau, *International Philosophical Quarterly*, Fall 1991.

3. Daniel Walsh, *Gethsemani Archives Document 3*, p. 8. (Much of the Walsh material is unpublished, but is available through Brother Anthony Distefano, OCSO, Abbey of Gethsemani, Trappist KY 40051.) See also *Document 4*, "Some Intimations of the Person in the Noetic of Knowledge and Love in the Doctrines of St. Thomas and Duns Scotus," p. 6.

4. Imperato, *Merton and Walsh on the Person*, pp. 70–71.

5. Ibid., pp. 63–64.

6. Walsh, *Document 5*, "Person and Community," p. 4.

7. Ibid.

8. Ibid. Also Walsh, *Document 3*, p. 8.

9. Bede Griffiths, "Christianity in the Light of the East," The Hibbert Lecture 1989, available also in Aide Inter-Monastères, North American Board for East-West Dialogue Bulletin #36 (October 1989), p. 7. (To receive the Bulletin, apply to: Abbey of Gethsemani, MID Bulletin, 3642 Monks Road, Trappist KY 40051–6102.)

10. See Beatrice Bruteau, "Freedom: If Anyone Is in Christ, That Person Is a New Creation," in *Who Do People Say That I Am?*, ed. Francis A. Eigo, OSA (Villanova PA: Villanova University Press, 1980), esp. p. 135.

11. Griffiths, "Christianity in the Light of the East," p. 7.

12. Karlfried Graf Dürckheim, "Werk der Übung-Gerschenk der Gnade," in *Geist und Leben*, vol. 45, no. 5 (Oct. 1972), tr. by John C. Maraldo into English in Heinrich Dumoulin's *Zen Enlightenment* (New York: Weatherhill, 1979), pp. 63–64.

13. See Beatrice Bruteau, "In the Cave of the Heart: Silence and Realization," *New Blackfriars*, vol. 65, nos. 769/770 (July/August 1984), pp. 310–313.

14. Robert E. Carter, *The Nothingness Beyond God: An Introduction to the Philosophy of Nishida Kitaro* (New York: Paragon, 1989), p. 89.

15. Cf. Keiji Nishitani, *Religion and Nothingness* (Berkeley: University of California Press, 1982), p. 279. "Circuminsessional" means the reciprocal existence of one another of the three persons of the Trinity (*Random House Dictionary of the English Language, Unabridged*, 1967).

16. Robert S. Hartman, "The Logic of Value," *Review of Metaphysics* XIV (March 1961), p. 408.

17. Thomas Aquinas, Summa Theologiae I, Q. 50, Art. 3.; cf. also Hebrews 12:22.

18. Radhakrishnan, in his commentary on the Chandogya Upanishad VI.8.7, carefully points out that "The text 'That art thou' applies to the inward person, *antah purusa*, and not to the empirical soul with its name and family descent." *The Principal Upanishads*, edited by S. Radhakrishnan (London: George Allen & Unwin, 1953), p. 458.

19. Raimundo Panikkar, *The Silence of God: The Answer of the Buddha*, tr. from the Italian by Robert R. Barr (Maryknoll: Orbis, Faith Meets Faith Series, 1989), pp. 134ff.

20. Abhishiktananda, *The Secret of Arunachala* (Delhi: ISPCK, 1979), p. 82.

21. George A. Seielstad, *At the Heart of the Web: The Inevitable Genesis of Intelligent Life* (New York: Harcourt Brace Jovanovich, 1989), p. 124.

22. Cf. Abhishiktananda: "This individual form that *we* speak of as the body of such and such a jnani, does not seem to *him* his own any more than any other form belonging to the

created world whether human or something else." *Guru and Disciple*, tr. Heather Sandeman (London: SPCK, 1974), p. 45.

23. David Bohm, *Wholeness and the Implicate Order* (London: Routledge & Kegan Paul, 1980), pp. 147, 149.

24. Ibid., p. 178.

25. Ibid., p. 185.

26. Ibid., p. 178.

27. Cf. P. C. W. Davies, *The Accidental Universe* (Cambridge University Press, 1982); John D. Barrow & Frank J. Tipler, *The Anthropic Cosmological Principle* (Oxford University Press, 1988).

28. Cf. James Lovelock, *The Ages of Gaia: A Biography of Our Living Earth* (New York: Norton, 1988); Elisabet Sahtouris, *Gaia: The Human Journey from Chaos to Cosmos* (New York: Pocket Books, 1989).

Poems from Jonah: Warning from the Earth, Poem #30

Albert J. LaChance

Poem #30 from Jonah traces the history of creation/evolution and allows Earth herself to issue a solemn warning that we intelligent ones, the precious product of evolution's long struggle, must exercise our creative powers with reverence for the holy Whole.

To The People of Nineveh

I am Mother of all the mothers.
I am Mother of all the Marys.
I am Mother of all the fathers.
I am the Bride of Great Heart.

I am the Earth

. . . today I speak . . .

Disarm the entire planet . . . . NOW.
Stop polluting the soils . . . . NOW.
Stop poisoning the waters . . . . NOW.
Stop degrading the air . . . . NOW.
Stop ravaging the forests . . . . NOW.
No longer desecrate the animals.
Stop killing the preborn young.

—or—

The heavens will withhold their showers and the
soils will begrudge their bounty when they turn
to dust. All life will undergo the great collapse
of nature's increase. Famines will visit the life-
planet like never before, starvation in all the
lands where there was plenty. The waters will
flush poisons over the land; all flesh will boil
with hideous growths and stink in corruption. The
stench will ascend to the highest atmosphere and
will churn upon every wind. The bodies of monsters
will appear among you and among the animals bodies
not willed by Great Heart in the grand genesis of
all beauty and all generosity since the beginning.

Albert J. LaChance

In the Beginning

We were dark, enfolded, in the infinite cold
of the Great Heart's lonely dreaming.
A dream within a dream within a dream unfurled,
the fireball and galaxies of stars
were hurled, in one spasm of delight Great Heart ended
endless night, the planet Earth
then life then human consciousness uncurled in an
everlasting scream that would
engender every dream: "HOC EST CORPUS MEUM"

There Was Light

The lightless, endless night became the rite of endless
morning, and cooled to dust adorning
our emerging galaxy. And I was with
the virgins in attendance
of the sun, Who in his second birth would seed
my ceaseless pregnancies. I
harbored you within my heart, along with every
living thing. I formed a veil for all to
breathe. A veil to give you gathering. I made the rain
to fill the seas; I filled the soils
with ecstacies; I poured perfumes on every breeze
and filled the trees with harmonies.
The moon was midwife to the brine that rocked and sloshed
with energies. My one desire
was just to give, my only longing was to please.
The Great Heart with his spilling will
willed a thrill within my seas, that formed a billion willing
wives who birthed a billion trilling lives.

Then There Was Life

Dreaming dust married dreaming dust; plants and animals

—\|l/—

appeared. My oceans burst aflame
with lives, my soils and then my atmosphere. I am
the snake who eats her tail; I am
the flabby mother whale. I am the breath that you
inhale; I am the mind of fairy-tale.
I am the tree who shelters you, the nourishment
you suck and chew. I am the teeming
ocean floor, the shark who lurks, The Ancestor.
I breathed within the dinosaur;
I was their life and death and more . . . I am the governed
and the governor. I am
the eagle and his flight, the insect and amphibian.
I am the moonlight and the night,
the monkey sleeping on the limb. I am the pelican
and gull and all that thrives on
every shore, the fish, the worm and the fisherman . . .
the Goddess who gave birth to man.

Then There Was Consciousness

And you, you are my darling ones, my laughing ones,
forever young. You are my dream
within my dream, your cultures are my mother-tongue.
And it is ours to praise the sun
through all the throats of every faith, ours to marvel
at the ONE of whom all creatures
are the wraith. In you I love all body-souls, all lands,
all rivers, sky and sea. But you
forget that I'm of Great Heart and you are born of me.

Will There Then Be Death?

Civilizations rise and fade away, rise and fade
away, like leaves. With them the tyrants come and go
and the greedy and the cruel. It begins with the
destruction of the soil. People of Nineveh, I am not

your whore! I have watched the soils die and turn to dust. I have watched the waters abort the lives for which they are the womb. I have seen the air at noon darken over the Great City. People of Nineveh, I am not your whore! I have watched your machines devour the woodlands and wetlands the farmlands and meadowlands. The animals and children are dying. The birds and fish are dying. The planet of life becomes a tomb. People of Nineveh, I will watch you no more.

—for—

I am Mother of all the mothers.
I am Mother of all the Marys.
I am Mother of all the fathers.
I am the Bride of Great Heart.

I am Earth.

. . . Great Heart speaks . . .

Jonah is sent with this message:

"Change or the Great City will collapse.
The human is to live, a single family
among the other families of Earth."

Let this be a warning unto you,
. . . a prophecy against you . . .

O people of Nineveh.

Spirituality for a New Era: A Dialogue

Matthew Fox and Bede Griffiths

This dialogue offers a chance to hear the words of Dom Bede himself. Matthew Fox was a good friend of Father Bede's, and the two enjoyed many stimulating conversations, of which the following is a sample. It touches on all three of Bede's areas of interest—the interreligious, the gender polarity, and the concern for science. Fox is founder of the Institute of Culture and Creation Spirituality at Holy Names College in Oakland, California, and author of Original Blessing *(1983),* Coming of the Cosmic Christ *(1988), and* Creation Spirituality: Liberating Gifts of Peoples of the Earth *(1991).[1] This dialogue took place at the Institute in the fall of 1992.*

J would like to begin this dialogue with a quote from Father Bede Griffiths. When we met for the first time last winter he said this to me and I've been quoting it all over the country because I was very touched by it. "If Christianity cannot recover its mystical tradition and teach it, it should simply fold up and go out of business—it has nothing to offer." I think this is a very strong statement and a very truthful one. Religion is dying in the West to the extent that it has lost its source, its spiritual tradition. Thomas Aquinas said in the thirteenth century, "The experience of God should not be restricted to the few or to the old." And if our religious traditions are failing to usher us in to the ways to experience divinity, then indeed they need to be let go; because today spirituality is needed everywhere. It offers humankind and this planet its greatest signs of hope. I would like to address four issues in the spiritual awakening that to me seems to usher in a new era for human consciousness and therefore some hope for planetary healing.

The first is the need to teach mysticism—to draw it out of ourselves, to draw it out of our ancestors who are present with us in what we call the communion of saints. E. F. Schumacher, in the epilogue of his classic work *Small Is Beautiful*,[2] ends the book this way: "Everywhere people ask, 'What can I actually *do?*' The answer is as simple as it is disconcerting. We can, each of us, work to put our own inner house in order. The guidance we need for this work cannot be found in science or technology, the value of which utterly depends on the ends they serve; but it can still be found in the traditional wisdom of humankind." The issue of putting our inner house in order, it seems to me, is not just a personal issue but a community issue, and indeed today, a species issue. As individuals and as communities and as a species, our houses need to be put in order. Or as Hildegard of Bingen put it in the twelfth century, "Search out the inner wisdom of your heart."

Today in the West this search for wisdom requires a reinvention of models of education—models that are consciously and deliberately nonreductionist. In the West, in the last three hundred years since the enlightenment, we have been practicing reductionist education; we have taken away our right hemisphere from our minds, from the classroom and therefore from worship as well. We need wisdom schools instead of just knowledge schools or information factories. Wisdom schools will come far closer to the ancient traditions of learning that we find among Native Americans, Native Africans, and Native Celtic centers of learning, and certainly in the kind of ashram learning that Father Bede has been so committed to for so many years in Mother India.

A reinvention of education would guarantee a reinvention of work. Getting our own inner houses in order will create whole fields of new jobs—new jobs especially for artists of all kinds who are called to bring forth our images, our deep experiences, our darkness, and our brilliance. Hildegard of Bingen said, "There is wisdom in all creative works." We are trying to do this at the Institute of Culture and Creation Spirituality—to develop a wisdom school that depends so much on the artists who teach massage as meditation, dance as meditation, drama as meditation, and clay and painting as meditation. Because you cannot lie—you cannot lie to the artist inside of you or the images inside of you. They speak the truth that is ours.

We hear moaning in this country—we hear it in the Bay Area—that we are closing down military bases; we hear moaning that we are closing down factories in our country. When I look around the world I think we need a very finite number of factories and military bases. I think we have enough cars to go around for the most part. Instead of moaning, we should be investing in training our workers, including our military people, to become teachers in wisdom schools. Recently, I saw a statistic that pointed out how we could pull back 162 billion dollars from our weaponry because the East/West Cold War has melted. I propose that some of this could surely go into replacing crack houses with wisdom schools and communities of learners in all of our cities and in all countries—wisdom schools where the heart is instructed and not just the head. As Rilke said early in this century, "The work of the eyes is finished, go now and do heart work." So, our mystical education would be primarily an education of our hearts. As a species, our hearts have become grossly underdeveloped in the last three hundred years while our left brains have become bloated.

A second dimension to a spirituality for a new era is to enter more deeply into an experience of earth spirituality, which for us humans means into our own bodies. Wendell Berry, a poet, farmer, and prophet in our country, said, "I've long suspected that Christianity is not earthy enough." Sexuality is not an obstacle to the Divine. It is one of the ways to theophany and the Divine experience. Sexuality is a way to the experience of the sacred wilderness. The body is no obstacle to the spirit; it is one of the paths to the Divine and of the Divine to us, and all of us to the whole earth body today—to recover the holiness of matter, the sacredness of matter, the new cosmic story, the new cosmology. We are hearing about how our bodies got here through supernova explosions five and a half billion years ago, how our food is all dependent on the sun, through photosynthetic processes. All of this awakens our reverence because it awakens our awe for our own earthiness and the relationship of our bodies to all the other bodies in this universe.

Our religious tradition has a book in the Bible that is as holy as any other book—The Song of Songs—that celebrates the mysticism and the theophany of sexual love, and indeed, of love as an experience of the sacred wilderness. Holy passion leads to compassion, and it all begins with wonder and amazement and awe. We need to rediscover gratitude for matter. This is a blessing consciousness that I'm speaking of: the realization of the deep down goodness of things, the deep down goodness of being here and the deep down goodness of being in all its reality. It seems to me that Einstein, in declaring at the beginning of this century that energy and matter are convertible, set us on a new path away from Hellenistic dualisms, back to a Jewish appreciation of the spirit as present in matter and in all forms of energy. Indeed, in the thirteenth century Aquinas attempted to celebrate this new relationship of matter and spirit for the West, but he failed; he was condemned three times because he tried this. Aquinas said, "Vice does not come from the body to the soul, but vice goes from the soul to the body." I think much of Western religion has missed that point, of the deep down goodness of matter. And so today we need to try again, and today we cannot afford to fail as they failed at the end of the thirteenth century, because we need a "spirituality as if creation mattered"—a spirituality as if *matter* mattered.

This leads to a third point: the development of teaching what I would call the ecological virtues. In the past in the West we have had political virtues to think about, civic virtues to think about, domestic virtues to think about; but today around the globe we need to wake up to and instruct one another in what I would call ecological virtues. What are ecological virtues?

These are the habits that allow us to walk lightly on this planet and to pass it on, with beauty and with cherishing, to the next generation and those that will follow them. I will list a few of these ecological virtues that I think are challenging us today. First, vegetarianism, or semi-vegetarianism: It seems to me that the addiction to meat in the West has run its course. It is folly, it is immoral, and we all have to ask how we can cut back on the amount of meat we are eating and therefore the amount of water and the amount of land that we are utilizing to produce that meat. As John Robbins has demonstrated in his book, *Diet for a New America*,[3] if North Americans alone would cut back just ten percent on our meat consumption, sixty million people around the world who are starving could eat. And so a raised consciousness about our food and our diet seems to me to be integral to the pursuit of ecological virtue.

Another ecological virtue is learning to bicycle or walk whenever we can, to carpool and take public transportation, and to work, as much as possible, where we live or near where we live. Today an ecological virtue we are hearing about, especially from our children, is recycling. Another is simply learning reverence and awe for water, for healthy soil, for healthy air, and healthy forests. The basic lesson on reverence for water that I was taught several years ago by a Native American was this: "Go without it for three days." A little fasting goes a long way—you return to water with great reverence.

To practice conviviality where we live is an ecological virtue—to develop our own entertainment, our own acts of drama and music and gardening, at home and in our neighborhood. To plant trees would be an ecological virtue. And it would be virtuous to interfere with political folly by organizing to defend the creation—even practicing civil disobedience when that is called for.

These are ecological virtues for our time, to be expressed in our ritual making, so that we can rediscover, in our communities and in our groups, the power of imaging the sacred times and the sacred spaces and the sacred experiences of our natures, and of the rest of nature of which we are a part.

We need to remember that an authentic mystic develops into a prophet; that is how it happens—passion becomes compassion. As William Hawking said early in this century, "The prophet is the mystic in action." The test of authentic spirituality is not levitating. The test of authentic spirituality is justice-making. It is healing, it is celebrating, and therefore it is compassion. Aquinas says, "In compassion, the human imitates God." That is an ancient Jewish and biblical teaching and indeed we find this around the world. Therefore, the new spirituality will educate us not just into being mystics but into being prophets as well. The groundwork for being a prophet is to be a mystic, because if our actions for transformation in society do not flow from nonaction—from our experience of being and from the sense of letting go—then they are not truly radical. We would not go deep. We would be exchanging one anger for another anger, one slogan for another slogan.

Unless we change our hearts, we will not truly be affecting our species. And so, a spiritual education will teach us effective ways to interfere. That is what Rabbi Heschel says the prophet does—"interferes." Today's prophets should be interfering with the devastation of this planet, with the devastation and despair in our souls and especially in those of our children and those of displaced native peoples; interfering with the devastation of all the other species of living things so jeopardized on this planet today.

Recently, I heard information from Holland that their legislature tried to put through laws about lifestyle changes. And after several years they gave up and they made this statement, "You cannot change lifestyles through legislation." They are right, you can change lifestyle only through spirituality. Spirituality is the most radical form of social transformation. Ask Mahatma Gandhi—he demonstrated that spirituality can transform society because it can absorb the wrong patterns of responding and thinking and recycle them. That was Gandhi's brilliance.

There is no prophet, of course, who has not entered the dark. The entering of the dark needs to be undergone in our time. We need to find a new reverence for the dark—for silence and for entering into the dark night of the soul that all of us are involved in today. It takes a strong heart, a big heart—courage—for us to enter the dark night and not to deny it, not to run to the plethora of addictions that our culture offers to help us flee from the dark.

Father Bede has written about how despair itself is a yoga. He puts it this way: "It is significant that the experience of despair is a yoga. Despair is often the first step on the path of the spiritual life, and many people do not awaken to the reality of God and the experience of transformation in their lives until they go through the experience of emptiness, dissolution and despair." This is something we can all expect in the nineties. Alcoholics Anonymous and other base communities invented in the North are good examples of the healing power that emerges when people gather, not to parade their egos, but to share what they've undergone in the dark. It is from the breakdown that breakthrough happens. From a "via negativa" we are led into the "via creativa"; from Golgotha into Easter.

This is what the new spirituality will teach us about what Aquinas calls the "sins of the spirit." And the new spirituality will teach us with the same eagerness and zeal with which our Western church has over-taught us about the sins of the flesh. Indeed Aquinas said, "The sins of the spirit are far more dangerous than the sins of the flesh. For the sins of the spirit lead us away from something and the sins of the flesh still lead us to something." Consider for example, how many of us even know what the phrase "the sins of the spirit" means? What are sins of the spirit? Try despair. In some places we are now suffering an epidemic afflicting youths: nine, ten, and eleven-year-olds are killing others in our cities these days. That's what happens when the human heart falls into despair, loses hope. Or consider the spiritual sin floating through our culture of fear. Think how much damage is caused by religious fundamentalism because of the fear it engenders. Consider the spiritual sin called acedia, which is, as Aquinas says, "The refusal to begin new things," because we don't have the energy for it. We're tired, we're cynical, we've seen it all before. That's acedia.

These are issues of the nineties, and now I especially want to discuss one sin, and that is the spiritual sin called avarice, or greed. Our whole culture, I propose, is built on a consciousness of avarice and greed. We call it consumerism, and we call it luxury living. In the eighties we saw many examples of avarice: the Savings & Loan crisis, the bank crisis, the growing gap between haves and have-nots, and so many other obvious examples. What I'd like to share briefly is how a spirituality can provide us an analysis and a liberation from this one example of a spiritual sin, that of avarice.

Aquinas says this about avarice: "The greed for gain knows no limit and tends to infinity." I was absolutely struck dumb when I read this sentence because I had always thought of avarice and greed in terms of materialism, where people want more things. But he says that avarice is not about materialism, it is about the quest for the infinite. And that is what spirit is in us humans. You know, there is no avarice in other creatures. The whales, the trees are not greedy. But we humans fall easily into it. Carl Jung says, "The decisive question for the human being is this, are we related to something infinite or not? That is the telling question of our lives."

I propose that greed or avarice is the kind of quest for the infinite that will not satisfy. You know it's infinite because every year our culture comes out with a new model. How dare anyone die before the next year's car comes out? How do you cure this disease of the quest for the infinite in terms of greed for what Aquinas would call the unnatural gifts of the earth—those that humans make, such as consumer items? But, he goes on to say, "God has shared infinite goodness with each one of us. The gift is infinite on the part of the giver."

In Aquinas' analysis the human is infinite in a healthy way, in three ways: First, he says, each human *mind* is infinite, for it is capable of knowing an infinite number of things, and the proof of this is that you never learn too much. Even on your deathbed you're getting curious about the next journey. So our *mind* can touch the infinite. He says we're also infinite in our *hearts*: "It is not possible to place any limits to the increase of love in this life." As long as our mind is alive and feeding our heart with objects to love, there are no limits to what our hearts can love. And the third example of authentic human experience of the infinite is our *imagination*. Aquinas says, "Our imagination connected to our hands can produce an infinite variety of artifacts."

Consider that there have never been two musicians in the history of the human race who wrote the same piece of music, or two painters who painted the identical picture, or two potters who gave birth to the same pot. Or dancers who danced the same dance, or poets who birthed the same poem. He's absolutely correct: Our imaginations connected to our hands can give birth to an infinite variety of artifacts. There is where our new civilization must invest its education, its efforts in ritual and worship to reawaken the human capacity for the infinite that is healthy: our minds, our hearts, and our imaginations. And that will displace the quest for the infinite that is being fed to us in a sick and avarice-based society.

Pat Schroeder, a Colorado congresswoman, has said, "When the people lead, the politicians will follow." I would like to adapt this and propose the following: When authentic spirituality leads, religion will follow . . . maybe. If it does not, it ought to move aside, as Bede Griffiths said, for spirituality is coming. As Carl Jung stated, "It is only the mystics who bring what is creative to religion itself. It is the reawakening of mysticism that will in fact reawaken our religious traditions." And as Wendell Berry puts it, "We must fight the worst with the best." And the best, according to Jung again, is the mystic, "who may have been a cross to the churches but who represents the best in humanity."

When I use the word "mystic," I mean the mystic inside every one of us, who wants to dance and play in the universe, to recover the sense of erotic delight with divinity that is our birthright as a species. But we are failing in this. Rabbi Heschel defines sin as humanity's failure to be who we are. In the nineties we need to reawaken to who we are. We are mystical, delightful, charming, prophetic, and very dangerous beings. And we need to pay attention to all this power in our midst.

If spirituality cannot ignite and spread this wild fire, then I believe our young will die—they will die of despair, they will die of being deprived of adventure that is worthy of the size of their souls. And when that happens, when the young die, the species dies. And because of the inherent violence in our species, we will die bringing down thousands of other species with us. That, I think, is what is at issue in recovering a living mysticism.

Regarding mystics to whom we owe what is best in humanity, I look forward to hearing what Father Bede will share with us. I would like to say a personal word of introduction because back in 1967, when I wanted to study spirituality, I wrote to Thomas Merton and asked where I should go to study. He sent a long letter back and said to go to Paris and gave me this long list of things I had to learn. And then he said, "Someday, you must meet Father Bede Griffiths in India." The winter of 1991 is when I first had the pleasure of meeting Father Griffiths, although I had heard of him and his works for years. It was a wonderful and powerful experience. I happened to be in the process of writing a tome on Thomas Aquinas' mysticism, and Father Bede said he would like to see what I was doing. In his unbelievably generous manner he read through an eight hundred page manuscript twice and corrected all the stiff translations, putting them into the Queen's English and smoothing out the biblical translations. I am indebted to him for his generosity and patience in helping me with that.

BEDE GRIFFITHS:

I am very glad to be with you and with Father Matthew. I have the greatest admiration for the work he's doing. In our little ashram in India, we read his *Original Blessing* about two years ago and then we read his *Coming of the Cosmic Christ*. And when I first met him last year, I said "I think his creation spirituality is the spirituality of the future and his theology of the Cosmic Christ is the theology of the future," and I firmly hold that this is so. I therefore think it is extremely important that we meet together and share this vision of the future of a new age that is really dawning in the world and dawning here in America and dawning here in California. Something is happening in California, and in America and in the world today.

Perhaps I should begin where I started. I've been a Benedictine Monk for almost sixty years. I became a monk when I was a young man in England because I was disillusioned with the world around me. After the 1914 war there was a great feeling of disenchantment and disillusionment everywhere, especially at Oxford where I was studying. When I left Oxford, I had no understanding of any meaning or purpose in life, and I went to live with two friends in the country to try to discover some meaning in life—to get back to roots. We had a little cottage, and a garden and a cow, and we tried to live a very simple life. We began to read the Bible, and for the first time, the Bible meant something to me. I think I read it three times and it changed our lives—all three of us.

When I came out of that, I had to find somewhere to live this experience that had come, and by the grace of God I found the Catholic Church—through Newman largely—and then I found a monastery in South England. And it was a wonderful experience. I'll never forget it and never cease to be thankful for it. It gave me everything I wanted at the time, and the first thing was what Father Matthew has been talking about: the mystical dimension of religion and in life. I had no idea of it. My friends and I were lovers of poetry and lovers of nature, but beyond that we had nothing. And now this experience suddenly showed me there is something beyond nature and poetry. There is a presence of God that can be discovered and it was in that monastery. I've never questioned it. It was in the community—it was really a community of love. I've never felt so much love as I met in that community.

And so we had a very balanced life. We had prayer seven times a day; we chanted the Gregorian chants and it was wonderful music—it went into your heart and into your mind—it was beautiful. We also had a wonderful library; we could study anything we liked. And we did manual work every day for two or three hours. There was almost nothing I didn't do: making stone, mixing concrete, helping in the building, and working in the fields and in the garden. That was wonderful too, because it wasn't only the mind, it was also the body and the earth, and that experience was in me from that time onward. So, I'm very thankful for that monastery, and I was there for twenty years.

In the course of that time I began to get interested in Eastern thought, and I met a very wonderful woman called Toni Sussman. She was a German and one of Jung's first disciples, so she knew Jungian psychology, and she also had all the books on Eastern mysticism and Eastern religion. That was in 1940, and it opened a new world for me. From then on I began to look towards India as the land of promise, and by the grace of God again, I met an Indian Benedictine monk from Canada who came to our monastery and asked me if I would come and start a foundation with him in India. So in 1955 I realized my dream and I said to a friend, "I'm trying to find the other half of my soul." Because, you know, our Christian tradition develops your spiritual mind and the upper faculties wonderfully, but it neglects the lower faculties—the earthly faculties—and it neglects the feminine. It masters the masculine and neglects the feminine. And I was searching for this other side of my being, and that's what I found in India.

India has this mystical tradition, but it has not broken with the earth, with matter, with life. It's in the villages—the people in the villages in India have the sense of the sacred. In America it's very rare to find that sense. The Native Americans have that wonderful sense of the sacredness of the earth, of the water, of the plants and animals, and that is mysticism— mysticism not in the head or in the mind alone but in the body and in the whole being. And so I began to discover a much more holistic mysticism, a holistic experience altogether, and it's very wonderful in our ashram—we're so integrated. We have a little hut among the coconut trees—it's extremely natural and beautiful—by the river they call the Ganges of the South, the Kavery. We live a life of prayer, meditation, and study, and also of communion with nature as a whole—with the earth, the trees and the world around us, that is really what I've grown up with.

What I feel people are looking for today in different ways is an awakening to that need for wholeness—body, soul, and spirit. Body is the physical organism and part of the physical universe. Father Matthew is bringing out the ecological problem—that we've lost that sense of belonging to the whole. We are part of the physical universe—the electromagnetic energy that is flowing through everything and flowing through our bodies. We're all part of this physical universe, and we have to realize that.

And then there is the soul, the psyche—that is not only the mind or even the will, but the whole heart and feelings and senses, the whole psychological being. That is also part of your human being. You're a physical and psychological being, and this is a point we all have to face.

Beyond the physical and psychological is what in English we call the spirit; in Sanskrit we call it the Atman, the inner self. We have a physical self, a psychological self, and a spiritual self—your real being. In India we often ask "who am I?" Am I this thing sitting here while you are sitting there? or am I this thing that is talking and thinking? But beyond the body, beyond the mind and the psyche is this transcendent spirit that is present everywhere in everybody here and now. The spirit is among us and we're trying to realize it. We don't neglect our bodies; we realize their sacredness. And we don't neglect our human contacts; human relations are sacred also. But they become sacred only when we transcend our body and our soul and open to the Holy Spirit, the transcendent mystery, the Divine, the Word, the Tao, the Brahman.

All these words are pointing to something beyond, and I think the need of America today and the world today is to discover this Being beyond. We're locked into the body-soul, and it's so difficult to realize that this infinite eternal wonder of the spirit is present everywhere to everybody at every moment. We forget about it. We're imprisoned and asleep in our present state. But we can be awakened. That's what India did for me—it awoke the sense of mystical reality, and to me it still remains. We also have our mystical tradition in the West, and Father Matthew has been one who has revived it for us. It's not only John of the Cross, it's Eckhart, it's Cusa and all the Rhineland mystics, Hildegard and Mechtild; it's a new world we're discovering of Christian mysticism. And don't forget that it was Christian mysticism that built the cathedrals. All the wonderful cathedrals!—they're really expressions in stone of a mystical experience—that's why they're so powerful.

But I feel we cannot recover the fullness of mystical reality unless we open ourselves to Asia, to India and China in particular. And that is the challenge to the churches in the world today: to open ourselves to the mystical traditions of India and China. I've been trying to do that for many years, and I have found that it changes your whole being as you begin to realize the depth of it all, the incredible depth. And I often like to emphasize that it is not difficult to contact those traditions.

I'm planning to produce a book of readings from the scriptures of the world [see *Universal Wisdom: A Journey through the Sacred Wisdom of the World* cited in the Bibliography]. I am giving the full text of six Upanishads—all written from the eighth to the sixth centuries before Christ. That's the time of breakthrough, when the mystical wisdom broke into humanity. I will include Upanishads that can be found in the Penguin classics translated by Mascaro, an excellent English edition.[4] I will give the whole of the Bhagavad Gita; this was an attempt to show how the mystical wisdom can be brought into daily life. The lesson of the Gita is do your work day by day, your dharma [vocation], whatever it is—but do it in the spirit of total surrender to the Lord. Surrender yourself, let go and allow the Lord, allow the spirit, allow the Atman, the Brahman to take possession of you. That is what we're seeking. So the Gita is for everybody. I wrote a commentary on it—it's called *The River of Compassion*, and I'm not ashamed to advertise it because it's a wonderful guide to life for everybody! And I've put it into the context of Christian faith.

Then I've given the Dhammapada of the Buddha. The Buddha was another great breakthrough. Just as the Christian religion went right through Europe and spread to America, Buddhism spread from India and from Sri Lanka right through Thailand and Viet Nam, through China, Tibet, and Japan; the whole of the Eastern world was transformed by the mystical experience of the Buddha, which he gained by simply sitting under the Bodhi tree and realizing that all this world is passing away and that there is something real behind it all. He called it simply "Nirvana" [the state of liberation in which the fire of the ego-oriented desires has "gone out," like a candle that has burned down] and wouldn't give it a name, but it was a liberation from the prison of this world and an opening to this divine reality. It has no name but it is everything. That's what the Buddha did.

And then the Tao Te Ching, which is, I think, the most wonderful book in the world in some ways. It's an extraordinary book, and it has an extraordinary insight, especially into the feminine. My appreciation of this, you know, is partly the masculine Western mind finding the feminine Indian mind. Of course, all minds are both masculine and feminine, and there's a strong masculine element in India; but in South India where I am they are essentially a more feminine people, and their worship is of the Mother Goddess. In all our villages, the Mother Goddess is the object of worship, and it's a beautiful community of women there who all worship the Mother. Their whole life centers on that.

So we have this tradition of the feminine, and in the Tao Te Ching it is marvelously developed. My idea of the feminine is that the feminine is receptive while the masculine is active. The feminine is receptive—it's an active passivity. In China it is called Wu Wei ["not action"]. Again, it's an active passivity; it's not a dull passivity but passivity that is totally open, sensitivity that has awakened. And that's what we are seeking—to be awakened. The Taoists compare it to emptiness; there's a wonderful chapter in the Tao that says, "We take clay and make a pot, but it's the empty space in the pot which makes it useful. And we take bricks and mortar and wood to make a house but it's the empty spaces of the windows and the doors that make it habitable." That is the feminine. It makes things useful and habitable.

We're trying to recover this balance. The mystical tradition of India and China can give the West the fullness of mystical reality that we are seeking. We have our Christian tradition and the Sufis in Islam have developed a marvelous mystical tradition as well, but I think all the world now needs this oriental mysticism. And it is part of the whole global movement today. We can't live any longer as Western people or Eastern people; we belong to a common humanity. That is where the mystical tradition is opening up.

The danger is that it tends to be very individualistic. In the past, if you wanted to be a mystic, you went into a monastery and you lived a very austere life and you separated yourself from the world. Today we believe that the mystical experience is open to everybody. We all have this capacity for God, deep in ourselves. It's buried in most people. It's coming to life in some, but it's possible for every human being to find that in the depths of their being lies an openness to transcendent mystery, the Divine Holy, the Tao, the Brahman, whatever word you give it. That is what we're seeking, how to open humanity today to this other dimension of reality.

And that involves, as Father Matthew was saying, two things. One is an understanding of the body. This has been a great weakness in Christian mysticism. I don't think I know any Christian mystic who really seriously takes the body into consideration. Hesychasts [from *hesychia*, quietness] among the Orthodox mystics did the breathing. At least they got to the point of using the breathing as something that would help. But in yoga—which is one of the great gifts of India to the world—in yoga, it's the total being that has to be transformed. The body and the soul are totally integrated.

Amaldas, one of our brothers in our ashram, was a wonderful brother who came to us twenty years ago and didn't know anything about yoga. But he learned by studying under several masters and became a master yogi and went on to teach meditation as a result of that. He published two books—*Yoga and Contemplation* by Swami Amaldas and *Jesu Abba Consciousness*. Jesu Abba was his mantra—"Jesu" as you breathe in, "Abba" [Father] as you breathe out. And he taught people to meditate by using that mantra: taking all the suffering and the needs of the world into your heart in "Jesu" and surrendering it all to the Father in "Abba." He did a great work as a Christian yogi and was invited all over the world to Europe, America, and Australia to teach this Christian Yoga.

So, we are beginning now to open ourselves to the place of the body in spirituality, and of course, as Matthew said, of sexuality. Now that is where the other Indian tradition comes in, that of Tantra. The main Hindu doctrine is Vedanta. The Vedas are the original Sanskrit scriptures—Vedanta is the philosophy that was developed out of the Vedas and took shape over a period of fifteen hundred years. And it has gone right on to the present time with the great Sri Aurobindo. But in the third century C.E., this movement of Tantra came into Hinduism and Buddhism. It was a movement from below and must have come from the pre-Aryan people. It's not Aryan, which is patriarchal, but pre-Aryan—it comes from the earth, from matter. And the whole teaching of Tantra was that you must learn to discover the spirit, the eternal, the reality in the earth, in matter, in life, in your body, in your breath; and when you meditate, you must learn to be aware of your body, be aware of your breathing. I use a mantra as well. Then one enters into the breathing through the mantra, and the whole body has to be transformed and the whole sexuality.

This has been a great problem in Christianity. I can understand it is a difficult subject and you can get carried away by it, and the Church from the time of Jesus onwards has certainly aimed at transcending sexuality. Marriage was allowed, but virginity, celibacy, was to be the ideal. And so there was a tremendous urge to get beyond sex and rest in virginity, to realize God in celibacy. Most of our Christian saints did that, almost all of them. But today we are realizing that it has very great dangers, because it's all very well to say you are going to get beyond sex, but what you may actually do is suppress it so that it becomes a negative force, a destructive force in your life.

So today we are trying to find how we can open up this sexual energy—not suppress it, not indulge in it, but open it up to this rhythm of life. It has to flow, according to the Tantra, through the chakras from the base of the spine through the sex center, the emotional, the heart, the throat, the head, up to the Supreme. The energy has to flow through all the chakras. And we have to open ourselves to this energy. In the base of the spine is where we contact the whole physical universe—all the electric energy in the universe is vibrating up the base of our spine. And then in the sex center, all the vital energy in the universe—of plants, and animals and human beings—is all centering there. Then in the emotional center—in Japan they call it the Hara—we are emotionally tied to one another. We know today how a child is emotionally tied to its mother, for good and for evil of course, but the emotional ties are tremendously powerful. We have to bring all of these into our spirituality, into our meditation.

We become aware of our physical energy, and the whole environment in which it works. We become aware of our psyche, our sexual energy, and see it as a positive force in our lives, rather than negating it, trying to get rid of it. On the other hand, it is not good to indulge in it; that's not the answer. But in the Tantra there is a way through meditation, through the breathing, of letting the energy flow, letting it rise through the chakras, from the base of the spine through the sex center; through the emotional, to the heart, which is the vital center. All the energy is really centered in the heart.

That's where our energies from above meet the energies from below. And then in the throat chakra you open up the whole world of transcendence through words, song, and music. It's where we begin to transcend the limits of this world and open ourselves up to the higher energies. It takes place in the throat.

Then you come to the sixth chakra, which is the mind. We have overdeveloped the mind—we're all centered on this chakra and we've neglected the lower chakras, but we must learn to integrate. It's no good giving up the mind. The mind has a controlling force and we must use it. All Western science is of great value and we must make use of it. But we must not stop with that. The mind must be integrated with the heart, with the emotions, and with the sexual and physical energies, and finally and above all, with the whole organism. The body and soul have to be opened up to the transcendent. The Tantriks call it the thousand petalled lotus at the crown of the head. You have to open up your whole being, and your being with others, and your being with the universe—open up to the transcendent mystery that in our Christian tradition is "coming down." The Spirit descends; it came down upon the Apostles at Pentecost. And if we open ourselves to the Spirit, this rushing Spirit comes down upon us. And that is transforming, and that is how the human being is transformed.

When you let your whole being let go and open itself up, you allow in the power of the Spirit, the energy that is in the creation, in the whole of humanity, in the soul, in the body, and yet that transcends it all. I like to relate this to the Holy Spirit. Unfortunately in our Christian tradition we have no feminine aspect of God. It's because we come out of a patriarchal tradition in which God the Father is a masculine image, the Son is a masculine image, and even the Holy Spirit (though the word is neuter in Greek, it's masculine in Latin) is still "He, the Holy Spirit."

But there is no reason why we should not think of and image God the Supreme as Mother. Many people are doing that today—even in the "Our Father" we can say "Our Father, Mother"; we need not stop at the Father. God is neither male or female, but we can use a male image or a female image and we need to use both. In India it is very common for a devotee to say "my Father, my Mother"; they would say both. So we are trying to get an integrated spirituality that integrates the whole human being, the body and the soul, and opens up to the transcendent and then begins to discover the richness of the Divine.

In the West we've got such a narrow view of God, and it's a big problem. It's the question of the personal God: In the Bible, Yahweh is a personal God; in Islam, Allah is a personal God; even in India we have many personal Gods—Shiva, Krishna, and Vishnu. But in India it's been understood from the beginning that we need a personal form of God and we need to go through and beyond the person to the transcendent. As Eckhart said, "Through God to the Godhead." If we stop at the personal God, it's a projection of our minds and it's a limited thing. We worship an idol, really, because any image or form or concept of God is an idol. God has no name; God is beyond all this. And all our prayer, our meditation, and every word we use should take us beyond the word, the thought and the image to the transcendent mystery. Then our whole being is liberated and the whole of humanity can be liberated, if we go beyond.

That brings me to the last point Father Matthew made, this question of avarice. I would put it in another way: the question of egoism. The real problem that faces all of us is the separated self, the ego center. We have our body with its senses, we have our soul, and we have our mind, all centering on the ego, the "I," which is perfectly normal and natural. A child has to acquire an ego, a personality, to be somebody. That becomes our center. But the point is you shouldn't stop at your ego. It's only a stage, and as you grow to adolescence and beyond you have to open your ego to others and then to the transcendent. However, what has happened is that we're all imprisoned in our ego, and we're all seeking our own ends. We try to be open to others but we clash with others all the time.

These terrible conflicts come from all over the world. And of course they are in religion just as much as outside religion. The ego gets into all our religions—my religion is right and your religion is wrong. We get these terrible religious conflicts, and it all comes from the ego. The self-centered personality is your ego. But your ego has to die. That is the meaning of the crucifixion. What Jesus did on the cross was to die to his ego, to die to the whole created reality, to all the limitations of his mind and his body, and let go completely and surrender. That is how we get free of the ego, by making this total surrender of the ego.

And that, I feel, is a challenge to America today. If you don't mind my saying so, it's a terribly ego-centered society. The fact that you all go about in little cars by yourselves is a sign that you all want to be alone, doing your own thing. It's wonderful in a way, but you have to go through that stage and then get beyond this ego-personality, this separated self, and discover that at a deeper level, beyond the psyche, we are united with the Atman, the spirit, and that actually we are all already in union with one another at this deeper center. If we stop with the body and the mind, we feel we're all separate. But when we let go of that, we realize that at the deepest level of our being, in our true selves, we are in communion with everybody and everything. There is something deep in us that is open to the whole of creation and the whole of humanity. And this is the spirit. The spirituality of the future must be open to the whole of creation and the whole of humanity.

I would like to say for those who are Christians, and most of us have a Christian background, that I think you will find all this in the New Testament, and particularly in St. John's Gospel and the Letter to the Ephesians. Ephesus was a center of Gnosis and Gnosis is wisdom. In Sanskrit it is *jñana*. It's almost certain that this wisdom came from India through Persia to Asia Minor and had its center in Ephesus. The Fourth Gospel was written in Ephesus and the Letter to the Ephesians was written in Ephesus. And at that point, Christian doctrine with its Jewish background came into contact with this wisdom, the wisdom of Asia—the wisdom of the world, really.

And it opened up the whole horizon so you get wonderful sentences in the Letters to the Ephesians and to the Colossians—the two of them go together. For instance, Colossians says, " . . . in Christ—in Him and through Him and for Him all things were created and in Him all things hold together." The whole universe is held together in this Cosmic Person. That's a wonderful figure—the Cosmic Person. In Sanskrit it's *Purusha*, and in Islam it's called the Universal Person, and it's one of the basic features of Islamic or Sufi doctrine. When the early Christians came in contact with this understanding of the Cosmic Person, they saw that Jesus embodied this— he is the Cosmic Person. And in him the whole creation comes together and in him is the fullness of humanity.

Humanity is one; this is very important. The Fathers understood it: Adam is humanity and all humanity is one. As a result of sin, of falling away from reality, from the truth, from the One, we became separated, disintegrated, and we live in this disintegrated world. But we are all being urged to get beyond this disintegration, to open ourselves to one another and to discover the union that actually exists among us. The whole creation—the sun and the moon and the stars—all things come together to form a fullness. And the whole of humanity, all the races of humanity, all religions of humanity, all come together in this fullness. The Letter to the Colossians [1:19] says that in Christ all "fullness was pleased to dwell," so Jesus Christ is a symbol of the fullness. And there are other signs and symbols of this fullness, such as the Buddha and Krishna. But for a Christian, Jesus is the symbol of this total fullness.

We are all trying to enter into the fullness. In the Letter to the Ephesians we see that the Church has this *mystery* in it—behind all the weakness of the Church and all the sins of the Church, there is this mystery of Divine Life and Truth. It has been there all the time. We are all being called into that fullness—that's really our calling. And only then can we get rid of our egoism, our avarice; as Father Matthew said, the searching for the satisfaction of our own individual self. We go beyond that by allowing this great mystery to take possession of us and by sharing our lives with one another.

So that's the kind of spirituality that I think we're being called to and that I think is being taught in this Institute of Culture and Creation Spirituality. I feel it is very important that we should all share this vision together and share it with others. All the religions have their limitations and we must recognize this, but I think that in all the religions there is always the basic truth. They all emerge from this original truth, this primordial truth. Then it gets developed in different ways and it gets lost in many ways. But it's there and we can all look behind our own religion and discover the mystery that was at work in it all and that can bring humanity together today. No one religion can do it, but when we open ourselves to that truth and mystery in all religions, then we can begin to come together as a whole.

We're living in a very critical time. It's an extraordinary time; things are breaking down politically and economically and a new vision is emerging. One of the things that comes to me from being in America these last few months and the same last year [1991] is that materialism is probably at its worst in America, but the search for a deeper reality is stronger here than anywhere. People are searching for some deeper meaning, a deeper reality. And I think Creation Spirituality is one of the ways to open people to this new vision that is coming to us all.

So I hope and pray that this really may grow, that it's part of a movement of humanity today and the spirit today—bringing people together, opening their hearts to one another, showing them the possibilities of the future and making it possible to create a new world. We can have a new humanity and a new world that will respond to this marvelous mystery that we have cut out of our lives. We've cut it out, but now we're beginning to discover that we will destroy ourselves if we don't recover it. If we can recover it, we can recreate the world.

NOTES

1. Matthew Fox, *Original Blessing* (Santa Fe, NM: Bear & Co., 1983); *Coming of the Cosmic Christ* (San Francisco: Harper SF, 1988); *Creation Spirituality: Liberating Gifts of Peoples of the Earth* (San Francisco: Harper SF, 1991).

2. E. F. Schumacher, *Small Is Beautiful: Economics as if People Mattered* (New York: Harper-Collins, 1989).

3. John Robbins, *Diet for a New America* (Walpole, NH: Stillpoint, 1987).

4. *Upanishads*, trans. by Juan Mascaro (New York: Viking Penguin, 1965).

Mysticism and the New Science

Rupert Sheldrake

At this point, the anthology moves on to authors who highlight Dom Bede's final area of interest: science and spirituality. Rupert Sheldrake, British biologist, is the author of the widely discussed A New Science of Life: The Hypothesis of Formative Causation *(1981) and more recently,* The Rebirth of Nature: The Greening of Science and God *(1990).[1] He develops the thesis of the latter book in this essay— that "living organism" is a better model of What Is than "mechanism." Sheldrake further comments that if nature is seen as living rather than as mechanistic, a mystical sense of close connection with nature cannot so easily be dismissed as romantic projection.*

Sheldrake further explains that autonomy, spontaneity, and creativity are the characteristics of the living; if these are appropriate categories in which to view the universe, then it may be seen as "an organism of organisms." And if this approach characterizes the new science that is now being shaped—as seems to be happening—then an opening may be found for a new relationship between natural science and mysticism. Such a prospect was very much part of Father Bede's triple integration ideal, and he and Sheldrake spent many hours discussing it during the months the latter stayed at Shantivanam. Sheldrake feels that there is now the possibility that the sense of the sanctity of the natural world may be recovered, thus also retrieving the holiness of the body. This is being accomplished by the Creation Spirituality movement and others.

S cience bears a closer relationship to mystical experience than many scientists themselves recognize. Even the mechanistic worldview is rooted in an intuitive, mystical vision of the order and unity of the natural world.

The mystical vision of a harmonious order underlay the intertwined Pythagorean and Platonic traditions. Copernicus, Kepler, Galileo, and the other founding fathers of modern science were inspired and motivated by this intuition. The vision of the material world as a vast mathematical system, the prototypic mechanistic cosmology, came to Descartes as mystical revelation on the eve of St. Martin's Day in 1619, and was, he believed, shown to him by the Angel of Truth. He at once made a vow to undertake a pilgrimage of gratitude to Our Lady of Loretto, fulfilled on a visit to Italy three years later.

Newton too, and indeed most great physicists ever since, have believed that through mathematical physics they have been privileged to glimpse something of the transcendent, eternal mathematical order that underlies the changing phenomena of the universe, organizing it through the mathematical laws of nature. They thought of this order as inherent in a transcendent mathematical mind. Indeed, for many of the mathematicians and mathematical physicists who have shaped the mechanistic worldview, God is a mathematician; consequently, mathematicians are capable of direct conscious insight into the Divine Being.

This Platonic or Pythagorean kind of mysticism is not in opposition to mechanistic science; on the contrary, it has been a major, enduring source of inspiration for scientific progress. Albert Einstein spoke of it as "cosmic religious feeling":

What a deep conviction of the rationality of the universe and what a yearning to understand, were it but a feeble reflection of the mind revealed in the world, Kepler and Newton must have had to enable them to spend years of solitary labour in disentangling the principles of celestial mechanics! Those whose acquaintance with scientific research is derived chiefly from its practical results easily develop a completely false notion of the mentality of men who, surrounded by a sceptical world, have shown the way to kindred spirits scattered wide throughout the world and the centuries. . . . It is cosmic religious feeling that gives a man such strength.[2]

The mechanistic worldview of Newtonian physics grew out of the synthesis of the Pythagorean-Platonic tradition with atomistic materialism, propounded in ancient Greece by Democritus and Epicurus. The world consisted of eternal, indestructible, inanimate corpuscles of matter in motion; but this unconscious, material world was entirely governed by nonmaterial mathematical laws of nature, present everywhere and always. Thus there was a cosmic dualism between the material world and the transcendent mathematical laws that governed it.

The discoveries of twentieth-century physics have revealed that atoms are not solid and homogeneous, as they were originally imagined to be. Rather, in the words of Werner Heisenberg, "the smallest units of matter are, in fact, not physical objects in the ordinary sense of the word; they are forms, structures, or—in Plato's sense—ideas, which can be unambiguously spoken of only in the language of mathematics."[3] The quantum theory extends the Pythagorean approach into the very heart of matter, and indeed appears to confirm the theory that eternal mathematical relationships are the basis of all physical reality. The ancient intuition of the harmony of the spheres finds its microcosmic reflection in the harmonic series of orbitals made up of electron waves around the atomic nucleus, itself a harmonious system of vibratory patterns. Everything is rhythmical, vibratory, made up of waves.

The old science depended not only on a sense of the rationality of nature, but also of its unity; all parts of the universe were governed by the same universal laws of nature, all were contained within the same mathematical system of space and time, and all matter was interconnected according to Newton's law of universal gravitation. The fundamental unity of nature was emphasized by the philosophers of ancient Greece as well as the theologians of the Judeo-Christian tradition, and again this presupposition of mechanistic science has its source, directly or indirectly, in mystical experience.

In addition to the intuition of the rationality and unity of nature built into the foundations of Newtonian science, there is another related assumption directly or indirectly rooted in mystical experience: beyond or behind the changing world of sense-experience is a timeless realm of Being. The transcendent, eternal reality of the Pythagoreans and Platonists, like eternal mathematical laws of nature, is one aspect of this timelessness. The other, derived from atomistic materialism, is enshrined in the principles of conservation of matter and energy: the total quantity of matter and energy in the universe is always the same. And so is the total amount of electric charge, angular momentum, and all other quantities subject to conservation principles. Hence the most fundamental physical realities neither come into being nor pass away. Consequently, classical physics is nonevolutionary; and insofar as the second law of thermodynamics introduces an arrow of time into the universe, the direction of development is not evolutionary but devolutionary. We discovered that the machine-like universe we inherited from the nineteenth century was running down, but was nevertheless eternal—it would continue to exist forever even after it had run out of steam, its indestructible particles of matter and its inexhaustible energy eternally governed by immutable laws.

THE MECHANISTIC ABOLITION OF THE SOUL

For Aristotle and his medieval followers, the world of *phusis*, nature, was a living world with its own inherent principles of growth, organization and movement, a world containing many kinds of animate beings. By contrast, the mechanistic theory of nature asserted that the physical world of matter in motion was inanimate—devoid of life, mind, spontaneity, and creativity. Mother Nature became dead matter, and souls were withdrawn from the natural world, leaving all plants and animals, like the world as a whole, nothing but mechanisms devoid of life and mind.

As part of this same process, the soul was withdrawn from human bodies until all that remained was the rational, conscious mind located in a small region inside the head. Descartes thought that it interacted with the body in the pineal gland; over the last three centuries its presumed location has migrated a couple of inches to the cerebral cortex, but the basic theory has remained the same. This rational mind, the only truly living thing to be found within the material world, and then only in a very small part of it, was capable of participating in the Mind of God. Through it humanity could come to know the mathematical truths that governed the world—and gain a God-like power over nature in the process.

Both Descartes and Newton realized that this new theory of nature inevitably involved a new conception of God and the spiritual world. They welcomed this change, and thought that by denying any life, creativity, and spontaneity to nature, they were arriving at a more elevated conception of God. This God of the world machine was the source of all matter and motion, all design and purpose in the world. Nature was not self-organizing; it was designed and made by an external intelligent creator, just as human-made machines are designed and made by people to serve human purposes.

This view of nature was not only accepted by many theologians, particularly within the Protestant tradition, but it was used as an argument for the existence of God. The contention was thus: Assuming that animals and plants are mere inanimate machines, the beauty of their structure and their purposive adaptations must mean that they are intelligently designed by an external designer, and in an inanimate world devoid of any trace of creativity or intelligence, the only possible source of their design is a transcendent Author of Nature. This is the argument against which Charles Darwin reacted. He shared with natural theologians such as Paley the assumption that nature was inanimate and mechanistic, but thought he had found a blind, unconscious creative principle within it in the form of natural selection.

The mechanistic worldview has proved to be compatible with strongly dualistic forms of mysticism and religion: on the one hand the kind of gnosticism that emphasizes a transcendent realm of spirit while downgrading the physical world and bodily life; on the other hand the religious attitude, strongly marked in some of the Jewish prophets and in the Protestant tradition, which emphasizes the divinely ordained superiority of humanity to the rest of the natural order. Through fear of falling under the influence of the old goddesses and gods, or through fear of relapsing into animism or pantheism, the powers inherent in the natural world tended to be denied or ignored, or else attributed directly to God, or even to Satan. The mechanistic worldview is not merely compatible with these dualistic mystical and religious attitudes, it has grown out of them. Even in its atheistic form, it retains a fundamental duality of mind and matter. This duality is reflected in the theoretical dichotomy between the material universe and the nonmaterial laws that govern it, in the problematic relationship between human bodies and minds, and on a practical level in humankind's attempted conquest of nature.

Nature Comes to Life Again

Although the mechanistic worldview has developed in close association with mysticism of the Platonic and Pythagorean variety, it has been opposed for over two hundred years by the romantic attitude toward nature, which was inspired by another kind of mysticism. Rather than emphasizing the mathematical intelligibility of the physical universe, the romantic poets and other nature mystics have responded to the *life* of nature. They have affirmed rather than denied the experience that comes to us through our senses and feelings, the qualitative rather than the quantitative experience of the world.

In fact, many modern people are influenced by both the mechanistic and the romantic attitudes, but at different times. The mechanistic worldview usually prevails from Monday to Friday during working hours, while the romantic attitude comes into its own on weekends and holidays. This has led to a fundamental split in our civilization. Many people who work in cities want to become rich, even if they help despoil the natural world by doing so; but a common reason for wanting to be rich is to buy a house in the country in order to "get back to nature."

A fundamental romantic intuition is that there is living spirit in all things—that nature is alive, we are in her, we participate in her, and she is all around us. This life of nonhuman nature is known to us not through mathematical reasoning, but through our intuitions, senses, and feelings, through our own experiences of animals, flowers, forests, mountains, the sea, the sky, the weather. Such direct experiences, even those with a deep sense of truth, are nowhere to be found in the worldview of orthodox science, except as unusual patterns of physiological activity in the brain. Hence, from a romantic point of view, mechanistic science is at best incomplete, at worst life-denying.

—ⱳ—

But what if the worldview of science changes from one in which nature is regarded as inanimate—essentially dead, blind, unconscious—to one in which the world is recognized as living? What if nature has a life of her own? The transition from the idea of a dead, machine-like universe to a living natural world has in fact been going on by stages within science itself for over two hundred years. Here, in brief, are some of the steps:

1. To start with, in the "mechanical philosophy" of the seventeenth century, nature was composed of inanimate matter, made and set in motion by God, always following God's inexorable laws. There was no freedom or spontaneity at any point in the physical world; freedom, creativity, and spontaneity were to be found only in the realm of the spirit. To Newton, it seemed absurd to endow inanimate matter with attractive and repulsive powers, capable of acting at a distance; he considered several possible explanations of gravitational, electrical, and other forces, either in terms of "aetherial spirit" or the agency of God.[4]

2. During the course of the nineteenth century, the causes of electrical and magnetic attractions and repulsions capable of acting through seemingly empty space came to be thought of in terms of *fields*. At first, electromagnetic forces and waves were thought to be carried by fields in a subtle, nonmaterial medium, the "aether." Through Einstein's special theory of relativity, published in 1905, the electromagnetic fields were separated from the concept of the aether, and through his general theory of relativity, gravitational effects were explained in terms of geometrical properties of gravitational field. Subsequently, further kinds of fields were introduced beneath the level of the atom in quantum field theory. Through these developments in twentieth-century physics, matter has ceased to be regarded as the fundamental reality; fields and energy are more fundamental. As Karl Popper, a philosopher of science, has put it, through modern physics "materialism has transcended itself."[5] Material bodies are now thought to be forms of energy bound within fields. Fields, like souls in the Aristotelian and medieval worldview, are immanent organizing agencies, and have a wholeness and autonomy that was banished from the realm of nature by the original mechanistic theory.

3. In one sense, quantum theory was a further step towards realizing the traditional Pythagorean ambitions of mechanistic science. But the

price that had to be paid for it was the recognition of the action of spontaneity within the natural world, because quantum events were predictable only in terms of probability. Within the last twenty years there has been a growing recognition that spontaneity and indeterminism are to be found almost everywhere— in the weather, for example. The complete determinism and predictability assumed by Newtonian physics now looks like an extreme idealization; even simple mechanical systems like pendulums turn out to behave in a non-Newtonian, "chaotic" manner.

4. Newton's principle of Universal Gravitation affirmed that everything in the universe is interconnected, and further kinds of interconnections have been discovered in the contexts of electromagnetism and quantum theory. The phenomenon of quantum nonlocality involves an instantaneous connection between quantum particles that came from a common source, but which may be yards or miles apart. The wider significance of this new kind of interconnectedness is still obscure.

5. According to classical, Newtonian physics, the physical world had no inherent creativity. Everything was designed and created by God. But the discovery of convincing evidence for biological evolution indicated that there was in fact a creativity inherent in nature. The Darwinian theory of evolution attempts to explain how this can happen in an inanimate, machine-like universe. But since the 1960s, the old idea of an eternal world machine has been discarded in favor of an evolutionary cosmology; biological and human evolution are now seen against the background of a cosmic evolutionary process. Today the cosmos seems more like a developing organism than a machine. Nature involves not just *natura naturata*, the complex natural changes and processes, but also *natura naturans*, an immanent creative principle.

6. The coming-into-being of form, of morphogenesis, can be understood in plants and animals only in terms of holistic organizing principles, often thought of as morphogenetic fields. Such organizing principles may well be at work in systems at all levels of complexity, including molecules, crystals, cells, tissues, organs, organisms, societies, plants, solar systems, and galaxies. According to the hypothesis of formative causation first proposed in my book, *A New Science of Life*[6] (written at Shantivanam, and dedicated to Father Bede), all such self-organizing systems are associated with morphic fields, which shape and sustain their

patterns of organization. Such fields are not determined by transcendent laws of nature, but rather contain an inherent memory of previous similar systems. This memory depends on a process called morphic resonance, involving an influence of like upon like, through or across space and time. Through morphic resonance, organisms draw upon a collective memory of their species, and in turn contribute to it. If rats, for example, are trained to do a new trick in one place, rats elsewhere should subsequently be able to learn the same thing more quickly, even in the absence of any known type of connection or communication. The more rats that learn it, the greater this effect should become. In its most general terms, the hypothesis of formative causation proposes that the regularities of nature depend not on transcendent, eternal laws, but rather on immanent habits.[7] The evolutionary process involves an interplay of creativity and habit, and we experience just such an interplay in our own lives. This hypothesis is still very controversial, and is currently being tested experimentally.

7. The failure of attempts to explain human behavior mechanistically has led to the increasing influence of nonmechanistic systems of psychology, such as Jung's postulate of the existence of a collective human memory, the "collective unconscious." Like the hypothesis of formative causation discussed above, this theory emphasizes the importance of interconnections, not only through space but through time as well, from the past to the present.

8. The baleful effects of the exploitation of nature through science and technology, together with the use of scientific knowledge to develop ever more powerful means of destruction of life, have finally led to a widespread realization that we are not separate from nature—somehow over and above the world we inhabit. We are a part of a natural order that we are threatening and disrupting at our own peril. One aspect of this realization is the growing influence of the Gaia hypothesis, the idea that Mother Earth is a living organism; another aspect is the rising political importance of the Green movement.

The "new science" is still taking shape, and scientific orthodoxy, especially within the biological sciences, is still officially mechanistic. But it seems clear that we are on the threshold of a new view of nature in which autonomy, spontaneity, and creativity are recognized at all levels of organization; a view in which the cosmos is seen as an organism of organisms, alive rather than dead.[8] This growing scientific recognition that we live in a living world opens up the possibility of a new relationship between mysticism and natural science, a relationship that has hardly begun to be explored.

HUMANISM, RATIONALISM, AND MYSTICISM

For over two hundred years, we in the West have grown used to the coexistence of seemingly opposed kinds of mysticism: the Platonic-Pythagorean variety so important for the development of mathematics and physics, and the nature mysticism of the romantic tradition, influential in the private lives of the many people who find inspiration in nature. The former kind of mysticism extols reason but has little place for other realms of human experience; the latter is fed by intuitive experiences that seem far deeper and richer than those accessible to the mere intellect. To rationalists, romanticism seems irrational, while to romantics, rationalism seems life-denying.

Secular humanism is the official worldview of secular society, the dominant ethos of modern public life. Religious belief is usually regarded as a private affair, a personal option. Humanism puts humanity above the rest of nature: human beings have more conscious understanding than anything else in the world, and hence they have great power, ever growing with the advance of civilization, technology, and science.

In this secular, humanistic context, rationalism is of central importance. Reason makes human beings human, and scientific reason has given modern humanity its power. At the same time, reason, and especially its purest form, mathematical reason, is what makes us God-like. But from a humanist point of view, there is no need to assume that a transcendent mind really exists, a mind in which human reason can participate mystically. This seemingly divine realm of reason is simply the highest aspect of the human mind, part of our uniquely human nature, one of the crowning glories not of God but of humanity.

Just as Pythagorean and Platonic mysticism can be assimilated by secular humanism, so also can romantic mysticism. It is construed such that mystical esperience does not mean that human beings can gain direct intuitive insights into the flow and the power of nature. This would be to fall into the trap of anthropomorphic projection. In this view, poetic and artistic insights inspired by nature are simply examples of the range and creativity of human imagination. Art as well as science reflects the glory of humanity, providing yet further evidence for human superiority.

Humanism thus puts itself above religions and religious faith. It sees humanity as a higher principle than inanimate nature or human-made gods. There is a strong incentive for secular governments and educational institutions to take this humanistic stance, so that they can appear to rise above sectarian interest groups and thus maintain authority over populations with a variety of religious and antireligious beliefs. Humanism derives much of its contemporary credibility from the power of science, and the mechanistic worldview is generally taken for granted by modern humanists. But what is happening to humanism as the orthodoxy of science changes, and nature comes to be seen as alive rather than inanimate?

For a start, the mystical experience of connection to nature cannot simply be dismissed as a projection of human subjectivity onto an inanimate world. In a living world, perhaps real connections are possible in a manner undreamt of by humanists. Moreover, the surviving forms of shamanism, rooted in archaic traditions, may be a more valuable guide to understanding these connections than romanticism. There has indeed been a recent renewal of interest in the insights and abilities of peoples such as Australian aborigines and Native Americans, who in the past were regarded as too primitive to teach us anything worth knowing.

Second, the breaking down of mechanistic humanism leaves a vacuum that makes the question of the relationship of the mystical experience of nature to the great religious traditions more urgent. In Hinduism and Buddhism, especially in Tibet, old shamanistic and animistic practices have survived and still coexist with more recent forms of religion; the same was true of Christianity to some extent in the middle ages and before. Even today in Roman Catholic countries such as Ireland there is a strong sense of sacredness of the land, inherited from the pre-Christian past; for example, there are hundreds of holy wells. But especially in Protestant countries, much of this heritage has been lost. How can a sense of the sanctity of the natural world be recovered? And what part can Christian mysticism play in this process? Father Bede Griffiths made some fruitful suggestions;[9] another approach to these questions is being made by the Creation Spirituality movement, which has drawn attention to the aspects of the Jewish and Christian traditions that place a strong positive value on bodily experience and on the natural world, including mystics such as the medieval abbess Hildegard von Bingen.[10]

Third, there is the question of the relationship of not just mystical experience but of all conscious experience to the world of fields and energies described by modern science. Even if the organization of molecules, or trees, or brains could be proved to depend on morphic fields containing an inherent memory, there would still be the question of how these fields are related to consciousness. What is the relationship of the field to the knower of the field?

THE FIELD AND THE KNOWER OF THE FIELD

Science as we know it as a matter of principle does not account for the consciousness of scientists, and assumes that consciousness plays no part in the physical world. Science is supposed to be dealing with objective facts, freed as far as possible from the emotions, beliefs, hopes, expectations, and personality of any particular scientist. When doing science the minds of scientists are supposed to function in a mode of superhuman objectivity, dealing with physical facts as they really are, uncontaminated by human minds, or indeed by any kind of mind. The data are imagined to inhabit an objective world that does nothing but follow the objective laws of nature without the least transgression. Although this world does indeed involve many kinds of events that are unpredictable in detail, these are just a matter of blind chance.

In fact, even a slight acquaintance with the history of science or with living scientists reveals that scientists are subject to normal human emotions, hopes, and fears. They are not disembodied observers of a material world from which their minds have somehow become detached—no such human beings exist. We know the physical world through our bodies and our senses; our bodies and experience are not everywhere and always, but in particular places at particular times. And insofar as we know the material world, or know anything at all, we know it through our conscious minds.

Our knowledge is not independent of our minds, with their intrinsic human limitations.

In the context of quantum theory there has been a general recognition of the simple fact that observations depend on observers, and that conscious human beings are therefore involved in the process of scientific measurement. This is a general point that applies to all branches of science. But, in practice, science is still pursued as if nature is mindless and as if human minds can observe objectively without affecting what they observe.

Father Bede wrote in a letter to me in 1988: "I sometimes feel when reading the theories of those who believe in a mechanistic universe that it is like watching a game of blind man's bluff. To try to explain the universe without reference to human consciousness is really to blindfold oneself." But what will happen if this blindfold is removed? What will happen if science takes into account not only fields but the knowers of fields?

As a starting point for the exploration of this question, I take Father Bede's commentary on an opening verse of the thirteenth chapter of the Bhagavad Gita, which states, "This body, Arjuna, is called the field. He who knows this is called the knower of the field." In Father Bede's words:

> The field is the whole world of nature, or what contemporary physics calls a "field of energies." The spirit is the knower, it is the principle of consciousness which pervades this field.[11]

And then in verse thirteen we read, "His hands and feet are everywhere, he has heads and mouths everywhere; he sees all, he hears all. He exists, encompassing all things." Father Bede adds the commentary that

> The one person, the one Purusha, the one reality, is manifested in all creation, in every person, in every thing, and all human beings are as it were, his hands, his feet, his heads. He is in you and me; he is acting through our hands and feet, our heads and our mouths. All these are his members, as it were. In the Christian tradition there is the understanding that the universe is the body of Christ. Christ has assumed the whole creation in himself and he now acts in and through the whole creation. Christ is present in every human being.[12]

—⚡—

It is interesting to compare this commentary with Sir Isaac Newton's conception of the relationship of God to the universe. In the second edition of the *Principia*, he wrote as follows:

> He is eternal and infinite, omnipotent and omniscient; that is, his duration reaches from eternity to eternity; his presence from infinity to infinity; he governs all things and knows all things that are or can be done. . . . He endures forever and is everywhere present; and by existing always and everywhere, he constitutes duration and space. . . . He is all similar, all eye, all ear, all brain, all arm, all power to perceive, to understand, and to act; but in a manner not at all human, in a manner not at all corporeal, in a manner utterly unknown to us.[13]

Newton suggested that the medium of God's omniscience was Absolute space, which was, in other words, the divine sense organ: "[T]here is a Being incorporeal, living, intelligent, omnipresent, who in infinite space, as it were with his sensory, sees the things themselves intimately, and thoroughly perceives them, and comprehends them wholly by their immediate presence to himself."[14] God not only perceives all things, but can act through them. According to Newton, God "being in all places, is more able by his will to move the bodies within his boundless uniform sensorium, and thereby to form and reform the parts of the universe, than we are by our will to move the parts of our own bodies."[15]

For Newtonian physics, Absolute space was the container of all things and the medium through which gravitational forces acted. Einstein replaced Absolute space with the gravitational field. This universal field is now the container of all things and the medium of gravitation; the entire physical universe exists within it, and so do space and time. The gravitational field is not *in* space and time, it *is* space and time, or rather space-time. In these senses the gravitational field takes over some of the essential features of the soul of the world, the *anima mundi*, as conceived by the neo-Platonist school in general, and in particular by the seventeenth-century Cambridge Platonists, who influenced Newton in his youth. Newton replaced the world soul with space directly sustained by God, and now we have a world field instead.

In the spirit of the Bhagavad Gita or of Newton, we can look for a relationship between this universal field and the knower of this field. We see at once that if there is a knower of the gravitational field then the knower is indeed omnipresent. All material bodies and all relative movements occur within this field and are thus known to the knower of the field; no things or events in the physical universe can ever be outside or beyond or be hidden from him or her.

But the gravitational field is not the only universal field of interrelationship; the universe is pervaded by the electromagnetic field, in which visible light and invisible radiations have been traveling ever since the birth of the universe. If the universal consciousness can instantaneously feel where everything is within itself through the gravitational field, it can also instantaneously see what is happening everywhere, and at all scales of organization, from electrons to molecules, from cells to brains, from planets to galaxies. Electromagnetic fields are within and around all things, and nothing physical can happen without affecting them. Moreover, all mechanical and acoustic vibrations are inevitably registered in the gravitational and electromagnetic fields through the movements of electrically charged matter. Through these fields, the knower of the fields could feel all rhythms and hear all sounds. Every chemical molecule and every kind of chemical interaction is characterized by specific patterns of activity in the electromagnetic fields of the atoms and molecules; a knower of these patterns can smell and taste everything.

In addition to the fields of universal extent—electromagnetic and gravitational—there are the fields of quantum field theory, the basis of subatomic particles. A knower of these fields would know the internal structure of all particles and atoms. And if organized systems at all levels of complexity are organized by morphic fields containing an inherent memory, then the knower of these fields will also know all organisms from within, and will know their habits, too.

Morphic fields are similar in certain respects to Aristotelian souls or entelechies; most of the time they may organize the bodies and behavior of organisms unconsciously, just as so much of our own bodily development and habitual behavior is unconscious. In such cases the internal knower does not know itself, but it can be known through its relationship to the fields of the more all-embracing organisms within which it is living—the gravitational and electromagnetic fields pervading the universal organism, the fields of greater organisms around it—the fields of galaxies embracing those of solar systems, solar systems of planets, and so on down through ecosystems, societies, individual animals and plants, organs, tissues, cells, molecules and atoms. Here we have a nested hierarchy of fields, through which the knower of the fields can know every level both from within and from without.

In a like manner, a nested hierarchy of fields seems to structure and organize the working of our own bodies and minds. This hierarchical structure is found in our systems of classification, languages, measuring systems, myths, social patterns, and indeed thought in general. We ourselves are the knowers of these fields.

An essential feature of all these fields is that they are fields of probability: the fields always contain more possibilities than are actualized. In quantum theory the actualization of the activity of an electron, photon or any other particle involves the collapse of all the other possibilities open to it, the so-called collapse of the wave function. Only through such a collapse can a particle be observed. The knower of the particle field presumably knows both the field of possibilities and the continual collapse of these possibilities into observable actualities. And this should be true of the fields at all levels of organization, including those in human minds.

ENERGY, LIGHT, AND SPIRIT

According to modern physics, physical reality depends on two fundamental kinds of entities: fields and energy. Material bodies consist of energy bound within fields. Fields confer form and organization, and energy is the basis of bodily existence and activity in space-time. This duality recalls the Aristotelian distinction between form and matter, where matter was regarded as potentiality, capable of being actualized in various bodily forms. Energy, the basis of all physical change and activity is, like Aristotelian matter, capable of entering into any bodily form or physical activity. In physics, the standard definition of energy is not in terms of what it actually is, but in terms of what it can do, its capacity to cause change: "Energy is the property of a system that is a measure of its capacity for doing work."[16]

The modern concept of physical energy unifies several historical strands of thought. One stems from the idea that a quantity related to motion is conserved whenever there are changes of motion; in seventeenth-century mechanics this quantity was called living force, *vis viva*, and defined as mv^2, the mass times the square of the velocity. The modern name for living force is kinetic energy, meaning the energy possessed by virtue of motion. A second strand was the eighteenth-century idea of a "universal fluid" responsible for the phenomena of heat, light, electricity, and magnetism. Third, there was the concept of an imponderable fluid called caloric, proposed by Carnot, one of the founders of thermodynamics. A unified concept of energy was developed in the latter half of the nineteenth century incorporating all three traditions, and this concept was taken further by Einstein. He showed that energy and mass are equivalent, and can be interconverted according to his famous equation $E=mc^2$, where c is the velocity of light. Mass can be converted to light energy, electromagnetic radiation, as in nuclear explosions; conversely light energy can be converted to mass. Note that the term mc^2 is the same as the term for living force or *vis viva* with the velocity of light.

Even if it is possible to start developing a theory of consciousness on the basis of fields and the knower of fields as discussed above, the question remains: What is the relation of the energy in the fields to the spirit? The same energy can exist in many different forms, within many different fields; it is always a flowing, moving on; it is all part of the universal field of energy. Then how does energy differ from spirit? Both are flowing principles—a primary meaning of spirit is breath or wind—and both pervade all fields.

The parallels between energy and spirit are close. Returning to chapter thirteen of the Bhagavad Gita, we read of Purusha, the Spirit: "He is far and he is near, he moves and he moves not, he is within all and he is outside all" (v. 15). Father Bede commented: "He is the mover, everything moves, acts, works, behaves, through his presence, through his power and yet he himself remains unmoved, the 'unmoved mover.'"[17]

The same paradox of that which "moves and moves not" underlay Einstein's insight into the nature of light. As a boy, he is said to have wondered what would happen if he chased a beam of light faster and faster. When he was moving alongside the beam at the speed of light, what would he see? A stationary ripple.

According to Einstein's theory of relativity, photons, the units of action of light, in some sense escape from time. From the point of view of a photon of light leaving the sun and being absorbed by the leaf of a banyan tree, no time has passed; the connection is instantaneous. In the world of light, there is no time, space, charge, or mass. Yet light travels at a constant velocity, and never rests.

Although physical energy in general resembles the spirit pervading the universe, light is the particular form of energy most commonly associated with consciousness, both human and divine. We speak of God as light, and also of the light of the mind, of illumination, and enlightenment. According to Eastern and Western mystical traditions, the light of God and of consciousness and the physical light through which we see are not separate kinds of light. In the words of the Bhagavad Gita, "He is the Light of all lights which shines beyond all darkness. It is vision, the end of vision, to be reached by vision, dwelling in the heart of all" (13:17). The one light shines through the stars, the sun, and through earthly fire; they have no light in themselves. But this light is also vision or knowledge, and it dwells in the heart of all.

Light and vision are like polar aspects of the same spirit who "moves and moves not." They have a reciprocal relationship: light goes one way and vision the other. This is the way our own sense of vision works. Light comes to us from objects that emit it—like fires or stars—or reflect it—like trees or the moon; it travels into our eyes, patterned by the object from which it has come. But at the same time vision moves outwards from the one who sees to what is seen: we see things through our eyes and our vision reaches out to them. When we look at distant stars, we touch them with our minds.

We can think of matter as frozen or as condensed light, as flowing, vibrating energy bound within the fields of material particles, atoms, molecules, and so on. In this sense there is indeed light in all things. If this light or energy is not just physical activity, but also vision, then both light and vision dwell in the heart of all.

Bodies of all kinds derive their physical activity and material existence from the flowing energy within them; their natures—their form and organization—depend on their fields, which as morphic fields contain an inherent memory; they are pervaded by spirit in its aspect as seer and knower. All fields are limited in spatial extent and duration, and hence the spirit within them is limited by the nature of the field. The energy and the knowing within a hydrogen atom, the spirit in the atom, is much more confined than is the spirit in a snowflake, which in turn is far simpler than the spirit in a skylark, and the spirit of the lark is much more limited than the spirit in a person. In Father Bede's words:

> The one Spirit is received in a different way in each person and in each thing according to its capacity. Every inorganic object receives the power of the Spirit but it does not receive life. The living being receives the power and the life but it does not receive consciousness. The human being also receives the power, the life and consciousness—but only a limited mental human consciousness. The whole purpose of creation is that the human being should develop his capacity until he receives the fullness of divine consciousness into himself. . . . That is our goal, to be one with the One who appears as many.[18]

The reason that the one spirit appears as many is that it is moving—and not moving—within nature. The Bhagavad Gita says of nature, *prakriti*: "Nature is the source of all material things: the maker, the means of making, and the thing made" (13:20). Nature is the cause, the activity, and the effect. The fields of nature shape the patterns in which the spirit flows. And the circulations and vibrations of the spirit within these fields—their sounds—become more and more habitual through repetition, more unconscious.

CONCLUSIONS

There are a variety of ways in which connections can be seen between modern science and mysticism. The two I have explored here relate to fields and energy; fields play many of the same roles as souls did in the premechanistic philosophy of nature, and energy is an aspect of the spirit in all things. The relationship of fields to energy is like the relationship of souls to spirit. Hence we can know directly through our own experience something of the relation of spirit to nature, and of the relation of conscious experience to the fields of our minds and bodies. Science provides another way of deepening our understanding. The mystical and the scientific ways of knowing are potentially complementary, and the history of science contains many examples of mystical visions, intuitions, and insights that have played an essential role in scientific discovery.[19]

One of the greatest unsolved problems of science is the relationship of our own minds to our bodies. We know a lot about the physical and chemical aspects of our bodies, but so far have understood very little about ourselves as living people. This problem can never be solved if science fails to take into account our own conscious experience, while at the same time simply taking for granted the conscious experience and activity on which science itself depends. The new science needs mystical insight if it is to flourish, and mystical insight may in turn be enriched by science.

NOTES

1. R. Sheldrake, *A New Science of Life: The Hypothesis of Formative Causation* (London: Blond and Briggs, 1981); and idem, *The Rebirth of Nature: The Greening of Science and God* (London: Century, 1990).

2. Quoted in Ken Wilber, ed., *Quantum Questions* (Boulder: Shambhala, 1984), p. 103.

3. Ibid., p. 51.

4. R. S. Westfall, *Never at Rest: A Biography of Isaac Newton* (Cambridge: Cambridge University Press, 1980).

5. K. Popper and J. C. Eccles, *The Self and Its Brain* (Berlin: Springer International, 1977).

6. R. Sheldrake, *A New Science of Life*.

7. R. Sheldrake, *The Presence of the Past: Morphic Resonance and the Habits of Nature* (London: Collins, 1988).

8. R. Sheldrake, *The Rebirth of Nature*.

9. B. Griffiths, *The Marriage of East and West* (1982); idem, *A New Vision of Reality: Western Science, Eastern Mysticism and Christian Faith* (1989).

10. M. Fox, *Original Blessing* (Santa Fe: Bear and Co., 1983).

11. B. Griffiths, *River of Compassion* (1987).

12. Ibid., p. 238.

13. Quoted in E. A. Burtt, *The Metaphysical Foundations of Modern Physical Science* (London: Kegan Paul, 1932), p. 257.

14. Ibid., p. 258.

15. Ibid., p. 259.

16. V. H. Pitt, ed., *The Penguin Dictionary of Physics* (Harmondsworth: Penguin, 1977).

17. Griffiths, *Marriage of East and West*, p. 240.

18. Ibid.

19. Sheldrake, *The Presence of the Past*, pp. 265–269.

The Ecozoic Era

Thomas Berry

"Greening" is a concern of Thomas Berry. Professionally a historian of culture, he also calls himself a "geologian" (as distinct from a "theologian") and is very much a prophet for an age called upon to rethink the relation of our species to the earth. He amply develops this theme in The Dream of Earth *(1988) and* The Universe Story *(1992), the latter coauthored with cosmologist Brian Swimme.[1] Sharing Dom Bede's commitment to the integration of our fundamental polarities and diversities, he has worked in interreligious dialogue for many years, including the masculine/feminine integration.*

In recent years, Berry has devoted himself to awareness of the ecological threat and to speaking on the need to save the earth. He, like others, sees a global cultural transformation as upon us, but with implications and dire consequences far beyond earlier instances of cultural shift. By disturbing the biosystems of the planet at their most basic level, human beings have endangered the earth as a habitat. Berry feels that we need to consider how the human-mind sphere, and its offspring, the industrial-commercial-technological sphere, can be developed in compatibility with earth's land, water, air, and life spheres. He elaborates that the earth's troubles are much deeper than those that can be helped by solutions such as recycling and pollution penalties. The whole carbon cycle of the planet has been altered, the rainforests are under attack, the ozone shield has been pierced, and the human population, with its built-in demands for things that cause these troubles, continues to grow at a tremendous rate. A great wave of extinctions is flooding over us, declaring the termination of the Cenozoic Era.

Berry thus hopes for the dawn of an "Ecozoic Era" of mutually—enhancing functioning among living systems, regarded as a communion of subjects rather than a collection of objects. As a differentiated unity, all members must respect the right to life of all other members, acknowledging that the planet is primary and all the rest of us derivative, and that we thus form a single community. To coax this new Era into reality, human beings need a new myth, a "new story of the Universe" that will put us again into a right relation of reverence before the deep mystery of life. Berry believes that science can enable us to tell this story in the way it needs to be told to modern people, but that we also need to listen to different cultures telling their Universe stories. In Berry's view, the interreligious theme is interwoven with the science/religion theme. And insofar as ecozoic concern is seen as a feminist issue, with the multivalent language and diverse symbolic meanings used to speak it, that polarity is present as well.

The changes presently taking place in human and earthly affairs are beyond any parallel with historical change or cultural modification as these have occurred in the past. This is not like the transition from the classical period to the medieval period or from the medieval to the modern period. This change reaches far beyond the civilizational process itself, beyond even the human process, into the biosystems and even the geological structures of the earth itself.

There are only two other moments in the history of this planet that offer us some sense of what is happening. These two moments occurred at the end of the Paleozoic era, 220 million years ago, when some 90 percent of all species living at that time were extinguished, or 65 million years ago at the terminal phase of the Mesozoic era when there was also a very extensive extinction.

Then in the emerging Cenozoic period, the story of life on this planet flowed over into what could be called the lyric period of earth history. The trees had come before this, the mammals existed already in a rudimentary form, the flowers had appeared perhaps 30 million years earlier. But in the Cenozoic period there was wave upon wave of life development, particularly with the flowers and the birds and the trees and the mammalian species, all leading to that luxuriant display of life upon earth such as we have known it.

In more recent times, during the past million years, New England, for example, went through its different phases of glaciation, also its various phases of life development. In its trees, especially, it developed a unique grandeur. Possibly no other place on earth has such color in its fall foliage as this region. It was all worked out during these past 65 million years. The songbirds that we hear also came about in this long period.

The Ambivalent Human

Then we, the human inhabitants of the earth, arrived with all the ambivalences that we bring with us. Throughout the planet we have become a profoundly disturbing presence. In New England to the north and in southern Quebec, the native maple trees are dying out in great numbers due to pollutants in the atmosphere, and in the soil and the waters of the region. This is largely due to the carbon compounds, especially petroleum, that we have loosed into the atmosphere through our use of fossil fuels for heat and energy. Carbon is the magical element. The whole life structure of the planet is based upon it. So long as the life process is guided by carbon's natural patterns, the integral functioning of the earth takes place.

The wonderful variety expressed in marine life and land life, the splendor of the flowers and the birds and animals, all these, through the mediation of the carbon cycle, were enabled to expand in their gorgeous coloration, in their fantastic forms, in their dancing movements, and in their songs and calls that echo over the world. To accomplish all this, however, nature had to find a way of storing immense quantities of carbon in the petroleum and the coal deposits, and also in the great forests. This was worked out over some hundreds of millions of years. A balance was achieved and the life systems of the planet were secure in the interaction of the air and the water and the soil with the inflowing energy from the sun.

But then we discovered that petroleum could produce such wonderful effects. It can be made into fertilizer to nourish crops, it can be spun into fabrics, it can fuel our internal combustion engines for transportation over the vast highway system that we have built, it can produce an unlimited variety of plastic implements, it can run gigantic generators and produce power for lighting and heating our buildings. It was all so simple. We had no awareness of the deadly consequences that would result from the residue that would be produced by our use of petroleum for all these purposes. Nor did we know how profoundly we would affect the organisms in the soil with our insistence that the patterns of plant growth be governed by artificial human demands achieved by petroleum-based fertilizers, rather than by the spontaneous rhythms within the living world. Nor did we understand that biological systems are not that adaptable to the mechanistic processes we imposed upon them.

I do not wish to dwell on the devastation we have brought upon the earth but only to make sure that we understand the nature and the order of magnitude of what is happening. While we seem to be achieving magnificent things at the microphase level of our functioning, we are devastating the entire range of living beings at the macrophase level. The natural world is more sensitive than we have realized. While we have thought our manipulations to be of enormous benefit for the human process, we now find that by disturbing the biosystems of the planet at the most basic level of their functioning we have endangered all that makes the planet Earth a suitable place for the integral development of human life itself.

Unaware of what we have done or its order of magnitude, we seek to remedy the situation by altering our ways of acting on some minor scale, by recycling, by diminishing our use of energy, by limiting our use of automobiles, by fewer development projects. The difficulty is that we do these things not primarily to cease our plundering of the earth in its basic resources, but to make possible a continuation of these plundering industrial life patterns by mitigating the consequences. We mistake the order of magnitude of what we are dealing with.

MACROPHASE BIOLOGY

Our problems are primarily problems of macrophase biology. Macrophase biology, the integral functioning of the entire complex of biosystems of the planet, is something that biologists have given almost no attention to. Only with James Lovelock and some of our more recent scientists have we even begun to think about this larger scale of life-functioning. This is not surprising since we are caught in the microphase dimensions of every phase of our human endeavor. This is true in law and medicine and in the other professions as well as in biology.

Macrophase biology is concerned with the five basic spheres: the land sphere, the water sphere, the air sphere, the life sphere, and how these interact with each other to enable the planet Earth to be what it is. Then we have a very powerful sphere—the mind sphere, the human mind sphere. Consciousness is certainly not limited to humans. Every living being has its own mode of consciousness. We must be aware, however, that consciousness is an analogous concept. It is qualitatively different in its various modes of expression. Consciousness can be considered as the capacity for intimate presence of things to each other, through knowledge and sensitive identity. But obviously the consciousness of a plant and the consciousness of an animal are qualitatively different. The consciousness of fish and the consciousness of birds or insects are all distinct. So too with the human. For the purposes of the fish, human modes of consciousness would be more of a defect than an advantage, and the consciousness of a bird would not suit a tiger.

It is also clear that the human mode of consciousness is capable of unique intrusion into the larger functioning of the planetary life systems. So powerful is this intrusion that the human has established an additional sphere that might be referred to as a technosphere, a way of controlling the functioning of the planet for the benefit of the human at the expense of the other modes of being. We might even consider that the technosphere in its subservience to industrial-commercial uses has become incompatible with the other spheres that constitute the basic functional context of the planet.

The biggest single question before us at present is the extent to which this technological-industrial-commercial context of human functioning can be made compatible with the integral functioning of the other life systems of the planet. However, we are reluctant to think of our activities as being inherently incompatible with the integral functioning of the various components of the planetary systems. It is not simply a matter of modifying our energy use with such things as "re-cycling," because this presupposes a "cycling" that is already devastating in its original form. Nor can we resolve the situation simply by mitigating the pollution so that the system itself can continue in its same basic form as at present. The system in its present plundering phase is certainly over with—it cannot continue. The industrial world on a global scale, as it functions presently, can be considered to be definitively bankrupt.

There is no way out of the present recession within the context of our existing commercial-industrial processes. Any recession now is not simply a financial recession or even a human recession. It is a recession of the planet itself. The earth cannot sustain such an industrial system or its devastating technologies. In the future the industrial system will have its moments of apparent recovery but these will be minor and momentary. The larger movement is toward dissolution. The impact of our present technologies is beyond what the earth can endure.

We can differentiate an acceptable technology from an unacceptable technology quite simply: an acceptable technology is one that is compatible with the technologies of the natural world. An unacceptable technology is one that is incompatible with the integral functioning of the technologies that govern the functioning of the natural systems. Nature has its own technologies. The entire hydrological cycle can even be considered as a vast engineering project, although it is an engineering project vastly greater than anything humans could devise with such beneficent consequences throughout the life systems of the planet.

The error has been to think that we could distort the natural processes for some immediate human benefit without incurring some immense penalty, a penalty that might eventually bring the well-being of humanity and of most other life forms into danger. This is what has happened in this twentieth-century petroleum economy that we have developed. The petroleum base of our present industrial establishment at its present rate of use might last another fifty years, probably less, possibly more. But a severe depletion will occur within the lifetime of young people presently living; the major portion of petroleum will be gone. Our youngest children could see the end of it. They will likely see also the tragic climax of the population expansion. With the number of automobiles on the planet estimated at 600 million in the year 2000, we will be approaching another saturation level in the technological intrusion into the planetary process.

It is awesome to consider how quickly events of such catastrophic proportions are happening. When I was born in 1914 there were only 1.5 billion people in the world. Children of the present will likely see 10 billion. The Petrochemical Age had hardly begun in my early decades. Now the planet is saturated with the residue from spent oil products. There were fewer than a million automobiles in the world when I was born. In my childhood the tropical rainforests were substantially intact. Now they are devastated on an immense scale. The biological diversity of the life forms was not yet threatened on an extensive scale. The ozone layer was still intact.

In evaluating our present situation, my judgment is that we have already terminated the Cenozoic period of the geobiological systems of the planet. Sixty-five million years of life development are over. Extinction is taking place throughout the life systems on a scale unequaled since the terminal phase of the Mesozoic.

A renewal of life in some creative context requires that a new biological period come into being, a period when humans would dwell upon the earth in a mutually enhancing manner. I describe this new mode of being of the planet as the Ecozoic Era, the fourth in the succession of life periods thus far identified as the Paleozoic, the Mesozoic, and the Cenozoic. But even when we propose an emerging Ecozoic Era to succeed the Cenozoic Era, we must indicate the unique character of this emergent period.

CONDITIONS FOR THE RISE OF THE ECOZOIC ERA

First, regarding the name, Ecozoic: I propose Ecozoic as a better designation than Ecological. Eco-logos refers to an *understanding* of the interaction of things. Eco-zoic, a newly selected term, is a more biological term that can be used to indicate the integral *functioning* of life systems in their mutually enhancing relations.

If other periods have been designated by such names as the Reptilian or the Mammalian periods, this Ecozoic Period must be identified as Era of the Integral Life Community. For this to emerge there are special conditions needed for humans, for although this period cannot be an anthropocentric life period, it can come into being only under certain conditions that dominantly concern human understanding, choice, and action. Here we might enumerate some of the particular conditions to be fulfilled on the part of the human if the Ecozoic Era is to come about.

The *first condition* is to understand that the universe is a communion of subjects, not a collection of objects. Every being has its own inner form, its own spontaneity, its own voice, its ability to declare itself, to be present to other components of the universe in a subject-to-subject relationship. While this is true of every being in the universe, it is especially true of each component member of the earth community. Each component of the earth is integral with every other component of the earth; this particularly applies to the living beings of the earth in their relations with each other.

The termination of the Cenozoic period of earth history has been brought about by the incapacity of humans in the industrial cultures to be present to the earth and its various modes of being in some intimate fashion. Ever since the time of Descartes in the early sixteenth century, Western humans, in their dominant life attitudes, have been autistic in relation to the nonhuman components of the planet. Whatever the abuse of the natural world by humans prior to this time, the living world was recognized until then in its proper biological functioning as having an "anima," a soul. Every living being was by definition an ensouled being with a voice that spoke to the depths of the human of wondrous and divine mysteries, a voice that was heard quite clearly by the poets and musicians and scientists and philosophers and mystics of the world, a voice also heard with special sensitivity by the children.

Descartes, we might say, killed the earth and all its living beings. For him the natural world was mechanism. There was no possibility of entering into a communion relationship. After Descartes, Western humans became autistic in relation to the surrounding world. There could be no communion with the birds or animals or plants since these were all mechanical contrivances. The real value of things was reduced to their economic value. A destructive anthropocentrism came into being.

This situation can be remedied only by a new mode of mutual presence between the human and the natural world, with the plants and the animals of both the sea and the land. If we do not get that straight then we cannot expect any significant remedy for the present distress experienced throughout the earth. This capacity for intimate rapport needs to be extended into the atmospheric phenomena and the geological structures and their functioning.

Because of this autism, my generation never heard the voices of that vast multitude of inhabitants of the planet. They had no communion with the nonhuman world. They would go to the seashore or to the mountains for some recreation, a moment of aesthetic joy. But this was too superficial to establish any true reverence or intimate rapport. No sensitivity was shown to the powers inherent in the various phenomena of the natural world. There was no depth of awe that would have restrained their assault on the natural world in order to extract from it some human advantage, even if this meant tearing to pieces the entire fabric of the planet.

The *second condition* for entering into the Ecozoic age is a realization that the earth exists and can survive only in its integral functioning. It cannot survive in fragments any more than any organism can survive in fragments. Yet the earth is not a global sameness. It is a differentiated unity and must be sustained in the integrity and interrelations of its many bioregional contexts. This requires an immediacy of any human settlement with the life dynamics of the region. Within this region, the human rights to habitat must respect the rights to habitat in the region possessed by the other members of the life community. Only the full complex of life expression can sustain the vigor of any bioregion.

A *third condition* for entering the Ecozoic Era is recognition that the earth is a one-time endowment. We do not know the quantum of energy contained in the earth, its possibilities or its limitations. We must reasonably suppose that the earth is subject to irreversible damage in the major patterns of its functioning and even to distortions in its possibilities of development. Although there was survival and further development after the great extinctions at the end of the Paleozoic and the Mesozoic eras, life was not so highly developed as it is now. Nor were the very conditions of life negated by such changes as we have wrought through our disturbance of the chemical balance of the planet.

Life upon earth will surely survive the present decline of the Cenozoic Era, but we do not know at what level of its development. The single-celled life forms found throughout the planet, the insects, the rodents, the plants, and a host of other forms of life—these will surely survive. But the severity of devastation as regards the extinction of rainforests, the fertility of the soils, species diversity, survival of the more developed animals, the consequences throughout the animal world of the diminishment of the ozone shield, the extension of deserts, pollution of the great freshwater lakes, the chemical balance of the atmosphere, these are all subject to disturbance that might not ever be restored to their present grandeur, certainly not within any time scale that is available to human modes of thinking or planning. Almost certainly in these past centuries we have witnessed a grand climax in the florescence of the earth.

A *fourth condition* for entering the Ecozoic Age is a realization that the earth is primary and that humans are derivative. The present distortion is that humans are primary and the earth and its integral functioning can only be a secondary consideration, and thus the pathology manifest in our various human institutions, professions, programs, and activities. The only acceptable way for humans to function effectively is by giving first consideration to the earth community and then dealing with humans as integral members of that community. In economics the first consideration cannot be the human economy, since the human economy does not even exist prior to the earth economy. Only if the earth economy is functioning in some integral manner can the human economy be in any manner effective. The earth economy can survive the loss of its human component, but there is no way for the human economy to survive or prosper apart from the earth economy.

The absurdity has been to seek a rising Gross Human Economy while diminishing the Gross Earth Economy. This primacy of the earth community applies also to medicine and law and all the other activities of humans. It should be especially clear in medicine that we cannot have well humans on a sick planet. So in jurisprudence, to poise the entire administration of justice on the rights of humans and their limitless freedoms to exploit the natural world is to open the natural world to the worst predatory instincts of humans. Medicine must first turn its attention to protecting the health and well-being of the earth before there can be any effective human health. So in law, the prior rights of the entire earth community need to be assured first, then the rights and freedoms of humans can have their field of expression.

A *fifth condition* for the rise of the Ecozoic Age is to realize that there is a single earth community. There is no such thing as a human community in any manner separate from the earth community. The human community and the natural world will go into the future as a single integral community, or we will both experience disaster on the way. However differentiated in its modes of expression, there is only one earth community, one economic order, one health system, one moral order, one world of the sacred.

A New Myth

As I present this outline of an emerging Ecozoic period I am quite aware that such a conception of the future, when humans would be present to the earth in a mutually enhancing manner, is mythic in its form, just as such conceptions as the Paleozoic, Mesozoic, and Cenozoic are mythic modes of understanding a continuing process, even though this continuing process is marked by an indefinite number of discontinuities amid the continuity of the process itself. The effort here is to articulate the outlines of a new mythic form that would evoke a creative entrancement to succeed the destructive entrancement that has taken possession of the Western soul in recent centuries. We can counter one entrancement only with another—a counter-entrancement. Only thus can we evoke the vision as well as the psychic energies needed to enable the earth community to enter successfully into its next great creative phase. The grandeur of the possibilities ahead of us must in some manner be experienced in anticipation; otherwise we will not have the psychic energy to endure the pains of the required transformation.

Once we are sufficiently clear as to where we are headed, once we experience its urgency and the adventure of what we are about, we can get on with our historic task; we can accept and even ignore the difficulties to be resolved and the pains to be endured because we are involved in a great work. In creating such a great work the incidentals fall away. We can accept the pathos of our times, the sorrow that we will necessarily go through. Hopefully we will be able to guide and inspire the next generation as it takes up this creative effort. Otherwise they will simply survive with all their resentments amid the ruined infrastructures of the industrial world and amid the ruins of the natural world itself. The challenge itself is already predetermined. There is no way for the new generation to escape this confrontation. The task to which they are called, the destiny that is before them, is, however, not left simply to themselves. The human is supported by the entire universe, as well as by every earthly being on earth. Not only is the entire planet involved, but the successful emergence of the Ecozoic age on earth can be considered as part of the great creative task of the universe itself.

This destiny can be understood, however, only in the context of the great story of the universe. All peoples derive their understanding of themselves by their account of how the universe came into being in the beginning, how it came to be as it is, and the role of the human in the story. We in our Euro-American traditions have through our observational studies in recent centuries created a new story of the universe. The difficulty is that this story was discovered in the context of a mechanistic way of thinking about the world and so has been devoid of meaning. According to this model, supposedly everything has happened in a random meaningless process. It is little wonder then that we have lost our Great Story. Our earlier Genesis story long ago lost its power over our historical cultural development. Our new scientific story has never carried any depth of meaning. We have lost our reverence for the universe and the entire range of natural phenomena.

The difficulty is that our scientific story of the universe has no continuity with the natural world as we experience this in the wind and rain and clouds, the birds and animals and insects that we observe. For the first time in all of human history, the sun and moon and stars, the fields and mountains and streams and woodlands fail to evoke a sense of reverence before the deep mystery of things. These wondrous components of the natural world are somehow not seen with any depth of appreciation. Perhaps this is why our presence has become so deadly.

But now all this is suddenly altered. Shocked by the devastation we have caused, we are awakening to the wonder of a universe never before seen in quite the same manner. No one ever before could tell in such lyric language the story of the primordial flaring forth of the universe at the beginning, the shaping of the immense number of stars gathered into galaxies, the collapse of the first generation of stars to create the ninety-some elements, the gravitational gathering of scattered stardust into our solar system with its nine planets, the formation of the earth with its seas and atmosphere and the continents crashing and rifting as they move over the asthenosphere, the awakening of life. Such a marvel this 15 billion year process, such infinite numbers of stars in the heavens and living beings on earth, such limitless variety of flowering species and all forms of animal life, such tropical luxuriance, such natural scenery in the mountains, such springtime wonders as occur each year!

What is needed now is that we be able to tell this story, meditate on this story, listen to this story as it is told by every breeze that blows, by every cloud in the sky, by every mountain and river and woodland, by the song of every cricket.

TELLING THE STORY

The role of elders at the present time is to assist the next generation in fulfilling their role in this transformation moment. We can, I think, assist them mainly by indicating just where they can receive their instructions. Here I would like to speak of an incident on Cape Croker along Georgian Bay in northwest Ontario. Some years ago I was invited to participate there at a meeting of the indigenous Native American peoples, mostly Ojibwa,

Cree, and Six Nations, concerning their future and what direction their lives should take.

When I spoke with them I mentioned that the previous night I was watching the moon flickering on the waters of the bay and I asked the moon, "What should I say?" and the moon answered "Tell them the story." I asked the wind "What should I say?" and the wind said, "Tell them the story." Then before I came into the big tent I asked the clover in the meadow, "What should I say?" and the clover said, "Tell them the story, my story, the mountain story, the river story, the bird story, your story, their story, the Great Story." Then I remarked to the people, "What I say here is not important. But what the mountains and the rivers say is important. What the birds and the animals and the creatures in the sea say, what the flowers and the trees say and the sands of the shore, what the wind and the sun and the moon and the stars say—all this is important." Of course the indigenous peoples all knew this. I was in a manner speaking to myself and to the society from which I come.

I mentioned then that my generation had been insensitive in relation to the entire range of natural phenomena. Since we could not enter into evocatory relations with these surrounding powers, we found it necessary to plunder these sources in order to survive, but the more we plundered the less fertility was found in the soils and the less abundant the natural resources, the less available water suited for drinking or air for breathing. Because we could not listen we could not learn.

We have lost contact with our Story, with the Great Story, and that is why the instruction being given to me by the moon and the wind and the clover was to *tell the story*—to remind us all what is happening and where we must look for guidance. For we can come together—all the peoples of Earth and all the various members of the great Earth community—only in the Great Story, the story of the universe. For there is no community without a community story, no Earth community without the Earth story, and no universe community without the universe story. These three constitute the Great Story. Without this story the various forces of the planet become mutually destructive rather than mutually coherent.

We need to listen to each other's way of telling the Great Story. But first, we in the West—with our newly developed capacity to listen to the universe through our vast telescopes and to hear the sounds of the universe as these come to us from the beginning of time and over some billions of years—really need to listen to this story as our own special way of understanding and participating in the Great Story.

Whenever we forget our story we become confused. But the winds and the rivers and the mountains—they never become confused. We must go to them constantly to be reminded of the Great Story, for every being in the universe is what it is only through its participation in the Story. We are resensitized whenever we listen to what they are telling us. Long ago they told us that we must be guided by a reverence and a restraint in our relations with the larger community of life, that we must respect the powers of the surrounding universe, that only through a sensitive insertion of ourselves into the great celebration of the Earth community can we expect the support of the Earth community. If we violate the integrity of this community, we will die.

THE HUMAN ROLE

The natural world is vast and its lessons fearsome. One of the most severe expressions of the natural world has to do with nuclear energy. When we go deep into the natural world and penetrate into the inner structure of the atom and in a sense violate that deepest mystery for trivial or destructive purposes, we may get power, but nature throws its most deadly consequences at us. We are still helpless with regard to what to do once we have broken into the mysterious recesses of nuclear power. Forces have been let loose far beyond anything we can manage.

Earlier I mentioned five conditions for the integral emergence of the Ecozoic Era. Here I would continue with a sixth condition: that we understand fully and respond effectively to our own human role in this new era. For while the Cenozoic era unfolded in its full splendor entirely apart from any role fulfilled by humans, almost nothing of major significance is likely to happen in the Ecozoic Era that humans will not be involved in. The entire pattern of earth functioning is altered in this transition from the Cenozoic to the Ecozoic. We did not even exist until the major developments of the Cenozoic were complete. In the Ecozoic, however, humans will have a pervasive influence on almost everything that happens. In the entire modality of earth functioning we are crossing over a critical threshold. While we cannot make a blade of grass, there is liable not to *be* a blade of grass unless it is accepted, protected, and fostered by humans—protected mainly from ourselves, so that the earth can function from within its own dynamism.

Finally, the question of language for a new Era needs to be addressed. A new language, an Ecozoic language is required. Our late Cenozoic language is radically inadequate. The human mode of being is captured and destroyed by our present univalent, scientific, literal, unimaginative language. We need a multivalent language, a language much richer in the symbolic meanings that it carried in its earlier forms when the human lived deeply within the world of natural forms and the entire range of earth phenomena. As we recover this early experience in the emerging Ecozoic Era, all the archetypes of the collective unconscious attain a new validity and new patterns of functioning—especially in our understanding of the symbols of the heroic journey, the death-rebirth symbol, the Great Mother, the tree of life.

Every reality in the natural world is multivalent; nothing is univalent. Just as sunlight carries within itself warmth and light and energy, everything has a multitude of aspects and meanings. Sunlight awakens the plenitude of living forms in the springtime. Sunlight is not a single entity. It awakens poetry in the soul, it evokes a sense of the divine. It is mercy and healing, affliction and death. Sunlight is irreducible to any scientific equation or any literal description.

But all these meanings are based on the physical experience of sunlight. If we were deprived of sunlight, the entire visible world would be lost to us and eventually all life and immense realms of consciousness would be lost, too. We would be retarded in our inner development in proportion to our deprivation of the experience of natural phenomena, of mountains and rivers and forests and seacoasts and all their living inhabitants. The natural world itself is our primary language as it is our primary scripture, our primary awakening to the mysteries of existence. We might well put all our written scriptures on the shelf for twenty years until we learn what we are being told by unmediated experience of the world about us.

So too we might put Webster on the shelf until we revise the language of all our professions, especially such professions as law and medicine and education. In the discipline of ethics we need new words such as biocide and geocide, words that have not yet been adopted into the language. In law we need to define society in terms that include the larger community of living beings of the bioregion, of the earth and even of the universe. Certainly human society separated from such contexts is an abstraction. Life, liberty, habitat, and the pursuit of happiness are rights that should be granted to every living creature, each in accord with its own mode of being.

The Exodus Symbol

I might conclude with a reference to the Exodus symbol that has exercised such great power over our Western civilization. Many peoples came to this country believing they were leaving a land of oppression and going to a land of liberation. We have always had a sense of transition. Progress is supposedly taking us from an undesirable situation into a kind of beatitude. So we might think of the transition from the terminal Cenozoic to the emerging Ecozoic as a kind of exodus out of a period when humans were devastating the planet to a period when humans began to live upon the earth in a mutually enhancing manner.

There is a vast difference, however, in this present transition. It is not simply a transition of humanity but of the entire planet, its land, its air, its waters, its biosystems, its human communities. This exodus is a journey of the earth entire. We hope we will make the transition successfully. Whatever the future holds for us, however, it will be a shared experience among humans and all other earthly beings. There is but one community, one destiny.

Notes

1. Thomas Berry, *The Dream of Earth* (San Francisco: Sierra Club Books, 1988); Thomas Berry & Brian Swimme, *The Universe Story* (San Francisco: Harper SF, 1992).

Father Bede's Favorite Scriptures

I KNOW THAT GREAT PERSON
of the brightness of the sun
beyond the darkness.
Only by knowing him
one goes beyond death.
There is no other way to go.

Svetasvatara Upanishad
India, 800–400 BC

THOU ART THE IMPERISHABLE,
the highest end of knowledge,
the support of this vast universe.
Thou art the everlasting Ruler
of the law of righteousness,
the spirit who is and was
at the beginning.

Bhagavad Gita
India, 300 BC

HE IS THE IMAGE OF THE INVISIBLE GOD,
the First-born of all creation.
In him everything in heaven
and on earth was created,
things visible and invisible,
thrones and dominations,
principalities and powers.
All were created in him and for him.
He is before all things
and in him everything continues in being.

Letter to the Colossians

Appendix

Before his death Father Bede founded a Trust to oversee and care for his publications, manuscripts and tapes, to further disseminate his spiritual vision to the world, and especially to encourage and support the renewal of contemplative life throughout the world. The Trust has established study and meditation centers on several continents, where Father Bede's commitment to contemplative prayer can be experienced and where his books, articles, tapes, as well as documentaries and studies on his life work are available for consultation or purchase. The Trust archives are housed at Graduate Theological Union in Berkeley, California.

Several doctoral and masters theses have already been written on Father Bede's teaching and life, and the Trust seeks to promote further study in this area. His many books and articles offer abundant possibilities for scholarly work.

The Trust also promotes local and national conferences on Father Bede's teachings, and on East/West and ecological themes. It publishes a worldwide newsletter, "The Golden String," and also helps Father Bede's ashram community in South India, Saccidananda, and the village projects for the poor supported by the ashram. In these ways, the Trust seeks to further Father Bede's spiritual ideals.

The four centers in the United States, all within the context of contemplative monastic communities, are:

New Camaldoli Hermitage
c/o Fr. Robert Hale, OSB Cam.
Big Sur, Ca 93920
(408) 667–2456
(408) 667–0209 (FAX)

Osage Monastery
c/o Sr. Pascaline Coff, OSB
18701 W. Monastery Road
Sand Springs, OK 74063
(918) 245–2734
(918) 245–9360 (FAX)

Incarnation Monastery
c/o Br. Cassian Hardie, OSB Cam.
1369 La Loma Ave.
Berkeley, CA 94708
(510) 548–0965
(510) 845–0601 (FAX)

Epiphany Monastery
c/o Fr. Romuald Duscher, OSB Cam.
96 Scobie Rd.
New Boston, NH 03070
(603) 487–3700
(603) 487–3020 (FAX)

Other centers of the Trust are:

in India:
Saccidananda Ashram
c/o Br. John Martin, OSB Cam.
Tannirpalli 639107
Kulittalai—Trichiappali Dist.
Tamil Nadu, South India
(011) 91–4323-3060

in Germany:
Shantigiri/Mount of Peace
c/o Roland Ropers, Obl. OSB
D-83707 Kreuth/Teghernsee
Germany
(011) 49–8029-8235
(011) 49–8029-8888 (FAX)

in Italy:
Monastero di San Gregorio
c/o Fr. Bernardino Cozzarini, OSB Cam.
Piazza di San Gregorio al Celio
Rome, Italy 00184
(011) 396–700-8227
(011) 396–700-9357 (FAX)

in Australia:
Christ by the River Hermitage
c/o Fr. Douglas Conlan, Obl. OSB
PO Box 35, Pinjarra 6208/W
Australia
(011) 09–5311-227
(011) 09–5312-480 (FAX)

Bibliography

Jesu Rajan with Judson Trapnell

This up-to-date bibliography of Father Bede's works and secondary sources about him was compiled by Father Jesu Rajan, a close friend of Bede's and author of the book Bede Griffiths and Sannyasa *(1989). Pascaline Coff and Wayne Teasdale also helped in this joint effort. Additional sources were provided by Judson Trapnell, who also updated the material. A number of items listed here are annotated "unpublished." These are included because we believe that persons interested in Father Bede will want to know about them. They, and all of Father Bede's works, published or unpublished—are available in the Archives at Incarnation Monastery in Berkeley, California (see Appendix). Items here noted as unpublished may soon be published. Readers wishing to keep abreast of ongoing publications and newly discovered or composed materials relating to Father Bede may write to their nearest Trust center (see Appendix), and ask to be put on the mailing list for* The Golden String, Bulletin of the Bede Griffiths Trust, *referred to in the Appendix.*

PRIMARY SOURCES

BOOKS BY BEDE GRIFFITHS:

The Golden String: An Autobiography. Springfield, Illinois: Templegate Publishers, 1954, 1980.

Christ in India: Essays Towards a Hindu-Christian Dialogue. Springfield, Illinois: Templegate Publishers, 1966, 1984.

Vedanta and Christian Faith. Clearlake, California: Dawn Horse Press, 1973, 1991.

Return to the Center. Springfield, Illinois: Templegate Publishers, 1976.

The Marriage of East and West: A Sequel to the Golden String. Springfield, Illinois: Templegate Publishers, 1982.

The Cosmic Revelation: The Hindu Way to God. Springfield, Illinois: Templegate Publishers, 1983.

River of Compassion: A Christian Commentary on the Bhagavad Gita. New York: Continuum, 1995 (formerly published by Amity House, 1987).

A New Vision of Reality: Western Science, Eastern Mysticism and Christian Faith. Edited by Felicity Edwards. Springfield, Illinois: Templegate Publishers, 1990.

The New Creation in Christ: Christian Meditation and Community. Edited by Robert Kiely and Laurence Freeman. Springfield, Illinois: Templegate Publishers, 1995.

Universal Wisdom: A Journey through the Sacred Wisdom of the World. Edited by Roland Ropers. San Francisco: HarperCollins, 1994.

ARTICLES AND PUBLISHED LECTURES BY BEDE GRIFFITHS:

"The Power of the Imagination," "The Power of Intuition," & "The Process of Knowledge." Photocopies from Griffiths' typewritten unpublished manuscripts, 1930s.

"The Poetry of St. Benedict." *Pax* 25 (August 1935), 101–106.

"St. Justin's Apology." *Pax* 27 (March 1937), 289–293.

"A Pilgrim to Jerusalem." *Pax* 28 (1938), 7–11, 30–35.

"The Mysticism of Mary Webb." *Pax* 28 (October 1938), 161–165.

"Integration." *Pax* 28 (November 1938), 185–189.

"The Church of England and Reunion." *Pax* 29 (1939), 36–46.

"The Poetry of the Bible." *Pax* 29 (1939), 124–128.

"Christian Democracy." *Pax* 29 (1939), 255–262.

"The Platonic Tradition and the Liturgy." *Eastern Churches Quarterly* 4, no. 1 (January 1940), 5–8.

"The New Creation." *Pax* 36 (1946), 15–23.

"Pluscarden: September 8th." *Pax* 36 (1946), 111–113.

"The City of God." *Catholic Mind* 46 (1948), 410–413.

"The Mystery of Sex and Marriage." *Pax* 39 (1949), 77–80.

"Catholicism To-day." *Pax* 40 (1950), 11–16.

"The Priesthood and Contemplation." *The Life of the Spirit* 5 (April 1951), 439–446. (Reprinted in *Orate Fratres* 25, no. 8 [July 1951], 347–355.)

"The Divine Office as a Method of Prayer." *The Life of the Spirit* 6, nos. 62–63 (August-September 1951), 77–85.

"Liturgical Formation in the Spiritual Life." *The Life of the Spirit* 6, no. 69 (March 1952), 361–368.

"The Mystery of the Scriptures." *The Life of the Spirit* 7, nos. 74–75 (August-September 1952), 67–75.

"Swiss Monasteries." *Pax* 42 (1952), 166–172.

"The Divine Office as a Method of Prayer." *Theology Digest* 1 (1952), 42–44.

"A Catholic Commentary on Holy Scripture." *Pax* 43 (1953), 76–78.

"Christian Existentialism." *Pax* 43 (1953), 141–145.

"The Cloud on the Tabernacle." *The Life of the Spirit* 7, no. 83 (May 1953), 478–486.

"The Enigma of Simone Weil." *Blackfriars* 34, no. 398 (May 1953), 232–236.

"Monks and the World." *Blackfriars* 34, no. 404 (November 1953), 496–501.

"The Incarnation and the East." *The Commonweal* 59, no. 12 (25 December 1953), 298–301. (Reprinted in *Christ in India*, 69–76.)

"On Reading Novels." *Pax* 44 (1954), 124–128.

"The Transcendent Unity of Religions." *The Downside Review* 72, no. 229 (July 1954), 264–275.

"Our Lady and the Church in the Scriptures." *Liturgy* 23 (1954), 87–92.

"The Meaning of the Monastic Life." *Pax* 45 (1955), 132–137.

"Experiment in Simplicity." *The Commonweal* 61, no. 18 (4 February 1955), 471–474. (An excerpt from *The Golden String*, 65–73.)

"For a Hindu Catholicism." *The Tablet* 205, no. 6000 (21 May 1955), 494–495.

"Fulfillment for the East." *The Commonweal* 63, no. 3 (21 October 1955), 55–58. (Reprinted in *Christ in India*, 77–85.)

"The Missionary Today." *The Commonweal* 64, no. 4 (27 April 1956), 90–92. (Reprinted in *Christ in India*, 86–93.)

"The Taena Community." *Pax* 46 (1956), 112–115.

"Kerala." *Pax* 47 (1957), 90–94. (Reprinted in *Christ in India*, 48–54.)

"Vinoba Bhave." *Blackfriars* 38 (1957), 66–71.

"Symbolism and Cult." In *Indian Culture and the Fullness of Christ*. Madras: The Madras Cultural Academy, 1957.

"Catholicism and the East." *The Commonweal* 68, no. 11 (13 June 1958), 271–274. (Reprinted in *Christ in India*, 94–103.)

"Experiment in Monastic Life." *The Commonweal* 68, no. 26 (26 September 1958), 634–636.

"Kurisumala Ashram." *Pax* 48 (1958), 128–133.

"John Cassian." *The Month* 21, no. 6 (June 1959), 346–362.

"The People of India." *The Commonweal* 71, no. 4 (23 October 1959), 95–98. (Reprinted in *Christ in India*, 115–125.)

"Role of the Layman." *The Commonweal* 71, no. 5 (30 October 1959), 119–121.

"Eastern and Western Traditions in the Liturgy." *The Clergy Monthly Supplement* 4 (1959), 223–228.

"The Church Universal: Efforts Toward Reunion." *The Commonweal* 71, no. 14 (1 January 1960), 387–390. (Reprinted in *Christ in India*, 235–242, with slight changes.)

"The Language of a Mission." *Blackfriars* 41, no. 478 (January-February 1960), 20–27.

"The Kerala Story." *The Commonweal* 71, no. 26 (25 March 1960), 692–694.

"Walking with Vinoba." *The Commonweal* 73, no. 1 (30 September 1960), 14–16. (Reprinted in *Christ in India*, 126–133.)

"Hinduism and Christianity in India." *Blackfriars* 41, no. 485 (October 1960), 364–372. (Reprinted in *Christ in India*, 55–65.)

"A Letter from India." *The Life of the Spirit* 15, no. 172 (October 1960), 178–182.

"Liturgy and the Missions." *Asia* 12 (1960), 148–154.

"An Ecumenical Movement in Kerala." *The Star of the East* 21 (1960), 10–12.

"An Ecumenical Movement in Kerala." *Arunodayam* 16 (1960), 18–19.

"The Seed and the Soil." *Good Work* 23 (1960), 59–64.

"The New Creation." *Sponsa Regis* 31 (1960), 223–230.

"The Ideal of an Indian Catholicism," 425; and "Indian Catholicism and Hindu Culture," 633–634, *The Examiner* 111 (1960).

"Three Roads to Unity." *The Commonweal* 73, no. 26 (24 March 1961), 651–653.

"Non-violence and Nuclear War." *Blackfriars* 42, no. 490 (April 1961), 157–162. (Reprinted in *Christ in India*, 143–150.)

"Non-violence and Nuclear War." *Bhoodan* 6 (1961), 6–7.

"Non-violence and Nuclear War." *Pax Bulletin* 86 (1961), 1–3.

"The Ecumenical Approach to Non-Christian Religions." *The Catholic World* 193, no. 1157 (August 1961), 304–310.

"The Contemplative Life in India." *Pax* 51 (1961), 105–111.

"The Goal of Evolution." *Sponsa Regis* 32 (1961), 125–134.

"Paradise Lost." *Sponsa Regis* 32 (1961), 210–219.

"The Promised Land and Paradise Regained." *Sponsa Regis* 32 (1961), 278–288.

"The World Council and the Syrian Church." *The Star of the East* 22 (1961), 55–59.

"The Church Universal." *The Star of the East* 22 (1961), 16–22.

"The Ecumenical Movement in the Roman Catholic Church." *Arunodayam* 17 (1961), 17–18.

"The Birth of Christ in India." *The Examiner* 112 (1961), 783.

"Gandhi's India, Mao's China." *The Commonweal* 77, no. 12 (14 December 1962), 309–312.

"Meeting at Rajpur." *The Clergy Monthly Supplement* 6 (1962), 137–151. (Reprinted in *Christ in India*, 179–190.)

"The Challenge of India." *Good Work* 25 (1962), 82–87.

"The Meeting of East and West." *Good Work* 26 (1963), 100–109. (Reprinted in *Christ in India*, 163–178.)

"Report from India." *Jubilee* 11, no. 1 (May 1963), 2–3.

"Christian Witness in India: Ways of Knowing God." Lecture given on "The Catholic Hour" radio program, November 10, 1963. Washington, DC: NCCM, 1963. Transcript available in Archives.

"The Church and Hinduism." *Jubilee* 11, no. 7 (November 1963), 30–35. (Reprinted in *Christ in India*, 179–190.)

—⟨⟩—

"Placing Indian Religion." *Blackfriars* 44, no. 521 (November 1963), 477–481.

"The Church of the Future." *The Examiner* 114 (1963), 821–822. (Reprinted in *Christ in India*, 243–249.)

"Liturgy and Culture." *The Tablet* 218, no. 6471 (30 May 1964), 602–603.

"Background to Bombay." *The Month* 32, no. 6 (December 1964), 313–318.

"Kurisumala Ashram." *The Eastern Churches Quarterly* 16, no. 3 (1964), 226–231. (Reprinted in *Christ in India*, 41–47.)

"The Vatican Council." *The Star of the East* 25 (1964), 9–12.

"Indian Spirituality and the Eucharist." In *India and the Eucharist*, edited by Bede Griffiths and Co. Ernakulam, India: Lumen Institute, 1964, 9–18.

"Dialogue with Hinduism." *The Clergy Monthly Supplement* 7 (1964), 144–149.

"The Ecumenical Approach to the Missions." *India* 15 (1964), 64–67.

"India after the Pope." *The Commonweal* 81, no. 20 (12 February 1965), 641–642.

"The Dialogue with Hinduism," *New Blackfriars* 46, no. 538 (April 1965), 404–410. (Reprinted in *The Catholic Mind* 63 [1965], 36–42.)

"The Church and Non-Christian Religions." *The Tablet* 219, no. 6552 (18 December 1965), 1409–1410.

"The Ecumenical Approach to Hinduism." *The Examiner* 116 (1965), 505.

"Light on C. S. Lewis." *The Month* 35, no. 6 (June 1966), 337–341.

"Monastic Life in India Today." *Monastic Studies* 4 (Advent 1966), 117–135.

"The Declaration on the Church and Non-Christian Religions." *The Examiner* 117 (1966), 117, 122.

"The Dialogue with Hindus." *The Examiner* 117 (17 December 1966), 821–822.

"The Sacred Cow." *The Commonweal* 85, no. 17 (3 February 1967), 483–484.

"The Christian Doctrine of Grace and Freewill." *The Mountain Path* (April 1967), 124–128.

"The New Creation." *The Examiner* 118 (1967), 809.

"Further Towards a Hindu-Christian Dialogue." Bede Griffiths & A. K. Saran. *The Clergy Monthly* 32, no. 5 (May 1968), 213–220. (A response by A. K. Saran to *Christ in India*, followed by Griffiths' reply.)

"Forest of Peace in South India." *The Tablet* 223, no. 6716 (8 February 1969), 130–132.

"The Meeting of Religions." *The Tablet* 223, no. 6745 (30 August 1969), 856.

"St. Benedict in the Modern World." *Pax* 59 (1969), 77–79. (Reprinted from *Church and People* "nearly twenty years ago," according to the editors.)

"The Ecumenical Situation in Kerala Today." In *The Malabar Church: Symposium in Honour of Rev. Placid Podipara, C.M.I.*, edited by J. Vellian. Rome: Pontifical Institutum Orientalium Studiorum, 1970, 307–310.

"Man and God in India." *The Tablet* 225, no. 6813 (2 January 1971), 5–6.

"Indian Christian Contemplation." *The Clergy Monthly* 35, no. 7 (August 1971), 277–281.

"Where World Religions Meet." *The Tablet* 226, no. 6877 (1 April 1972), 314–315.

"Eastern Religious Experience." *Monastic Studies* 9 (Autumn 1972), 153–160.

"Salvation in India." *The Tablet* 226, nos. 6912–6913 (23 & 30 December 1972), 1221.

"Erroneous Beliefs and Unauthorised Rites." *The Tablet* 227, no. 6928 (14 April 1973), 356, 521.

"The Sources of Indian Spirituality." In *Indian Spirituality in Action*. Edited by R. B. Pinto. Bangalore: Asian Trading Corporation, 1973, 63–67.

"The One Mystery." *The Tablet* 228, no. 6975 (9 March 1974), 223.

"Experience of God and Eternal World in Asian Religions." *Cistercian Studies* 9 (1974), 273–276.

"Kurisumala and Indian Monasticism," 37–42; "Swami Parama Arubi Ananda," 65–67; "Shantivanam: A New Beginning," 75–76; "The Future of Christian Monasticism in India," 110–113. In *Kurisumala: A Symposium on Ashram Life*. Edited by M. F. Acharya. Bangalore: Asian Trading Corporation, 1974.

"The Universal Truth." *The Tablet* 229, no. 7022 (1 February 1975), 101–102, 347.

"Revelation and Experience." *The Tablet* 229, no. 7023 (8 February 1975), 136–137, 1167–1168.

"Indianisation." *The Examiner* 126, no. 19 (10 May 1975), 233.

"Indianization of Liturgy." *The New Leader* 65 (25 May 1975), 7.

"Non-Christian Scriptures in Liturgy." *The New Leader* 65 (15 June 1975), 7.

"The Benefits of Indianization." *The New Leader* 65 (6 July 1975), 4, 9.

"Unity and Diversity." *The Tablet* 229, no. 7047a (26 July 1975), 702, 847–848.

"In Defence of Indianization." *The New Leader* 65 (17 August 1975), 9.

"Shantivanam." *The Spirit and Life* 70 (1975), 24–27.

"Dialogue with Hinduism." *Impact* 11 (May 1976), 152–157.

"Village Religion in India." *The Tablet* 230, no. 7098 (24 July 1976), 726–727.

"'Dear Thomas' Again." *The Tablet* 230, no. 7105 (11 September 1976), 879–880.

"The Indian Spiritual Tradition and the Church in India." *Outlook* 15, no. 4 (Winter 1976), 98–104.

"A Christian Ashram," 14–20; "Shantivanam: An Explanation," 44–48; "An Open Letter to Father Anastasius Gomes," 67–70. *Vaidikamitram* 9 (1976).

"The Laity Congress." *The Examiner* 127 (1976), 381.

"Indianization or Hinduisation?" *The Examiner* 127 (1976), 485.

"The Vedic Revelation." *The Tablet* 231, no. 7165 (5 November 1977), 1053–1054.

"Communion in the Hand." *The Examiner* 128 (1977), 280.

"The Mystical Dimension in Theology." *Indian Theological Studies* 14 (1977), 229–246.

"Christian Monastic Life in India." *Journal of Dharma* 3, no. 2 (April-June, 1978), 123–135. (Reprint, with revisions, of "Monastic Life in India Today." *Monastic Studies* [1966].)

"Intercommunion Now," *The Tablet* 232, no. 7200 (8 July 1978), 660–661.

"In Filial Disobedience." *New Blackfriars* 59, no. 701 (October 1978), 463–466.

"The Advaitic Experience and the Personal God in the Upanishads and the Bhagavad Gita." *Indian Theological Studies* 15 (1978), 71–86.

"Moksha in Christianity." In *Interfaith Dialogue in Tiruchirapalli.* Edited by X. Irudayaraj and L. Sundaram. Madras: Siga, 1978, 15–18.

"The Monastic Order and the Ashram." *American Benedictine Review* 30, no. 2 (June 1979), 134–145.

"The Search for God." *The Tablet* 233, no. 7251 (30 June 1979), 620–621.

"Mystical Theology in the Indian Tradition." *Jeevadhara* 9, no. 53 (September-October 1979), 262–277.

"The Birth in a Cave." *The Tablet* 233, nos. 7276–7277 (22 & 29 December 1979), 1252.

"The Benedictines in India," *The Examiner* 131, no. 12 (22 March 1980), 178–179.

"Death into Life." *The Tablet* 234, nos. 7291–7292 (5 & 12 April 1980), 336–338.

"The Two Theologies." *The Tablet* 234, no. 7299 (31 May 1980), 520–521, 677.

"Saint Benedict: His Significance for India Today." *Vidyajyoti* 44, no. 9 (October 1980), 432–436.

"Dialogue Between Faiths." *The Tablet* 234, no. 7324 (22 November 1980), 1145–1146.

"Quest for Truth and Authentic Living." *Akasavani* 45 (1980), 13–14.

Foreword to *The Child and the Serpent: Reflections on Popular Indian Symbols*, Jyoti Sahi. London: Routledge and Kegan Paul, 1980.

"Death and Resurrection." *The Tablet* 235, nos. 7345–7346 (18 & 25 April 1981), 386–387.

"The Benedictines in India." *Indian Theological Studies* 18 (1981), 346–353.

"The Church of the Future." *The Tablet* 236, nos. 7396–7397 (10 & 17 April 1982), 364–366.

"The Mystical Tradition in Indian Theology." *Monastic Studies* 13 (Autumn 1982), 159–173. (Same article as printed in *Jeevadhara*, September 1979.)

"Science Today and the New Creation." *The Examiner* 133 (1982), 137–138.

"The Emptying of God." *The Examiner* 133, no. 51 (18 December 1982), 811–812.

"Indigenisation of Religious Life in India from a Benedictine Point of View." *Word and Worship* 15 (1982), 149–153.

"Science Today and the New Creation." *The American Theosophist* 71 (1983), 412–417. (A slightly revised version of Griffiths' talk at the February 1982 conference in Bombay on "East and West: Ancient Wisdom and Modern Science," printed in *Ancient Wisdom and Modern Science* [1984].)

"The Trinity and the Hologram." Unpublished talk concluding a conference at Shantivanam in 1983, entitled "Religion in the Light of the New Scientific View."

"Avatara and Incarnation." *The Examiner* 135 (1984), 805.

"Science Today and the New Creation." In *Ancient Wisdom and Modern Science*. Edited by Stanislav Grof. Albany: State University of New York Press, 1984, 50–58.

"Inner Disarmament and the Spiritual Warrior." *Contemplative Review* 17 (1984), 17–21.

"The Ashram and Monastic Life." *Monastic Studies* 15 (Advent 1984), 117–123 & *In Christo* 22 (1984), 217–222.

Preface to *Yoga and the Jesus Prayer Tradition: An Experiment in Faith*, Thomas Matus. Ramsey, New Jersey: Paulist Press, 1984.

"Christian Ashrams." *Word and Worship* 17 (1984), 150–152.

"Transcending Dualism: An Eastern Approach to the Semitic Religions." In *Tantur Year Book*. Jerusalem: Ecumenical Institute for Theological Studies, 1983–1984, 93–111.

"A New Vision of Reality: Western Science and Eastern Mysticism." In *G. R. Bhaktal Memorial Lecture*, 1–16. Bangalore: Indian Institute of World Culture, 1984.

"Emerging Consciousness for a New Humankind." *The Examiner* 136 (9 February 1985), 125, 128.

"The Church of Rome and Reunion." *New Blackfriars* 66, no. 783 (September 1985), 389–392.

"Emerging Consciousness and the Mystical Traditions of Asia," 48–64; & "Reflections and Prospects," 122–125 (with slight revision, this is the same summary of a January 1985 conference in Madras published in *The Examiner* [February 1985]). In *Emerging Consciousness for a New Humankind: Asian Interreligious Concern*. Edited by Michael von Brück. Bangalore: Asian Trading Corporation, 1985.

"Avatara and Incarnation." *The Examiner* 136 (1985), 161, 233, 403. (Three responses by Griffiths to letters reacting to his article of this title in *The Examiner* [1984].)

"Transcending Dualism: An Eastern Approach to the Semitic Religions." Edited by Wayne Teasdale. *Cistercian Studies* 20, no. 2 (1985), 73–87. (Reprinted in Griffiths, *Vedanta and Christian Faith* [1991 edition], 73–93. An edited version of talk printed in *Tantur Year Book* [1983–1984].)

"Dialogue and Inculturation." *The Examiner* 137, no. 33 (16 August 1986), 777–778.

"The Gifts of the Magi." *The Examiner* 137, no. 51 (20 December 1986), 1211.

"A Meditation on the Mystery of the Trinity." *Monastic Studies* 17 (Christmas 1986), 69–79.

"Transformation in Christ in the Mystical Theology of Gregory of Nyssa." *The American Theosophist* 74 (1986), 156–160.

—⟋⟍⟋—

"A Symbolic Theology." *New Blackfriars* 69, no. 817 (June 1988), 289–294.

"The Christian Ashram." *The Examiner* 139 (1988), 1235.

"The Meaning and Purpose of an Ashram." In *Saccidananda Ashram: A Garland of Letters*. Tiruchirappalli, India: Saccidananda Ashram, 1988, 4–9.

"The Significance of India for Camaldolese Monasticism." *American Benedictine Review* 40, no. 2 (June 1989).

"Christianity in the Light of the East." The Hibbert Lecture, 1989. London: The Hibbert Trust, 1989.

"A Benedictine Ashram." In *Saccidananda Ashram: A Garland of Letters*. Tiruchirappalli, India: Saccidananda Ashram, 1989, 3–5.

"The M-Word." *The Tablet* 244, no. 7830 (11 August 1990), 1002.

"Monk's Response to the Document on Christian Prayer from the Congregation for the Doctrine of the Faith." *N.A.B.E.W.D. Bulletin*. Trappist, Kentucky: Abbey of Gethsemani (1990), 11.

Foreword to *Christ as Common Ground: A Study of Christianity and Hinduism*, Kathleen Healy. Pittsburgh: Duquense University Press, 1990.

"Swamy Amaldas," 1–2; & "Renewal of Monastic Life," 3–6. In *Saccidananda Ashram: A Garland of Letters*. Tiruchirappalli, India: Saccidananda Ashram, 1991.

"Oblates of Shantivanam." Unpublished guidelines for lay contemplative communities, 1991.

"The Silence and Solitude of the Heart: Communion with God." Unpublished talk at Shantivanam. Edited by Roland Ropers, 1991.

"For Those without Sin." *The National Catholic Reporter* 28, no. 36 (14 August 1992), 20.

"In Jesus' Name." *The Tablet* 246, nos. 7915–7916 (18 & 25 April 1992), 498–499.

"The Human Condition." *Monos* 4, no. 8 (September 1992), 1–4.

Afterword to *Sheer Joy: Conversations with Thomas Aquinas on Creation Spirituality*, Matthew Fox. San Francisco: HarperCollins, 1992.

"A Center of Contemplative Living." Unpublished description of a lay contemplative community of oblates of Shantivanam, 1992.

"The New Consciousness." (Acceptance speech for the John Harriott Memorial Award.) *The Tablet* 247, no. 7954 (16 January 1993), 70.

"Dzogchen and Christian Contemplation." *A.I.M. Monastic Bulletin*, no. 55 (1993), 122–125.

"The Ashram as a Way of Transcendence." In *Christian Ashram: A Movement with a Future?* Edited by Vandana Mataji. New Delhi: ISPCK, 1993, 30–33.

"Jñana Marga," 184–185; & "Prayer in Christian Ashram," 217–221. In *Praying Seminar.* Bangalore: I.S.P.C.K. (n.d.).

RECORDED LECTURES OF BEDE GRIFFITHS:

Riches from the East. East-West Monastic Conference on Formation, Kansas City, Kansas, 1983. NCR: Credence Cassettes, 1983:

> "Dialogue with the East."
> "Contemplative Theology and the Experience of God."
> "The Personal God and the Absolute Godhead."
> "This World and the Absolute Reality."
> "The Church and the New Science and New Theology."

Christian Meditation: The Evolving Tradition. The John Main Seminar, New Harmony, Indiana, 1991. Chevy Chase, Maryland: The John Main Institute, 1991:

> "The Ideal of Monastic Life in John Main's Teaching."
> "The Extension of the Monastic Ideal to Lay Groups."
> "Meditation with a Mantra according to Fr. John."
> "Mantra Meditation in the Eastern Tradition."
> "The Contemplative Life in the Church Today in the Light of John Main's Teaching."

(The tape series also includes two cassettes entitled "Plenary Group Discussions" in which Griffiths answers questions. Both the talks and the questions and answers have been edited and published in England as *The New Creation in Christ.*)

INTERVIEWS WITH BEDE GRIFFITHS:

"Intervista a Beda Griffiths." Interview by R. Nava. *Missione Oggi* 1 (1979), 30–32.

"Interview: Bede Griffiths." Interview by Guilio Cattozzo, Padua, Italy, September 1979. *Messenger of St. Anthony* 83 (1980), 28–29.

"Mission is Dialogue: An Interview with Bede Griffiths." *Indian Missiological Review* 3 (January 1981), 43–53.

"On Poverty and Simplicity: Views of a Post-Industrial Christian Sage." Interview by Renée Weber. *ReVision* 6, no. 2 (Fall 1983), 16–30. (Reprinted in Renée Weber, *Dialogues with Scientists and Sages: The Search for Unity.* Arkana, 1990, 157–180.)

"Benedictine Ashram: An Experiment in Hindu-Christian Community." Interview by Fred Rohe and Ty Koontz, California, 1984. *The Laughing Man* 5, no. 3 (1984), 34–37.

"Interview: Father Bede Griffiths, O.S.B." Interview by Johannes Agaard and Neil Duddy, Europe, Summer 1984. *Update* 9 (1985), 22–36.

"Interview with a Spiritual Master: The Trinity." Interview by Wayne Teasdale, Shantivanam, India, December 1986. *Living Prayer* 21, no. 3 (May-June 1988), 24–31.

"Reincarnation: A Christian View." Interview by Wayne Teasdale, Shantivanam, India, December 1986. *Living Prayer* 21, no. 5 (September-October 1988), 22–28.

"Contemplative Community and the Transformation of the World." Interview by Wayne Teasdale, Shantivanam, India, December 1986. *Living Prayer* 22, no. 1 (January-February 1989), 11–15.

"Father Bede Griffiths." Interview by Malcolm Tillis, January 27, 1981, Shantivanam, India. In *Turning East: New Lives in India: Twenty Westerners and Their Spiritual Quests.* Edited by Malcolm Tillis and Cynthia Giles. New York: Paragon House, 1989, 119–126.

The Universal Christ: Daily Readings with Bede Griffiths. Excerpts from interviews by Kathryn Spink and Peter Spink, and from recorded talks. Edited by Peter Spink. London: Darton Longman and Todd, 1990.

VIDEO RECORDINGS OF BEDE GRIFFITHS:

Christ in the Lotus: An Interview with Bede Griffiths. Interview by Laurence Freeman, Shantivanam, India. Produced by Mark Schofield. Christian Meditation Media, 40 min., videocassette.

The Space in the Heart of the Lotus. Series of talks at Shantivanam. BBC TV.

Christian Meditation: The Evolving Tradition. The John Main Seminar, New Harmony, Indiana, 1991. Chevy Chase, Maryland: The John Main Institute, 1991.

Exploring the Christian-Hindu Dialogue: A Visit with Bede Griffiths and Russill Paul. Interview by Tyra Arraj. Chiloquin, Oregon: Inner Growth Videos, 1992.

The Wisdom of a Prophet: The New Vision of Reality. Talks and questions in Perth, Western Australia, May 1992. Sydney, Australia: More Than Illusion Films, 1993, videocassette.

The History and Interpretation of the Bible. Talk at Shantivanam. Sydney, Australia: More Than Illusion Films, 1993, 40 min., videocassette.

Discovering the Feminine. Talk at Shantivanam. Sydney, Australia: More Than Illusion Films, 1993, 32 min., videocassette.

A Human Search: The Life of Father Bede Griffiths. Documentary and interview by Andrew Harvey and John Swindells. Produced by John Swindells. Sydney, Australia: More Than Illusion Films, 1993, 59 min., videocassette.

SECONDARY SOURCES ON BEDE GRIFFITHS

Bruteau, Beatrice, ed. *As We Are One: Essays and Poems in Honor of Bede Griffiths.* Pfafftown, North Carolina: Philosophers' Exchange, 1991. (*Bede Griffiths: The Other Half of My Soul: Bede Griffiths and the Hindu-Christian Dialogue* is an expanded edition of this work.)

Fastiggi, Robert, and Pereira, Jose. "The Swami from Oxford." *Crisis*, March 1991, 22–25. (A revision of Pereira's article in *Dilip* [1990].)

Fernandes, Albano. "The Hindu Mystical Experience according to R. C. Zaehner and Bede Griffiths: A Philosophical Study." Ph.D. dissertation, Gregorian Pontifical University, 1993.

Freeman, Laurence; Sheldrake, Rupert; and Ropers, Roland. "Obituary." *The Tablet* 247, no. 7971 (22 May 1993), 667–668.

Gheddo, P. "Bede Griffiths: Un 'guru' Cristiano in India." *Mondo e Missione* 107 (1979), 231–253.

Helsing, S. B. "Bede Griffiths och religionsdialogen." *Svensk-Missionstidskrift* 73 (1985), 27–33.

Hoblitzelle, Harrision. "India's Christian Guru: A Visit with Father Bede Griffiths." *New Age* 9 (1983), 37–43.

Kalliath, Antony. "Inward Transcendence: A Study on the Encounter of Western Consciousness with Indian Interiority Based on the Works of Fr. Bede Griffiths." Masters dissertation, Dharmaram Pontifical Institute, 1986.

Panikkar, Raimon. "The Wider Ecumenism: An Explorer Crosses the Borders." Review of *River of Compassion*, by Bede Griffiths. In *The Tablet* 246, no. 7938 (26 September 1992), 1192–1193.

Pereira, Jose. "Christian Theosophists?" *Dilip*, November-December 1990, 11–19.

Rajan, Jesu. *Bede Griffiths and Sannyasa*. Bangalore, India: Asian Trading Corp., 1989. (Originally a doctoral dissertation submitted to the Pontifical University of St. Thomas Aquinas in Rome, 1988.)

Rice, Ed. "Christian Monks on an Inner Journey to the Hindu Experience of God." *The Sign*, April 1968, 36–43.

Rodhe, Sten. "Christianity and Hinduism: A Comparison of the Views Held by Jules Monchanin and Bede Griffiths." *Vidyajyoti* 59, no. 10 (October 1995), 663–677.

Smith, R. "Religious Diversity, Hindu-Christian Dialogue and Bed Graffiti." In *Proceedings of the Eighth International Symposium on Asian Studies*. Hong Kong: Asian Research Service, 1986, 1413–1429.

Spink, Kathryn. *A Sense of the Sacred: A Biography of Bede Griffiths*. Maryknoll, New York: Orbis Books, 1989.

Teasdale, Wayne Robert. "Bede Griffiths and the Uniqueness of Christianity." *Communio* 9, no. 2 (Spring 1984), 177–186.

———. "Bede Griffiths As Mystic and Icon of Reversal." *America* 173, no. 9 (September 30, 1995), 22–23.

———. "The Other Half of the Soul: Bede Griffiths in India." *The Canadian Catholic Review* 3 (1985).

———. *Towards a Christian Vedanta: The Encounter of Hinduism and Christianity According to Bede Griffiths*. Bangalore, India: Asian Trading Corp., 1987. (Originally a doctoral dissertation submitted to Fordham University in Bronx, New York, 1986.)

———. "Forest of Peace: Shantivanam at the Heart of the World." *The Canadian Catholic Review* 7 (June 1989).

Trapnell, Judson B. "Bede Griffiths' Theory of Religious Symbol and Practice of Dialogue: Towards Interreligious Understanding." Ph.D. dissertation, The Catholic University of America, 1992.

———. "Bede Griffiths, Mystical Knowing and the Unity of Religions." *Philosophy & Theology* 7, no. 4 (Summer 1993), 355–379.

————. "Bede Griffiths as a Culture Bearer: An Exploration of the Relationship Between Spiritual Transformation and Cultural Change." *American Benedictine Review*, 1996.

————. "Two Models of Christian Dialogue with Hinduism: Bede Griffiths and Abhishiktananda." *Vidyajyoti* 60 (1996).

List of Illustrations

QUEST BOOKS
are published by
The Theosophical Society in America,
Wheaton, Illinois 60189-0270,
a branch of a world organization
dedicted to the promotion of the unity of
humanity and the encouragement of the study of
religion, philosophy, and science, to the end that
we may better understand ourselves and our place in
the universe. The Society stands for complete
freedom of individual search and belief.
For further information about its activities,
write or call 1-800-669-1571.

*The Theosophical Publishing House
is aided by the generous support of
THE KERN FOUNDATION
a trust established by Herbert A. Kern
and dedicated to Theosophical education.*